CHINA'S MEDIA
IN THE EMERGING
WORLD ORDER

Hugo de Burgh has a deep knowledge of the Chinese media scene, and in this engagingly written book he examines everything from the official print media to TV reality shows to web blogs. He also analyses the cultural underpinnings of the Chinese media, as well as the government's mentality and the ways it exercises controls. de Burgh succeeds admirably in this insightful portrayal of China's media world.

Jonathan Unger, Editor, *The China Journal,* Professor of Political Science, Australian National University

This is an important and timely book on a critically important topic in the evolving relationship between China and the West. This thoroughly researched and wide-ranging book will greatly assist Western readers to deepen their understanding of China's rich and complex cultural evolution under the policies of reform and opening up.

Peter Nolan, Sinyi Professor of Chinese Management, University of Cambridge

In *China's Media*, Hugo de Burgh has provided a timely and thoughtful contribution to the required reading list for any student of global communication. de Burgh's new book provides more than an introduction to the evolving state of media in the world's most populous nation. He has made a compelling case for the central importance of understanding the state, history and future direction of media in China.

John V. Pavlik, Professor of Journalism and Media Studies Department, Rutgers University

The book moves beyond dogma while sidestepping obligations to validate Western democracy as the benchmark. de Burgh's impartial account of China's media will arouse considerable debate but such debate is surely needed to bring us closer to understanding the complexities of China's media. Required reading.

Michael Keane, Professor and Principal Research Fellow/ Australian Research Council Centre of Excellence for Creative Industries and Innovation, Queensland University of Technology

I have fond memories of watching Hugo de Burgh handle the Chinese media and I can think of no one better qualified to tell us about a subject of ever growing importance.

Boris Johnson MP, Secretary of State for Foreign Affairs, United Kingdom

CHINA'S MEDIA
IN THE EMERGING
WORLD ORDER

Hugo de Burgh

University of Buckingham Press

Published in 2017 by

The University of Buckingham Press
Yeomanry House
Hunter Street
Buckingham MK18 1EG

A CIP catalogue record for this book is available at the British Library

ISBN 978-1-908684-34-9

"Nations do not escape from their past merely by making a revolution"

George Orwell, *The English Revolution*

Contents

Hugo de Burgh is Professor of Journalism at the University of Westminster, where he set up the China Media Centre in 2005. He is also Professor in the School of Media & Communications at Tsinghua University. Previously he worked for Scottish Television, BBC and (the UK's) Channel4.

His books include *Investigative Journalism, The Chinese Journalist, Making Journalists, China, Friend or Foe?, China's Environment and Chinese Environment Journalists, China and Britain: the potential impact of China's development* and *Can the Prizes Still Glitter? The Future of British Universities in a Changing World.*

Introduction

Early one morning, Shanghai Media Group (SMG) 上海文广 *held a 'Report Back' meeting* 节目创新创意赴英培训汇报会, *in which 15 of its producers presented to several hundred colleagues what they had learnt during a six-week workshop on Programme Development, held in London some months before. The Group Vice President opened the session with the words, 'Comrades! Our studying abroad is bearing fruit. Thanks to the efforts of [the 15 producers] in studying hard and applying the examples and lessons learnt abroad, four new television series will now be made for our satellite channel.' Following his introduction, the team members made illustrated presentations of the different skills and knowledge they had absorbed on the course, before going on to show the pilots that had been made of the four programmes.[1] They were all in the light entertainment category, one being a comedy competition, another a dog show.*

At the end of the proceedings, the Party Secretary of SMG made a speech in which she praised the creativity of the team and the contribution that they were making to their company, to the development of television and 'to the rise of our country in the world'. Such a mixture of patriotism, commercialism and politics epitomises China's media today.

As China increasingly influences the economies and international relations of every country, it also seeks to have its media seen on a par with those of the rest of the world. China's media, in their various forms, are becoming ubiquitous. This book is for people who need to know about this new force in the world but are unlikely to consume much of it, if any.

The first academics to write about the Chinese media saw themselves as studying propaganda and techniques of mass persuasion. They also assumed that media reflected only the political system, that the Chinese media were controlled from the centre monolithically.[2]

This book takes a different tack. The theme is that the way the Chinese media work can be understood as a reflection of culture as much as of political economy. The purpose is to help normalize discussion of the subject. Inevitably I see with an Anglophone perspective, but have tried to liberate myself from ideological prejudices as far as I am able.

When Anglophone observers have looked at China's media, they have often done so through particular assumptions, such as that only commercial media can be free, or that the media and the state are antagonists; media that do not fit into familiar categories are found wanting.[3] Here I try to explain the Chinese

1

equivalents in their own terms and to understand them within the context of their own society and history rather than seeing them as underdeveloped or perverted expressions of 'universals'.

China's media are distinct, different not just because they are under the control of a communist government which, for a long time, sought to force on its people an alien creed, but also because Chinese society is different from the Anglophone world in some quite fundamental ways.[4]

Moreover, since the state religion is Marxism, Chinese intellectuals and leaders alike need to use its vocabulary as camouflage lest what they advocate be taken as heretical. For example, in promoting what they regard as pro-social moral behaviour, likening the nation to a family, objecting to the commodification of relationships, eulogising inter-generational solidarity, pointing to the dangers of contamination from materialism and hedonism, and calling for respect for nature, they often appear to be expressing traditional Chinese nostrums, yet advance them as 'socialist values'.

The Chinese media are arms of the state but not a 'Fourth Estate'. This is because the different functions of government are not separated in the way they are in the Anglosphere. This does not mean that the media do not have roles in 'supervising' governance, but the ways in which they should do this are differently defined. The media are not adversaries but parts of the apparatus itself.

Some commentators like to suggest that today's China is capitalist 'red in tooth and claw', writing off the predominance of the state in the economy as a dwindling relic of communism. Recent measures to reduce the extent of direct state management or to mix the shareholdings of State Owned Enterprises (SOEs) are taken as moves towards a free market economy. In fact, they might better be interpreted as moves to incorporate useful lessons into a system unchanged in principle.

Some have been known to apply the logic of the free market philosophers[5], as well as what they learnt from the failures of the Soviet experiment, to propose that China's achievements have come *despite* the state. From within China, however, the situation can look very different. Youthful entrepreneurs, graduates from the Anglosphere and CEOs of global high tech companies alike do not necessarily question their subordinate status. In traditional Chinese society, the rules of the economy were set by the state and the commercial classes were permitted to become rich as and when it suited it. So, state-controlled industries are no more an anomaly now than they were under the empire. Ultimate power resides, as ever, with the representatives of the realm. The precariousness of vastly rich industry leaders and entrepreneurs, who are regularly reported as having been cut down to size, illustrates the point.

Today, it can seem that a system of governance closely related to indigenous tradition is being reasserted with modern adaptations.[6] It is only so long that an alien ideology – in this case Marxism – can survive in unsuitable soil. It is easier to get people to recite its tenets than to believe in them. Governance, in the long term, is a reflection of the moral soil of a culture. Later in the book, we will look at how China's traditional culture might come to accommodate greater participation, along with the accountability and transparency which modern developments make both possible and desirable. For the moment, though, we should remind ourselves that Chinese officials proudly proclaim the nation to be 'the foremost country in the world that practices a political system fundamentally different from the Western parliamentary democracies',[7] and have no intention of being made to feel ashamed of that.

Chapter by chapter

Difference and the intention to remain different are among the motivators of the 'going out' strategy 走出去战略, by which the government is encouraging engagement abroad, so we start with the nuts and bolts of media projection outside of China. Why such great effort and expenditure to replicate what the BBC and CNN do already, and very successfully? And, given that this is a state enterprise, what problems arise in competing with established commercial operations? How are the Chinese equivalents different? Chapter 1 attempts to answer these questions, while identifying some of the difficulties that China's media are facing.

The causes of these lie not only in the official ideology of media, restated in uncompromising terms by the President in 2016, but in how the modern Chinese media came about. In chapter 2, the reader is reminded of the history of the Anglophone media, and the contrasts between the background and assumptions that gave rise to it and those that that have operated in China. The media have not always been as subservient to the state as the CCP would like them to have been, but the relationship between them has never been the same as in the Anglosphere.

Were I writing about the American or British media, much of the background knowledge of the readership could be taken for granted. I could refer to newspapers, TV programmes and so forth knowing that my readers would either be familiar with the names or could become so in minutes through the Internet. Not so with China, at least not yet. Chapters 3 and 4 provide some of the missing background, giving the reader a sense of what the most significant manifestations of Chinese media look and sound like. When I draw attention to specifics, I tend to do so in terms that derive from the equivalents in my own country and, to that extent, my view is inevitably partial and biased.

When my Chinese students think of New Media, their minds will turn to setting up fashion businesses through Taobao 淘宝, or summoning up their favourite singers, or gossiping with their mothers on Weixin 微信. Anglophones, because of the way China has been framed in their countries, will in all likelihood be looking for dissidence and disharmony. They will not be consoled by being told that 99% of Internet traffic ignores politics. I am not immune to such tendencies, though I try to compensate for them.

Having collected some facts about how the media work in China we will look at the environment they reflect and create, which I term 'The Networksphere'. In the last century, the collapse of the great totalitarian powers of Germany and Russia led to claims that the Anglophone political model [8] was superior and a manifestation, not of English culture, but of universal values. Conforming to that model has been considered essential to being modern. Two of its central features are a 'public sphere', in which large numbers of citizens participate in policy making, and 'civil society', or those associations and little platoons which stand between family and state. The existence of a media independent of political or commercial pressure, run by professionals operating according to occupational norms and ethics, is regarded as an essential condition for these features to survive.

Having established in earlier chapters that China's media operate on different principles – public ownership, overt political guidance, cultural self-censorship – in Chapter 5 (*The Networksphere*),we ask whether a *public sphere* and *civil society* can be present in China in the same way as in the Anglophone model. In 17th century England, John Milton advanced that a media independent of authority is a prerequisite for, as well as fruit of, what Anglophones think of as a free society. Can such a society exist in China?

We will see that the cultural fundamentals behind the Anglophone model are different from those of China, resulting in differing contingent institutions. Crudely simplified, whereas Anglophone culture is dominated by the notion of individualism, the equivalent force in China is communitarianism.[9] The media of The People's Republic are at least as subject to its influence as they are to technological and economic pressures.

This approach requires explanation because Anglophones have become accustomed to seeing their system as the one towards which all the others are evolving. The philosopher, Larry Siedentop, explains why:

'Since the 16th century and the advent of the nation state, people in the west have come to understand 'society' to mean an association of individuals. Until recently that understanding was accompanied by a sense of difference, a sense that other cultures had a different basis of organisation, whether that was caste, clan or tribe. But in recent decades the western impact on the rest of the world through capitalism, the spread of democracy and the language of human rights has weakened such [sense of] difference.'[10]

It has therefore been assumed that the divergences between Chinese and Anglophone societies, and the rejection of universal values as advocated by the Anglosphere,[11] are due not to local culture but to the Communist Party (CCP). This is only partly true, and becomes less so day by day.

When the Chinese Communist Party took power in 1949, it imposed a Russian-inspired system of control over society, using the media as its principal tool for changing behaviour and obliging conformity. Since 1978 the media have been easing their way back to a relationship with society that has as much in common with tradition as with Marxism. The methods of censorship and regulation that illustrate this are examined in Chapter 6, *Defending identity*. I have deliberately given a provocative spin to this subject, despite my belief that censorship is often reprehensible, in reaction to the customary but ideologically charged condemnations of it.

The history of the Chinese media, their political context and the characteristics of the society of which they are a manifestation, suggest that they are likely to remain different from their Anglophone equivalents. But could the political situation change? Frustration with the defects of government at home and influence from outside, including the propagation of the Anglophone model, have given rise to constant discussion about political change. In the final chapter, *The future and its past*, I bring the reader's attention to the ongoing debates about the kinds of polity and media the Chinese envisage for their future.

Much of what I write may at first sight seem too rosy in the light of current developments in China, where stricter controls on expression are being imposed than have been seen for many years. To some, this is a temporary expedient brought about by the leaders' funk when confronted with what Matthew Arnold called the 'melancholy, long, withdrawing roar' that denotes a change of *zeitgeist*. To others, the clampdown represents a concentrating of power for its own sake. It has been deemed a ploy to distract attention from grand plans for reform, while for others it is a logical concomitant of Xi's overall policies and a proud affirmation of China's difference. It can also be explained as tactical 'tightening'

– the direction of travel has not changed but tactics demand alternating approaches of 'tightening' and 'relaxing'. Now is a time for squeezing. While suspending judgment on this big question, I try to show the to's and fro's of conceptualisations of the media since 1949, and of reflections on their inadequacies.

The limitations

There is now a good deal of writing on China's media. I have not done it justice, particularly the Chinese literature on the subject (there have been organisations for research into the media since 1918!)[12] I can only plead that the topic is too big for one book because the Chinese media encompass so much.

Why *China's Media* and not 'Chinese Media'? Chinese media exist in as many parts of the world as there are Chinese communities. Some of the best examples are based in Hong Kong, Malaysia or Taiwan. BBC Chinese and *Voice of America* must also be taken into account. These subjects need separate treatment. *China's Media* are here defined as those which originate in the Peoples' Republic of China.

My limits are not just geographical. Media are spoken of as embracing a vast range of communication modes, from exhibitions to emoticons, news aggregation websites to Valentine cards, not to mention film and literature, genres which are only given the odd mention in this book. The all-encompassing nature of the present understanding of media is a good thing but it makes generalization difficult. I have therefore restricted myself to what are typically called the mass media (also 'conventional' or 'legacy' media) and New Media. I have focused more on journalists than on other kinds of media workers, partly because they make more noise and partly because they are pervasive as managers as well as producers throughout all media systems. To compensate for these limitations, I have tried to give as many references to further reading as possible.

My hope is that the reader will have a useful 'map', to use James Carey's analogy.[13] 'Different maps', he writes, 'bring the same environment alive in different ways; they produce quite different realities.' The global traveller might do well to consult maps other than those supplied by his own culture. I see China's media as providing an alternative map of the world. At the same time, I ask you to consider this book as just one map of China's media.

Notes

[1] The 4 programme concepts were: 笑傲江湖 *Comedy Competition*, 天梯 *Reach High!*, 狗狗向前冲 *Go Doggie!* and 蜜密约会 *Disguised Meeting*.

[2]Polumbaum, Judy (2010) Looking Back, Looking Forward: The Ecumenical Imperative in Chinese Mass Communication Scholarship. *International Journal of Communication* 4 (2010), pp 567-572.

[3] Anglophones often betray the premise that they see Chinese media as the polar opposite of the 'free' media. Discussing this issue, Polumbaum suggests that, notwithstanding the 'rhetoric of individual freedom and independence for journalists in the U.S.', research in fact shows that despite the 'overt political controls' on the media in China, Chinese journalists can surmount those constraints such that they are not as determining as those placed on US journalists. I am not sure I agree with the point, but it is a useful cue. Ibid.

[4] It is quite difficult to explain the connections between substructure and superstructure, of which media are a part, because relatively little academic attention has been paid to this. Some leading writers on the media (all of whom are cited in this book) have referred to the need to do so, James Carey, Michael Schudson, Zhao Yuezhi, Daniel C. Hallin and Paulo Mancini and Rogier Creemers, but the challenge has hardly been taken up, perhaps because it requires stepping outside the modernist assumptions with which we were typically brought up.

[5] Principally Friedrich von Hayek and Ludwig Edler von Mises.

[6] The principal exponent of this view is Zheng Yongnian in his (2012) *The Chinese Communist Party as Organizational Emperor: culture, reproduction, and transformation.* London: Routledge

[7] de Burgh, Hugo (2006) *China Friend or Foe.* Cambridge: Icon, pp 26.

[8] They did not call it 'the Anglophone political model' but 'democracy'. In the speeches of Messrs G.W. Bush and T. Blair a crusade to remake the world in this model was indicated; the real reason for the attack on Iraq is more likely to have been old fashioned imperialism. See: http://www.theguardian.com/environment/earth-insight/2014/mar/20/iraq-war-oil-resources-energy-peak-scarcity-economy (Accessed: 17 March 2016)

[9] I prefer the term 'communitarianism' to 'collectivism' both because the latter is loaded with negative associations in the Anglophone mind, and because 'communitarianism' better describes how Chinese tend to think of the world and the place of the individual. Of course there are exceptions, just as there are also aspects of Anglophone societies that are communitarian. 'Communitarian' also best connects Chinese traditional ideas about society with socialist ideals, something we touch upon later.

[10] Siedentop, Larry (2015) *Inventing the Individual, The Origins of Western Liberalism.* London: Penguin, pp 7.

[11] This is rather ironical since it was Communists who previously promoted universal values over the narrow national values of the old nation states.

[12] Nip, J., Qiu, Z. (2012), *A Meta-Review of Chinese Media Studies: 1998-2008* : China Media Report. pp 113-114.

[13] Carey, James (2009) *Communication as Culture: Essays on Media and Society.* NY: Routledge. pp 22. My colleague Vivien Marsh reminded me of this.

1 China Comes Out

China is challenging the existing order of the information age; not yet the position of English as its predominant language, but certainly its dominant position. From being barely visible outside the homeland, China's media have rapidly become ubiquitous. It is not just that the Internet allows us to access them. Their non-Internet forms are being promoted everywhere: magazines, newspapers and broadcast channels are competing with established media, and the news agencies, and drama and entertainment producers are selling their wares with enthusiasm.

In part the state has mobilised the media for long-term, commercial reasons; it wants them to compete in the global market. But there are more pressing geopolitical reasons: China has vast interests abroad which need to be defended and represented.

The Chinese position is that, until now, the international media have been dominated by Anglophones who denigrate China. What are therefore needed are media that put forward China's story on the issues of the day, whether development in Africa or reform at home, turbulence in the Middle East or global warming. And China wants the world to believe that, unlike its aggressive competitors, it is cooperative, peaceful and respectful of difference.

Then, there is the matter of survival. China rejects the Anglophone presumption that its values are better and universal, suggesting that this claim serves as a cover for commercial and political expansion. They see Anglophone crusades as self-interested subversion. The intention to remain different is one of the main motivators of the going out strategy and is not necessarily, as some assume, camouflage for politicians' self-interest.

1.1 Overview of China's Media Abroad

The origins of the ascendancy of the Anglophone media lie in the commercial expansion of Europe and the USA in 19th century. The 'going out' of China's media today is also partly a consequence of economic development, but unlike the Anglophone equivalent in the 19th century, it is state directed. The policy was set in motion in the 1990s when the State Council Information Office 国务院新闻办 took responsibility for communication with foreign nations. Many government news websites were inaugurated, including in 1997 the China National Network (China.Com.cn), formed to be the main national overseas publicity platform.[1]

Media organisations were made to prepare for the competition that it was anticipated would follow entry to the World Trade Organisation in 2001, and exhorted to think how they might export their products. Because of their value to

8

domestic industrial development, the government had encouraged Internet applications from the start. By 2015, half the population was online and, notwithstanding some limits on interconnectivity, capable of communicating globally. Government departments and businesses have web presences in English and some other languages.

Xinhua bureaux worldwide

image: Dan Strassburg

The state has provided large resources.[2] The launch of the US edition of the *China Daily*, in 2009, was followed by an English language version of the *Global Times*. China Radio International has developed multilingual websites for overseas. Xinhua News Agency sells its services alongside Reuters, AP and other long-established agencies and also has its own broadcaster, China News Channel (CNC).

The major investment is in CCTV. China Central Television's first international channel was in Chinese, targeted at the diaspora, but in 2009, CCTV launched channels in five languages.[3] In 2011, it established the *Documentary Channel* 纪实 频道, which broadcasts 24 hours a day in both Chinese and English to 60 countries. Later that year, the 24-hour global satellite English channel, earlier called CCTV-9 or CCTV News but now China Global Television Network (CGTN)中国国际电视 台, became, along with the multilingual China National Network, 'the new vehicles for China to realise the objectives of "foreign propaganda" and to pursue soft power'.[4]

CCTV stations worldwide

image: Dan Strassburg

CGTN offers several current affairs programmes, including *China Today*, *World Wide Watch* and *Asia Today*. Nottingham University specialist Zhang Xiaoling has commented: 'An examination of the [news] programmes shows that CCTV-9 [sic], the first TV media organisation in Asia that can beam its signals to every corner of the globe, not only provides more extensive coverage on China, Asia and other developing nations than is offered by other international channels, but is also set on presenting its own version of issues and events happening in China, Asia, the developing world and other world affairs as an insider and as an alternative voice to the dominating Western voice, just as Asia Today's mission statement goes: "We report on Asia from the perspective of Asians."'[5]

Non-Chinese reporters are being taken on in major cities around the world, including Miami, Chicago, Houston, San Francisco, Toronto and parts of Latin America, as CCTV attempts to compete with international broadcasters such as CNN, BBC and Al Jazeera.[6] CCTV increased its overseas staff from 280 in 2012 to 500 in 2016, in 80 bureaux.[7]

In January 2012, China Central Television inaugurated a Media Hub in Nairobi; and at roughly the same time launched a substantial centre in the USA; a European Hub is formally to open in London in 2018. While Western countries' newsgathering presence overseas is diminishing, China is spending $4bn to

10

expand abroad.[8]

1.2　African and other markets

In countries with well-established indigenous media of high quality, it may be difficult for China to gain customers. Recognising this, managers have put their main efforts into attracting African, South East Asian and Latin American audiences. At the beginning of 2012, CCTV started up its English Language channel, CCTV Africa, which soon expanded from a one-hour a week show to two hours a day.[9] China had thus already embarked on this media battle at a time when BBC was reducing its worldwide coverage.[10] CCTV executives claim that its pan-Africa programmes, researched and reported by Africans, have outshone BBC programmes of a similar kind.[11]

How successful have these efforts really been? Although CCTV professes 98% coverage, surveys conducted in the UK showed less than 5% of the potential audience around the world use Chinese media.[12] The market is today very crowded; rivals are well-established and it would be hard for any incomer to shift customers. It is particularly difficult for China, as her culture and affairs have typically been known through critical Anglophone filters.

Because of two other initiatives taking place hand in hand with media expansion, language teaching and promotion of culture, it may be that, in a generation when these have been thoroughly instantiated, people will be more receptive to China's media. There are also three new tacks which may have more appeal.

The first is overseas product sales. 'Dynasty dramas had saturated a pan-Chinese media market by the early 2000s[13] but subsequently other markets have been addressed. Agreements have been reached with Mongolia, Argentina, Tanzania and other Asian and African countries. 80 films and television shows were dubbed into multiple languages (including Swahili and Mongolian) during 2013. Initially they were distributed free, in order to develop the market. The most popular themes are domestic dramas based on large families and stories about young people struggling to get on in the world. Martial arts have also been popular but other kinds of historical topics are likely to be marketed in the future. Chinese TV formats are being sold abroad: in 2014 the British group ITV bought the licence for *Sing my Song* 中国好歌曲, a talent show first broadcast on CCTV3. At the time of writing *In the Name of the People* 人民的名义, a saga of about an anti-peculation unit 反贪局 (a section of the Provincial Scrutiny Office 检察院) investigating corruption in the administration, has attracted such online attention worldwide that consideration is being given to an English language version. *Nirvana in Fire*, 琅琊榜 a historical drama which has had over 13 billion views and 3.55 billion posts on

11

Sina Weibo, is reported as having been unexpectedly successful in the USA, suggesting that a taste for Chinese historical drama may be being acquired there too.[14]

The footprint of CCTV

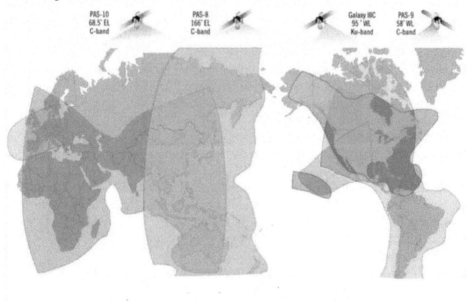

image: Dan Strassburg

Secondly, Chinese media companies are buying equity in existing media abroad and working with companies producing local media.[15] A very large acquisition was Wanda Group's purchase of Hollywood studio Legendary Entertainment in 2015. StarTimes is a distributor of TV programmes to Africa which include Chinese channels and was set up in China specifically to provide programmes in Hausa and Swahili.

Thirdly, broadcasters are undertaking co-productions with foreign producers who can help them provide Chinese culture in forms digestible by non-Chinese audiences.[16] One of the most visible of these has been the BBC/CCTV co-production *Wild China* 美丽中国.

Media conglomerates such as Hunan Satellite have their own reasons for wanting to expand internationally; though rich enough, they are constrained from expanding at home. Thus they readily respond to calls from the government to develop products that sell abroad. Profit from these ventures is a secondary factor: 'Rather, China fundamentally connects the thesis of national security to cultural policy and industry'.[17] Cooperative ventures with foreigners are good if they spread Chinese culture abroad but the Chinese authorities are not prepared to allow the culture or its transmission to be dictated by commercial interests, particularly when these are foreign commercial interests.

Media people: a foreign correspondent

A celebrated war reporter and then presenter of international affairs, Shui Junyi 水均益graduated in English Literature from Lanzhou 兰州 University before joining Xinhua News Agency in 1984. Here he worked for ten years, including two as a war correspondent in the Middle East.

In 1993 Shui joined CCTV as a Reporter and then as the Presenter of CCTV's, *Oriental Horizon*, 东方时空 the first breakfast programme. He continued to report from abroad and is one of the very few Chinese war journalists to have been at the frontline in Iraq, Bosnia and Afghanistan.

Shui is renowned for his interviews with world leaders, covering almost every kind of topic, from politics to the economy, from celebrities to scientists. His programmes are widely thought to have greatly increased awareness and understanding of international affairs.

Image source:
http://www.gov.cn/wszb/zhibo20070306/content_543450.htm

The government likes to sell historical films abroad because they promote the image of China as a 'grand and ultimately united civilisation with a long and distinguished history' although the University of California's Michael Curtin doubts whether they are an effective means to promote China, as they point up the distance between the modern and ancient worlds. Moreover, thus far non-Chinese viewers have little or no knowledge of Chinese history so that their level of understanding is shallow.[18] Nevertheless, epics such as *Crouching Tiger, Hidden Dragon* 卧虎藏龙 or *The Great Wall* 长城 have appealed for their grandeur and derring do. On the other hand, modern urban comedies such as *Go Lala Go!* 杜拉拉, about a white-collar girl's travails in love and at work, are more transferable. And there is plenty more of that genre, some of it set in the USA or Europe. Domestic television series such as *Snailhouse* 蜗居, *Coming and Going* 来来往往 and *Divorce Chinese Style*[19] 中国式离婚 deal with universal concerns and, if made with foreign audiences in mind, might help to humanise and soften the image of China.

Independent film and documentary[20] work, such as that of Jiang Wen 姜文,[21] will appeal to a different, albeit limited, audience for its emotional sensibility and moral depth. Films recently popular abroad have included *I am not Pan Jinlian!*

我不是潘金莲. It is a complicated tale of a wronged woman who takes on the whole legal and government system to try to right a wrong. Then there is *Mr Six* 老炮儿 which shows how a simple man from the backstreets of old Peking attempts to save his son from gang revenge. For the factually-minded there are documentaries such as *The Mayor* 中国市长, by CCTV's Zhao Qi 赵琦, which tells the story of an official and his controversial battle to improve a city.[22]

In sum, China now has a growing presence in the global mediascape and the potential for much more. Broadcasters are fine-tuning their approach to product aimed at overseas with the intention of bringing Chinese culture onto our screens in digestible ways. The journalists are working on their craft with the same ambitions, as we shall see shortly. These initiatives are propelled by the state. Why?

1.3   The defence of China's interests abroad

In the 16th century the English started to 'go out', as traders, colonists and rulers. Two hundred years later, their institutions and language and customs took precedence in very many countries. A further hundred years' later Anglophones pulled the strings in much of the world, backed by the wealth, leadership and ingenuity of the United States.

Today China's is the world's second-biggest economy and its purchasing power has displaced that of the United States. A fifth of humankind is Chinese and the language is used by many more than those who speak English. Few are the traders, policy-makers, designers, teachers or producers who can think ahead without taking China into account.

Domestic growth is only part of the story.[23] The Chinese economic revolution is being exported. A feverishly toiling, sharp-minded and creative diaspora connects China with the economies and polities of much of the world, from Venezuela to Sicily and Nigeria to Pakistan.[24]

Most manufactured goods sold in Central Asia come from China, as with many developing countries.[25] As China produces more and more sophisticated goods and services, its penetration of the developed markets will also grow. China does not have to import finished goods to achieve this, but rather the wherewithal to produce them and/or the capital to fund them abroad. From European textile industries to wine production, a growing number of owners are Chinese.[26] New Zealand dairy production has been integrated into the Chinese economy[27] In Argentina, Chinese own 8,900 supermarkets; China controls a third of the world's furniture trade; one telecommunications company, Huawei 华为, which has only been operating for 25 years, competes in 140 countries with world leaders Cisco Systems, Siemens and Nokia.[28] Four of the ten top New Media companies are Chinese, the others are American.

The Media Abroad

In the early years of the 21st century many innovations came about intended to improve communications overseas, today the mainstream media titles have all launched their Apps for smart phone users:
A revamped *China Daily.*
Xinhua newspaper app for mobiles/cell phones.
Overseas editions of *The Peoples' Daily.*
China's multilingual website, China National Network (www.china.com.cn).
English edition of *Global Times.*
China Watch, a regular supplement in *The Washington Post, New York Times* and (the UK's) *Daily Telegraph.*
Xinhua News Agency now competes internationally for business previously shared among western agencies.
A 24-hour global English language news channel, CNC World, established by Xinhua, and available in the UK on Sky and free to air satellite; in the USA it is on Time Warner Cable.

Various innovations have also been made by China Central Television (CCTV), with the aim of reaching overseas audiences:
- International channels in Arabic, English, Spanish, French, Chinese and Russian.
- The CCTV Documentary Channel, set up in 2011 and broadcasting 24 hours a day in Chinese and English. The English channel broadcasts mainly six programmes, featuring the life in China, culture, history and a daily top story. The programmes includes, *Today's Top Pick, Humanities and Geography, Living China, Special Edition, Journeys and Discoveries* and *History in Frame.*
- China Global Television Network (CGTN) has been established to incorporate CCTVNews, its own CGTN Apps, new website, and accounts on Facebook, Twitter and WeChat. CGTN comprehends CCTVNews Channel, the documentary (English) channel, plus French, Spanish, Arabic and Russian Channels. CRI has been incorporated.
- Regional Hubs in Washington, Nairobi have their output branded as CCTV Africa and CCTV America. They make news programmes locally, using local reporters and producers and having a relatively loose editorial control from Beijing. They include the daily African news show *Africa Live, a* 30-minute weekly talk show *Talk Africa* and documentaries on people in Africa, such as *Faces of Africa.* The head office produces programmes including *News Hour, China 24, World Insight, Dialogue* and *Asia Today, The Point with Xin, Asia Assignment, Sports Scene* and *Culture Express.*

But China also needs to buy. The combination of its restricted capacity to produce food and its enormous population, ever more urbanised and expecting to eat better than previous generations, make the sourcing of food abroad essential. In Argentina, already the third largest supplier of food, huge areas are soon to be farmed entirely for the Chinese, and often by them. The government backs these agri-businesses with financial and diplomatic support. To guarantee its water supplies, China has been reordering the great rivers in ways which can have adverse effects upon its neighbours when they too rely upon those rivers.[29]

The immense expansion of industry at home, the frenzied building of houses, offices and infrastructure, more air travel, higher expectations for cars and household goods – all have created unprecedented demand for raw materials.

The country's need for energy drives its activities in Africa, Latin America and the Middle East. All this brings Chinese companies into contact with countries to which business with the People's Republic becomes more and more significant. In early 2016, the downturn in China's economy was blamed for the financial crises of countries which depend heavily on China buying their raw materials: crude oil (Venezuela), natural gas (Russia and the Central Asian 'stans'), and timber and critical minerals (Mozambique, Papua New Guinea, Indonesia, Burma, Congo, Madagascar, Gabon, Equatorial Guinea and others). China imports aluminium, cement, copper, zinc, lead, nickel, iron ore and steel, the processing and utilisation of which lead to increased requirements for gas and oil. China has become the world's second largest oil importer after the United States.[30]

Even before the announcement of the Belt and Road Initiative, the degree of involvement in the development of other countries was extraordinary.[31] 'In Africa alone, China has contributed to the construction of 2,000 km of railway tracks 3,000 km of roads, dozens of football stadiums and 160 schools and hospitals. It is building or financing 300 dams across the world,[32] and funding thousands of kilometres of strategic oil and gas pipelines in places such as Sudan, Kazakhstan and Burma, the re-construction of housing in war-torn countries such as Angola, and railway projects in Argentina and Venezuela'.[33] 'Chinese firms are already by far the biggest international infrastructure contractors, strongly entrenched in dominant position throughout Africa and Eastern Europe in particular.'[34] China is providing aid for economic and social development and for coping with climate change.[35] China's 'policy banks'[36] have been lending more to developing countries than the World Bank for many years.[37]

Bryan Gould, the New Zealander who has been an influential left politician in Britain, has noted that Chinese leaders 'see trade, aid and influence as complementary elements in a single integrated drive to ensure that China will have the access and control it needs to claim a much greater share of the world's resources.' 'The economies of other, smaller countries could in effect be absorbed into the greater Chinese economy and be directed from Beijing.'[38]

Ordinary Chinese citizens are connecting with the wider world too. In the first nine months of 2016, 122 million Chinese travelled abroad,[39] and 174 million are predicted to travel abroad in 2019.[40] About 4 million of the country's students have gone abroad for full-time study since 1978.

Media People: A campaigner

Ma Jun 马军 became established as an authority on China's environment with the publication of *China's water crisis* 中国水危机 in 1999. At the time, he was a reporter on Hong Kong's *South China Morning Post*, where he specialised in environment stories.

Mr Ma later set up the Institute of Public and Environmental Affairs公众环境研究中心, where he created the *China Water Pollution Map* 中国水污染地图, the first ever such database, and became a tireless campaigner at home and abroad, promoting transparency, citizen participation and mobilisation.

In 2012 he wrote: 'Beijing's lung cancer rates have risen by 60% over the last 10 years. In the words of Zhong Nanshan, an academician at the Chinese Academy of Engineering, because of air pollution, "everyone over the age of 50 in Guangzhou has black lungs!"'.

Image source:
http://en.wikipedia.org/wiki/
File:Ma_Jun_-
_Annual_Meeting_of_the_Ne
w_Champions_2012_crop.jpg

Ma Jun decided to concentrate on ensuring that people concerned about pollution had access to the information on which to base protests. He compiled databases of environmental law violations, and in particular targeted foreign companies as being most sensitive about their reputations in China. Quoting Isabel Hilton, who founded *China Dialogue*中外对话, to which Ma Jun is a prominent contributor, the *Christian Science Monitor* wrote: 'Ma understood that information is key. He saw that protest without information tends to make noise, not impact.'

Being involved in so many ways in so many countries and competing with others for resources and trade deals increases the potential for misunderstandings, even conflict. The competition between China and Japan for influence and contracts in Central Asia and Africa may be as much the source of hostility between the two nations as their rivalry in the South China Sea. There has been hostility towards China from US labour unions and business interests for many years, and European criticism of China's dealings in Africa. 80% of oil imports travels through the Strait of Malacca, which is policed by the US Navy, and American ships also patrol very near China's shore.[41]

In 2006, the Cambridge economist Robert Rowthorn predicted that Chinese demand for resources would cause shortages and higher prices, that the technological lead of the hitherto more advanced economies would be eroded as China emerges as a centre of science and technology, and that as labour in China becomes more expensive the advanced economies would have to pay more for their imports, forcing them to reconsider their balance of payments. Rowthorn predicted that demand for sophisticated products from the West would grow in China but that in order to continue to be competitive in attracting investment, the West would need to reform its economies. None of his predictions have proved unfounded[42] and all have the potential to cause anguish and resentment in many other countries.

17

To present China's point of view, defend its interests and provide information on what is happening in countries where its investments are great, information sources and providers are needed which are not arms of foreign states or representatives of commercial competitors. This is the most urgent requirement that propels China towards developing an international media. But China also wants to be seen differently for other reasons. What are they?

1.4   Esteem

When Li Changchun, the Politburo member then in charge of propaganda, visited CCTV in 2008, he said 'in the modern age, whichever nation's communication methods are most advanced, whichever nation's communication capacity is strongest, it is that nation whose culture and core values are going to spread far and wide, and that nation that has the most power to influence the world'.[43] He was alluding to soft power.[44] This became a hot topic in China in the late 1990s following publication of a book by Joseph Nye.[45] The USA's success in soft power was thought in China to point up its own failure to relay its story.

Ever since the 19th century, when the educated classes in China were forced to recognise the material superiority of Europe and their inability to defend their civilisation from it, their ambition for the nation to be a leader in the world and a model for others once again has blazed. The extraordinary achievements since the 1980s have convinced many that they deserve, if not leadership, then at least respect. Instead, many consider their country traduced, misrepresented and insulted by the very nations which assaulted China over a century ago.

In 1989 particular hostility was provoked by the Tiananmen Massacre. This concentrated minds in China's policy world on how to get their point of view across. Policymakers blamed the relative weakness of China's mass media on the international stage for the failure to improve perceptions of China.[46] Among many initiatives intended to put this right, the biggest was the 2008 Olympic Games.

Yet the international response to the Tibet riots of the same year almost ruined the Games for their hosts. The riots in Tibet were framed by many foreign media operations as liberation struggles. Some Europeans demonstrated against the Olympic torch relay or threatened to boycott the Games, and great prominence was given to them in the Anglophone media. This shocked many Chinese, to whom the riots were no different from those that have from time to time blighted American or European cities, particularly those connected with ethnic tensions. They were unprepared for the vehement criticism of their country and the failure to take account of its point of view.

Television: Applying international programme concepts

Multi-channelling and the variety of platforms have led to audience fragmentation 受众细分. Furthermore, foreign programming has been easily available online. Light entertainment shows, particularly Korean, have become very popular.

So, on the one hand, domestic pressure has intensified competition among media conglomerates; while, on the other, challenges from overseas are stimulating broadcasters. They have been looking abroad for ideas, motivated too by the government's 'going out' strategy 走出去策略 and the lure of foreign markets, which, given the limitations on their right to expand domestically, are the only opportunities for expansion once they have made a national success of their satellite channels. Regional broadcasters whose nominally subsidiary satellite channels had national reach and therefore competed with each other for advertising revenue, started with unauthorised imitation, copycatting foreign television programme formats, because to adapt a successful format was less risky and less expensive than creating from new. In 2005 Hunan Satellite TV sent some 15 producers to the UK, where there is a long-established record of innovation in light entertainment (LE), to study LE production from the various companies which had made the British format industry the world leader. The format industry has grown rapidly and as much as 65% of its global revenue may be earned by Britain. As a consequence of what its staff learnt abroad, instead of copying, Hunan by 2007 was buying the rights and producing authorised local versions of *Strictly Come Dancing* and *Just the Two of Us*.

Format purchasing and adaptation attracted attention from more and more broadcasters after the outstanding success of *China's Got Talent* 中国达人秀 in 2010, and there have been more than 40 authorised reproductions of foreign television formats, almost all of which originated from Europe. South Korean light entertainment shows have also been localized, with Chinese versions, such as Running Man，2 Days & 1 Night and Go Fighting!.

Voice of China 中国好声音 has been the most successful yet. In another departure, Shenzhen Media Group and Hengdun Chuanmei co-produced the British-originated *The Gadget Show* 一键启动, a fast-moving technology consumer series.

As format importation and adaptation have become the trend, so audience ratings have been on the rise. The teams which have worked on adapting and realising foreign formats claim that they have gained advanced expertise, improving their competencies through Chinese-foreign co-operation, and can turn these to account in creating original concepts. They are keen to develop and export; the first exported format from China was *Challenge Microphone* 挑战麦克风, produced by Hunan Satellite TV and sold to Thailand's True Visions TV in 2009.

Starting in 2016, there has been a rash of original innovations. In *The Readers* 朗读者 people from different professions read and comment on traditional and classical Chinese literature. *Letters Alive* 见字如面 explores behind historical letters or letters written by famous writers and *Challenge the impossible* 挑战不可能 is a programme that explores the courage and inspiration of ordinary people.

In 2015 SARPPFT issued a notice that no video streaming websites may broadcast foreign films or TV series, without license. To encourage more original programming, SAPPRFT issued a further rule in 2016 that from regional broadcasters may broadcast only one imported light entertainment show during the 19:30-22:30 slot.

Students in particular interpreted this as an attack, motivated by prejudice and jealousy, and driven by ignorance.[47] The Chinese Ambassador to London, Fu Ying 傅莹, later Vice Minister of Foreign Affairs, complained of demonization.[48] It was assumed that anti-Chinese propaganda held sway because China did not have the means to project its own views.

In consequence 'soft power' has become one of the most common expressions in public life. Hu Jintao 胡锦涛, President 2003-13, was in no doubt of its importance and that it was in China's interests to promote itself overseas.[49] When so opining, Chinese leaders revealed – perhaps as much to themselves as to the world – that they have an identity, a cultural and social system and a polity that are different to those of the Anglophones and that they intend this remain so.

They reject the characterisation of their country as one that has failed to modernise to Anglophone standards and do not accept that Anglophone political institutions are universal aspirations, as we shall see in Chapter 7. They wish to defend Chinese culture from what they see as pollution from 'mercenary' interests. They also appear to want to re-establish the pre 20th century order in East Asia, in which China was the model and moral leader. Their vision of the world is very different from that of Anglophones, in which countries cede power to global institutions and follow America's lead.

In historical maps, China is depicted as the middle of concentric circles; there are close countries, such as Korea, and others further away such as the principalities that now constitute Malaysia. According to sociologist Gary Hamilton 'The circle within a circle within a circle is a recurring motif in Chinese society. Take for example the Ivory ball within a ball within a ball. This type of carving has a philosophical meaning; it depicts the Chinese world order, the innermost sphere is the family and the outermost is *tianxia* 天下, all under heaven'.[50]

Today's vision is surely influenced by this.[51] Neither universalism nor utopias have much place in traditional Chinese thought. From China's perspective, it is not unreasonable to think that it should be the leader in East Asia. Today though, to become such, it has to persuade its neighbours – China shares borders with 14 countries – that it is worthy of respect and less dangerous than the USA and its 7th Fleet.

Diplomats try to do so, for example, by emphasising that China has not been aggressive, at least compared to the Europeans. It is this idea which underlies the promotion of Admiral Zheng He 郑和, the Ming Dynasty sailor whose voyages, unlike those of many European explorers, were peaceful and made no conquests. This appeals to countries which have been afflicted by imperialism, as does China's foreign policy of 'peaceful development' and respect for the sovereignty of others, a direct challenge to the 'Blair doctrine' or 'Liberal interventionism' espoused by leading US and British politicians. As Mark Leonard of the European Council on Foreign Relations, has it:

Where the USA is bellicose, Chinese policy-makers talk about peace. Whereas American diplomats talk about regime change, their Chinese counterparts talk about respect for sovereignty and the diversity of civilizations. Whereas American foreign policy uses sanctions and isolation to back up its political objectives, the Chinese offer aid and trade with no strings attached. Whereas America imposes its preferences on reluctant allies, China makes a virtue of listening to countries from around the world.[52]

This line has not been so easy to pursue since disputes in the South China Sea have become more heated.

Another selling point is the Chinese model 'in which a liberal market economy exists under an authoritarian political system', often referred to as the 'Beijing Consensus'.[53] This appeals to countries in which electoral democracy has not been tried, or is unstable. The implication is that China is successful because it has government focussing on what matters most to people, their economic conditions, rather than dissipating its energies in political competition. Such a government, the world must be told, is too fully occupied in solving domestic problems to be a threat to other countries.

China wishes to emphasise that it joins forces to contribute to the resolution of shared problems.[54] It has helped set up new international cooperation organisations, such as the Shanghai Cooperation Organisation (on Central Asia), the Forum of China and the Community of Latin American and Caribbean States, the Forum on China-African Cooperation, the Asian Infrastructure Investment Bank and the Belt and Road Initiative, to work with other countries, excluding the USA. The Belt and Road Initiative, in particular, seems bound to increase China's influence and stature as it promises massive infrastructure projects intended to hasten the development of many countries in Eurasia, of which China is likely to be principal partner or initiator.

Among the innumerable cultural initiatives taken to 'brand' China have been exhibitions, student exchanges, exports of performance, video billboards in New York, events of every kind in the capitals of Europe, foreign aid (especially of infrastructure) in poorer countries and substantial participation in international organisations, especially UN peacekeeping. Through the 500 Confucius Institutes,[55] many people are learning Chinese and becoming better informed about China.

Media people: a journalist and polemicist

Source of the image:
http://gb.cri.cn/27224/2011/
08/09/342s3331924_8.htm

Chai Jing 柴静 is a former CCTV presenter and journalist who now works as independent producer and environment campaigner.

From 2001, she was the presenter of *Oriental Horizon* 东方时空 in CCTV and become the leading journalist on *News Probe* 新闻调查 in 2003. Chai is famous for her courage and determination to go to the frontier of investigative journalism, such as exposing deaths in a mine disaster in Shanxi province and challenging peculation by officials. She was the first journalist to go into the isolation zone to interview SARS patients in 2003. In 2011, her book *Insight* 看见 became a best-seller.

After leaving CCTV in 2014, Chai undertook a self-financed independent investigative documentary *Under the Dome* 穹顶之下, on the effect of pollution on health and life in China. The documentary is reported to have got over 6 millions views within 12 hours and over 200 million views within 48 hours via the main Chinese streaming video websites. She challenged the weakness of environmental protection departments and questioned state owned energy companies. *Under the Dome was* banned in March 2015 and Chai was attacked by some netizens for deploying misleading statistics and being used by US interests.

Implicit in all these offerings are positive messages about China: economic progress as the consequence of benign state policies harnessing the market; foreign policy centred on peaceful development 和平发展 and non-interference 不干扰, the respect for diversity which Chinese consider that Anglo-America lacks; and Chinese civilisation as the culmination of several thousand years of achievement, to which the current President, Xi Jinping, constantly refers.[56]

This model can be understood as an equivalent of the 'American Dream'. President Xi has given us his version of the good life, which seems to be of a prosperous country which re-establishes itself as a leader in science, technology and the arts, amid a resurgence of Chinese civilisation, culture and defensive strength. This will undoubtedly appeal at home, but will it have resonance abroad? Some consider that it cannot, because China suffers from an identity crisis.[57] According to this view, it is trying to project itself as bearer of ancient values and civility abroad while at home it is shoring up a Marxist polity, with all the attendant injustices and violence. As long as China is confused about what it is, it media cannot project itself with confidence. The respect sought may be elusive.

1.5 Countering hostile propaganda

In the British Parliament, in 2012, Zhao Qizheng 赵启正, Chairman of the Foreign Relations Committee of China's upper house, the Consultative Conference 中国人民政治协商会议 (CPPCC), and former head of the State Council Information Office, reiterated a point he has been making for a very long time: the Anglophone-dominated global media 'demonises' China rather than presenting an impartial picture of it to the world. Because of this, China must provide 'accurate' sources of information.[58] In the same year, President Hu Jintao opined that 'we must clearly see that international forces are intensifying the strategic plot of westernising and dividing China'. He considered that that they wished to subvert his country through ideology and cultural imperialism.[59]

Anglophone observers tend to write this attitude off as paranoia or blame the Chinese for deluding themselves. International Relations specialist William Callahan considers that 'patriotic education' in schools, which emphasises humiliation at the hands of foreigners, 'United States as the evil hegemon, Japanese as devils, Taiwan as the renegade province, and the Dalai Lama as a ravenous wolf' has perverted China's vision. 'China has created for itself a sea of enemies'. [60] Yet from a Chinese perspective, influential foreign media misrepresent the nation by emphasising the negative and framing reporting of it detrimentally. Phillip Deans, also an IR specialist, says: 'The international media [are] always complaining about the riots, they're complaining about Tibet, they're saying that China is developing this great big strong army … the Chinese are sick to death of all of this negative coverage. They say, why isn't there more talk about how we've lifted hundreds of millions of people out of poverty? Why aren't people talking about China as a model for developing countries?'[61]

Two Influential Television Series

River Elegy 河殇; transmitted by CCTV in 1988, was a polemic against Chinese civilisation. From the 1920s to the extremity of the Cultural Revolution, radicals had claimed that it was China's culture that held their country back, a theory based on no discernible evidence. According to Mark Leonard, *River Elegy*, in which the destructive attitudes engendered in the 1920s reached their apogee ,'was quite likely influential in the rising tide of fervour for radical change which culminated in the disaster of the Tiananmen Massacre of 1989'.

River Elegy was well out of favour by 2006 when an equally remarkable television series captured the imagination of the country, *The Rise of the Great Powers* 大国崛起.

The passionate ignorance and anger had gone; this programme sought to understand why countries such as Spain and Portugal in their days, England, Japan and the USA later, had achieved economic and international success. One of the discoveries was that the Anglophone countries had long incubated certain valuable social institutions and that the traditional culture of those countries was the key to understanding their achievements. This was most welcome news to those who had begun to realise that their successes since the 1980s had come about once they had stopped trying to destroy their indigenous culture and, in practice if not in theory, rejected the totalising – and foreign – ideology that purported to lead to modernity via utopianism and repudiation of the past.

It can be difficult to accept that the Anglophone media are reporting in good faith. Since the invasions of Iraq and Afghanistan caused terrible suffering, to say nothing of the Vietnam War a generation ago, the Western media's 'obsession' with 'China's human rights violations' can be seen as hypocritical. The constant reiteration of the Tiananmen Massacre of nearly three decades ago, of the Tibet issue, and the bigging up of 'dissidents' are rather as if the USA were to be written off as iniquitous by those whose only reference points were the Trail of Tears, the My Lai Massacre, and Abu Ghraib.

That the US media evaluate foreign countries according to their own ideology and, as Lee Chin-ch'uan, eminent scholar of Chinese affairs, puts it, justify US interests abroad while 'undermin[ing] the legitimacy of its rivals', is not in question.[62] Empirical research backs up Chinese beliefs that the Anglophone press is hostile to China,[63] and indeed that political discourse in the USA is permeated by the notion of a 'China threat'.[64] In their book, *China's Search for security*, eminent political scientists Andrew Nathan and Andrew Scobell state: 'The United States constantly pressurises China over its economic policies, and maintains a host of government and private programmes that seek to influence Chinese civil society and politics.' They go on to say that 'Chinese officials consider that the United States uses the ideas of democracy and human rights to delegitimise and destabilise regimes that espouse alternative values, such as socialism and Asian-style developmental authoritarianism. And that it is only a short step from this to attack'.[65]

International Journalism students at Tsinghua University, who are the foreign correspondents of the future, have asked why it is China that is pilloried as a danger, when, they say, the USA and its allies have been so aggressive and violent, have subverted other countries and instigated or condoned the unrest and civil wars that have blighted the Muslim world over the last few years. Young people regard the USA as a thoroughly belligerent country, with the UK as its poodle, and they are more hostile than their elders.[66] The 'avalanche of negativity' seems to them like a 'softening up' or prelude to much worse.[67] During the US election periods of 2012 and 2016, a great deal of rancour against China was expressed by the political élites. Some of their advertisements are available on YouTube, one of the most unsavoury of which was 'The Chinese Professor', in which Chinese students (actually Korean and other actors) are shown laughing over their clever schemes to destroy the USA.[68] Hostility to, and denigration of, China has reached a new nadir since the election of President Trump.[69]

This is not to say that the Chinese government does not give plenty of openings to those who want to ridicule or condemn it. The persecution of the Falungong 法轮大法 meditation practitioners, the countenancing of harsh measures of population control, allowing rights activists to be maltreated and the demonisation of critics all provide ammunition. And when China's media are obliged to propagate such stuff, they can seem absurd or sinister. Those tyro correspondents at Tsinghua are, though, very conscious of the deficiencies of their own media. What they reject is the Anglophones' assumption that the media in their countries are impartial or free of propaganda. To illustrate common attitudes to the Anglophone media, here is a cynical passage from *The Inner Court* 后院, a recent novel, in which a doughty investigative reporter has been working on his editor to back him in a sensitive investigation of official corruption and malfeasance:

> *Editor:*
> For heaven's sake don't bring up that 'freedom of the press' stuff, it turns my stomach. It's too false: you just tell me, what country really has a free press? USA?

> *Reporter:*
> USA? Some freedom! The US media all just follow the cue of the big corporations, the corporations are their father and mother and food and drink; the media are just the throat and tongue of different profit grubbers, mere spokespersons. Americans know perfectly well that their press freedom is a fraud.[70]

Many are of the conviction that the Anglophone media treat China as an enemy and are intentionally ignorant of that which they vilify.

At a seminar on public service media in January 2013, CCTV's best known current affairs analyst, Bai Yansong, asked a prominent Anglosphere TV anchor, Jeremy Paxman, what the Chinese media should learn from the BBC. After a long answer, a disquisition on the wonders of a free press and, by implication, condemnation of China's, Paxman politely asked what he should learn from China. Bai Yansong replied, tersely, 'Chinese'.

1.6   Current evaluations of the Chinese media abroad

Such is the climate in which the Chinese media abroad have to operate, and in which they are expected to undermine the idea that somehow the Anglophone media are reliable whereas theirs are not. Can they succeed?

Foreign journalists employed by Chinese media companies acknowledge the challenge of attracting viewers who may be sceptical about news sources controlled by the state.[71] The prescribed role of the media in the 'guidance of public opinion' could impede its ability to wield soft power because Anglophones are sceptical of state controlled media,[72] although where rival news organizations have commented on CCTV coverage of international events, they have accounted them balanced.[73]

Media people: The Debater

Image source:
http://cctv.cntv.cn/lm/dialog
ue/host/yangrui/

A native of Jilin but brought up largely in Heilongjiang, Yang Rui 杨锐 graduated from Shanghai Foreign Studies University in 1986 with degrees in English Literature and International Journalism. He started his professional career as a journalist at China Central People's Radio Service. In 1988, he moved to CCTV and began his career as an English-language TV reporter, quickly becoming presenter of *Focus*. Between 1993 and 1994, he studied at Cardiff College of the University of Wales and obtained the master degree in Global Media.

Yang has been working at CCTV's English services for over 20 years and is best known as the producer and presenter of its most famous talk show *Dialogue*, broadcast every weekday. This show enjoys the highest rating on the English service. He is best known for his aggressive and sharp style, witty arguments and broad knowledge. On *Dialogue* has interviewed many leading scholars, scientists, and politicians including the UN Secretary General and former US Presidents Clinton and Carter. He covers controversial domestic matters such as human rights, religious freedom, the death penalty and government and political reform as well as all major international issues.

His English is flawless and his vocabulary extensive, such that he can interview in a probing and unpredictable manner if he so wishes; those who accept his invitations need to be prepared for unexpected changes of tack. Anglophones should not imagine that because he is able to move easily in English speaking company, his opinions coincide with theirs. The nationalistic way in which he expressed his condemnation of lowlife behaviour by some foreigners in the seedier parts of Beijing, shocked foreign followers when they saw them posted on his blog.

Yang was involved in reporting the return to China of Hong Kong and Macao, the 2000 Sydney Olympics and other major events and has won many awards, including one from CNN for *Tea House* 茶馆, which examined local culture in Peking and Shanghai.

China also faces problems of media management and technical virtuosity. While other countries were developing their creative industries in the 1960s and 1970s, China's stood still. Although they are catching up very fast, the state-run institutions are slow movers. The education, training and recruitment of foreign correspondents is unsystematic[74] and inimical to good work. Their conditions of work are not good and as a consequence inexperienced young people tend to take on many of the jobs, putting them at a great disadvantage to seasoned reporters from other countries.

In her ongoing comparisons of CCTV and BBC international news, former BBC producer Vivien Marsh finds some interesting differences, though the gulf is not as great as polemicists would surmise. CCTV reports very much more of Asia, the BBC very much more of Europe. As to Africa, CCTV especially attends to countries in which it has interests, while the BBC emphasises former British colonies. The BBC appears to make a conscious effort to diminish reporting of

China's contributions in Africa, for example by devoting a mere 25 seconds to the visit of a Chinese Prime Minister notwithstanding the huge array of infrastructure projects that he had come to initiate or propose. Not surprisingly, CCTV gave the trip a great deal more airtime. Reporting by the Chinese media on the Charlie Hebdo killings was not homogenous: some media echoed the Anglosphere/EU line that all good and true should unite against this attack on free speech, but at least one English language newspaper from China suggested that the murdered Charlie Hebdo journalists could be seen as warriors in a war against Islam. The Hong Kong demonstrations of 2015 were reported from the perspective of the authorities (or the 'silent majority' who thought the demonstrations a nuisance), contrasting with the BBC's unremitting bias in favour of the demonstrators whom they framed, uncritically, as fighters for democracy.[75]

Taking a helicopter view, Phillip Deans[76] considers that the Chinese media will in time provide an acceptable alternative, particularly in the developing world. The Anglophone assumption that a country with an authoritarian government cannot produce high quality media is not necessarily true: 'CCTV does very good coverage of issues, unless they are related to China. I think people will increasingly turn, especially in the developing world, to a Chinese news channel as much as they would turn to the BBC. It'll be problematic, and it may never be [that events are covered in] the way that many people in the United Kingdom or the United States think is appropriate for journalism, but that doesn't mean it's not going to work, and that doesn't mean it won't be successful. Are the Chinese media, at their worst, any worse than the American media at their worst at times for bias on content, coverage and presentation? Probably not. It's not as sophisticated, [and] standards in terms of the quality aren't there yet, but they'll close up, they'll narrow that gap with technical standards. And it will be a heavily biased perspective, but probably no more biased a perspective than Fox News or even in its own peculiar way the BBC, which has a very strong bias in favour of liberalism and human rights and democracy'.[77]

When these issues were put to him, the Deputy President of CCTV replied:

> 'Individual stories will be handled impartially and truthfully; an earnest of our determination in this respect is that we will be employing professional journalists from the BBC and good quality US media, people with reputations to defend. These are not people who will change their standards of professionalism when they join a rival broadcaster. Where we may differ is in the selection of stories to cover. We believe that Western news organisations often betray a bias in selection, even when they are excellent at reporting. Not surprisingly, since we are Asians, from a developing country, with a different set of priorities from Europeans or

Americans, our selection of what matters may be different. There is no harm in that'…[78]

Chinese Journalists Find their Voice

From August 22nd 2017, CCTV war correspondent Yu Peng 余鹏 ran a series of reports *Syria War Diary* from the front line of Kurdish Peshmerga fighting ISIS.[79] Individual reports included the recently reopened bus journey from Qamishhlo to Damascus; the frontline of Yekîneyên Parastina Gel (YPG) snipers in Qarah; interviews with a former ISIS member about brainwashing and threats used on ISIS recruits.

CCTV's Xu Dezhi 徐德智 contributed to an exposure of the 'White Helmets'.[80] In August 2016, many international media (CNN,[81] BBC[82] and *The Guardian*[83]) featured pictures of a five-year old boy, Omran Daqneesh, wounded and covered in blood and dust, stated to have been victim of Russian or Syrian government forces' indiscriminate attacks in Aleppo and then rescued by the 'White Helmets', an organisation of impartial rescuers. Xu later interviewed the boy's father and found that he had been offered money to blame the Syrian government. [84] Xu reported the father alleging that the 'White Helmets' had been mainly interested in taking photographs and had held the boy against the wishes of the family in order to use him for publicity.

Xu is not alone among correspondents in questioning this the veracity of this, or other, stories coming out of Syria. The great American investigative journalist Seymour Hersh, in 'Whose Sarin?',[85] examined the attribution of blame for a poison gas attack on Damascus' Eastern Ghouta . He alleged that blame had probably wrongly, and mischievously, been attributed to the Syrian government.

China's media abroad are starting to tell stories their way and to equate with the established international media in such a manner that other media treat them seriously. In 2017, several Chinese frontline correspondents were written up in a [British] *Guardian* feature. [86]

1.7   Responsible media?

CCTV journalism claims to be different in other respects. First, the impact of what it reports is taken into consideration. Second, it judges itself by its ability to promote peace and development rather than 'the need to bear witness and write the first draft of history from the front line'. [87] CCTV Editors think that Anglophone media are too adversarial, too combative; they want to be positive and useful.[88] Practitioners distinguish such journalism from both the negative approach they consider to be favoured in the Anglosphere and also its reviled antithesis, positive journalism.[89] In so doing, CCTV Africa 'promote[s] a view of Africans seeking their own solutions.'[90] CCTV is saying that it wants to 'give a new kind of balance and shine a new kind of light on the continent'.[91]

There are, though, restrictions on CCTV's ability to provide the 'new type of journalism', often termed 'constructive', to which they aspire. These include not only the oft-cited subservience to the political line, at least when covering China issues, but also a lack of confidence among its reporters when making selections and assessments. This can make their reports anodyne or drive them to rely heavily on Anglophone agencies or NGOs whose material reflects Anglophone agenda and values. [92] As a consequence, CCTV is probably not reflecting a Chinese understanding of the world, something that has been suspected by academics such as Li Xiguang[93] and has been given empirical underpinning both by Jirik and Marsh.

John Jirik,[94] an American journalist who worked in the Chinese media before becoming an academic, finds that, far from being Party propaganda, CCTV's international news is barely distinguishable from that of its competitors. He suggests that this is in part because it sources so much of its material from international agencies. 'Management's claim that CCTV-I provided Chinese perspective on world events was not supported, unless a story involved Chinese interests.' This observation reflected Chang & Chen's finding, a decade earlier, that the conformity of news to the 'Party line' was contingent on the relationship of the story to PRC interests. In line with their findings, when the 'national interest' was not part of the story, reports tend to be standardized according to international criteria. [95]

The value to the rest of the world in having a Chinese media presence is that it might offer an alternative perspective to the dominant framings of international affairs. On the other hand, it might fail in this endeavour, 'follow[ing] the same market-driven, infotainment-oriented model with its roots in the commercial media system of the US'.[96]

Whether the Chinese media will enrich us, paying attention to what others have ignored, talking in new terms and becoming an antidote to CNN or the BBC, probably depends upon how China resolves the identity problem mentioned a few pages ago. Is it a benign lodestar of ancient values or just a greedy state? Without such a resolution, the media will not be able to represent with confidence the revitalised Chinese culture which they aim to promote.

1.8   Will China succeed in accumulating 'soft power'?

American academic David Shambaugh has done a thorough audit[97] and is of the opinion that China's influence, and hence its soft power, is very limited for several reasons. First, he considers that the Chinese government is itself unclear as to what it should establish as the Chinese image or brand and that this problem derives from the inconvenient fact that while the official ideology is the discredited Marxism Leninism, the proclaimed philosophy amounts to modern Confucianism. President Xi appears to be attempting a fusion, but Shambaugh sees the contradiction is thus far unresolved. Secondly, the government is inconsistent in declaring itself benign while allowing the persecution of various individuals and minorities.

Some Foreign Formats Reproduced in China up to 2016

Hunan Satellite:

- *Your Face Sounds Familiar* 百变大咖秀: 2012, a celebrity imitation show, Endemol, the Netherlands
- *Top Gear* 最高档: 2011, a car-based television series, the BBC, UK
- *Take Me Out* 我们约会吧: 2009-2012, a dating show, FrementleMedia, UK
- *1 vs. 100* 以一敌百: 2008-2010, a game show, Endemol, the Netherlands
- *Just the Two of Us* 名声大振: 2007-2009, a reality singing contest, the BBC, UK
- *Strictly Come Dancing* 舞动奇迹: 2007-2011, a celebrity dancing show, the BBC, UK
- *Divas Hit the Road* (花儿与少年): 2014-2016, travel-reality show, Sisters Over Flowers , tvN, South Korean
- *Where Are We Going, Daddy?* (爸爸去哪儿): 2013-2016, reality TV show, Dad! Where Are We Going? MBC, South Korea
- *I Am a Singer* (我是歌手), 2013-2016, singing competition program, I Am a Singer, MBC, South Korean
- *Takes a Real Man* (真正男子汉), 2015, Military variety shw, Real Men, MBC, South Korean

Shanghai's Dragon TV:

- *The Cube* 梦立方: 2012, a game show, All3Media, UK
- *MasterChef* 顶级厨师: 2012, a cooking show, the BBC, UK
- *Sing It* 我心唱响: 2011-2012, a reality singing show, Talpa Media, the Netherlands
- *China's Got Talent* 中国达人秀: 2010-2012, reality singing contest, FremantleMedia's *Britain's Got Talent*, UK

Zhejiang Satellite:

- *Tonight's the Night* 中国梦想秀: 2011-2012, a game show, the BBC, UK
- *The Voice of China* 中国好声音: 2012, a reality singing contest, Talpa Media's *The Voice*, the Netherlands
- *I'm the Winner* 冲关我最棒: 2012, a quiz show, *101 Ways to Leave a Gameshow*, Endemol for the BBC
- *The More You Dance, The Prettier You Are* 越跳越美丽: 2012, a weight-loss dancing competition, 495 Production's *Dance Your Ass Off*, US
- *Hurry Up, Brother or Running Man* 奔跑吧兄弟: 2014-2016, game-variety, *Running Man*, SBS, South Korea

Jiangsu Satellite Channel:

- *Husband can do* 老公看你的: 2010-2011, a game show, SevenOne International's *My Man Can*, Germany
- *Quarrelsome Lovers* 欢喜冤家: 2010-2011, a reality show based on marital disputes, Endemol's *The Marriage Ref*, the Netherlands
- *Who Dares, Sings* 谁敢来唱歌: 2009, a karaoke style game show, ITV, UK
- *A Bright World* 世界青年说, 2015-2016, talk show, Non-Summit, JTBC, South Korean
- *Hidden Singer* 蒙面歌王, 2015, entertainment TV program, Hidden Singer, JTBC, South Korean

Southeast Satellite Channel:

- *Happy Choir* 欢乐合唱团: 2011, a game show, the BBC's *Last Choir Standing*, UK
- *Let's Go Tomorrow* 明天就出发:2011-2012, a game show, the BBC's *This Time Tomorrow*, UK

Shenzhen Satellite Channel:

- *Generation Show* 年代秀: 2011-2012, a celebrity quiz and game show, DRG International, UK

Anhui Satellite Channel:

- *Don't Stop Me Now* 势不可挡: 2012, a talent show, FremantleMedia, UK

Liaoning Satellite Channel:

- *Sing With Verve* 激情唱响: 2011-2012, a reality singing contest, FremantleMedia's *The X Factor*, UK

Hubei Satellite Channel:

- *I Love My Country* 我爱我的祖国: 2012, a celebrity quiz show, Talpa Media, the Netherlands

Guangdong Satellite Channel:

- *Dating in the Dark* 完美暗恋: 2011, a dating show, Talpa Media, the Netherlands

China Central Television:

- *Great Challenge* 了不起的挑战, 2015-2016, television entertainment program, Infinite Challenge, MBC, South Korea.

Thirdly, Shambaugh considers that China's reputation is unattractive to the rest of the world on account of its political system. Odd Arne Westad, of Harvard University, goes further: 'in cultural terms, China is singularly lacking in soft power: no young person of sound mind in Tokyo or Seoul, or even in Taipei or Singapore, is looking to the PRC for music to download, films to watch, or ideas to latch on to'.[98] I am not so sure. Martial arts and exercises, massage, the art of food and medical practices are well established in many countries; exported films, though few, are popular; design, fashion, telenovellas and pop music are not far behind. Very large numbers are studying Chinese at school and will be consumers before long. And within a generation, China's equivalents of *The Economist* and *Wall Street Journal* are likely to become influential abroad, if only because Chinese business matters.

Are the media succeeding in altering perceptions of China? China's position has undeniably improved in the eyes of many. Opinion polls show a growing respect for the country; the more countries have to do with China, the more they appear to be well disposed towards it.[99] The Chinese model of development is admired[100] and it is very probable that in many areas of the world, when doing business and politics, it is Chinese norms that now determine how things should be rather than Anglophone ones. In Britain (and elsewhere) many schools have not only introduced Chinese as a second language but also adopted Chinese methods of teaching mathematics. Immersion schools, seeking to soak children in Chinese culture as well as language, are sprouting up: There are now over 200 Chinese immersion schools in the USA alone.

Having looked at China's media 'going out', we will now turn to how they have evolved to reach this point and the parts they have played in the nation's rise in recent decades.

Notes

[1] Zhang, Xiaoling (2009) Chinese state media going global. In: *East Asia Policy*, pp 42-50, pp 44.
[2] There have been PRC-backed Chinese language media in many countries for a long time. See Zhu Ying (2016) 'Transnational Circulation of Chinese-Language Television Dramas' in Zhu Ying and Berry Chris (2090) *TV China*, Bloomington : Indiana UP p 229
[3] Zhang, Xiaoling. Personal communication; 23 January 2012.

[4]Zhang, Xiaoling (2009). From 'foreign propaganda' to 'international communication': China's promotion of soft power in the age of information and communication technologies. In: Zhang X, Zheng Y. (eds.) *China's information and communications technology revolution: social changes and state responses*. New York; London: Routledge, pp 103-120.

[5] Zhang, ibid., pp 110.

[6] Farhi P. (2012) In DC China builds a news hub to help polish its global image. *Washington Post*, 16 January 2012.

[7] Branigan T. (2011) Chinese state TV unveils global expansion plan: CCTV to increase overseas staff tenfold by 2016 as English Language services spearhead Beijing's soft power push. *The Guardian*, 8 December 2011.

[8] ibid.

[9] For an overview of China's media in Africa, see Gagliardone, Iginio, Repnikova, Maria and Stremlau, Nicole (undated) *China in Africa: a new approach to media development?* , Oxford: PCMLP

[10] Fesmedia-africa. How do you say 'good morning Africa' in Chinese? [Online] 2012 [cited 27 February 2013]. Available at: http://www.fesmedia-africa.org/what-is-news/africa-media-news/news/article/how-do-you-say-good-morning-africa-in-chinese/. (Accessed: 17 March 2016). On 18 June 2012 the BBC World (TV) launched Focus on Africa, attracting a weekly audience of 77 million; this put a question on the CCTV claims.

[11] BBC. BBC to launch focus on Africa TV programme. [Online]. 2012 [cited 27 February 2013]. Available at: http://www.bbc.co.uk/news/world-18375291 (Accessed: 17 March 2016).

[12] Zhang, ibid., pp 47.

[13] Zhu Ying (2016) 'Transnational Circulation of Chinese-Language Television Dramas' in Zhu Ying and Berry Chris (2090) *TV China*, Bloomington : Indiana UP, pp 221.

[14] http://www.scmp.com/tech/enterprises/article/1886420/legend-miyue-smashes-online-video-viewing-record-china-700-million (Accessed 31 July 2017)

[15] Since the 1990s Chinese language services in many countries have been incorporated or initiated by PRC companies. For example, backed by CCTV, American Eastern TV has had a 12-hours a day Chinese language service in the US since 1993. I have deliberately excluded Chinese language services abroad; for more information, see Zhu et al (2009), pp 229.

[16] Wang Jianjun, the head of SMG, said at a London seminar for UK media executives, held on 21 October 2015 at the China Media Centre: 'SMG has active working relationships with BBC, RSC, Disney and Dreamworks, among others, yet the relationships are not equal. We buy 300 hours of TV from the UK but the UK buys virtually nothing from us, partly because there is a dearth of reciprocal respect and interest. We need to learn from our British counterparts how to develop Chinese content in such ways that it will be acceptable and attractive to you.......... European audiences are largely ignorant of the huge corpus of Chinese literature and history. My ambition is to find ways of encouraging them to enjoy the *Water Margin, The Tale of the Three Kingdoms, The Journey to the West* and gradually to make our heritage as appreciated here as is yours in China.'

[17] Fung, Anthony Y.H. (2008) *Global Capital, Local Culture* New York: Peter Lang, pp 193.

[18] Lobato, Ramon (2007) quoting Michael Curtin in his review of 'Rising in the East? Playing to the world's biggest audience: the globalisation of Chinese film and TV' in *Book Reviews* Issue 45, November 2007.

[19] Liu Liu 六六 (2007) 蜗居 *WoJu* (Snailhouse). 武汉 Wuhan: 长江文艺 Changjiang Wenyi; 池莉 Chi Li (2009) 来来往往 *Coming and Going*. 北京出版集团公司北京十月文艺出版社 Writers' Publishing House, China; 王海岭 Wang H (2004) 中国式离婚 *Divorce, Chinese style*. 北京 Beijing: 北京出版社 Beijing Publishing House.

[20] see Robinson, Luke (2013) *Independent Chinese Documentary: From the Studio to the Street*, Oxford: Palgrave

[21] I am thinking of, in particular, *In the Heat of the Sun* 阳光灿烂的日子. Wang has also made patriotic historical dramas, such as *The Building of the Nation* 建国大业。

[22] Zhao Qi's *The Chinese Mayor* won a Special Jury Prize at the Sundance Festival in 2015.

[23] For a well-informed overview, see Stiglitz J, Yusuf S, editors. (2001) *Rethinking the East Asian miracle*. New York: OUP.

[24] Cardenal JP, Araujo H. (2013) *China's Silent Army*. London: Allen Lane.

[25] Ibid.

[26] 'Se il padrone e Cinese' (When the Boss is Chinese), *L'Espresso*; 20 June 2013.

[27] Gould, Bryan (2013) *Myths, Politicians and Money* London: Palgrave Macmillan, p136

[28] Cardenal, JP. (2013), pp 228.

[29] Choi R. (2011) The push to dam China's rivers. [Online]. 19 May 2011 [cited 10 Aug 2013]. Available at: http://blogs.ei.columbia.edu/2011/05/19/the-push-to-dam-china%E2%80%99s-rivers/ (Accessed: 17 March 2016).

[30] SCMP. [Online]. 15 August 2012 [cited 2 July 2013]. Available at: http://www.scmp.com/article/992533/help-china-drive-resources-us-body-says (Accessed: 17 March 2016). See also Burgos Cáceres Sigfrido. *Understanding China's global search for energy and resources*. Central European Journal of International and Security Studies. 2013; 7(1).

[31] There are many sources of information on China's investments abroad, from the World Bank onwards. See, for example the World Resources Institute, (Accessed: 17 March 2016). http://www.wri.org/blog/closer-look-china's-overseas-investment. (Accessed: 17 March 2016).

[32] Sinohydro 中国水电集团 is the world's most experienced builder of dams.

[33] Cardenal, JP. (2013), pp 8.

[34] Gould, op cit, p137

[35] Bernasconi-Osterwalder N, Johnson L, Zhang J. (2012) *Chinese outward investment: an emerging policy framework*. Winnipeg: International Institute for Sustainable Development, pp 24.

[36] China Development Bank, Exim Bank, People's Bank of China.

[37] https://www.chinadialogue.net/article/show/single/en/8947-China-becomes-world-s-biggest-development-lender , accessed 290517

[38] Gould, op cit, p138

[39] http://www.travelchinaguide.com/tourism/2014statistics/outbound.htm
 By November of 2014 China's yearly outbound tourists reached 100 million for the first time, a milestone in China's outbound tourism. In the whole year, the outbound tourists reached 117 million, an increase of 19.16% over 2013. (Accessed: 17 March 2016).

[40] Li Jing and Yang Feiyue (2016) 'Going Mobile' in *China Daily*, 20 January 2016, pp 19.

[41] That navy 'is superior and operating only a few miles from many of China's major cities', writes Dyer. The pentagon has a war plan directed at China, called *Air Sea Battle* . See Dyer, Geoff 'Is this the new cold war?' FT Com: 22 to 23 February 2014.

[42] Rowthorn R. 2004. *The renaissance of China and India: implications for the advanced economies*. UNCTAD working paper. [Online]. Available at: http://unctad.org/en/docs/osgdp20071_en.pdf. (Accessed 7 March 2016). See also Robert Rowthorn & Kenneth Coutts (2013) *De-Industrialisation and the Balance of Payments in Advanced Economies*, Cambridge: Centre for Business Research, University of Cambridge Working Paper No. 453

[43] Richard Sambrook on 6th February 2015 in his keynote address to the first annual conference of the *UK China Media and Cultural studies Association*, quoting from a report to the US Congress.

[44] The theory of soft power is generally taken to mean that military and economic power is buttressed, even sometimes trumped, by what an American politician has referred to as 'the civilian instruments of national security – diplomacy, strategic communications, foreign assistance, civic action, and economic reconstruction and development'.

See Shanker T. 'Defense Secretary [Robert M Gates] urges more spending for US diplomacy'. [Online]. *New York Times*. 27 November 2007 [cited 30 July 2013]. Available at www.nytimes.com/2007/11/27/washington/27gates.html (Accessed: 17 March 2016)

[45] Joseph Nye's book, *Bound to Lead: The Changing Nature of American Power;* the concept was later refined in Nye, JS. (2004) *Soft power: the means to success in world politics.* New York: PublicAffairs™ (Perseus Books).

[46] Li, Mingjiang (2009). Soft power in Chinese discourse: popularity and prospect. In: Li Mingjiang (ed.) *Soft power: China's emerging strategy in international politics.* Lanham, Md.: Lexington Books (Rowman & Littlefield), pp 21-44.

[47] Wang, Yu (2009). *What makes a successful online community? a case study of the Powerapple forum, an overseas Chinese online community.* Unpublished MA dissertation. London: University of Westminster.

[48] http://www.telegraph.co.uk/comment/personal-view/3557186/Chinese-ambassador-Fu-Ying-Western-media-has-demonised-China.html (Accessed 19 March 2016)

[49] 'President Hu Jintao, for instance, noted at the Central Foreign Affairs Leadership Group meeting on 4th January 2006 that the increase of China's international status and influence depends both on hard power, such as the economy, science and technology, and defence, as well as on soft power, such as culture. Hu again highlighted soft power in his political report to the 17th Party Congress in October 2007, stressing the urgent need to build China's cultural soft power to meet domestic needs and increasing international challenges' (see, *passim,* Li Mingjiang (2009) *Soft power: China's Emerging Strategy in International Politics,* Plymouth: Lexington).

[50] Hamilton, Gary G. (2015) 'What Western social scientists can learn from the writings of Fei Xiaotong' in *Journal of China in comparative perspective* volume one number 1 June 2015 pp 143 to 160, pp 125.

[51] Threre has been much discussion of the *Tianxia* concept and its relevance to the modern world, by, among others Zhao Tingyang, whose writings can be found through the Internet.

[52] Leonard, Mark (2008) *What does China think?* London: Fourth Estate, pp 99.

[53] Ramo, JC. (2004) *The Beijing consensus: how China's authoritarian model will dominate the twenty-first century.* London: Foreign Policy Centre.

[54] Ambassador Wu Jianmin, speaking at LSE *Ideas* on 22 December 2014, emphasised that China had learnt the lessons of the 20th century that the 'daunting' problems of the present (nuclear proliferation, pandemics, climate change, terrorism, the widening gap between North and South) required not war and revolution but cooperation. He was expressing the national policy in terms with which Anglophones can identify.

[55] *The Diplomat.* Re-examining the Confucian Institutes. [Online]. 2012. Available at: http://thediplomat.com/china-power/reexamining-the-confucian-institutes/ (Accessed: 17 March 2016); Opponents have been doing their best to undermine efforts to have cultural outreach programmes similar to those that European governments have long had. There is a campaign against Confucius Institutes in the USA and something similar involving US academics in the UK. ['Confucius says', *The Economist,* 13 September 2014 pp 35 to 36].

[56] for example, see Xi Jinping (2014) *The Governance of China,* Beijing: Waiwen pp 179 and other sections of the same volume; also his selected speeches on literary and artistic work, in 习近平总书记（2015）在文艺工作座谈会上的讲话（学习读本）北京：中国美术学院党委宣传部 General Secretary Xi Jinping *Talks on Cultural Work* (Study Text)Peking: Publicity Office of the Central College of Art.

[57] Callahan, WA & Barabantseva E. (2011) *China orders the world: normative soft power and foreign policy.* Baltimore: Johns Hopkins University Press; pp 201 passim.

[58] Zhao Qizheng at the Westminster Forum: *Soft Power and the Creative Industries: China and Britain,* 25 April 2012 in the House of Commons.

[59] Rawnsley, Gary (2015) Chinese international broadcasting, public diplomacy and soft power. In: Rawnsley, Gary D. and Rawnsley Ming-yeh T. (eds.) *Routledge Handbook of Chinese Media,* London: Taylor & Francis, pp 466.

[60] Callahan, William A. (2010) *China: The Pessoptimist Nation* Oxford and New York: Oxford University Press, pp 194.

[61] Deans P. Personal communication; 2012 Feb 14.

[62] Lee, Chin-chuan (1991) Mass Media: Of China, About China. In: Lee, Chin-chuan (ed.) *Voices of China: The Interplay of Poitics and Journalism.* London: The Guildford Press, pp 20.

[63] See Sparks 2010. But see also: Cao Q. Signification of Hong Kong's handover: the case of the British press. *Journal of International Communication.* 1999; 6(2):71-89.; Mawdsley, E. (2008) Fu Manchu versus Dr Livingstone in the Dark Continent? Representing China, Africa and the West in British broadsheet newspapers. *Political Geography.* 2008; 27:509-529. Yang YE, Liu X. The China threat through the lens of US print media 1992-2006. *Journal of Contemporary China.* 2012; 21(76):695-711. Sullivan J, Renz B. Representing China in the South Pacific . [Online]. East Asia. 2012. [cited 2013 Aug 10]. Available at: http://www.academia.edu/1628681/Representing_China_in_the_South_Pacific (Accessed: 17 March 2016); Cao Q. (1999) Signification of Hong Kong's handover: the case of the British press. *Journal of International Communication* 6(2), pp 71-89. [Online]. Available at: http://www.tandfonline.com/doi/abs/10.1080/13216597.1999.9751890 (Accessed: 10 Aug 2013).

[64] Nathan, AJ & Scobell, A. (2012) *China's search for security.* New York: Columbia University Press.

[65] Nathan AJ, Scobell A. (2012), pp 39. James Dobbin (former Assistant Secretary of State) argues that 'A climate of mutual distrust and suspicion clouds the US-China relationship, and is producing a potent security dilemma. If ignored, this dynamic could spiral out of control. Altering it will require both the United States and China to fundamentally rethink their national security goals and strategic assumptions in Asia and beyond.'

[66] Westad, OA. (2012) *Restless empire: China and the world since 1759.* London: Bodley Head, pp 457.

[67] For further discussion of this phenomenon, see O'Connell, AB. (2012) The permanent militarization of America. *New York Times.* 4 November 2012, pp 10.

[68] https://www.youtube.com/watch?v=OTSQozWP-rM (Accessed: 17 March 2016)

[69] Edward Luce informs us that influential Trump's advisers have form as China-haters, Luce, E. (2017) *The Retreat of estern Liberalism* London: Little, Brown, pp145-153.

[70] 高和著 Gao He (2006). 后院 *The inner court.* 北京 Beijing: 中国友谊出版社 China Friendship Publishing Company, pp 47.

[71] Farhi, P. (2012) In DC China builds a news hub to help polish its global image. *Washington Post.* 16 January 2012.

[72] 'Any reports on breaking news are organised and managed by the State Council Information Office, which drafts the reportage on the incident, and after approval from the Central Government and the State Council, it will organise the reporting of it to the outside world. It is difficult for the Chinese media, with their lack of competitiveness, caused by strict government restrictions, to win large audiences abroad' (Zhang, X. (2009) From Propaganda to International Communication: China's promotion of Soft Power in the age of Information and Communication Technologies. In: Zhang, X. and Zheng, Y. (eds.) *China's Information and Communications Technology: Social changes and state responses.* London: Routledge, pp 114)

[73] Dong, SG & Shi, A. (2007) Chinese news in transition. In: Thussu DK. (ed.). *Media on the move: global flow and contra-flow.* London; New York: Routledge (Taylor & Francis Group), pp 183.

[74] The comment is the result of many conversations with dissatisfied CCTV and CNC employees. As far as I am aware, the only research into current Foreign Correspondents has been undertaken by Pal Nyiri, who expressed very similar concerns in an address 'China's New Generation of Foreign Correspondents: Cosmopolitan Lives, Sinocentric Stories' given at *China and the Changing Geopolitics of Global Communication*, conference in London's China Media Centre on 09 April 2016.

[75] Marsh, Vivien (2016) presentation to postgraduate students of 28 January 2016, based on her, 'Mixed messages, partial pictures? Discourses under construction in CCTV's *Africa*

Live compared with the BBC.' Chinese Journal of Communication (November 2015). http://www.tandfonline.com/doi/abs/10.1080/17544750.2015.1105269 (Accessed: 17 March 2016); 'Africa through Chinese eyes: new frames or the same old lens? African news in English from China Central Television, compared with the BBC.', Chapter in the Routledge anthology, Africa's Media Image in the 21st Century: from the 'Heart of Darkness' to 'Africa Rising'. (eds. M Bunce, C Paterson, S Franks); 'Looking global, acting national? CCTV-News (English) and BBC World News compared.' , 2nd Chinese Intercultural Communication Annual (2016).

[76] Deans P. Personal communication; 14 February 2012. Phillip Deans, former Head of the Contemporary China Institute, is now Professor of International Affairs at Richmond University.

[77] Ibid.

[78] Sun Yusheng. personal communication; 12 November 2011.

[79] CCTV. 2017. Talk to the father of Aleppo's 'boy in the ambulance'. [Online]. Available from:http://m.news.cctv.com/2017/06/20/ARTI6qCcEHcEDfgstH7STWrC170620.shtml [Accessed 27 August 2017]

[80] For an apparently impartial discussion of the White Helmet phenomenon, by a former US Intelligence agent, see: https://www.truthdig.com/articles/the-white-helmets-and-the-inherent-contradiction-of-americas-syria-policy/ [accessed 070917]

[81] CNN. 2016. Story of Syrian boy moves CNN anchor to tears. [Online]. [Accessed 22 July 2017]. Available from: https://www.youtube.com/watch?v=PJOzBRy7dWs

[82] BBC News. Battle for Aleppo: Photo of shocked and bloodied Syrian five-year-old sparks outrage. *BBC.* [Online]. 18 August 2016. [Accessed 27 July 2017]. Available from: http://www.bbc.co.uk/news/world-middle-east-37116349

[83]Hunt, E. 2016. Boy in the ambulance: shocking image emerges of Syrian child pulled from Aleppo rubble. *Guardian.* [Online] 18 August 2016. [Accessed 27 July 2017]. Available from: https://www.theguardian.com/world/2016/aug/18/boy-in-the-ambulance-image-emerges-syrian-child-aleppo-rubble

[84] CCTV. 2017. Syria War Diary. [Online]. Available from: http://tv.cctv.com/2017/08/22/VIDEhnrFbwJtZZiusurIN5Oo170822.shtml [Accessed 27 August 2017].

[85] Hersh, S.M., 2013. Whose sarin?. *London Review of Books*, 35 (24), pp.9-12. Available from: http://newspdfs.com/uploads/download/603/Seymour_M._Hersh_-_Whose_sarin.pdf

[86] Phillips, T. 2017. China's new generation of war correspondents hit the front line. *Guardian.* [Online]. 26 April 2017. [Accessed 27 July 2017]. Available from:
 https://www.theguardian.com/media/2017/apr/26/chinas-new-generation-of-war-correspondents-flock-to-the-front-line

[87] Marsh, Vivien (2015) Mixed messages, partial pictures? Discourses under construction in CCTV's Africa Live, compared with the BBC. *Chinese Journal of Communication.* [Online]. Available at: DOI: http://dx.doi.org/10.1080/17544750.2015.1105269), (Accessed: 7 March 2016).

[88] *Africa's media image in the 21st century: from Heart of Darkness to Africa Rising*, edited by Melanie Bunce, Suzanne Franks and Chris Paterson (Routledge, 2016) contains an article by James Wan, 'Propaganda or proper journalism: China's media expansion in Africa' which goes into greater detail on CCTV's challenge of 'constructive journalism'.

[89] Zhang Yanqiu (2014) Understand China's Media in Africa from the perspective of Constructive Journalism, Paper presented at the international conference *China and Africa Media, Communications and Public Diplomacy* on 10 September 2014. Available from: http://www.cmi.no/file/2922-.pdf, (Accessed: 7 March 2016).

[90] Ibid., pp 11.

[91] Ibid.

[92] Discussed in Xie, Shuang and Boyd-Bareet, Oliver (2015) 'External-National TV News Networks' Way to America: Is the United States Losing the Global "Information War"? ' in *International Journal of Communication* 9 (2015), pp 66–83.

[93] Li, Xiguang (2005) Who is setting the Chinese Agenda? The Impact of Online Chatrooms on the Party Presses. In: *China sees the world sees China, Media and Power in China Today*, School of Communication, Tsinghua University

[94] Jirik, J. (2009) The PRC's 'going out' project: CCTV International and the imagination of a Chinese nation. Lehigh, PA: Lehigh University. [Online]. Available at: https://global.cas2.lehigh.edu/sites/global.cas2.lehigh.edu/files/Jirik_lecture.pdf (Accessed: 6 November 2013).

[95] 'systematic typification', is the term used by sociologists Galtung and Ruge and which Jirik applies to foreign news at CCTV-1. Galtung, Johan and Ruge, Mari Holmboe. (1965) The Structure of Foreign News: The Presentation of the Congo, Cuba and Cyprus Crises in Four Norwegian Newspapers *Journal of Peace Research* March 1965 vol. 2 no. 1 pp 64-90.

[96] The words are those of my colleague Daya Thussu.

[97] Shambaugh, David (2013) *China Goes Global*. Oxford: OUP, pp 263-267

[98] Westad, Odd Arne (2012) *Restless Empire: China and the World since 1759*. London: Bodley Head, pp 459.

[99] http://www.pewglobal.org/2013/07/18/chapter-3-attitudes-toward-china/ (Accessed: 18 February 2016).

[100] Leonard, op cit, pp 121.

2   Media in the making of modern China

The English media, and thus all the media of the Anglophone world, were incubated in domestic conflict, in the 17th century, when monarchical authority and traditional ideas about popular rights were pitted against each other. Writers and publishers began to see themselves as adversaries to those in power and as the representatives of their fellow citizens.

The Chinese experience was quite different.[1] In the 19th century, journalism was the patriot's weapon of resistance to foreign aggression and the media were the means by which suffering China was to be enlightened and mobilized to join together in the struggle to make the country rich and strong once more. The contrasting roles of both sets of media in modern history reflect their origins.

2.1   Genesis

The origins of the Anglophone media lie in seventeenth-century England, in particular the period of the Civil War between the Monarchy and Parliament.[2] Pamphleteers of the time took up a variety of positions on the issues of the day and contradicted or championed the ideas of the authorities, religious and political. The Puritans, advancing ideas that were revolutionary for the times, saw that freedom of speech was essential to their interests. John Milton theorised that society could not develop and progress without media free of state control.[3] Yet, if freedom from state control is a necessary condition for the free flow of ideas, it is not a sufficient one. Commercial media or media independent of government can also be selective, unreliable and polemical. The assumption that 'free' and 'unfree' media are as distinct as good and evil is questionable. In China, the commonly held view is the opposite to the Anglophone convention: only state regulation can guarantee 'free' media, i.e. media serving the public rather than particular interests, especially commercial ones. In the Anglosphere, Milton's idea has motivated and mobilised journalists and writers ever since, although it took another two centuries for the media to be free of state interference in the way that he envisaged.

The struggles which made independent media possible, along with the stimuli from Protestantism and the Enlightenment,[4] meant that, when the Industrial Revolution allowed the media to expand, through mass printing equipment, the telegraph and improved transport, they were controlled by individual entrepreneurs. Advertising increasingly funded periodicals, specialist newspapermen took over publishing from printers and a journalism profession came about. The modern media had arrived. By the 1850s, they were being exported around the British Empire, and to China.

38

Media People: The journalist philosopher

Image source:
http://big5.xinhuanet.com/g
ate/big5/news.xinhuanet.co
m/book/2012-
11/01/c_123901563.htm
(Accessed 11/03/2016)

Foremost of the early journalists and regarded as one of nation's intellectual leaders, Liang Qichao梁启超 (1873-1929) was a disciple of Kang Youwei 康有为in the 1890s and active in the early reform movement.

Between 1902 and 1904 he visited Italy, where he was inspired by the example of an ancient civilisation renewing itself, and identified with the scribbler-activists of the *Risorgimento*. When he returned, he founded the *Criticism Daily* 清议报, named after an intellectual movement among civil servants of the Eastern Han Dynasty (AD25 - AD 220) and would edit other newspapers, *Public Affairs at Home and Abroad* 中外纪闻, *The Times* 时务报 and *The New People's Gazette* 新民丛报. He was the first Chinese to express views on what roles journalism might play in society and saw the press as performing a supervisory or scrutinising function in society and as mobilising public opinion to try to influence government.

Under his editorship, *The Times* mobilised people against the government's railways policy and published articles defending the revolutionary Qiu Jin 秋瑾, condemning her execution by the government.

When forced to deal with the West in the mid 19th century, China already had government gazettes and popular pamphlets similar to those of Western Europe in earlier centuries.[5] As European and American businesses were setting up in China and missionaries arrived alongside them, the expatriates wanted to be served by what they were accustomed to: what we recognise as modern newspapers. Enterprising publishers adopted Anglophone models and China's media developed rapidly. By the 1940s, they would be modernised to the highest technical standards pioneered elsewhere, and yet their character was different because of their distinctive origins.

At the turn of the 20th century Chinese writers and journalists were often dissatisfied with government. But the overwhelming issue was how to overcome and, if possible overtake, the foreign aggressors who were establishing colonial enclaves in their country, ordering the government about and re-organising China as it suited them.[6] For the doyen of journalism, Liang Qichao, who had talked with the 'scribblers' of the Italian Risorgimento and learnt of the part played by journalism in divesting Italy of occupying imperialist powers, 'The press was not simply a transmission belt of information, but an intellectual instrument for China to rid itself of widespread ignorance, weakness, and imperialist humiliation'.[7]

2.2 The 'Golden Period'

The energies of journalists were channelled into putting backbone into the

39

government and uniting the people in the national struggle. That does not mean to say that the media were homogenous; there were always divergent views as to how to improve government and tackle abuses until the 1930s, when they became overwhelmingly biased against tradition and pro-'modernist'.[8] In the early years of the 20th century, critical journalists, like their literary forebears, strove to point out that detached commentary on affairs and proposals for improvement in government are of benefit to the state.[9] They thought of themselves as a 'loyal opposition', to use the English term. By the 1920s there was a vigorous, opinionated press, whose products travelled all over the Chinese Empire.[10] The media matured during the years of political division (1911-1937), civil war and savage invasion from Japan (1937-1945), to the extent that this can be referred to as a 'Golden Period'.[11]

Lee Chin-ch'uan reports the *Workers' Daily* 大公报 as the most impressive of the era. Its moral values came out of Confucianism but its professionalism was similar to that of the better Anglophone newspapers. In 1931, it propounded four principles: nonalignment; no commercial influence; the serving of no interests but the public's; and not being blinded by ideology or emotion.[12]

There were flaws in the Republic's governance and China suffered a calamitous Japanese invasion during its era, yet its achievements were many. The foreign powers eventually gave up their concessions and extra-legal rights, a great triumph of Chiang Kaishek's 蒋介石 government and an aim of all patriots. With judicial reform, the development of modern education, scientific research and scholarship, voluntary associations and inquisitive media, China was rapidly becoming a modern country. The expansion of the Chinese industrial and enterprise economy benefitted the poorer classes, and agriculture advanced to such an extent that nutrition improved between 1870 and 1930.[13] China was fortunate in not having a significant class of landlords with large estates, but wide distribution of land, with enterprising farmers who could be very successful when free of money-lenders or levies by officials.[14]

The historian Frank Dikötter writes that 'Freedom of association, freedom to travel, freedom of religion, freedom to trade, and relative freedom of speech ... wrought profound changes in the texture of everyday life, from the appearance of huge metropoles to a lively press, while the introduction of the rule of law, constitutional government, democratic elections and oppositional politics constituted an extraordinary transformation of the realm of politics'.[15]

In the 1920s a new factor entered into the relationship between authority and the media. I use the shorthand term 'utopianism' for it. The Nationalist Party, (Kuomintang, KMT) had been founded in 1912 to bring several democratic and revolutionary groups together under the leadership of Sun Yatsen 孙中山, the first President of the Republic. Although much admired, he was given little or no help by Britain, then the world's pre-eminent superpower, let alone by other Western countries, all of whom were chary of becoming enmeshed in internal Chinese politics. The KMT was obliged to look elsewhere.

Media People: A pioneer investigative journalist

Image source:
http://news.ifeng.com/histor y/zhongguojindaishi/detail_2 010_12/28/3734611_0.shtml (Accessed 11/03/2016)

While a student in Zhejiang, Shao Piaoping 邵飘萍 (1884-1926) established his first newspaper, *The Daily* 一日报, in 1909. On graduation he worked for several other newspapers, and two years later established the *Hanmin Daily* 汉民日报. In 1918 he launched the influential *Capital Daily* 京报, radical and independent.

Shao was a courageous investigative journalist who also worked hard to promote professionalism through lectures at Peking University and textbooks. In 1918 he founded *The Journalism Study Society* of Peking University 北京大學新聞研究會.

According to Li Lubo 李路波, Shao 'believed in a free and independent press, with a public interest as its highest consideration. He argued that the reporter should act as "a king without a crown" or a "fair minded judge" who takes no sides. "Truthfulness is the backbone of news, while human interest serves as flesh and blood", he wrote.' [quoted in de Burgh, H (2003) *The Chinese journalist*, London: Routledge pp 147-148.]

Some intellectuals, inspired by the October Revolution and taking the Bolshevik's claims of being a popular movement at face value, became amenable to their overtures and began to absorb the Marxist catechism. That Lenin's régime had, in 1917, promised to withdraw Russian forces from Chinese territory and abrogate the unequal treaties, greatly disposed young Chinese towards Russia and its seemingly internationalist and modernising ideology. Under Russian guidance, the Chinese Communist Party (CCP) was founded in Shanghai in 1921. The ruling orthodoxy of the Russian Marxists was that only industrial workers could spearhead revolution. Yet China had very few of these, compared with the number of peasants. As a result of this confusing contradiction, the CCP did not attract much support until, some years later, Mao, noticing that his country had rather more peasants than workers, argued that if the CCP wished for a large political movement it should take account of the majority of the population and its grievances.[16] Meanwhile the Russians decided that, while it would be useful to have a Chinese Communist Party to run errands, they could best pursue their ambition of making China a complaisant satellite by using the KMT.

The weaknesses of the politicians who inherited the state from the Qing Dynasty, and their differences and lack of experience when faced with innumerable problems, made for a difficult situation. The failure of Sun Yatsen to win support from the predominant powers, and the dismissal at the Treaty of Versailles, of China's expectation of having territories occupied by Germany returned to it in appreciation of its contribution to the Allied victory, helped to make the position of the KMT, the leading political party, very tenuous. Thus, when Russia's ruthless international agency, the Comintern, offered to assist the KMT leaders with organisational reform, ideological training and military education, they gratefully accepted. In 1923, Russian agents became active in all aspects of the party, re-organising it on the model of the Soviet parent, and encouraging the establishment of a Propaganda Institute which instilled Soviet attitudes to the media. But the KMT was never as rigid or as ruthless as the CCP would become, as the flourishing intellectual life under the Republic testifies.

What did undermine the press were Marxist theory and Russian management methods. As reformists turned into revolutionaries, both KMT and CCP activists stopped believing in an open society. Marxists adjudged that there was no such thing as free expression, only the expression of class interests, and the KMT found this theory useful because it excused the bullying of journalists.

2.3   1949 – The Great Leap Backwards

Led by Chiang Kaishek, the Republic fought a titanic struggle against Japanese aggression until 1945. The Japanese behaved much as did the Germans in Eastern Europe, reducing the natives to slavery, expropriating or mismanaging industry and liquidating many. Not surprisingly, local government became ineffectual and the military debilitated, especially since the CCP undermined from behind. The CCP, which many had expected to survive only as a bandit gang on the fringes of a new China led by the nation's hero and defender, Chiang Kaishek, was surprised to find, in 1948-9, that, with supplies from Russia and merciless assaults on the cities, it was able to knock out the exhausted national armies and banish them to Taiwan.[17]

The Chinese Communist Party (CCP) in 1949 was utopian, in that, like other 20th century movements it claimed that, in extirpating legal and political rights, it was progressing towards a communist utopia. It came to power committed to the abolition of private property, the centralisation of economic power and the state control of everything, though these processes were to be staged. Along the way the buildings and the very ecology of the culture were to be obliterated.[18] The Party leader, Mao Zedong, was a devotee of (what is now called) the blank slate theory,[19] holding that everything wrong with society was the consequence of bad social institutions and that human beings had no innate predispositions which might explain culture but were 'blank sheets of paper' to be refashioned by him. The media were the means by which people were to learn their new identities. His tactics were largely cribbed from the USSR, whose propaganda had persuaded many Chinese, as well as much of the credulous Western intelligentsia, that its murderous and incompetent government was successful, and even a role model.

Private enterprise was abolished and so was civil society, that accumulation of voluntary and charitable associations, self-help groups, religious and recreational societies that are the foundation of sophisticated societies, as well as expressions of popular initiative and culture. Only one view of the world was to be tolerated, there was only one source of money and power, and only one route to advancement was even to be discussed. A black fog of ignorance and fear suffocated China. The media, when not promoting 'strike-hard' campaigns against enemies, were deployed to create a picture of glorious success and unbounded happiness.[20]

Those newspapers not closed down were subsumed into the propaganda system. Journalists were sacked and some were murdered in the course of imposing central control. All channels of communication were exploited thoroughly to mobilise and deliver the new thinking: radio transmitted on loudspeakers in every square and alley, big character posters, travelling propaganda teams, newsprint and tracts, unending meetings at which participants were pressurised into conformity with the latest policy and the 'mass line'.[21]

The importance ascribed to the media by the CCP is difficult to exaggerate. Its leaders, as Chinese intellectuals, had been brought up in the literary tradition and believed that education transforms lives and is the foundation of civilised society. They had seen how modern media had opened the eyes of their own families, hitherto ignorant of the world beyond China. They now intended that the thousands of peasant communities, dispersed and benighted, their horizons confined to the next village, should be made conscious of belonging to the nation and contribute to its struggle for survival. Their Russian advisers reinforced this and advised them of the latest tools they could use in propaganda.

Although Lenin's prescription that the media should be 'a collective propagandist, a collective agitator, and a collective organiser'[22] was the orthodoxy, there were always those who argued that media which functioned as reporters and advocates rather than mouthpieces would serve the Party better by revealing problems and discovering what people really thought. A leading advocate of less subjugated media was committed communist Liu Binyan 刘宾雁, whose investigative journalism was bold. It was not really until the disadvantages of having supine media became obvious at the time of the Great Leap Forward 大跃进 that politicians started to take notice of the damage caused by suppression.

Media People: an investigative journalist in bad times

Image source:
http://www.mingjingnews.co
m/MIB/Blog/blog_contents.a
spx?ID=0000803700000180

Under the patronage of his editor Hu Yaobang 胡耀邦, Liu Binyan 刘宾雁 (1925-2005) first published exposures of bureaucratic incompetence in 1956, as well as a now famous story about Restricted Circulation Publications, RCPs, and how the life of a young journalist is blighted when her investigative work ends up ignored in some obscure filing cabinet. In *News from Inside the Paper* 本报内部消息, reporter Huang wants to reveal the reality of a coal mine but is pressurised to depict it in a manner approved by the Party, far from what she observes. Another typical tale tells of a man who fakes being deaf and dumb, so that he does not have to participate in any meetings. Since factual reporting was impermissible, Liu deployed a mode called *Reportage Literature* 报告文学.

Liu was expelled from the Party in 1957 and sent to a labour camp, returning to *China Youth Daily* during 1961-1969. He was imprisoned again in 1969. Rehabilitated in 1979 and given a post on *The Peoples' Daily*, he wrote his most arresting work, *People or monsters?* 人妖之间, about a vast network of corruption.

In 1985, Liu published *A higher kind of loyalty* 第二种忠诚, the story of a minor official who denounces corruption. Out of the country at the time of the Tiananmen Massacre, he was placed on a wanted list by the government, but did not return and later denounced the government.

2.3.1 Campaigns

The Great Leap Forward 大跃进 (1958-61) was one of the largest of a long succession of destructive campaigns which amounted to permanent revolution (a list of the main campaigns and their targets is on page 45). Leaders would start them off with speeches and the newspapers would produce editorials setting out the purposes of the campaign; other media would follow. There would be wall posters and sometimes drama troupes, party leaders at all levels would promote the campaign throughout their jurisdictions and there would be large and small rallies at which people would be expected to get up and show by what they said that they had understood and would put into practice the purposes of the campaign.

Campaigns still take place, though they are less harsh than their predecessors. As I write, an anti-corruption campaign is underway; leading figures in various professions have been summarily sacked after being denounced by colleagues for corruption, and officials have found their dossiers blotted because they took part in dinners reported by informers to have been paid for out of public funds.[23] Following much fanfare in the media and the President's speeches at the principal national media, rallies have been held within the media organisations at which workers have spoken of their rapture at receiving their mission from on high.[24] A gripping TV saga, *In the Name of the People* 人民的名义, transmitted by Hunan TV in early 2017, dramatises the efforts of young police investigators exposing corruption up to the highest levels of government and Party.

Eleven Major Political Campaigns

The media drummed up many vicious campaigns before Deng Xiaoping came to power; those listed below were probably the most extensive. In these campaigns a given percentage of people in any particular community were deemed 'rich peasants', 'spies' 'counter-revolutionaries', 'exploiting class', 'bourgeois' or whatever was the target of the moment; campaign leaders had to fill a quota, regardless of reality and have the quota hauled out for public humiliation, torture and/or death. The campaigns were intended to terrorise everybody and make as many citizens as possible complicit, for not to take part was to risk being targeted. They naturally brought to the fore the hooligans and the sadists. Mao's campaigns killed far more Chinese than did the Japanese in their barbarous invasion. They certainly set back China's development. There have been campaigns since the Cultural Revolution, but without the cruelty.

Dates	Campaigns	Target
1947-1952	Land Reform 土地改革	Against (often imaginary) landlords and 'rich peasants'. Conducted with great brutality, it resulted in several million deaths.
1950-1953	Suppression of Counter- Revolutionaries 镇反	Former members of other parties, intellectuals, religious. Between 1 and 2 million deaths.
1951-1952	Three-Anti / Five-Anti Campaigns 三反五反	Business people.
1951-1953	Rejecting Religious Movements 退道运动	Adherents of all kinds to religious beliefs and organisations.
1953	New Three-Anti Campaign 新三反	Intellectuals, especially within the Party.
1955	Elimination of Counter-Revolutionaries 肃反	Campaign against hidden enemies within the bureaucracy.
1956	Hundred Flowers Movement 百花运动	Ostensibly a campaign to encourage criticism, it allowed Mao's people to identify doubters and attack them.
1957-9	Anti-Rightist Movement 反右派运动	Against doubters, especially engineers and technicians.
1958-1961	The Great Leap Forward 大跃进	Collectivisation of agriculture, persecution of independent peasants, and the attempt to industrialise the country without experts and technicians, causing about 45 million deaths.
1963-1966	Socialist Education Movement 社会主义教育运动	'Cleansing' of the Party and administration.
1966-1976	The 'Great Proletarian' Cultural Revolution 文化大革命, including the 'Destruction of the Four Olds' Campaign 破四旧 (customs, culture, habits and ideas) and the 'Learn from the Peasantry' 上山下乡 Campaign, and several others.	It is believed that several million people died, and it is clear that innumerable people suffered. With this movement, as brutal and barbarous as anything before, the rejection of humanity and civilisation reached its apogee. The damage to social morality must surely have been as severe as it was to culture.

Today's campaigns are shorn of the public cruelty typical of those mobilized by the media before 1980.[25] Those earlier campaigns were the means for the repression of the population, and the media were essential tools. The purpose was threefold: to destroy people who might question the Party by ruining them in public 'struggle sessions' 批斗会, sentencing them to slave labour or just killing them in quotas; to seize their wealth and that of any community organisations, and to make as many people as possible complicit by pushing them to abuse their neighbours and colleagues, loot their homes and beat them, breaking down all reticence and moral sense. As with the persecution of the Jews in Germany a few years earlier, others had to be made to share the guilt and benefit from the suffering of the victims. Two novels of the 1950s, published in Hong Kong by Zhang Ailing 张爱玲 (Eileen Chang), an escapee who is arguably one of the 20th century's greatest writers, portray this.[26]

The Great Leap Forward caused mass starvation. A death toll of at least 45 million people is now officially admitted.[27] It was a campaign against reality, rather than just terrorisation of people. Mao held that the slow process of development since 1949 was the fault not of fatuous policies, but of failure of will. Modernisation, he opined, could be brought about by total collectivisation, and by ordinary people abandoning farming to create industries from scratch. Whether he believed such tosh or whether he simply saw the campaigns as means to bolster his power is open to question. Such was his prestige and the enslavement of the media which he mobilised on his side that the campaign was continued even after the suffering it caused was well known among the leaders. The result was that agricultural production collapsed and industry regressed to pre-modernity, yet officials dared not give the peasants land from which to feed themselves or abandon the misery-making communal living arrangements.

Journalists were in the best position to know the real situation as they toured from county to county, a notable privilege in a country where movement was restricted. But after the hammering they had received in earlier campaigns, there were no journalists, that we know of, with the courage, confidence or authority to question what was happening. Recent novels by Yan Lianke, Yu Hua and Mo Yan have described these terrible years vividly.[28]

Mao's prestige in the Party took a knocking when the truth became known, at least to the ruling class. His colleagues attempted to marginalise him, lest he do any more damage. President Liu Shaoqi recognised that journalists, if they had been trusted to report impartially, would have been able to expose the problems, making it feasible to tackle them and change policy.[29] Unfortunately for China, Mao retained sufficient political influence to be able to mobilise young power-hungry leftists and launch, in 1966, the most destructive and savage of all the campaigns, the Great Proletarian Cultural Revolution 文化大革命 (GPCR), ostensibly directed against the 'Four Olds' 四旧: civility, expertise, legality and culture, or what was left of them.[30]

The Cultural Revolution lasted approximately ten years and involved media of every kind. The newspapers and magazines that had not been abolished became polemical tracts; radio and what television there was were used to mobilise the 'masses' against 'class enemies'; theatre, opera and musicians reduced their repertoires to agitprop. In the media, as in other areas of life, professionals were replaced by their persecutors, organised into 'Revolutionary Committees'. As in other revolutions, megalomaniacs, sadists and other dregs of society took power. Mao licensed thuggery through tasking young followers to eliminate 'traitors' and vaguely defined contrary ideas. They caused destruction of innumerable buildings, libraries, works of art, and the homes of millions of people who were tortured, killed or exiled. Local factions seized power and instituted rule by brute force. Eventually the chaos was so great that the army took charge to re-establish order. A 'Gang of Four' 四人帮 nominally ran the country, made up of Mao's wife, two journalists and a textile worker turned political activist.

2.4   1978: The Death of Mao and the Rebirth of China

Mao Zedong died in September 1976 and in October the wretched 'Gang' fell. Before long they were succeeded by a man capable of reversing the effects of a dysfunctional ideology.[31] In rejecting its main tenets, in effect if not in words, Deng Xiaoping began the process of liberating the Chinese from the thought cage into which Mao had immured them, inspiring astonishing achievements.

Over the period 1949-1978, living standards fell so far that by 1978 they were lower than they had been in 1936. By 1978 industrial production was lower than in the war-torn 1930s, housing stock was depleted and in appalling condition, much of China's education system was wrecked, and the gap between rich oligarchy and poor citizenry was far more extreme than it had been before 1949, or is today for that matter.[32] To add to this, people had passed through years of suffering and disruption caused by the political campaigns, and many millions had been murdered, especially the educated and the enterprising. No proper account of this has ever been provided by the media and people in China and abroad have assumed that, despite the campaigns, there were great achievements. It has been left to historians and some journalists to challenge this assumption in books.[33]

Not only had China failed to keep up with the rest of the world, it had also reversed its achievements of the first half of the century. Ordinary people, taught by their media that China was a world leader, would not dare to express scepticism after seeing the fate of doubters. How was Deng to emancipate them from the shibboleths that had been force-fed to them for so long? In 1978 he made possible the publication of a newspaper article entitled 'Practice is the sole criterion of truth' 实践是检验真理的唯一标准. This launched a campaign, whose proponents tactfully claimed to be inspired by Mao's writings, to liberate minds from 'modern superstition 当代迷信', from which we infer utopianism. His most famous sayings were outright rejections of dogma which became the mantras of the new era: 'Seek Truth from Facts' 实事求是 and 'It doesn't matter if a cat is black or white as long as it catches mice' 不管黑猫还是白猫，能抓到老鼠的就是好猫.

It was not enough to say that ideology had failed; he had to show it. Opening up to the rest of the world and allowing television to illustrate the advances of other countries were ways of emancipating China from its illusion that it was a success, and showing what to aim for.

Deng exhumed a bypassed manifesto of Zhou Enlai's 周恩来 entitled 'The Four Modernisations' 四个现代化. This proposed development routes for Agriculture, Industry, National Defence, and Science and Technology, and looked forward to China becoming a modern nation by the early twenty-first century. Deng was able to use the Four Modernisations as cover to release the economy from its ideological straightjacket. The peasants were allowed to cultivate the land which had previously been taken from them to be collectivised and internal trade was permitted. Private enterprise gradually returned and, little by little, China's economy began to be restored. Foreign trade was made easier and Deng visited the USA and sported a Stetson. By the mid 1980s, he was sufficiently powerful to be able to accelerate reforms, with the media re-emerging to champion what Canadian writer Zhao Yuezhi terms 'an ideological consensus around reform and opening up'.[34]

Deng also allowed what was to be called the 'Beijing Spring' 北京之春. People could recount and criticise the preceding period; many of those earlier hounded to death or imprisoned were pardoned, and the persecution of people merely on account of their 'class background' ceased. However, the relatively open atmosphere stimulated some to call for a 'Fifth Modernisation', democracy. The best known was the courageous and idealistic electrician-turned-magazine-publisher, Wei Jingsheng 魏京生, who discovered that this was a step too far for the authorities when he was imprisoned for fifteen years. Although the example made of Wei set limits to freedom of speech, the media during the 1980s would be far more open than at any period since 1949.

2.5   Journalism in the Aftermath of the Cultural Revolution

Under Deng, the Editor of the Party's and the nation's leading newspaper,

People's Daily 人民日报, was Hu Jiwei 胡绩伟. Not only did the newspaper promote Deng Xiaoping's pragmatic approach, it also published critical letters by readers and opinion pieces by non-journalists. The atrocities of the Cultural Revolution were exposed, drawing upon thousands of letters received daily. Hu also revived investigative journalism, with the two most influential investigations resulting in the resignations of the Ministers of Petroleum and Commerce respectively.[35] General Secretary Zhao Ziyang 赵紫阳 at this time adumbrated the theory of 'supervision by public opinion' 舆论监督, an extension of ideas proposed by Liu Shaoqi 刘少奇 in the aftermath of the Great Leap Forward.[36] He advocated that allowing the media to investigate independently and report impartially to the people should be acknowledged as essential to development.[37]

There were opponents. Hu Jiwei fell foul of left wingers and was forced to resign in in the Anti Spiritual Pollution Campaign 反精神污染运动, of 1983.[38] Two years later, China's foremost investigative journalist, Liu Binyan 刘宾雁, was expelled from the CCP.[39] Nowhere was journalism more bold or experimental than in Guangdong 广东. There were at least two reasons. In 1980, Shenzhen 深圳 was declared a Special Economic Zone 经济特区 (SEZ), where the inhabitants, whose numbers would grow from a few hundred to over 10 million (official figures) by 2017, were freed from restrictions common elsewhere and encouraged to take in foreign capital and expertise, and generally to learn from more advanced economies. Yet the purposes of the SEZs were not only economic; they were to liberate minds too.

The second reason was that Guangdong citizens were permitted to watch and listen to Hong Kong broadcasts. The small part of Guangdong then ruled by Great Britain was home to the most independent media in the Chinese world, yet since 1949 they had been largely closed to the rest of Guangdong. Their influence was to be galvanising.

Journalists and Officials[40]

A story from *Notes from the Civil Service*, a novel

The nine volumes of this saga tell the story of the career of Hou Weidong, whom we first encounter when he graduates in law from a minor university and seeks a job in local government. In the course of his career he comes across journalists several times, and in one case becomes a good friend of a senior provincial journalist. When they first meet, Hou fears him, because that journalist's newspaper has begun to investigate complaints against decanting householders from the enterprise zone for which he is responsible. However, mutual respect develops as Hou begins to understand what the investigating journalist does and why, and in turn the journalist realises that Hou is confronting difficulties, associated with large-scale development projects, in good faith. Here, Hou, now County Party Secretary, has required one of his subordinates, Cai, to hold a press conference to answer charges that government officials have maltreated petitioners. While a local mine owner, Fang, was being taken into custody by police officers, the vehicle in which he was travelling was involved in a car crash and Fang was killed. The man's extended family are demonstrating in order to gain compensation and prosecuting the officials on charges of abuse of office. In the course of this, Fang's family are first offered a bribe to desist by people posing as officials and then, when they had ceased the demonstration, were badly beaten by them. Hou and his colleagues believe that these were not government employees, but thugs hired by local mine owners intending to exacerbate the situation and malign the local authorities.

Having thoroughly prepared his statement, Cai, Deputy Head of the Propaganda Department of Chenxi, arrived at the Press Conference with a serious expression on his face. There were already 16 or 17 reporters present, including one from the Lingxi Legal News. In the province of Lingxi, Chengjin County generally is of no interest to the media. So many of the provincial and city media collected in Chengjin was something that had not been seen in 20 years. Once Cai had read out his pre-prepared statement, the reporters began to ask questions. Although he had never had this kind of experience before, Cai had prepared himself with great diligence. His office had assembled substantial briefing notes for him, to help him answer the questions they expected the journalists to ask. Nevertheless, as Cai saw them raise their hands he felt very tense.

Indeed, the first question came from the Lingxi Legal News reporter. A tall, thin young man asked:

'Secretary Cai, I am Lingxi Legal News reporter Zhao Jie. According to the Fang family, when they were in the provincial capital presenting a petition, employees of the county made a point of finding them and offering compensation of $20,000 on condition that they would cease their representations. Is that the case?'

Secretary Cai denied that this was the case.

With a cold smile, Zhao proceeded with his questioning:

'The government employees who did this were travelling in a car of which the registration number is known to us. And, from our investigations, your authority does indeed own this car. Not only are we clear about the registration number, but also the make, model and colour. All exactly the same as the one owned by local government. Moreover, many people who were there at the event identified this car. Please can the Secretary tell us how he would like to explain this?'

Cai silently cursed Party Secretary Hou for putting him in this predicament by obliging him to hold a press conference. 'Chengjin is such a small county, what the hell do we need a press conference for!' he had muttered to himself. But he was now in fighting spirit and he could not but respond, lest he make a fool of himself.

'Indeed you're right that this registration plate belongs to the local government, but the car itself has recently been in the workshop for repair and is still there. The police are currently investigating how this registration number came to be used fraudulently.'

Zhao from Lingxi Legal News had asked questions close to the bone. With a cold smile he concluded, 'My questions are done, thank you, Secretary Cai'.

As an experienced journalist, he did not really believe that the authorities could be so stupid as to do that of which they were being accused. However, some aspects of this case were difficult to fathom, and only when the truth came to light might the authorities clear themselves. This brief respite offered him a useful opportunity: once the press conference was over, Zhao did not hurry to leave, but sat smoking for a while, and then made his way to see the Deputy Head of the Propaganda Department. His conversation went something like this:

'Lingxi Legal News pays great attention to factual evidence so I would like to clarify the Secretary's explanation. For example, the Fang family were quite certain that they recognised that car and its number plate in the county capital, and yet the Secretary said that the car was being repaired. This is really quite difficult to elucidate, and all I can do is to give both sides of the story and let our readers decide whom to believe'.

The Deputy looked at Zhao's hard face and cursed under his breath: 'He wants money. He's got his snout in the trough. The fraud! If this business were to be stirred up, it would do a lot of harm to the county government'; and so he replied:

'Mr Zhao, I don't think it's right that, with the facts not yet fully established, you should make too much of it'. The reporter was an old hand and continued to lay out his reasons: 'I have a great respect for the facts and I intend to present both sides of the story, so that the readers can make their own judgements.'

There was a pause during which the reporter saw that the Deputy was hesitating. Taking advantage of this, he casually mentioned the fact that his laptop had been lost in the township when he was doing interviews. Would it be possible for the office to provide him with another? He made clear exactly which model it was. Now, this model was not available in Chengjin, although it could be bought in the county capital at the price of $17,000. The Deputy did not dare take a decision and went to talk it over with his boss. The boss, in order to keep the matter confidential and away from his assistant said with great aplomb: 'Don't you worry about this, I'll sort it out. Just get the reporter to come to my office. He hasn't got horns and hooves – he's just a man and he'll listen to reason'.

The reporter walked confidently into the Propaganda Director's office; after all he had rich experience in dealing with lower-level officials. All you need do is to take hold of the Achilles heel and you get what you want. From the government's point of view, to spend a little bit of money to cover up nastiness is always very sensible. And this time the officials had got into a bit of a muddle, so $20,000 shouldn't be any problem; he would just have to do a bit of bargaining and was certain to get at least $10,000.

The Director very courteously got his assistant to brew tea for this self-assured journalist.

Speedily the reporter got to the point: 'I've just told your deputy what happened, and so I do hope that you will sort this out. We journalists are running all over the place, never a moment's rest.'

Without raising his voice Director Liang replied: 'Lingxi Legal News is an organisation with which we have an excellent relationship. I even use your Chairman's mobile!' To make the point, he spoke out the number as if he used it every day. 'I've just been on the telephone to your Chairman Jiang, thanking him for the way in which his newspaper has covered our township; such a fine man, I'm so glad to know that he will be coming to visit us very soon'.

Half of what Director Liang said was true and half was not. Having been given the idea by Secretary Hou, Liang had used the contact to give the newspaper President a call of appreciation for his coverage of Chengjin. They had chatted a bit and got on well. But actually that was the first time he had ever spoken to the newspaper boss, and the projected visit had been invented in order to frighten the reporter.

Zhao was merely a reporter, and when he heard the Propaganda Director's claims his face changed colour. After quite a pause he gave a mocking smile:

'Director this whole issue requires further exploration, and at the moment I'm not in a position to write up the story. I need to get on with some interviews, and so I will leave you in peace.'

Once the journalist had left, Director Liang picked up the telephone and reported back to County Secretary Hou Weidong, that his trick had worked.

In 1978, the entire country had less than 70 newspapers. A very short time thereafter, Guangdong alone had 62. A great deal of free discussion appears to have taken place rather quickly, owing to encouragement from the top, where the leading positions were held, from 1978-1981, by the present President's father.[41] A later governor set a trend when he did not try to curb public criticism of himself in the *Shekou News* 蛇口通讯.[42] The *Shenzhen Youth Newspaper* 深圳青年报 called on Deng Xiaoping to retire.[43] In coastal Huizhou 惠州 a periodical called *Modern Life* 现代生活 included a column entitled 'Observing Zhong Nan Hai' 观察中南海, the equivalent of which might be 'Let's watch our Cabinet'.[44] Some articles even suggested the overthrow of the CPC and the establishment of democratic politics. The atmosphere was such that, in Shekou Industrial Zone, in the first democratic election since 1949, held in November 1985, an unprecedented 14 candidates made speeches about their policies and answered questions put to them by voters.[45] Newspapers and periodicals were founded regularly. The most durable and most distinguished was *Southern Weekend* 南方周末, (see table on p227).

Hong Kong's radio shows were much more populist than their mainland equivalents. They dealt with local and personal issues, featured presenters and audience members as personalities, and encouraged participation.[46] As soon as people in the PRC started listening to Hong Kong Radio, there was an almost complete collapse of audiences for local radio stations in Guangzhou 广州. In response, Pearl River Economic Radio 珠江经济广播电台 was launched in December 1986.

A particularly popular programme, *Social Hotline* 社会热点, which was transmitted all day, 'had listeners raising not only topics to do with their personal family lives, but also sensitive social and political issues, which the CPD censored using a delaying system. Despite the censorship, much criticism and dissatisfaction was aired'.[47] Audiences soared and Hong Kong stations suffered. They retaliated by being even more forthright, encouraging participants to air radical opinions and interviewing critics of the government.

Officials paid great attention, even establishing rapid response units to deal with issues of greatest public concern. The lively Guangdong services were copied by Shanghai's East Radio 上海东方广播电台 and later Central People's Radio 中央人民广播电台. Both invited officials on to their programmes, not merely to propound but to discuss.

Although they had talked about the media being given more latitude and professed themselves aware of the damage done under Mao by their gagging of media, the leaders maintained their belief in the media as mouthpieces of the elite who guide the nation's destiny.[48] Nevertheless, new ideas about functions of the media had begun to emerge. National debates were possible too: throughout the 1980s market liberalisation was 'greatly contested' in the media, and issues such as the public's right to know and the role of public opinion in policy-making were raised. 'Media laws were drafted' though never passed.[49]

2.6   Television

Television had existed in rudimentary form before the Cultural Revolution, with a few non-political programmes and tiny audiences. During the years of turmoil, media of every kind – drama troupes, film, opera, radio, ballads, wall posters – became the tools of mobilisation and denunciation. Television at one point was deployed to illustrate the beatings of so-called 'class enemies' by the so-called 'rebels', with a view to inciting further such activities. When these programmes, in which people were seen being humiliated, tormented and murdered, failed to elicit the desired response, they were discontinued.[50] Thereafter, television was used for the crudest form of propaganda. Promotion of Chairman Mao's publications (his earnings from royalties became enormous), and the 'eight model operas' 八个样板戏 devised by Mao's wife, Jiang Qing 江青, were almost the sum of acceptable entertainment. The most noteworthy programming in the immediate aftermath of the Cultural Revolution was the trial of Jiang Qing and the other members of the Gang of Four.

A month after Jiang's fall, the regulator held a conference on the quality of television news, and it was agreed to study and learn from Hong Kong. The first advertisements were permitted soon after, and programme production increased and had greater variety. It included drama, traditional operas, variety shows and even imported cartoons. These changes were not universally welcomed. The head of the regulating body expressed his concern that television had become merely a vehicle of entertainment, rather than a channel of political and economic information. [51] Possibly in response, the number of news programmes and bulletins increased. *National News* 新闻联播, remained the flagship programme, designed as a bulletin of official doings and pronouncements. Within news production units, the question of whether editorial rather than political judgement should determine story selection and ranking began to be debated. This question continues to animate newsrooms to this day.

Journalists became more daring: In 1979 a pioneering investigation of minor corruption was undertaken. 'Two young CCTV journalists, [] bravely recorded the registration plates of all cars parked in front of the Wangfujing Department Store. The reporters suspected that the government cars were parking there for the officials' private purposes (they were being used by their wives for shopping). The programme was edited for immediate showing on the evening of 1st May 1979, but it failed to survive further editing by the CCTV Director, the Deputy of News and later by the minister-level Director-General of the [then regulator]. Four months later, on12 September 1979, the story was finally on air, though not as "news". This ground-breaking story received the highest praise from viewers. For the first time, over 1,000 people wrote to CCTV about just one news item. Both the SAB and CCTV were relieved when, as a result, the 5th Plenary Meeting passed a new document regulating senior Party officials' political and private lives.' [52] Thereafter, CCTV established its Department of Current Affairs 评论部, which would incubate a new, revelatory journalism.

2.7   The Democracy Movement and 4th June 1989

By the late 1980s, something akin to the dissatisfaction felt by the peoples of Eastern Europe with their incompetent and corrupt Communist rulers had oozed its way around China. Triggered by the death of an admired official, Hu Yaobang 胡耀邦, demonstrations erupted in many cities, usually initiated by students but soon joined by others. The most significant was in Tiananmen Square 天安门广场, the heart of the capital and of the nation's government. Most wanted grievances specific to their own workplace or college to be addressed, or were protesting about corruption. A few students wanted 'American democracy' but many workers opposed 'American capitalist' market reforms. Joining the clamour were journalists calling for 'the freedom not to lie'. There was no coherent programme beyond demands for participation, and no credible leadership. Discussions were held with the authorities and compromises were brokered, but by late May 1989 there was deadlock. Despite many warnings, demonstrators refused to budge from their encampments and the government declared martial law.

A model of good conduct

Bao Qingtian 包青天 (999–1062) is one of several legendary heroes of Chinese public life, along with Judge Di 狄仁傑, Hai Rui 海瑞 and Qu Yan 屈原.

Bao came from a simple family but excelled at school; later on he passed the highest level examinations to become an official. He was to gain a reputation for the zealous and impartial pursuit of justice, prosecuting not only powerful courtiers but even members of his own family. He lived modestly, could not be accused of accepting even the smallest of gifts and reformed the petitioning system so that citizens might approach him direct, instead of going through potentially corrupt gatekeepers.

To round him off as the complete Chinese hero, Bao was particularly filial; he even postponed taking up an office for several years in order to care for his aged parents. Innumerable representations of Bao have been made in fiction, theatre, opera, film and television. Journalists hold 'Righteous Bao 包正 ' in high regard, and often mention him.

To the political establishment, which could not find a way of accommodating the often inchoate demands, the choice was not between reform and the CCP but between the CCP and anarchy. The leadership suppressed the anarchy. When the protestors occupying Tiananmen Square refused to disperse, the army cleared the streets with considerable loss of life. The full story has been written up many times, notably by Craig Calhoun, recently Director of the London School of Economics, who was present at the time, in his *Neither Gods nor Emperors*.[53] There is an impressive film record, produced in the USA but not adulatory of the demonstrators, some of whose leaders appear to have incited the carnage.[54]

2.8   The Southern Progress[55]

Following the massacre of 4th June 1989, those who had cavilled at Deng's reforms felt empowered. They had been right to resist the economic and social changes, because they would demonstrably only bring chaos and the downfall of the Party. So they attempted to rein in Deng.

Deng Xiaoping sought to refute them, but he was stymied. Just as Mao had been obliged to go south in 1966 to make his call to arms, having failed to get his ideas into the media, so Deng responded in the same way in 1990 when he was denied media access. In order to get the country moving again in the direction he believed essential, he went south in a 'progress' to promote his vision in a series of speeches and conversations with political allies. The media eventually published them.

It is not that there were no journalists keen for the kind of change for which Deng stood. The Tiananmen protestors of 1989 had included journalists carrying banners declaring them employees of the *People's Daily* or *New China News Agency* 新华社. But many had been purged and their successors were nervous.

Shortly after the 'progress' became public knowledge, changes took place which were so far reaching that the left appeared to have been side-lined. The number of 'special development areas', which were inspired by the four Special Economic Zones set up in 1980 and offered investors many advantages, leapt from 117 to 1,951 in a year.[56] The privatisation of land, commercialisation of housing, introduction of stock exchanges, and the possibility of a 'free' labour market all presaged a return to the kind of market society that the CCP had set out to abolish and surpass.

2.9   Media in the 1990s: Commercialisation

After Deng's reassertion of his strategy, the media resumed development along similar lines to the 1980s, though criticism was muted and wise journalists at first kept away from anything that might be construed as controversial. Media managers concentrated on the infrastructure. Concomitant with the economic developments following the Southern Progress, the media were thrust into the marketplace. As Joseph Chan, the notable Hong Kong academic, has recounted in detail, subsidies were to be (virtually) ended and the press to be subjected to competition.[57] This was in response to various pressures: the demand by domestic and foreign businesses for advertising opportunities. the unwillingness of the state to continue to subsidise the media, dissatisfaction of consumers identified by the Culture Minister Li Ruihan, the public demand for more media and the advent of new technology requiring extensive investment.[58]

At China Central Television, for example, two important reforms took place in the 1990s. Under the Producer System Reform 制片人制度改革, non-news producers were permitted to generate their own advertising and sponsorship. News producers were to be career journalists rather than, as often in the past, generic state officials, and they were given responsibility for specific programmes and programme segments, rather than being assigned to departments like clerks in a ministry. Human Resources Reform 人事制度改革 permitted managers to hire and fire as they wished. They were no longer required to limit pay to civil service scales and could award bonuses.

With these reforms CCTV was able, in effect, to become independent of state financing. Beijing Television 北京电视台 became self-sufficient in 1993. The result was a hybrid, combining state ownership, public service values and commercial discipline.

Media people: a media academic

Image source:
http://sgjc.swupl.edu.cn/xygk
/szdw/152049.htm
Li Xiguang李希光is a founder
of the School of Journalism
and Communication at
Tsinghua University.

One of the first generation of graduates after the Cultural Revolution, Professor Li Xiguang read English Literature at Nanjing University and obtained his master's degree in International Journalism from the Chinese Academy of Social Sciences. Before joining Tsinghua University, Li was for ten years at Xinhua News Agency, first as a science reporter specialising in environment stories, ending as Deputy Director of Central News Gathering and Production. In 1995, he moved to the *Washington Post* as an Alfred Friendly Press Fellow, and in 1999 was Research Fellow at the Shorenstein Center of Harvard University.

Li was Founding Dean of the School of Journalism and Communication at Tsinghua University and initiator of bold and imaginative projects to develop professionalism and scholarship. He has published many, often controversial, studies of the media. Two of his many books, *Journalism in Transition* and *Essential Journalism*, are the core text books for most journalism courses.

When Bo Xilai was appointed Mayor of Chongqing, Li was invited to set up various new units in the South Western University of Politics and Law there. He established centres dedicated to journalism, Trans-Himalayan affairs, Pakistan affairs and International Relations.

Returning from the South West, his expertise in environmental journalism led to his establishing the Institute of Health Communication at Tsinghua University. He has driven many initiatives, from encouraging open reporting of AIDS-related issues to getting student journalists to report from ethnic minority areas, and promoting media literacy among officials.

A policy of conglomeration was instituted by central government in the late 1990s, with the aim of strengthening Chinese media entities to enable them adequately to compete with international media groups.[59] This led to cross-media ownership in the audio-visual, print media and publication sectors through acquisition, merger and joint-venture. In 1998, for example, the Wuxi Broadcasting Group 无锡广播电视集团 brought together radio, television and cable resources in four cities, while in 2001 the Shanghai Media Group 上海东方传媒集团 combined all the city's cultural resources, including broadcasters, newspapers, new media, theatres, sports clubs and many other cultural operations. This process was to result in the creation of 20 media conglomerates by 2002.[60]

Great efforts were made to improve programme production and scheduling. In 1993 the ministry responsible called on CCTV to achieve international standards 'if it aspired to be influential in the world'.[61] Hu Zhengrong 胡正荣, in his history of the Chinese media, describes how in 1993 a junior TV producer thought up the idea of a programme which would tell stories about ordinary people, something which was then quite revolutionary. Although news programmes did not change, from the inception of his programme *Lifespace* 生活空间, the whole tenor of Chinese journalism began to alter. The programme was soon followed by a raft of others looking at problems and contradictions in society that mattered to ordinary people, In 1994 the *People's Daily* wrote that 'before *Lifespace* the only place where common people had a speaking part was on dating shows'.[62]

Media People: An official who changed the media

Ding Guangen 丁关根 (1929-2012), head of the Central Propaganda Department (CPD) in the 1990s, featured prominently in the remaking of the propaganda system by affirming party control of media after 1989.

Between 1985 and 1988 he was Minister of Railways and then, after a period in the Planning Commission, headed the State Council's Taiwan Affairs Office. He promoted cross-strait economic cooperation, and set up the Taiwanese investment zone in coastal areas of Fujian province to attract Taiwan investment.

From 1992 to 2002, he headed the CPD and in this capacity visited Singapore to investigate the media management system. He accelerated development of the Internet and formulated its rules in 1995 and 1996. During his tenure, he encouraged the media to speak for the public and report the truth. The flowering of investigative journalism in this period is attributed to his leadership. After retirement, Ding worked to promote Peking Opera, re-founding training programmes for young opera singers and advocating rescue and study of operatic traditions and their diffusion.

Image source:
http://media.itxinwen.com/2012/0728/419990.shtml
(Accessed 11/03/2016)

The slogan of *Lifespace* was 'Ordinary Peoples' Own Stories' 老百姓自己的故事. One item which seems to have stuck in many peoples' minds told how two elderly people transformed a little three-wheeled car into a caravan and went travelling around the country for pleasure. Not only was it immensely popular; it was admired by media professionals. As Hu Zhengrong puts it, 'The whole model of television changed, substituting for the former hypodermic model an approach which was much more horizontal and used popular language'.

In the same year, Sun Yusheng 孙玉胜 became Director of the Current Affairs Department 新闻评论部, following successes as an investigative reporter and as the first editor of *Focus Report* 焦点访谈. He recruited to CCTV some remarkable journalists such as Bai Yansong 白岩松, Cui Yongyuan 崔永元, Zhang Jie 张杰 and Yang Rui 杨锐 of whom more later, and some imaginative and innovative programmes were introduced under his watch. *Focus Report* had broken a number of taboos, from filming crime scenes to reflecting public opinion and criticising officials. It was much admired by President Jiang Zemin 江泽民 and Premier Zhu Rongji 朱镕基. *Simulcast* (national) *News* 新闻联播, which was transmitting 12 bulletins a day by 1993, followed suit in covering aspects of society heretofore considered too 'negative' to publish.

Other popular programmes emphasising revelation and investigation of matters close to daily life included *News Probe* 新闻调查 (see table on page 72) the remarkable investigative series launched by Sun Yusheng in 1996 with Zhang Jie 张杰 as its first Editor, and *Tell It Like It Is* 实话实说. They, along with *Focus Report*, set the agenda for the rest of the media.

It must have seemed to many that the new government which took office in 2002 would consolidate the position of the media as a respected and professional element of the body politic. After all, they could no longer be overridden by politicians if they expected them, in the Anglo-American idiom, to 'speak truth to power'.

2.10   Harmonious Society and media at the turn of the century

When President Hu Jintao and Prime Minister Wen Jiabao 温家宝 'ascended the dais' in 2002, they began the process of adumbrating their own manifesto, the 'Scientific Development Approach' 科学发展观; or 'Harmonious Society' 和谐社会. This can be seen as a logical extension of Jiang's 'Three Represents' 三个代表, which sought to make the enterprising and inventive feel that the CCP represented their interests. The Harmonious Society extended the embrace to the poor, while acknowledging concern for democracy and the rule of law 民主法制, fairness and justice 公平正义, order and stability 安定有序 and the environment, termed 'harmony between people and nature' 人与自然和谐相处.

From time to time, both leaders made statements demonstrating that they were aware of the value to government of media given free rein to report, investigate and analyse without political interference. In theory, they recognised that the media were essential to good government and future progress.[63] Also in 2002, the then head of the propaganda *xitong* 系统, or network of partner institutions, Li Changchun 李长春, exhorted the media to adhere to what he called the 'Three Proximities' 三贴近 :[64] be close to reality 贴近实际, close to the people 贴近群众 and close to life 贴近生活, He forbore from mentioning the 'throat and tongue', which was the orthodox way to express the relationship between Party and Media.

The first reminder of the damage that can result from stifling the media came with the SARS crisis of 2003. Severe Acute Respiratory Syndrome (SARS) is an acute form of pneumonia that the World Health Organisation (WHO) suspected was spreading in China, but although cases were detected there as early as November 2002, the information was suppressed. When SARS spread from China to other countries, the WHO was furious. In late April 2003, following revelations in the Hong Kong media, the government admitted that the number of SARS cases had been greatly under-reported, and apologised. The dismissal of the Minister of Public Health was a victory for investigative journalism.[65] Elsewhere, media exposure made it possible for the outbreak to be dealt with more quickly. The failings of China's media were perceived as having harmed other countries.

The Communication University of China

There are about 800 higher education institutions teaching media in China. Although journalism is the core subject in the oldest media departments (the earliest dating from the early 1900s), the whole gamut of media-related topics, from advertising and public relations to broadcasting engineering or presentation, may be included. Academic universities with the greatest prestige are Peking, Tsinghua, Fudan and seven others.

China also has a national, specialist, university (and some provincial equivalents), the Communication University of China 中国传媒大学 (CUC). Originally the technical college of the Central Broadcasting Bureau, founded in 1954, it was for a period the Beijing Broadcasting Institute 北广 before widening its scope and becoming CUC in 2004. CUC is the most important educator of media personnel and is ranked first in China for media; its alumni are chief executives, editors and presenter-reporters, as well as filling posts lower down the hierarchies throughout the media.

CUC is as competitive to get into as are the leading academic universities, and attracts particularly talented as well as particularly well-connected applicants for its 15,000 places in Peking and 9,000 places in Nanking where it has established the Nanjing Broadcasting Institute 中国传媒大学南广学院, an independent, undergraduate, institution. The Distance Learning Faculty has nine centres and over 60 other units around the country. CUC is a 'key' university, supported under the Project 211 of the Ministry of Education.

CUC now describes itself as 'a comprehensive institute of higher learning 综合性大学 with broadcasting, film production, journalism, drama, animation, advertising, news-casting, creative cultural industry, communications engineering, foreign languages, management and media law education as its major academic disciplines'. Just near its Peking campus, CUC houses media companies and branches of media companies able to give practical work experience to its students. CUC has arrangements of various kinds with about 300 foreign universities; its faculty members take professional development courses abroad and several summer schools are held annually for CUC third-year undergraduates in London.

Later, relatively full – and unusually rapid – coverage of an Avian Flu outbreak and the Sichuan earthquake of 2008 suggested that the government had learnt from the experience of handling SARS that suppressing such reports is self-defeating; the information eventually emerges anyway, and the failure to report it adequately from the start earns opprobrium.[66]

Despite that lesson, the Tibetan riots of 2008 were not handled well. The media did not source their own news reports, but regurgitated handouts from the Central Propaganda Department (CPD). Foreign media were kept out of Tibet as far as possible, and officials later concluded that this had contributed to the hostile reporting abroad.

The Sanlu Milk Powder 三鹿奶粉 scandal of September 2008 reflected well on the media but badly on the authorities and the Sanlu Company. Media reports emerged about thousands of children suffering from kidney stones, a rare disorder among neo-natals, and these cases were traceable to the Sanlu Company's milk powder. For a year, Sanlu denied the allegations and government health and safety authorities took no action. The scale of the problem was only taken seriously when a New Zealand politician, on a visit to the capital, raised the matter.

When ethnic disturbances took place in Xinjiang two years later, media organisations, including foreign ones, were given greater access. This may have been because, by then, the government had had the positive experience of the way in which the foreign media had covered the Wenchuan 汶川 (Sichuan) Earthquake, they having been generally impressed by the rapid and extensive relief efforts. Domestic journalists had initially been banned by the government from travelling to the scene , but they got there nevertheless, reporting disaster which had killed tens of thousands and rendered millions homeless. Extensive national and international coverage of the earthquake eclipsed the Tibetan riots.

The authorities later attempted to reassert control over reportage, because it appeared that the media were inflaming resentment against local officials, under whose watch schools and other community buildings had allegedly been poorly constructed, contributing to the high casualty rate.

Media People: A leader of the Party press today

Yang Zhenwu has been President and Publisher of the People's Daily Group 人民日报社 since 2014, succeeding Zhang Yannong 张研农 whose background was in the United Front Work Department of the CPCCC, the Central Propaganda Department and as Director of the Theory Department of the *People's Daily* (PD).

Yang Zhenwu graduated from Nankai University in 1978, where he studied Chinese Literature. Upon graduation he was appointed to the Editorial Department of the *People's Daily*. From 1984 to 1989, Yang was the Chief Journalist of the Hebei Bureau. In 1989, he became Vice Director of the Education, Science and Culture Department and thence Head of the Department of Journalists in 2001.

From 2004-9 Yang was a member of the Editorial Board, Editor-in-Chief of the Overseas Edition and Party Secretary of the newspaper. From 2009, Yang move out of *People's Daily* to head the Propaganda Department of the CPC Shanghai Municipal Committee (and became a standing member). In April 2013, he returned to the *People's Daily* as Editor-in-Chief. The following year he acceded to the top job in the group.

Image source:
http://www.people.com.cn/G
B/50142/208383/index.html

60

2.11   What are the media for?

In 2006, President Hu Jintao met with 450 media senior executives to reinforce his Harmonious Society message. 'Chinese television responded by filling its programmes with themes promoting wise leadership, a more egalitarian distribution of income, community harmony and state benevolence'.[67] In so doing, it was carrying out the conventional function of the media: explaining the authorities to the people.

The following year, Hu addressed the Party Congress with a manifesto differing from those of his predecessors in two key respects: it mentioned the word 'democracy' many times and acknowledged concerns about the expanding gap between rich and poor. The implication for the media was that they were partners in the exposure of social issues. That this was now their 'other; main function was to be further emphasised following the Party Congress of 2007, when internal briefings [68] emphasised accountability and transparency. President Hu wanted 'to guarantee that the powers vested in us by the people be used to the benefit of the people; to guarantee that powers are exercised correctly, authority should be exercised in the open'. Because the people have 'the right to be informed, the right to take part, the right to express opinion and the right to supervise, we need decision-making and implementation to be public, accountable and credible'. On the other hand, President Hu also stressed that the media are not independent but part of the formal apparatus for social monitoring.[69] This was a clear rejection of the 'foreign' idea, mooted from time to time, that the media should be outside the system of government. But it was also acknowledgment that the media were more than the 'throat and tongue of the Party'.

In another relevant political development, the 10th Five-Year Plan (2001-2005) had advanced innovation and creativity as fundamental to the future of society.[70] As early as the 1980s there had been programmes for 'key' laboratories, 'key' universities and the *Torch Programme* 火炬计划,[71] to stimulate enterprise in high technology, demonstrating that these attributes were recognised as essential to every area of society.[72] With these ambitions came an implicit understanding that, with the Internet forming an essential infrastructure for a new ideas-based economy, ideas themselves would be the currency and would require new techniques of management. Nobody raised the point that there might be a contradiction between this and the situation of the media.

Unfortunately, although media theory has regularly acknowledged the responsibility of the media to the public as equally important as its service to authority,[73] practice has not kept up. Any assessment of the early 21st century in China must acknowledge greater openness, but also the dismissal and occasional imprisonment of editors whose investigations have proved unwelcome, the curbing of journalists' freedom of movement, and the maltreatment of individual reporters exploring stories in the provinces. In 2016, President Xi complicated the situation by revising the understanding of Supervision by Public Opinion 舆论监督, the principle with which the media had been able to claim the duty to investigate and criticise. Not only did he remind the media that they served the Party foremost, but he enunciated that 'supervision by public opinion and positive propaganda are unified' 舆论监督和正面宣传是统一的, strongly suggesting that monitoring the power holders was out of fashion again. Elucidation in the Party press emphasised this.[74]

Eminent academic Hu Zhengrong, who now heads China's leading institution for the education of the media professions, says: 'Any topic may be discussed among friends and colleagues, and people do so, but the scope of discussion in the public media is still circumscribed: You can discuss policy – for example, media conglomeration. You can talk about that; you can discuss that on [the] general media or public media. But usually you need to, or you have to, discuss it from the positive angle. That means you just say good to this, and don't say bad to this. Sometimes, in academic journals, we experts and professors can criticise the policy. Within a small area, within the academic area, that's fine. But when you are on the public media, if you are interviewed by any kind of media discussing Chinese media policy, you cannot spell out its disadvantages. If I do, the media cannot use it, they cannot quote it. They have to censor it. So, discussing the policy, it's okay. But discussing it negatively, no.'[75]

According to Lee Chin-ch'uan, doyen in studies of the media, three conceptions of the media jostled together at the start of the Twenty First Century: 'the Confucian and liberal model treats the audience as the target of education, guidance, and enlightenment; the Maoist model, as the target of mobilisation and indoctrination; and the Communist capitalist model, as the target of ideological conformity and exploitation for profit'.[76] The idea that the people might also be participants had to wait for New Media.

Conversations with Editors of national and regional newspapers, and CCTV current affairs programmes, suggest to me that they overwhelmingly adhere to Lee's first model. Leading CCTV editor Zhang Jie, no puppet he, has several times vividly expressed his belief that he and his colleagues must seek to promote harmony in society and are there to guide and enlighten.[77]

As to journalists' views on the matters of the day, whatever different models there might be in peoples' minds, the mainstream media, according to Zhao, have been united in creating 'ideological consensus around reform and opening up'.[78] They have been polemicists on the great matters of their day, as were their forebears.

To ensure that they are 'on message', gatekeeping of the profession has become stringent. Being a graduate of one of the 800-odd media courses in higher education is not enough. There is a national system of certification and licensing, with compulsory training and refresher courses.[79]

A poem about news

重要新闻报道提纲 A selection of important news reports by Gao Ping 高平

火车若干天没发生重大事故
There have been no accidents on the railways
公仆若干年不曾受贿贪污
Bribery is unknown in the civil service
公民及时播了种
The farmers have sown the crops on time
收购粮全都入了库
And the harvest has been gathered into the granaries
药店没有买卖假药
Pharmacies never deal in fake medicines
医生没有收取红包
And our physicians have not taken bribes
没有拖欠教师的工资
Teachers' salaries are paid on time
不再给农民打白条儿
No longer are the farmers paid with credit notes
媳妇给婆婆端水
Sons in law respectfully serve their wives' mothers
毕业生服从分配
And graduates accept the posts they are allocated
挪用的巨额公款正在清退
Embezzled money is being returned to the public purse
中国人不肯给外国人下跪
And Chinese people have ceased to do obeisance to foreigners!

2.12 Summary

Over the last 150 years, the media have been much more than mere providers of news and information. Before and under the Republic, when they enjoyed a latitude later denied them, they created an awareness of Chineseness among a people who had not seen themselves as belonging to a nation; they alerted them to the dangers posed by the barbarians at the gates, galvanised them with new ideas and mobilised them to resist and strive so that China might regain wealth and power.

Once again, comparisons help to illuminate what else is specific about China's media. The Anglophone polity long ago exhibited the traits with which it is today associated – localism, equality before (God and) the law, critical thinking and participation – well before anything like the modern media existed. The modern media were products of the division of powers between executive and legislature and the rise of Protestantism, and were sustained by the rule of law. Over time, they became more detached in order to appeal to diverse interest groups. They guarded their independence from politicians and claimed to be free of untoward influences.

By contrast, the media came about in China as political actors, seeking to press for change, propagate ideas and give opportunities to the educated classes to participate in the great commitment to save Chinese civilisation from imperialism. At the turn of the 19th/20th centuries, the people who set up magazines and newspapers saw themselves as of the political class.

The evisceration of the media in 1949 and their transformation into obedient mouthpieces of the oligarchy was disastrous for China's development over the following thirty years. The pre-1949 media may not have been perfect, but they facilitated the flow of ideas and provided information on which at least part of the population could make decisions as citizens and consumers. They staged debate and discussion, analysed policy options and investigated malpractice. These are the main tasks of the media in successful societies today. After Mao, some decision-makers recognised this, which is why they authorised media competition and invested in information technology and the Internet, but they could not let go and trust the media to make judgments. This left Editors struggling between their 'two chieftains': the Party bosses and the people, or at least their own judgments of what the people wanted.[80] Moreover, although central leaders have supported the idea of 'supervisory' media, those in authority under them, whenever the media have conflicted with their interests or prerogatives, have taken the short view that detached reporting is heinous.

The Anglophone media have many blemishes but the fact that journalists are protected by law and custom has allowed political mistakes to be analysed, corruption exposed and timely alerts provided. Because of their orientation, as well the Party's power, it has been difficult for Chinese journalists to perform these functions through the public media.[81] Until 1949 there was sufficient pluralism for them to do so, albeit often in an attenuated way, but thereafter they risked everything if they stood out.

Many see themselves, not as adversaries of authority, but as in the great tradition of erudite counsellors to state and people.[82] Asked, in 2009, why he chose to study journalism rather than science, one Tsinghua student spoke for his comrades when he replied: 'China has many successful scientists and entrepreneurs, but we cannot explain ourselves to the world. China needs communicators who can put our point of view and show our achievements, and that is the biggest need now'. His sense of common purpose is not unusual. It can promote timid conformity but it can also inspire great work. It has long been a distinguishing mark of Chinese media.

Notes

[1] The most comprehensive work on the subject is Fang Hanqi's (2012) *A History of Journalism in China* Hong Kong: Enrich

[2] I have given a fuller description of the emergence of English journalism in de Burgh, Hugo (2008) *Investigative journalism*. 2nd ed. London: Routledge, Chapter 2.

[3] Milton J. (1644) Areopagitica: a speech of John Milton for the liberty of unlicenc'd printing, to the Parliament of England London.

[4] Chinese intellectuals' assumptions that religion underpins the European Enlightenment are not mainstream in the West, but there are authorities that concur. Vernon White has written to me that 'Bertrand Russell notably made the case for a Protestant origin for some enlightenment political developments. Other social and economic developments are attributed to Protestantism by Max Weber in his *The Protestant Ethic and the Spirit of Capitalism*. More recently Charles Taylor has an interesting take on it, mostly in his *Sources of the Self*. Michael Gillespie's even more recent *The Theological Origins of Modernity* is rather different. He sees roots of modernity more in the pre-Reformation theological-philosophical shift from scholastic realism to nominalism. From historians there has been Hugh Trevor-Roper and his *The Crisis of the Seventeenth Century: Religion, the Reformation and Social Change*. He stressed how the possibility of dissent and pluralism brought by the Protestant Reformation was crucial for opening up enlightenment ideals.' (abbreviated)

[5] For a thorough history, see Zhang, X. (2007) The Origins of the Modern Chinese Press: The Influence of the Protestant Missionary Press in Late Qing China. London: Routledge and Wagner, R. G. (2008) Joining the Global Public. New York: State University of New York Press.

[6] The early years have been dealt with in my (2003) *The Chinese journalist: Mediating information in the world's most populous country*. London: Routledge, Chapter 7. Since then, Zhang Xiantao has published (2007) *The Origins of the Modern Chinese Press* London: Routledge

[7] Lee, Chin-chuan (2005) 'The Conception of Chinese Journalists' in de Burgh, Hugo (2005) *Making Journalists* (ed) Routledge, p 108.

[8] Ibid., pp 107.

[9] A very interesting collection of essays is relevant here: 李金铨 Lee, Chin-ch'uan (2008) (ed) 文人论证，知识分子与报刊 *Intellectuals and the Press*. 桂林 Guilin: 广西师范大学出版社 Guangxi Shifan University Press.

[10] Gray J. (1990) *Rebellions and revolutions: China from the 1800s to 2000*. Oxford: Oxford University Press, pp 245.

[11] 曾虚白 Zeng Xubai (1978) 中国新闻史 *A History of the Chinese Press* 台北 Taipei : 三民书局印行 Sanmin. is among those who use this term. Chapter 11.

[12] Lee (2005), pp 111.

[13] Dikötter F. (2008) *The age of openness: China before Mao*. Berkeley, Ca: University of California Press, pp 90-92.

[14] Deng K. (2012) *China's political economy in modern times* London: Routledge.

[15] Dikötter, ibid, pp 101.

[16] This is a simplification. The outrider in standing up for peasant rights was Peng Pai 彭湃, but his career as an activist was cut short at his execution.

[17] This is very well described in Westad, Odd Arne (2012) *Restless Empire: China and the world since 1750*. The Bodley Head: London.

[18] The destruction of the fourteenth-century city of Peking, one of the wonders of the world up to 1950, did not come about merely through casual vandalism. Just as with the extirpation of people and culture, so with the environment: an architect trained by LeCorbusier in Paris, who had never lived in China, was in charge of the planned destruction (See Westad, op cit, pp 243-244). Following his energetic vandalism, Hua Lanhong retired to France in 1977, after which, in the 1990s, the further obliteration of the wonder took place, thanks to careless officials and greedy developers.

[19] The Blank Slate Theory, now thoroughly discredited if still powerful among politicians for whom it is invaluable, has been particularly effectively exposed in Steven Pinker's *The Blank Slate* London: Penguin (2002)

[20] This is a simplification; there were of course variations in policy over this long period.

[21] Yu, Frederick T. C. (1964) *Mass Persuasion in Communist China* London Pall Mall Press, pp 4. The most thorough analysis of the pre-GPCR period.

[22] Ibid., pp 103.

[23] In 2016 various problems were identified throughout the public service and campaigned against in the media. They included the 'four tendencies' 四风 of bureaucratism, formalism, hedonism and 官僚、形式、享乐、奢风. Then 三严三实. The 'three publics' 三公 were criticized, or the use for private purposes of public vehicles, buildings and facilities. 公车公房公务. People at the bottom of society are probably delighted to see the wealthy or the officials put in their place, such that these campaigns may be more about getting grassroots support than reform of the public service.

[24] A thorough review of the campaigns, ancient and modern, is to be found in Perry, Elizabeth J. 'From Mass Campaigns to Managed Campaigns: Constructing a New Socialist Countryside' in Heilmann, op cit, pp 30-61.

[25] There were others, though mainly internal to the Party; these eight were the ones which affected most people. It might be argued that the Land Reform campaign had a positive aspect ; land reform though was carried out in many other countries, Taiwan and Italy, for example, without the savagery of the CCP.

[26] The author of *Bare Earth* 赤地 and *The Rice Sprout Song* 秧歌 is Zhang Ailing 张爱玲 (Eileen Chang).

[27] Dikötter, F. (2011) *Mao's great famine: the history of China's most devastating catastrophe*, 1958-62. London: Bloomsbury, pp xii.

[28] 阎连科 Yan Lianke 坚硬入睡 （2009）*Tough Like Water* 台北：成都文化 Taibei: Chengdu Wenhua；莫言 Mo Yan (2006) 生死疲劳 *Life and Death are Wearing Me Out* 余华 Yu Hua （2012） 活着 *To Live*, 北京：作家出版社 *see* p78 onwards

[29] I discuss this in more detail in *The Chinese Journalist* (2003) op cit.

[30] The most illuminating compendium of materials on this is Schoenhals, M (1996) *China's Cultural Revolution, 1966-1969: Not a Dinner Party*, New York: ME Sharpe

[31] Being a practical man, it is quite possible that Deng never reflected on, let alone accepted, the thought that the disasters in which he had been implicated were consequences of the theory rather than of the failures of individuals. In any case, faced with a powerful constituency for the status quo, he could not possibly question the ideology but only try to circumvent it. His inability to reject the ideology did not matter at the time; the repercussions are now, when China arguably should be sloughing it off, but finds it difficult to do so.

[32] Deng K. (2012) *China's political economy in modern times* London: Routledge, pp 136-141.

[33] Deng (2012) confounds the myth of economic progress; Chen Guidi and Wu Chuntao in their remarkable investigation of poverty [(2006) *Will the Boat sink the Water?* London : Public Affairs Ltd] exposed the claims to social progress; most powerful in its revisionist challenge is the trilogy by Frank Dikotter *The Tragedy of Liberation*, *Mao's Great Famine* and *The Cultural Revolution: A Peoples' History 1962-1976*, of which the most provocative is *The Tragedy of Liberation: A History of the Communist Revolution 1945-1957*.

[34] Zhao, Yuezhi (2012) 'Understanding China's Media System' in Hallin, Daniel C. and Mancini, Paolo (2012) *Comparing Media Systems Beyond the Western World*, Cambridge: Cambridge University Press, pp 149.

[35] Jernow, AL (1993) Don't force us to lie: the struggle of Chinese journalists in the Reform Era China. *Times Center for Media and Social Studies*, pp18. [Online]. Available at: http://digitalcommons.law.umaryland.edu/cgi/viewcontent.cgi?article=1120&context=mscas (Accessed: 7 March 2016) .

[36] And not for the first time. For a discussion of attempts to give more discretion to media in the 1950s, see China Media Project http://cmp.hku.hk/2016/06/ (Accessed: 31 July 17)

[37] Polumbaum, Judy (1990) The Tribulations of China's Journalists after a Decade of Reform, in Lee Chin-chuan (ed) *Voices of China: The Interplay of Politics & Journalism*, New York: The Guildford Press, pp 41.

[38] Hu would be among the 23 party elders who issued a strongly worded petition to Congress in late 2010, calling for an end to media censorship.

[39] For more on Liu Binyan, again see de Burgh, (2003), pp 150-152.

[40] Xiaoqiao, Laoshu (2010)小桥老鼠 *Notes from the Civil Service* 官场笔记 Beijing: Fenghuang, volume 5, pp132-4

[41] Xi Zhongxun 习仲勋 was either Party Secretary or Governor or both 1978-1981.

[42] Zhang, Jige (2010) *Media evolution and reform politics in China: a case of Guangdong*. Thesis submitted in partial fulfilment of the requirements for PhD, The University of Auckland; pp 82. This thesis covers ground in detail that no published book or article – as far as I can tell – does. [Online]. Available at: http://librarysearch.auckland.ac.nz/primo_library/libweb/action/dlSearch.do?institution=UOA&bulksize=10&indx=1&dym=true&highlight=true&displayField=title&displayField=creator&vid=UOA2_A&tab=search_library&lang=eng&group=GUEST&fn=search&search_scope=Combined_Local&query=facet_local1,exact,Theses&query=any,contains,zhang%20jige&query=any,contains,Auckland+OR+%22University%20of%20New%20Zealand%22

[43] Ibid., pp 86.

[44] Ibid., pp 41.

[45] Ibid., Chapter 2 passim.

[46] Zhao, Yuezhi. (1998) *Media, market and democracy in China: between the party line and the bottom line*. Urbana: University of Illinois Press, pp 96.

[47] Zhang (2010), pp 170.

[48] Lee, Chin-chuan (1990) 'Mass Media: of China, about China' in Lee Chin-chuan (ed) *Voices of China: The Interplay of Politics & Journalism*, New York: The Guildford Press, pp 8-10.

[49] Ibid., pp 118-9.

[50] Dong GP. *Governing China with the news: television and national development in China since 1958*. Unpublished PhD thesis. University of Durham; 2009: Chapter 2. [Online]. Available at: http://etheses.dur.ac.uk/2161/1/2161_169.PDF?UkUDh:CyT (Accessed: 17 March 2016)

[51] Ibid.

[52] Ibid., pp 99

[53] Calhoun, C. (1997) *Neither gods nor emperors: students and the struggle for democracy in China*. Berkeley: University of California Press. The Democracy Movement which is now generally coupled with the Tiananmen Massacre of June 4th, 1989, was much more than a protest

in the capital. For what happened in several oher provinces and cities, see Unger, Jonathan (ed) (1991) *The Pro-Democracy Protests in China: Reports from the Provinces*, Armonk:ME Sharpe

[54] *The Gate of Heavenly Peace*, see: https://www.youtube.com/watch?v=1Gtt2JxmQtg (Accessed: 17 March 2016)

[55] The Chinese expression is 'Nanxun' 南巡 ('southern travel'), the word *Xun* historically being used for what in English history is termed a 'Royal Progress'.

[56] Schell, O. (1995) *Mandate of heaven: a new generation of entrepreneurs, dissidents, bohemians and technocrats lays claim to China's future.* London: Warner, pp 391.

[57] Chan, Joseph Man 'Commercialization without Independence: Tends and Tensions of Media Development in China' in Cheng, J.Yu-shek. and Brosseau, Maurice (1993) (eds) *China Review* HK : CUP, pp 25.1-25.21.

[58] This section is drawn from de Burgh (2003).

[59] On Document 17 and the conglomerate policy, see Zhu Ying (2012), p31

[60] Zhao has discussed the conglomeration policy and its application extensively, see Zhao, Yuezhi (2008) *Communication in China*, Langham: Rowman and Littlefield, pp 97-100, 105-107.

[61] Dong (2009), pp 110. The Ministry in the case was MFRT, formerly SAB, later SARFT, still later SAPPRFT, known usually by its abbreviation of 'Office of TV and radio 广电局'

[62] 胡正容 Hu Zhengrong (2010). 社会透镜，新中国媒介变迁六十年 *Society's lens: sixty years of vicissitudes in the Chinese media* 北京 Beijing：清华大学出版社 Tsinghua University Press, pp 300-303.

[63] For example: Sina News. President Hu encourages reporting to be more realistic [Online]. 2003 [cited 3 March 2013]. Available at: http://news.sina.com.cn/c/2003-04-08/1730986521.shtml (Accessed: 17 March 2016)

[64] Zhu Yingchi (2008) How Polyphony is Changing China in Sen, Krishna, et al *Political regimes and the media in Asia* London: Routledge, pp 49.

[65] Bandurski, David (2010*) Investigative Journalism in China: Eight cases in Chinese watchdog journalism* HK : HKUP, p10

[66] Hu (2010), pp 334.

[67] Zhu, Y. (2012) *Two billion eyes: the story of China Central Television*. New York: The New Press, pp 16.

[68] This section is based upon interviews held in 2010-11 and reported in de Burgh H, Rong Z, Mi M. 'Responding to an activist public: reconfiguring relationships between authority and media in a Chinese city'. *Media Culture & Society* (2012) Nov; 34 (8): pp 1013-27.

[69] Chan, Ying (2010) 'The Journalism Tradition' in Bandurski, David (2010) *Investigative Journalism in China: Eight Cases of Chinese Watchdog Journalism*. HK: HKUP.

[70] Li, W. (2011) *How Creativity is Changing China*. London: Bloomsbury Academic.

[71] For the Torch Programme, see http://www.ctp.gov.cn/ctp-eng/index.htm.

[72] For much more on this, see Keane, MA (2011) *China's new creative clusters: governance, human capital and investment*. London: Routledge. See also Li, W. (2011) *How creativity is changing China*. London: Bloomsbury Academic.

[73] Polumbaum (1990), pp 34.

[74] China Media Project http://cmp.hku.hk/2016/06/ (Accessed: 31 July 17)

[75] Hu Zhengrong. Interviewed by the author. Peking; 10 November 2012.

[76] Lee (2005), pp 108.

[77] See p 170 in this book for a quote from Zhang. Zhu Ying quotes him extensively in (2009) pp 59 et seq

[78] Zhao (1998), pp 149

[79] Ibid., pp 29.

[80] Polumbaum (1990), pp 44-45.

[81] They can do so through the Restricted Circulation Publication (RCP) system. See Chapter 3 for an explanation of RCPs.

[82] I have explored this in an earlier article: de Burgh, H (2003) 'The Journalist in China: Looking to the Past for Inspiration' in *Media History*, Vol 9 No 3 December ISSN 1368-8804.

3   The media today

China's domestic media are both an industry, and an arm of government. They provide news, information, analysis and evaluation but they also offer, through art and entertainment, explanations of life, role models, issues for debate, humour and emotion. They serve a public bigger than that of the USA and Europe (including Russia) combined and a huge market.

The organisation of the pre-Internet media has barely altered since the 1950s, though the quantity, technology, content and expectations have changed mightily. After the abolition of independent media, a hierarchical system was set up, with media in effect being units of government at each of the main levels of administration, plus providers of specialist publications for particular professions or industries. When new media are established, they must be under the patronage and supervision of a government or Party institution; even a city 'what's on' or hobby magazine must conform. Occasionally we hear reports of apparently independent local papers being set up and wonder at their survival.[1]

Xinhua News Agency 新华社, CCTV 中央电视台, *The Peoples' Daily* 人民日报, *China National Radio* 国际广播电台 and the Party Central Committee Journal *Seek Truth* 求是 are the best-known national organs of the Party in their respective media. Each province has its equivalents, for example *Gansu Daily* 甘肃日报 is the Party newspaper in that province. Complementing them at each level in the hierarchy, including counties and cities at the lower levels, are many newspapers from lightweight evening papers to local teachers' journals to thoughtful weekend papers, of which the most notably freethinking is probably *Southern Weekend* 南方周末.

After 1949, media workers became civil servants required to perform functions complementary to the executives of the administration generally. The latter sometimes looked upon them as 'creatives', usually as their publicists and occasionally as colleagues who could be dangerous because of their propensity to inspect and investigate. Their work units – Qinghai TV, *Dahe Daily*, Wenzhou Radio et cetera – were supervised by more elevated state entities. Producers and editors held (and hold) ranks in the civil service.[2]

As we will discuss in Chapter 5, it is more the custom for media workers to identify with their work unit or network within it than to seek to conform to professional principles enunciated by impersonal bodies. Today, journalists in particular are subjected to training and must earn a license, a continuation of the CCP's longstanding efforts to detach people's loyalties from their own networks. Whether these have succeeded for longer than brief bursts of ideological enthusiasm is open to doubt.

Pervasive loyalty to the smaller community gives a particular complexion to the media, regardless of whether the ownership and management is private or 'public'. Media workers are local in their attachments. More and more, the media are reflecting their provinces, counties' and towns' languages and identities, as before 1949. This is typified in Shanghai, whose local media Australian academic Sun Wanning describes as the 'promoter and custodian of Shanghai culture', 'its dialect, its place-based memory, and its collective sense of identity and pride'. The Southern Media Group distinguish themselves as trend setters.[3] The Hunan group vaunts itself as having the best entertainment shows and presenters on account of the province's long tradition of storytelling, ballads and performance.

Thus, whereas once you could be forgiven for imagining the media as homogenous and centrally controlled, this is no longer the case. Sun reminds us that there are over a thousand county level TV stations carrying advertising for local products and services, producing parochial news and reaching local audiences. She reports 'many examples' of small cities replacing national advertisements with local ones, and the regulator 'has no way of ensuring' that grassroots media adhere to its rule of national uniformity in their coverage of national events or crises.[4]

One consequence of the reduction or removal of subsidies was that those organs, often given the sobriquet 'Party media', which persisted in majoring on politics and policies lost customers to the point that they would have collapsed had the media groups not cross-subsidised them with the profits of their 'commercial' media.[5] This is a smart solution to a problem that is plaguing many countries: how to preserve public service values in an increasingly competitive commercial media marketplace. It was feasible because the media are still owned by authority (there is some debate as to whether they are owned by state or Party) and subject to the ordinances of the Central Propaganda Department, SAPPRFT (the regulator) and local Party committees.

3.1 Agencies

We start with Xinhua (New China) News Agency (NCNA) 新华社 because it has until recently supplied the bulk of serious news to every form of media in China. The authorities often require media to follow its lead or even, for political matters or information deemed sensitive, to carry only Xinhua formulations. Its reporters take precedence at all times and it reports directly to the State Council. Although the agency has many sources of revenue, the government continues to subsidise it, emphasising its official role in the provision of information.[6]

At home Xinhua has newsgathering bureaux in every province, and publishes over 20 newspapers and magazines, with circulations of up to 10 million. Its other output includes news in six languages and multimedia formats 24 hours a day, the most bought newspaper, Reference News 参考消息, a compendium of extracts from foreign media, and Xinhuanet.com 新华网. The latter is among the leading news websites, with 31 local channels, and it hosts the largest block of government websites, including gov.cn.[7]

Abroad, Xinhua supplies news and financial information to more than 130 countries in eight languages from 170 bureaux worldwide.[8] China Xinhua News Network Corporation (CNC) 中国新华新闻电视网, a television news network run by Xinhua, seeks to emulate CNN with its English Language channel CNC World.

In the recent past Xinhua was conservative in both adhering to the official line and in what it covered. It is now moving towards greater transparency and credibility.[9] Since 2008, the agency has been permitted to report on mass protests and has covered stories that might once have been suppressed. This is as much an indication of the authorities' confidence in Xinhua as of acceptance that such stories will inevitably be exposed anyway, through New Media.

News Probe

Like the other leading national programmes dealing with social and political issues, 東方時空 *Oriental Horizon* (1993) , 焦點訪談 *Focus Reports* (1994) and 實話實說 *Tell It Like It Is* (1995), *News Probe* 新聞調查 (1995) was founded in that great burst of creativity of the 1990s. These types of programmes are known collectively as 'Commentary', 评论, programmes, or sometimes as 'in depth reporting', 深度报道.

A leading vehicle of investigative journalism transmitted weekly on CCTV, *News Probe* now has an audience of up to 100 million, providing 52 programmes per year for 40 minutes each. The first transmission is late on Saturday evening (21.30) but subsequent transmissions are on weekend mid-morning. The audience, says founder-editor Zhang Jie 张洁, was originally expected to consist of intellectuals, but he and his team rapidly realised that they had a huge following among the peasants and migrant workers. Large numbers of them call in with harrowing tales of exploitation, expropriation and corruption. All the calls are logged and the tales told are pored over for possible programme stories. Every year the programme shines its torch on new subjects, supporting its claim that it is: 'in pursuit of justice; balanced and in depth; getting at the truth'. In 1998 the programme went so far as to argue that the Discipline and Inspection Commission was not competent to audit the executive because of the interference of the Party, although its staff say that such outspoken criticism is not at present possible. Some of its stories are listed on pages 161-2.

Xinhua also produces *Restricted Circulation Publications* (RCP). *Reference News* 参考消息 used to be one but it is now publicly available. RCPs, which fall into several categories, are the means by which sensitive information and investigations are circulated to limited classifications of recipients. Journalists (including TV and radio) often say that some of their best work is in the RCPs, and that this is also the most useful since it can influence policy. Their contribution to the RCPs is the clearest illustration of how differently Chinese journalists see their responsibilities compared with the impetus to total exposure favoured in the Anglosphere.

3.2   Newspapers

Party newspapers such as *Liberation Daily* 解放日报 date back to before 1949, when they were distributed in all Communist-held areas, pinned on noticeboards (or behind glass) for communal study, read out in the workplace and even broadcast on the radio.[10] In the 1980s, evening papers were revived to leaven this stodgy fare[11] and in the 1990s the 'city' category appeared. 'A new name was engraved on the consciousness of the Chinese newspaper industry, and that was *West China City News* 华西都市报' writes Hu Zhengrong, the media historian who is now President of Communication University of China: 'Earlier, the man who was to be its editor, Xi Wenju 席文举, had made a very thorough examination of existing newspaper provision in China. He divided the existing newspapers into three categories. The first included the traditional evening papers, such as *New People's Evening News* 新民晚报. The second type included those attached to organisations, such as the *Chengdu Evening News* 成都晚报, with their styles reflecting the organisation in question. These were influenced by the authorities, despite the newspapers' policy of allowing social news and the interests of ordinary people to take the lead. A third type, exemplified by the *Yangzi Evening News* 扬子晚报, represented the new wave of newspapers which reacted against the traditional papers, stressing that they were neither mere supplements of the dailies nor entertainment vehicles, but close to the basic concerns of ordinary citizens. They intended to strike a new path in the provision of practical down-to-earth news reporting, of value to everyone. Launched in 1995, *West China City News* fell into this category, was immediately successful and gained a reputation for creating a new model of newspaper,'[12] prepared to raise every social issue.

Many others followed the lead of *West China City News* and newspapers of its kind rejoice in the fastest growing circulations and revenues from advertising. There are also many specialist professional newspapers, some of which are listed in pages 74-76 to give a flavour.[13] Each of them has a sponsor and a regulator, consisting of government or Party departments, which have to approve and take responsibility for the functions and footprints of the newspapers.

The newspaper market is the strongest in the county towns and provincial capitals, where local city newspapers now compete with the Party dailies. They have high circulation figures, but readership traditionally has been low, particularly compared with Japan and the USA.[14]

A witticism about officialdom

> Witticisms about the bureaucracy are a staple of Chinese conversation and the story below illustrates how the system is mocked:
>
> A child sees the panels that, outside every state and Party office, declare what goes on inside, and he asks: 'City Party Committee, City Parliament, City Government, City Consultative Assembly – what do they all do?' His mother responds: 'City Party Committee, it's like your father, does nothing, stands with his hands behind his back, lecturing others. City Parliament, it's like Grandpa, enjoying his hobbies, but not actually managing anything. City Government, that's like your mother, hard at work every day and sometimes even having to put up with lectures from your papa. City Consultative Assembly, that's just like Grandma, grumbling all day, but nobody taking a blind bit of notice.'
>
> The child then asks, 'And what about the Discipline and Inspection Commission?' 'Oh,' says his mother, 'that's just like you, supervising and criticising your parents, even though we are in charge of you. But you eat the food and wear the clothing we provide, and so all that supervision and criticism mean nothing'.

The Party newspapers are essential reading for officials. Because of their political obligations, they are able neither to appeal to ordinary readers nor to attract much advertising. Had it not been for the policy of conglomeration and the requirement that the conglomerates keep the Party press going, many of them would have failed in the market. Hence the media managers' launching of popular papers and 'city' dailies, which can earn enough to subsidise their Party newspapers (otherwise funded by departmental subscriptions). *Southern City Daily* 南方都市报 from Canton/Guangzhou is now the best known of these, along with its sister paper *Southern Weekend* (see p227). How can we evaluate them?

Lacking an authoritative study of such a large field, it is difficult to make any reliable generalisation as to how the newspapers in China compare in content to their Anglophone equivalents. A student's comparison of *Global Times*, *New York Times*, *Beijing Youth Daily*, *The Australian*, *Southern Weekend* and *The Observer* (a UK weekend paper) revealed no significant differences in the numbers of stories in various categories, with the exceptions that Chinese newspapers had a higher proportion of 'local' stories and a predilection for reflective essays on cultural matters and political commentary by intellectuals, as in *Southern Weekend*. My own review of several local newspapers together gave a similar impression.[15] There are differences in tone and weight; on the day I compared two serious broadsheets, *Southern Weekend* had the discursive features for which is it renowned on (1) reform through labour, (2) the Chinese dream and (3) how citizens see democracy. *Beijing Youth Daily* had six pages on former President Mandela, following his death, covered more stories rather less portentously, such as regulatory changes in the examination system, traffic alleviation and expansion of the underground railway.[16] Overall, and in response to the immediacy of online news, Chinese newspapers are becoming more like magazines, with more discursive and weighty articles and substantial specialist sections, as in the

Anglosphere. In the next chapter, we will look at two trends which see a struggle by 'news organisations [to] recapture their role in society by exploiting the opportunities provided by digitalisation'.[17]

Some newspapers by category

1 Newspapers of National Political Organs 中央机关报

People's Daily 人民日报	Unity 团结报	Southern Daily 南方日报	Tibet Daily 西藏日报
Beijing Daily 北京日报	Liaoning Daily 辽宁日报	Public Daily 大众日报	Chongqing Daily 重庆日报
Liberation Army Daily 解放日报	Xinhua Daily 新华日报	Hebei Daily 河北日报	Hainan Daily 海南日报
光明日报 Guangming Daily	经济日报 Economic Daily	天津日报 Tianjin Daily	山西日报 Shanxi Daily
内蒙古日报 Inner Mongolia Daily	河南日报 Henan Daily	吉林日报 Jilin Daily	黑龙江日报 Heilongjiang Daily
浙江日报 Zhejiang Daily	安徽日报 Anhui Daily	福建日报 Fujian Daily	江西日报 Jiangxi Daily
湖北日报 Hubei Daily	湖南日报 Hunan Daily	南方日报 Sourthern Daily	广西日报 Guangxi Daily
四川日报 Sichuan Daily	贵州日报 Guizhou Daily	云南日报 Yunan Daily	陕西日报 Shaanxi Daily
甘肃日报 Gansu Daily	青海日报 Qinghai Daily	宁夏日报 Ningxia Daily	新疆日报 Xinjiang Daily

2 NPC, CPPCC and Overseas Affairs Newspapers 人大，政协和侨务报

Consultative Congress 人民政协报	People's Power 人民政权报	Guangdong Émigré 广东侨报	Sichuan CPPCC 四川政协报
Shanghai Émigré 上海侨报	Fellowship 联谊报	Hainan Émigré 海南侨报	Ningxia CPPCC Newspaper

			宁夏政协报
Member of Congress Daily 人民代表报	Zhejiang émigré Voice 浙江侨声报	Democratic Consultant 民主协商报	Yunnan CPPCC 云南

3. Sports Newspapers 体育

China Sports 中国体育报	Chess Weekly 棋牌周报	Sport Weekly Abstracts 体育文摘周报	China Football 中国足球报
Xinmin Sports Daily 新民体育报	Sports Weekly 体育周报	Football Weekly 足球周报	Sports Life 体育生活报
Football 足球	Southern Sports 南方体育报	Guangzhou Sports 羊城体育	

4. Law Newspapers 法制

Law Daily 法制日报	Beijing Legal Evening News 北京法制晚报	People's Public Security 人民公安报	Law Abstracts 法制文萃报
People's Armed Police 人民武警报	Procuratorate Daily 检察日报	Legal Evening News 法制晚报	People's Court News 人民法院报
Democracy and Law Pictorial 民主与法制画报(They stopped finilish in 2016)	Discipline Inspection and Supervision 中国纪检监察报	**法制周报** **Legal Weekly News**	**民主法治网** **www.mzyfz.com**

5. Education Newspapers 教育

China Education 中国教育报	Junior Science 青少年科技报	Shanghai Student English 上海学生英文报	China Junior Newspaper 中国初中生报
	China Adult Education Information 中国成人教育信息报	Primary School Study Weekly 小学生学习周报	English Coach 英语辅导报
Chinese Television 中国电视报	Pinyin Tabloid 汉语拼音小报	Shanghai Education 上海教育报	Essay Comment 作文评点报

6. Broadcasting and Film Newspapers 广播影视

Jiangsu Broadcasting	China Broadcasting	China Film	Heilongjiang

and Television 江苏广播电视报	中国广播报	中国电影报	Broadcasting and Television 黑龙江广播电视报
Hangzhou Broadcasting and Film 杭州广播影视报	China Television 中国电视报	China Education Television 中国教育电视	Daqing Broadcasting and Television 大庆广播电视报
Hubei Broadcasting and Television 湖北广播电视报	Drama and Movie 戏剧电影报	Wenhui Film Times 文汇电影时报	Huangshan Broadcasting and Television 黄山广播电视报

7. Science and Computer Technology Newspapers 科技，电脑

Computer World 计算机世界		Science Daily 科技日报	China Computer Education 中国电脑教育报
China Electronics 中国电子报	China Science 中国科学报	China Computers 中国计算机报	China Association for Science 中国科协报
Beijing Electronics News 北京电子报	Technicians' Scientific News 中国职工科技报	China Meteorological News 中国气象报	China Space News 中国航天报

8. Regional Newspapers 区域性综合新闻

Xinmin Evening News 新民晚报	China Daily 中国日报	Xinhua Daily Telegraph 新华每日电讯	Global Times 环球时报
Union Times 联合时报	Workers' Daily 工人日报	Beijing Suburbs Daily 京郊日报	Beijing Workers' News 北京工人报
The News 新闻报	Beijing Evening News 北京晚报	Beijing Weekend 北京周末报	21st Century 21 世纪报

9. Industrial and Professional Newspapers 产业，专业报

China Population 中国人口报	China Petroleum 中国石油报	China Textile 中国纺织报	China Military 中国军工报
China Construction 中国建设报	China Packaging 中国包装报	China Building Materials 中国建材报	China Auto 中国汽车报
China Communications 中国交通报	China Nonferrous Metals 中国有色金属报	China Green Times 中国绿色时报	China Petrochemical 中国石化报

10. Digests，Reference, Publishing Newspapers 文摘，参考，出版，书讯

Abstracts 文摘报	Xinhua Bibliographic 新华书目报	Technology Digest 科技文摘报	China Book Business 中国图书商报
Reference News 参考消息	Youth Reference 青年参考	Writer's Digest 作家文摘	Pensioner Digest 老年文摘报

Press and Publications	Health Digest	China Reader	Wenhui News
新闻出版报	健康文摘报	中华读书报	文汇报

11. Economic，Commercial and Consumer Newspapers 经济，商业，消息和信息

Market Newspaper	Economic Information	China Environment	China Trade News
市场报	经济参考报	中国环境报	中国贸易报
China Commercial	International Business	Economic Daily	China Industrial and Commercial
中国商报	国际经贸消息	经济日报	中国工商报
International Commerce	China Township Enterprise	China Business	Chinese Consumer
国际商报	中国乡镇企业报	中国经营报	中国消费者

12. Medicine, Health, Family and Travel Newspapers 医药，健康，家庭和旅游

Health News	China Medicine	Voice of Civic Administration	Shanghai Public Health
健康报	中国医药报	民政之声报	上海大众卫生报
China Tourism	Chinese Traditional Medicine	Safety Produce News	Shanghai Chinese Medicine
中国旅游报	中国中医药报	安全生产报	上海中医药报
Health Consultant	China Red Cross	Health Times	Travel Times
健康咨询报	中国红十字报	保健时报	旅游时报

13. Humanity, Life, Entertainment and Art Newspapers 人文，生活，娱乐和艺术

China Women	Music Weekly	China's Children	Literature Story
中国妇女报	音乐周报	中国儿童报	文学故事报
Chinese Youth	Farmers' Daily	China Flowers and Plants	China Labour
中国青年报	农民日报	中国花卉报	中国劳动报
Chinese Youth	Satire and Humour	Literature and Art	Chinese Culture
中国少年报	讽刺与幽默	文艺报	中国文化报

What significance does ownership have? Lee Chin-ch'uan suggests that 'media conglomerates'' economic interests are subordinated to their ideological mission; only by serving the party state's political interests would they be granted economic privileges (ranging from tax breaks and resource allocation and utilisation, to political and military awards). They are editorially and managerially controlled by Party committees and are not open to private or foreign investment'.[18]

To outsiders there appears to be a contradiction between being tied to the Party yet needing to serve customers. How this is managed is suggested by Lu Ye, from Fudan School of Journalism: 'within a press group, the "parent" papers are, by design, oriented towards the wishes of the Party bosses, while the "offspring" papers cater to the customers. Likewise, some pages of each of the newspapers

78

serve the party while other pages please the market. Party messages coexist with, but are clearly demarcated from, non-Party messages'.[19]

It is not the case, as is assumed by some detractors, that newspapers contain wall-to-wall politics. How could they? Nobody would read them, let alone buy them. So the editors manage a tricky balancing act of both satisfying their local Party controllers and respecting the interests and needs of their readers. The stand-off implicit in the term 'Party controllers' is not really appropriate. The managers of press groups and their editors will often have, or have had, jobs in the regulatory bodies or relevant Propaganda Department; so will the Deans of journalism schools. 'The media world' 媒体界 or profession comprises different roles and responsibilities, which the same person may hold at different points in his or her career; a local reporter in the twenties may become a fearless investigator in the thirties, a regulator for a few years and then an editor before ending up in a position running the marketing department.

Media People: newspaper editor

Image source:
http://www.ce.cn/xwzx/gnsz/
gdxw/200604/07/t20060407
_6634741_10.shtml

Editor-in-Chief Jiang Yiping 江艺平 served a five-year term on *Southern Weekend* 南方周末, during which time the newspaper became China's most influential and profitable investigative newspaper. By the late 1990s, *Southern Weekend* was earning more than 100m RMB per annum in advertising revenue, employing a journalistic staff of just fifty.

Jiang graduated in English Literature from Zhongshan University, and joined the Southern Newspaper Group during the 1980s. In 1996, she became Editor-in-Chief at *Southern Weekend*, where she employed and trained a group of journalists who became famous in China for their investigations. Both Jiang and her team championed disadvantaged groups and exposed wrongdoings.

Jiang was obliged to leave *Southern Weekend* in 2000 and went to run the newly-founded *21st Century* newspaper titles, which included the *21st Century Business Herald* and the *21st Century Global Report*. The *21st Century Global Report* was, however, forced to close after publishing an interview with the former secretary of Chairman Mao Zedong.

After the Sun Zhigang Case and the removal of its Editor, Jiang was appointed to run *Southern City Daily*, but she was soon afterwards demoted to the Research Department there. Her years of leadership (1996-2000) are still widely remembered by journalists and editors, and are regarded as that newspaper's 'golden years'. In September 2013 she retired early, but was employed two months' later by Zhongshan University as a Postgraduate Supervisor in Communication under the Dean, Hu Shuli, also Editor in Chief of the Caixin Group.

Nevertheless, as Zhao Yuezhi reminds us, the press have, from the early 1980s, regularly been the sites of noteworthy debates, for example on the free market model. In an analysis of 'the Lang Xianping 郎咸平 case', Zhao both illustrates the way political debates can take place in the media and reminds us of the ideological conformity of those same media. Privatization policies, reducing the involvement of the state in the day to day management of the economy and incentivizing the enterprising, met with some resistance in the 1990s. Since the consensus was to get away from Soviet style central planning and control, which had so clearly failed, the mainstream media forbore from giving space to that resistance, whose advocates found that they could only publish their ideas in small-circulation intellectual journals. In 2004, however, a foreign educated economist, Lang Xianping, attacked privatization, citing specific cases of what he regarded as misappropriation of public assets, in public lectures, excerpts from which were widely published in the mainstream press. The debate became fervent, conferences and seminars were held, Internet commentary burgeoned. 'By late August 2004...with the participation of tens of thousands of Internet users, economists, legal scholars and public intellectuals in other fields, the debate's scope of public involvement was second only to the Sun Zhigang[20] case in 2003'.[21] Although criticizing privatization amounted to questioning core state policy, the debates widened even further to include warnings against the dangers of oligarchy. Different newspapers and magazines had different emphases and championed different points of view.

Lang was taken to task by defenders of the privatization policies, in particular Zhang Weiying 张维迎, who attacked the media for advancing Lang's ideas, for abusing media freedom to create a climate of opinion detrimental to China's development.[22]

One of the consequences of the continuing and fractious debates was that arguments over socialism versus capitalism featured in the 2006 Congress at which the leadership had to take sides and re-commit itself to reform. Thereafter leading media declared, in effect, that the debate was closed and that the critics of reform had failed.

How well do newspapers serve ordinary people, whether as sources of information and in representing their concerns? In an interesting study of three newspapers and the way they covered taxation issues, media lecturer Gong Qian has found that there were limitations. For a start, while they reflected middle class consumers' concerns such as education, medical care, housing banks and telecommunications and so forth they tended, with a few exceptions such as stories about unpaid New Year bonuses, to ignore the poorest. Specifically in dealing with tax, *West China [City] News* was careful to skirt around the issue of how high ranking officials or State Enterprise (SOE) managers could avoid paying it, leading Gong to conclude that the newspaper was denied the opportunity to be truly a watchdog.[23] On the other hand *Southern Weekend* did discuss taxpayers' rights, arguing that people had a right to be informed, to express opinions and to participate in decision-making because they were the sources of public revenue.[24] Are there rules which determine this coverage? Gong interviewed a journalist from the *People's daily* talk to her about the guidelines for covering income inequality:

> 'our stories can talk about income inequality, but they cannot be 'systematic'. For issues which are already having very negative influences among the public, such as house prices, we have to consider the degree to which we can report. There are no written rules or regulations for reporting the income disparity, but there is common sense – the perspective of the report has to be constructively critical. Otherwise there are only negative influences.'[25]

Newspapers differ. In a study seeking to identify the differences in approach as between Party papers and the others,[26] Lee Hsiao-wen analyses four news stories and shows the variety of ways in which they were covered. It is difficult to see consistent policy behind the coverage, and she did not attribute differences to the status of the paper. It is apparent though that local government attempts to suppress 'negative' news and journalists sometimes try to reveal it, regardless of which paper. The reporting of mining disasters, which reflected badly on local government, spurred the authorities to rapid action. In general there is an expectation that all newspapers will follow the line laid down by Xinhua on all topics which might be regarded as sensitive. When they do not, as in cases analysed by Lee, they are punished.[27]

One great defect of the press, according to Zhao, is its failure to represent or even notice the majority of the population. Before the Opening Up, 'the parade of workers and farmers in traditional party propaganda was hollow and manipulative'. Now these people are no longer even mentioned, let alone given a voice. She carried out a study of 'nearly 500' newspapers on the WTO accession and found 'not a single piece that bothered even ceremonially' to interview a worker or farmer.[28]

On the other hand the book *Will the Boat sink the water?* 中国农民调查, a well-known examination of rural life by two eminent journalists, gives examples of journalists' exposing corruption by rural officials, including falsification of local accounts and pollution.[29] They worked for Xinhua, *Democracy & Law* 民主与法制 and *Southern Weekend*, prompting the thought that national media may find it easier to be critical over rural issues, as they are protected from local pressures. Anyway, no matter how impressive the investigative projects carried out by national media, they are not a substitute for consistent coverage of majority concerns. It is likely that many countries' media have the same defect, because of the social backgrounds of the personnel.

Confrontations with the authorities are commonplace, and are often the focus of those overseas websites (such as *Danwei, China Media Project* and *Reporters without Borders*) which publicise maltreatment of journalists. Sometimes they defy easy judgement. In 2013 Changsha's *New Express* 新快报 was involved in a

Most popular media: newspapers

Rank	Title	Publisher
1	Reference News	Xinhua News Agency
2	Peoples' Daily	People's Daily
3	Global Times	People's Daily
4	Southern Weekly	Nanfang Daily group
5	Guang Ming Daily	Guang Ming Daily group
6	Guang Zhou Daily	Guang Zhou Daily Group

Reference News 参考消息: comprises a selection from the world's press translated into Chinese, and has the largest circulation of any periodical, around 3 million. *Reference News* is mostly about current affairs, political and social life in China. It is published by Xinhua News Agency in Chinese, Uighur, Mongolian and some other languages spoken in China. Originally a Restricted Circulation Publication, it is now sold on newsstands.

Peoples' Daily 人民日报 is the official newspaper of the Chinese Communist Party. Its principal focus is Party policy. According to the World Association of Newspapers and News Publishers (WAN-IFRA) it has a circulation of nearly 2.5 million. Many of the subscribers will be work units whose members need to know the thinking of the centre.

The Global Times 环球时报 is a daily tabloid belonging to the *People's Daily* newspaper. It emphasises international issues from a CCP perspective and is one of only two newspapers permitted to select news articles from the foreign media and re-publish them in Chinese. The other is *Reference News*. [1][2] *Global Times* is sometimes described as populist and sensationalist.

Southern Weekend – see p227

Southern City Daily 南方都市报 is a daily newspaper published in Guangzhou and mainly circulated in the Pearl River Delta area. It is known for its investigative journalism and provocative commentary on social issues. It publishes the largest number of daily pages of any Chinese newspaper.

Guang Ming Daily, founded by CPC Central Committee in 1949 is now managed by the Propaganda Department. It focuses on new developments in education, science and technology, as well as intellectual life more generally.

confrontation after the arrest of a reporter who, it was alleged, had maligned an important Changsha company by unjustly accusing it of colluding with officials in corruption. The editorial staff stood behind their colleague and published with the headline 'Let him go! 请放人！' However, the reporter later confessed that he had fabricated the reports for gain.[30] The circumstances are curious and illustrate the issues attending local media, which are often accused of corruption.

In sum, Chinese newspapers are varied and variable. Being part of the state apparatus inhibits, certainly, but not as much as critics propound. Media workers generally are in agreement about their responsibilities, but clashes occur when their reporting touches on matters which affect their leaders or their leaders' networks, since there is no acknowledgment that professional responsibility might trump responsibility to authority, or work unit or friends. The editor has to use judgment of the situation because he or she cannot appeal to an Anglophone style right to publish regardless of the consequences to those concerned.

3.2.1   Newspapers and the digital revolution [31]

News organisations, trying to keep their role in society, have reacted in various ways to the challenge of the Internet.[32] through prompt reporting, by being more populist, by getting their journalists to write online, by contributing to the blogosphere to market their newspaper, and by setting up online editions and websites. The *Peoples' Daily*, for example, set up *Peoples' Network* 人民网 in 1997. The Hangzhou Media Group 杭州报业集团, in addition to the Party newspaper, *Hangzhou Daily* 杭州日报 controls seven other newspapers including *City Express* 都市快报, two periodicals and 19 websites.[33]

China News Weekly 中国新闻周刊 has its own microblog team, and education channel covering educational issues, a cultural channel for cultural matters, a health channel for health issues, venture channels dedicated to youth entrepreneurship and *Beijing Youth Forum* 北青新讲坛.'By doing these things' says the Editor, 'we build up our brand and set up a communication channel with the Internet population'.

Before New Media emerged, everything was generated in the newsroom by specialists in news and opinion production. There was limited interaction with consumers, compared with modern journalism, which is 'more open, more participative, more networked, and likely to give newspapers a better approximation of the truth'.[34] What the Editors call 'open journalism' encourages participation and encourages others to initiate debate, publish material or make suggestions. It helps to form communities with common interests. It also links to other material and services on the web, aggregates it, acknowledges voices of authority and expertise other than those of journalists, and is transparent and open to correction, clarification and addition.

Editors, exploring a hybrid approach blending traditional roles and new activities[35] say that news stories are no longer produced to a regular daily or weekly routine. Online content is updated instantaneously through contributions from staff journalists, editors, freelancers and readers too. Thus the traditional gatekeeping routine no longer fits. Staff journalists are required both to master multimedia reporting skills and to take more editorial responsibility. There is much more collaboration. Not only are the newsgathering and production teams involved in online news making, but so are the technical staff, digital graphic department and external production teams.

Convergence has not only given headaches to editors of traditional newspapers, but opportunities to entrepreneurs with new ones. *The Paper* 澎湃 and *Sixth Tone* 第六声 (also in English) are not just newspapers put on a website but genuinely original digital periodicals, on account of their unusual perspectives, aimed at a sophisticated, educated audiences.

3.2.2 Changing relationships with consumers

Traditional news production has been challenged by citizen journalism and user-generated content. In a study by Mi Miao, well-established newspapers describe how they have adapted to meet the users' demand for space for comment and news sharing.[36] Journalists from Sichuan, Hubei and Zhejiang assume that editors are keen to boost circulation by involving the readership. They encourage collaboration between reporters and readers and think up stunts such as participation through donations for good causes. They feel that a sense of community is fostered by such interaction. However, little user generated content is used in their own reports. Only one reporter could think of an example. That was of the local TV station using footage of the English footballer David Beckham, arriving at Tongji university, shot on a mobile because nothing else was available.

Now that so much news and information is at hand, shallow newspaper reporting is otiose. So, according to the editor of *News Weekly* 新闻周刊, the quality of reporting has increased greatly, There are many more in-depth and investigative reports, particularly on the websites. The leads for such journalism come from New Media, with microblogs being the most important source of stories, but the magazine has to be careful to refashion the material. According to an editor, 'The problem for a periodical such as ours is to get people to bother to come to us when they can get what's happening from a microblog. Some of our editors are really good at writing microblogs and making them more lively than the periodical. So we often do a follow-up report around a microblog event. However, the readers of magazines still expect it to be rigorous , as well as a model of Chinese writing. We weed network language out of the magazine. Our values are permanency and considered reflection. We distinguish very clearly between this and New Media'.[37]

Editors have to be careful to provide something different from the herd. 'When everyone is chasing the hot-spots 热点, we need to provide something meticulous, say an investigative report which is to give the readers a judgment and explain the event sociologically, and we have to give an authoritative opinion to win regular readers. At bottom the opinions are rooted in our firm values, so I believe the values we hold in common will ensure that our loyal readers cohere with us.' [38]

3.2.3 Building a brand

News managers interviewed are very conscious that their organisations are in the information business, and that to maintain their brand, they need to keep abreast of the different reasons consumers have to satisfy their interests from different media. *Attorney Daily* 法制日报, the legal profession's newspaper, has many special issues, and is constantly seeking to enhance the attractiveness of its reports in the print newspaper and its three magazines, whilst building a presence on the Internet. It is connected to the portal of the Supreme People's Procurate of China 中华人民共和国最高人民检察院 and itself owns the *Justice Network* 法制网, which comprises many products, such as three mobile newspapers. 'We do some public opinion analysis and find that local judiciary and government agencies do not quite grasp the seriousness of many breaking news stories, and lack systematic depth of judgment and understanding of public opinion and new trends. Our professional service can help them get on top of the issues quickly'.[39]

Why do people continue to follow these official, relatively formal publications? One reason is that they need to keep their professional knowledge up-to-date. The other, according to Wang, is that the organs fulfil a function known as 'authoritative confirmation' 官方认证. For information on such topics as food hygiene or legal matters, consumers need to go to a source that they really trust. *Attorney Daily* aims to be just such a one.

Selected periodicals

1. Philosophy, Social Science and Political Affairs 哲学，社科和政治时事

The Study of Philosophy 哲学研究	The World 环球	Outlook 瞭望	Aspect 纵横	Public Opinion 群言
International Issues 国际问题研究	Thought Today 当代思潮	Sociology 社会学研究	Marxism Research 马克思主义研究	Socialism with Chinese Characteristics 中国特色社会主义研究
Two Weeks 半月谈	Across the Taiwan Strait	Public 群众	Explore and Debate	Theory and Practice 理论与实践

	海峡两岸		探索与争鸣	

2. Life，Consumption，Travel and Health Care　生活，消费，旅游和保健

Health World 健康天地	Travel 旅游	Consumer Guide 消费指南	Chinese Cooking 中国烹饪
Scientific Health Care 科学养生	Popular Photography 大众摄影	Modern Clothing 现代服装	Furniture and Interior Decoration 家具与室内装修
Friend of Health 健康之友	Traveller 旅行家	Life 生活	Friend of Women 妇女之友

3. Military，Public Security and Law 军事，公安和法制

Chinese Militia 中国民兵	PLA Pictorial 解放军画报	Modern Weaponry 现代兵器	Modern Military 现代军事
China Firefighter 中国消防	National Defence 国防	Public Security Monthly 公安月刊	Morality and Civilisation 道德与文明
National and International Law Study 中外法学	Law Study 法学研究	Law and Life 法律与生活	Law Expo 法制博览

4. University Journal s　高等学校学报

Peking University News 北京大学学报	Tsinghua University News 清华大学学报	Beijing Normal University News 北京师范大学学报	Renmin University News 中国人民大学学报
Beijing Business School News 北京商学院学报	Central Conservatory of Music News 中央音乐学院学报	Beijing Traditional Medicine University News 北京中医药大学学报	Capital Medicine University News 首都医科大学学报

5. Culture and Art　文化和艺术

Chinese Poetry 中华诗词	Best Friend 知音	Personalities 人物	Chinese Music 中国音乐
Art of Film 电影艺术	Opera Arts 戏曲艺术	Chinese Calligraphy 中国书法	Literary Theory and Criticism 文艺理论与批评

6. General Interest and Digest　综合和文摘

Xinhua Abstracts 新华文摘	China Pictorial 中国画报	China Today 今日中国	National and International 海内与海外
The Ethnic Minorities 民族	Window on the South	Intelligence Today 现代情报	Automobile Abstracts 汽车文摘

86

	南风窗		
Speechmaking 演讲与口才	Military Abstracts 军事文摘	China Mechanical Engineering Abstracts 中国机械工程文摘	Palaeontology Abstracts 古生物学文摘

3.2.4   From the critical turn to 'screaming journalism'

Over 15 years, digitalization, like volcanic ash from a great explosion, has transformed everything and not all changes have been as reasonable as those mentioned above. One has been a slashing of costs, which is thought to have reduced the quality of journalism because reporters are fewer, less senior and have less time. Another has been the downgrading of 'serious' journalism by previously responsible newspapers in favour of sensationalism, gossip and revelation, previously the particular domain of scurrilous Anglophone 'tabloids' 小报.

So much, so universal. But are there other aspects of newspapers that mark them out as different from their Anglophone equivalents? Here are two instances. During the period leading up to the referendum on whether Scotland should leave the United Kingdom, the Chinese press took a very strong line influenced by Chinese ideas about 'unity'. As one journalist put it, 'we think your different peoples comprise a family and should strive to remain together'. Chang Ping of the *South China Morning Post* reports that the *Global Times* (and other national papers) presented the clamour for Scottish independence as threatening to all parties. It also claimed that secession would weaken the EU, which is seen as a potential bulwark against US imperialism. It was scathing about the politicians who had created this movement, suggesting them to be irresponsible.[40]

At the moment of the 2015 attacks on Parisians by adherents of Islamic State an Editor at CCTV headquarters told of how she and her colleagues were reporting the story. They were seeking to report without giving the impression that the attacks had been successful for the terrorists, without causing alarm with shots of carnage and without emphasising the links with Islam. They were focussed on the potential effects of their reportage, rather than on reporting the 'whole truth'. This illustrates several things: that decisions about what and how important or emotive matters are to be reported is not left to those on the ground but the responsibility of those thought to have 'the bigger picture'; that 'drama' is a value accorded low priority and that journalists consider it 'responsible' to withhold information if it is socially beneficial to do so. This may be an illustration of subordination to authority, but it may also reflect the principle that practical issues, for example of effects, must take precedence over any abstract ideals.

Chinese journalists have talked of the 'illusion of detachment' of which they find

BBC reporters seized. It is difficult to accept that reporting can be simply an impartial transmission of objective truth, no matter how hard you try to stress facts. Tuchman's notion that news is a constructed reality is a familiar idea to them.[41] It seems that when Chinese journalists, channel controllers and feature editors select and compose their stories, they are not so much imagining that they are revealing facts as helping to 'hold society together'. When you discuss the handling of stories with journalists, or even the censoring of foreign television and films, it is common to be told that it would be 'irresponsible' to publicise vicious or disgusting events or give publicity to ideas that subvert public morality. News, as sociologist Gaye Tuchman has observed, is not just a mirror, but helps shape society by defining and confirming what is normative or deviant.[42]

Most popular media: Magazines

Rank	English name	Chinese Title
1	The Reader	读者
2	Rayli	瑞丽
3	Cosmopolitan	时尚
4	Bestie	知音
5	Youth Literary Digest	青年文摘

The Reader is a general interest digest magazine and has the highest monthly circulation of any Chinese periodical. Founded in 1981, it went by the name *Reader's Digest* 读者文摘 until forced to drop the name by the American *Reader's Digest* 普知. It consists of articles, joke collections, short stories and witty quotations. There is also a supplement which publishes exclusive, original compositions, rather than excerpts from other magazines.

Rayli is a fashion magazine catering for affluent urban women. Most of the articles are taken from Japanese fashion magazines, with local advertisements for foreign merchandise. There are currently three versions of the magazine: twenties, thirties, and 'high fashion'.

Cosmopolitan is the Chinese edition of an international fashion magazine for women. It has developed rapidly in China over 13 years.

Bestie is a general interest magazine, published twice a month. Its circulation reached 6.36 million in 2008. It covers original reports based on real stories, mainly about family life, love affairs and adventures.

Youth Literary Digest is managed by the Central Committee of the Communist Youth League and operated by China Youth Publishing House. It is a collection of the famous essays and interesting stories from newspapers, books and periodicals.

3.3 Magazines

Of the approximately 8000 magazines,[43] some of which are described in Tables 3.12 and 3.15, among the most successful (and subscription-financed) are *Stories* 故事会, a wonderfully engaging 'all human life is there' pocketbook, *Bestie* 知音, which concentrates on fervid tales of struggle for survival and love, *Family* 家庭,

featuring romance and crime stories, and *Reader* 读者, a digest of stories which claims to be the most popular magazine in China, with a circulation of over 10 million.

There are numerous current affairs magazines, which mix stories about business success and enterprise with discussion of social issues, investigations of the corrupt and exposures of the shameful. As before 1949 on the mainland and always in Hong Kong and the Chinese diaspora, these current affairs magazines generate ideas in the world of public affairs in a similar manner to their equivalents in the Anglosphere. The most famous is *Caijing* 财经, which has often revealed sensitive stories such as the SARS epidemic 非典危机, the Shanghai social security fraud 上海社会保险欺诈案, and insider trading 内线交易. Of the many others, a few are described in tables, above and below.

Since the 1990s, the authorities have allowed foreign publications to enter via three routes, provided they eschew news: Publishing under contract, on condition that the content is legal and they are given away free; foreign imports distributed by a state-owned company, such as the China National Publications Import and Export (Group) Corporation 中国图书进出口(集团)总公司; or content licensed to a local publisher, with a maximum of 70% imported content.[44] Most foreign publishers have gained entry to the market either by publishing a Chinese language edition or through the licensing of a magazine's brand and content to a local collaborator.[45] The Haymarket Group, for example, publishes *Autocar China* 中国汽车, *Digital Media* 数字媒体, *Finance Asia* 亚洲金融, *Nursery World* 幼儿园世界 and *Stuff China* 数字时代. The percentage of original Chinese content varies.[46]

The magazines which raise the most advertising revenue are fashion titles targeting affluent women.[47] Women's magazines were well established before 1949, among them *Women's Magazine* 妇女杂志 (est 1915) and *Ling Long Women's Magazine* 玲珑 (est 1931),[48] both of which dealt with women's emancipation as well as contemporary women's lifestyle. After 1949, they were replaced by *Women of China* 中国妇女. Since the 1980s, both traditional magazines and those categorised as 'fashion', due to their consumerist agendas, have deployed capital not available domestically, along with advanced management and design skills. China had fallen behind after 1949 and although it has caught up in current affairs, its fashion sector is still considered to lack sophistication.

Foreign magazines have both reflected and created the market for luxury goods, advertisements for which earn vastly more than those for the more prosaic products in the more popular indigenous periodicals, owing to their appeal to well-paid young professionals. Chinese fashion magazines offer today's women an idea of how to be female at odds with the drabness of 'socialist woman', who was supposed to think about nothing but (what the Party classified as) work.

Media People: The magazine editor

Image source:
http://finance.qq.com/a/200
91203/004134.htm

Hu Shuli 胡舒立 was born in Beijing in 1950s into a family of eminent journalists. Her Grandfather was a famous translator and editor at *Reporting Daily* 申报 and his older brother was Chief Editor of *Guangming Daily* 光明日报 and later the Director of China's Press and Publishing Administration. Her mother was a senior editor at *Workers' Daily* 工人日報.

Hu is of the first generation of university graduates after the Cultural Revolution. She graduated from Renmin University in 1982 in journalism and joined the *Worker's Daily*, then the second largest newspaper. She joined *China Business Times* 中华工商时报 in 1992 as International Editor and became Chief Reporter in 1995.

In 1998, Hu Shuli became founding editor of *Caijing* 财经 which has become China's most influential and profitable financial magazine. It equates to *The Economist* in the Anglophone world and its guiding principle is to provide "independent standpoint, exclusive coverage, and unique perspective'. In 2000 and 2001, *Caijing* achieved fame with several investigative reports on investment funds and the stock market. Hu insisted that *Caijing* should cover national crises and important social issues too and champion reform. An in-depth investigation on SARS in 2003, joined with coverage done by other media, propelled the resignation of the then Minister of Health and the Mayor of the capital. After 10 years as the chief editor of *Caijing*, Hu left the magazine with her 60 editorial staff and set up a new business magazine, *New Finance* 财新. It is said that this was a consequence of disagreements with the Board over remuneration. Hu Shuli is currently Chief Editor of *Century Weekly* under the aegis of Caixin Media. She was also the Dean of the School of Communication and Design at Zhongshan University until July 2014.

One of the first Western magazines to enter the Chinese market was *Elle*, in 1988. From 1993, a version of the Japanese magazine, *Rayli* 瑞丽 was followed by joint ventures between local companies and *Cosmopolitan* 时尚杂志, *Harper's Bazaar* 时尚芭莎; *Marie Claire* 嘉人, *FHM* 男人装 and the Chinese edition of *GQ* 智族. There are now more than 50 foreign-brand publications in mainland China, taking up about 10% of the magazine market. Most are published by licensing deals or joint ventures with local companies, and many have set up advertising agencies. Hachette Filipacchi Médias, for example, has set up a joint venture advertising company in China called Beijing Hachette Advertising Co Ltd, which has a Chinese investment of 51%.

There are both good and bad consequences of this. The locals learn from the experience and sophistication of experienced management,[49] yet domination of the market by well-capitalised titles, soaking up the available revenues, denies opportunities to local publishers. Since they do not have to fear competition, the foreign companies can supply inappropriate, foreign, content, which will be accepted unquestioningly out of 'cultural cringe'. This acceptance may in turn influence other publishers, who associate the profits of foreign magazines with their content, whereas their monopoly position is the key factor. Thus it may be that a situation that the authorities feared but thought they had avoided in the media generally has come to pass in the periodical industry, namely the influence of commercially-driven values on Chinese attitudes and behaviour.[50]

Overall, magazine advertising accounts for only 3% of the total advertising market share, a figure which compares unfavourably with other countries.[51] This perhaps reflects the decline in readership from around 379,000 in 2000 (the high point) to 312,000 in 2011. In summary, the magazine industry is dynamic, with a wide selection of genres, but losing customers. Although the ability of foreign media to influence the market is curtailed, in one area at least – fashion – it may be having a deforming effect. From the large number of public affairs periodicals, we can infer that magazines remain an important medium through which educated people relate to the policy world.

3.4   Television

The only official national broadcaster is China Central Television (CCTV). All provinces have their equivalents and their satellite channels, with differing brands, compete nationally. Some services based in the Hong Kong and Macau SARs can be received in various parts of the PRC, famously Phoenix, which claims an audience of 170 million.[52]

Regarded as the most influential medium, television is most controlled of all. CCTV is the voice of authority and it seeks to lead in matters of taste and cultural content. This is tacitly disputed by the provincial satellite broadcasters, which compete to provide popular programming. They are sometimes reined in by the regulatory bodies, ostensibly on 'public service' grounds but possibly to protect CCTV's audience share.

3.4.1   News

The main network news programme on CCTV, *National* (literally 'simulcast') *News*, 新闻联播 goes out at 7pm to an average audience of 400 million, preceded by the provincial or local news. This programme is considered to be the flagship and, by the authorities at least, the role model for news programmes generally. It reflects the Party's take on events. Indeed, it can appear like a series of official pronouncements rather than detached reporting. This is not surprising since the authorities regard CCTV journalists as their assistants, giving them the kind of access that official spokespersons have in Anglophone governments. Reporters accompany Chinese leaders and are often granted privileged access to leading politicians. [53] Those posted abroad hold civil service passports and can be deployed to assist visiting political leaders when required.[54]

The Four Levels of Television

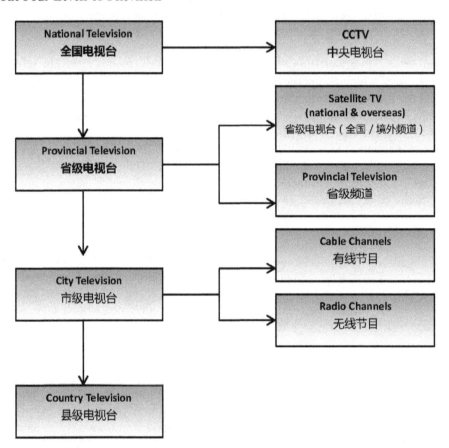

Because it is the voice of the establishment, customarily reporting first and foremost what the government is doing and generally emphasising the positive, CCTV news has tended to be mocked by sceptics. They parody its contents as 'the national leaders are busy, the people are happy and foreign countries are chaotic' 领导特忙，人民高兴，外国很乱， or 'all is well, China is victorious, our enemies are confounded' 中国是胜利的，我们的敌人是羞愧的. Even better, 'wouldn't it be jolly to live in the news?' 活在新闻联播里才幸福!

In 2012, CCTV managers tried to address the fact that their news can be unconvincing. Until then, political events linked to activities of the Party always led the news, followed by about 20 minutes of domestic news and five minutes of foreign news. During 2013, news programmes demoted the doings of the leaders, placing greater weight on stories which did not directly involve them and which had not been supplied by the CPD or Xinhua News Agency. Whereas it had been accepted that politics should take up nearly 40% of bulletins, with social news less than 50%, by January 2013 it was reported that politics had gone down to 16% and social news up to 64%. Remarkably, it was no longer axiomatic for politics and politicians to come first. Topics which had barely, if ever, been covered before, such as air quality measurement and demolitions, were now included.[55] However, by late 2015, it appeared that the former emphasis on central politics was being resumed, and by early 2016 the doings of the President dominated many if not all news bulletins.

The mockery of intellectuals may not be representative of public opinion. *National News* is criticised for being slow, but its managers claim that they would rather be accurate than immediate. The substantial audiences may be taken as showing that people by and large trust *National News*.[56] Unfortunately, it is guilty of omission. For example, at the time of the 2008 Sichuan Earthquake, CCTV failed to mention that negligent enforcement of building standards was being cited as a principal reason for the very high number of deaths,[57] although this issue was widely aired elsewhere. British academic Gary Rawnsley tells us how CCTV9 journalists were reprimanded for having tarnished China's international image by reporting on coal mining disasters.[58] There has been a number of corruption scandals in which companies have allegedly bought coverage or paid to spike it. In the early reporting of President Xi's meeting with Ma Ying-jeou 馬英九, President of the Republic of China (on Taiwan), in Singapore in 2015, Ma's words were not heard, though he was seen speaking for 7 minutes.[59]

3.4.2   Current affairs

Current affairs 深度报道 and talk shows have gone through very outspoken periods. The 1990s saw the birth of a remarkable suite of programmes, including the radical *Tell it like it is* 实话实说, the critical *Focus Reports* 焦点访谈 and the investigative *News Probe* 新闻调查. Local equivalents followed, such as *One out of Seven* (Shanghai) 七分之一, and *Citizen and Society* (Shanghai) 市民与社会.[60]

The prime-time *Zero Distance from Nanjing* 南京零距离 gets viewers to call in with reports, has enlisted 1000 amateur correspondents and cameramen. and carries out constant polls and sampling.[61] There are several law programmes, such as *Law Today* 今日说法, *Legal Lecture Theatre* (CCTV-12) 法律讲堂 and *East 110* 东方 (Shanghai), which are very popular. There are also many programmes, including *315 Latechat* 315 晚会, which champion consumers.

Some Factual TV Programmes and How they Work

You're my all 非你莫属

First broadcast on Tianjin Satellite Television (TJTV) in October 2010, You're my all is a job-hunting show, hosted by Zhang Shaogang 张绍刚, who is also a lecturer at Communication University of China.

In the 60-90 minutes show twelve company bosses sitting in front of the main stage, where the host will present each of about five candidates, seeking positions in one of the bosses' companies. One or two commentators sit to one side of the stage, and make suggestions to both bosses and candidates.

There are three rounds: the first is called the 'Introduction', the second 'I am talented', and the third 'Let's talk about the money'. First, a candidate introduces him or herself, and then the host asks the candidate questions relating to academic qualifications, work experience and areas of specialisation. This provides the bosses with more information about the candidate's relevance. The second round gives the candidates an opportunity to say more about their achievements and special skills. In the third round definite negotiations take place.

The show is controversial. Compere Zhang Shaogang is sarcastic and critical, and many think this unfair. In May 2012, thousands of viewers launched an online demonstration called, 'Stop Watching *You're my all*'. It also caused hot debate about degree fraud. Despite all this and the huge impact of *The Voice of China*, the show and its host have many fans, and audience ratings remain consistently high.

Strong Opinions 观点强中强

A 20-minute news commentary programme, hosted by Ji Zhiwei 籍之伟, first broadcast on Tianjin Satellite Television 天津卫视 TJTV in China on 25th May 2009. There are a many such news programmes in China, in the same format, including *Looking at Today* 今日关注 on CCTV-4.

Each programme focuses on one topic, which might be a news story, an important event, or a social issue. The topic is dissected in detail, probing beneath the surface, and exploring possible resolutions. There are two guests, usually experts or professionals in the area under discussion. To start, a video will usually be played to provide background and context to the topic, offering viewers different perspectives. *Strong Opinions* is one of the top rated programmes on TJTV.

News 1+1 新闻一加一

First broadcast on China Central Television's News Channel (CCTV-NEWS) in March 2008, *News 1+1* is currently hosted by Bai Yansong 白岩松 and Dong Qian 董倩, two highly regarded journalists.

It is broadcast live every weekday at 21.30, focusing on the most recent and significant stories. The production team reacts promptly to breaking news, and can gather enough information or do an investigative report fast. There are two main parts: video package presenting the topic/event, and one to one discussion.

Over 8 years, the audience ratings have remained constant at around 0.6%-0.9% (unofficial statistic), which is quite remarkable for a daily news programme. During significant breaking news, such as the earthquake in 2008, and the launch of the spaceship 'Shenzhou Seven', the average ratings of *News 1+1* have tripled or quintupled.

Face to Face 面对面

Launched on CCTV January 2003, *Face to Face* is a 45-minute interview-based programme, broadcast on CCTV-NEWS at 21.30 on Sundays, with Dong Qian as main host. It tells a current story through packaged interviews with main participants in a news event, or with people involved in or with influence on a particular news story, investigating the hidden background by questioning those involved face to face. Since it is impossible to invite all the relevant people to the studio, journalists are sent out to interview them, such that they are more important in creating the story than the host. *Face to Face* has been become very well-known since a shocking report on the SARS crisis.

Lecture series abound. The most successful has been *Learning from Confucius* by Yu Dan 于丹论语心得, transmitted in 2006. Its companion volume, *Confucius from the Heart*,[62] sold well and it was followed by another series of lectures by Yu Dan, this time on the philosophy of Zhuangzi 庄子. In 2017 the Israeli scholar Yuval Harari delivered lectures based on his controversial *Sapiens: a Brief History of Humankind* and *Homo Deus: A Brief History of Tomorrow* in the CCTV series *Architects of the Future* 未来架构师.

While there are numerous investigative and analytical programmes, there are some topics that are completely out of bounds and others that it would be wise to avoid. CCTV programmes are much freer to investigate than their regional counterparts, as they are not hampered by the rule that journalists must not pry into matters that are the provenance of provincial masters. They may, however, may be more circumscribed in the topics they address. It has been normal for regional journalists to exchange stories about their own areas with their equivalents elsewhere, although officials have regularly tried to stop this practice.

Discussion programmes work within similar parameters in avoiding the tendentious or giving offence to policy makers. The controversial presenter Cui Yongyuan 崔永元 lost his on-screen roles and became a media teacher for several years until finally returning to the screen in Shanghai in 2015. Another outspoken presenter, Bai Yansong 白岩松 was suspended for some weeks when his criticism of the Railway Ministry's handing of the 2011 Wenzhou rail crash was considered too sharp.

A recent addition to the many discussion shows, online video portal iQiyi's 爱奇艺 *Oddity Talks* 奇葩说, is also the most controversial. Its cheerful, irreverent style camouflages and popularises debate on serious issues such as the way older women are treated in society, how sick family members should be helped, career life balance, honesty in relationships, coming out as homosexual, should highly educated women become full-time housewives and whether single parenthood is a viable choice. The success has been phenomenal.

3.4.3 Drama

The largest bloc of viewers plumps for drama series. According to one account, on average 468 titles have been produced every year for five years.[63] Drama series tend to have upwards of 40 episodes, sometimes in the hundreds. In 2002, 90% of all revenue from television advertising came from drama series.[64] A few of the great variety produced are described on pp96-97. Independents make 90% of television drama.[65] Since the early 2000s at least, there has been strong competition from dramas imported from Taiwan, Hong Kong, Japan and Korea.[66]

Popular media: Television light entertainment

Rank	Title	Broadcaster	Genre	Targeted Audience
1	*Running Man* 奔跑吧兄弟	Zhejiang Television 浙江卫视	Game-variety show	Under 25
2	*Sing！China* 中国新歌声	Zhejiang Television 浙江卫视	Singing competition (rebranded version of the Voice of China)	Family
3	*Top Funny Comedian* 欢乐喜剧人	Dragon TV 东方卫视	Comedy show competition	Family
4	*The Negotiator* 王牌对王牌	Zhejiang Television 浙江卫视	Indoor games-variety show	Family
5	*Go Fighting!* 极限挑战	Dragon TV 上海东方卫视	Game-variety reality show	Family

Running Man (奔跑吧兄弟) is a variety show broadcast on Zhejiang Television, based on a South Korean original made by SBS. It is a game-variety show, where the presenters and guests complete missions in order to win a race. It was first aired in October 2014.

Sing! China 中国新歌声 is based on the singing competition format, *The Voice of Holland,* and was first shown in 15 July 2016 on Zhejiang TV, sponsored by Jiaduobao 加多宝. It consists of a blind audition, a battle phase and live performances. The four judges/coaches choose teams of contestants through a blind audition process. During each audition, the judge has to decide whether or not to choose the singer for his or her team. If two or more judges want the same singer (as often happens), the singer is given the final choice of coach。

Top Comedian 欢乐喜剧人 is a comedy show in which ten comedy teams compete with each other through various performances, such as comic dialogue, comedy sketches or other styles. The second season of *Top Comedian* was hosted by Guo Degang 郭德纲, a famouse Xiangsheng performer. At the end of each show, the audience votes for the best performance, those with least votes leave the programme.

The negotiator 王牌对王牌 is an original weekly indoor game-variety show produced by Zhejiang TV. Each episode focuses on a different theme, two fixed captains invite popular actors or pop stars to form two teams which compete through game and talent competitions.

Go Fighting! 极限挑战. Every episode is based on hotly debated social topics. In each episode the MCs and guest are given missions to work together, compete as teams to complete different tasks such as taxi driver or nanny.

Best known are period or 'dynasty' dramas[67] but there are also modern 'social issue' dramas, dealing with miscarriages of justice or set in the armed forces or female environments. Among the latter, which are referred to as 'pink dramas', are *Falling in Love* 好想好想谈恋爱, *A Mature Woman's Diary* 淑女日记 and *The Pink Ladies* 粉红女郎. [68] The recent family drama *Good Husbands* 大丈夫 (Anhui/LeTV) tells the story of two sisters and their relationships with their father and husbands, representing the women as assertive, dynamic and enterprising.

Northern audiences prefer historical themes, whereas southerners are addicted to stories set in the present. Fashions change: in the 1980s, amid enthusiasm for rebuilding the legal system, television became the means of promoting understanding of the conception of legality and the tasks of law enforcement agencies, and 'cops and robbers' dramas abounded. These were then superseded by historical dramas, but late in the 1990s, audiences sated by so many history plays, were provided with crime dramas again.[69] But by 2004, the regulator had become disturbed by the violence in such programmes and restricted transmission to after 23.00, whereupon the history dramas returned once more.[70] The interplay of official policy and drama themes has been studied by Zhu Ying and others.[71]

It is thought that the crime dramas are inspired by the tradition of 'investigating officials' stories,[72] published in China since 1000AD, based on historical characters such as Song dynasty magistrate Bao Zheng 包拯 and his Tang Dynasty peer Di Renjie 狄仁杰.[73]

To mark important commemorations there have been many great epic dramas, both feature films and series, in cinemas and on television. In 2009 there was a major film about Sun Yatsen, entitled *The Building of the nation* 建国大业. In 2010 the biopic *Confucius* 孔子 was screened, followed in 2011 by *Mighty Task: the Creation of the Party* 建党伟业 and *The 1911 Revolution* 辛亥革命. Older productions about Sun Yatsen were also retransmitted.[74]

What kind of television drama?

If the glory of US television is comic sitcoms and of the UK is nature documentaries, that of China must surely be its drama series, and in particular historical dramas. For over ten years, historical drama has not only been found to be favorite among audiences, but also raiose the most income.

Possibly the most famous is *Great Emperor Han Wu* 汉武大帝, a 58-part series about one of China's most competent leaders (156-87 BC), who both expanded China's territory and recast state administration. He is credited with establishing the Imperial Academy as the fount of Confucian orthodoxy. The series contains spectacular battle scenes, and celebrity actors from Greater China are employed to attract international audiences.

The First Emperor Of Qin 秦始皇 was shot by 2000 but not released until 2007, presumably because of political sensitivities. Over 32 episodes it tells the life of China's most controversial emperor, the man whom Mao 毛泽东 emulated in trying to destroy Confucianism by burying the scholars and burning the books. He also pulled together disparate Chinese kingdoms to create one empire with a central government and one written language, a project with a certain modern resonance.

The Story of the Empress 武媚娘传奇 is an 82 part TV series about China's only ruling Empress, how as a young girl she beguiled Tang Emperor Taizong with her intelligence and beauty and survived the court intrigues to become wife to one of the most able and intellectual rulers. After his death she was sent to a monastery, but brought back to court by Taizong's youngest son, Gaozong, who made her Empress. She shared his duties with him and succeeded him at his death.

97

These and many other historical dramas, including those set in the Republican period, the Anti-Japanese War and the Korean War 抗美援朝, are often of high quality and very popular despite growing competition from dramas with modern themes. One of China's most popular present day dramas has been The Good Wife 贤妻 which tells the tale of housewife Han Dayun 韩大芸 trying to keep her family intact while being nagged by her mother in law for not having a son, betrayed by her husband and generally exploited by the rest of the family.

Close To You And Make Me Warm 靠近你，温暖我 is a meditation on what it is to be a woman in today's society and how female-ness can persist despite masculinising pressures. It tells the stories of three women Ding Aiyu 丁爱羽, Fang Kezhou 方可舟 and Xie Xiangmei 谢香枚. One is a mistress, one's marriage has failed, one is a workaholic. Illicit love, emotional infidelity 精神出轨, sexual harassment 性骚扰, asexual marriage 无性婚姻 .....there's every possible crisis.

Gimme A Fag/ Night Rain 给我一只烟/夜雨 features hostesses in Shenzhen 深圳, their social position and how – when they have lost their youthful attraction – they move into more appropriate occupations. This is a sympathetic portrayal and an analysis of prostitution and the associated arts.

Divorce Chinese Style 中国式离婚 was adapted from the novel by Wang Hailing 王海鸰. A surgeon, fed up by being nagged to earn more money by his bad-tempered wife, eventually goes into a private health centre and finds himself much better paid but exhausted by the heavy workload. The deterioration of their relationship and the effects that this has on the wider family, are painfully revealed. It covers issues such as mid-life crisis, extramarital relationship, the single child family, the pressure to achieve and the stress which results.

The palace 宫: Luo Qingchuan 洛晴川 is a modest and sweet girl of the twenty-first century. One day she by chance travels through time and goes to the Forbidden City 故宫 during the reign of the Emperor Kangxi 康熙皇帝 in the 1700s. Although she encounters her hero from history, Prince Yin Zhen 胤禛, later to be the Yongzheng Emperor 雍正皇帝, her desire for him is not to be easily satisfied. Her knowledge of ancient history helps her remain safe amid the heated rivalry of the imperial concubines. Will she change the course of history?

Love apartment 爱情公寓: China's equivalent of *Big Bang Theory* or *Friends*. Seven young people of different backgrounds, identities and dreams live together. Much fun and many entertaining episodes occur, reflecting young people's living conditions and values. A similar series is *Ode to Joy*, 欢乐颂.

No delay 刻不容缓 plays on themes of justice and morality. It centres on a police officer's mission to clamp down on illegality and corruption. The drama delves into two main criminal cases, one of which tells the life of a professional robber and his involvement in a complicated love triangle. The other features a drug warlord, masked as a kindergarten principal, who is eventually exposed and prosecuted in the last episode. This action-packed drama keeps the audience entertained as it gradually reveals the complex web of clues that are central to deciphering the investigations.

The trail 天网追踪 is a police drama which sets the scene with a murder mystery when a bra is found buried in a nearby sand dune. This clue, the audience learns, reveals the story of a young female whose sudden disappearance in Guangzhou 广州 causes the series of incidents that led to her death. Another case ensues, a minibus of passengers are threatened and robbed by a professional gang on a motorway, causing unrest in the local community. In response to this, the police initiate an investigation and design a trap to capture the ringleader of the professional gang. In the final episode, the trap is successful, but the drama has a tragic end.

Heart Operation, 心术, a 36-part TV series, tells the stories of doctors and nurses from Jiangzhou City's Yunshan Hospital 江州云山医院 Neurosurgery Department. The characters, Liu chenxi 刘晨曦, Huo simiao 7, Zhang Xiaolei 张晓蕾 have their own distinct personalities and troubles: we get the real life of doctors and nurses, pharmaceutical reps, ticket scalpers and medical disputes. Issues covered include doctor-patient relationships,

> three-way relationships, attacks on staff and patients, mortgage slavery and the sex trade.
>
> *Naked Wedding* 裸婚时代 is a 30 part TV series about getting hitched without a marriage ceremony, diamond rings, party, or home to go to. Liu Yiyang 刘易阳 and Tong Jiaqian 童佳倩 have an 8 year relationship. When Tong gets pregnant, they decide to marry. But it has to be a naked wedding. Afterwards, they live with Liu's parents in a tiny flat, with constant conflict. Many issues are aired: young peoples' sense of family, ideas about marriage, work pressure, the exorbitant price of property and low salaries, the high cost of raising baby, the gap between the generations and single child dependency.

The CPD regularly provides lists of themes which it would like to see realized in dramatic form. Producers and directors will submit their treatments for review and discussion before going into production. There is a corpus of rules which dictates what subjects may not be dealt with and in what manner certain topics must be tackled.

3.4.4   Entertainment TV

Talent and dating shows, often based on formats developed abroad, have become popular and lucrative since the success of *Super Girl* 超级女声 in 2005. More than 100,000 contestants took part in this Hunan TV version of *Pop Idol* 流行偶像.[75] The final was viewed by 400 million people, with 3.5 million votes cast for the winner. The regulator, disturbed by screaming fans, the cult of celebrity and crass materialism, decided that in future this kind of programme should not be aired at peak time, i.e. between 19.00 and 22.30.

Games shows with prizes have been constrained on moral grounds. In a country with a large number of poor people, it is thought inappropriate to offer huge prizes. The British format, *Who Wants to be a Millionaire?*, was successful in 140 countries but failed in China. *Happiness Dictionary* 百万玩智多星, the localised version, offered prizes such as new schools for their villages or similar charitable donations instead of cash for contestants. Talent and dating shows have been closed down for being tacky, suggestive or corrupt. The most successful talent show, *Voice of China* 中国好声音, has been censured but not closed down for including a contestant who presented a fake case so emotive that one of the judges wept, while the others were overcome with sympathy for the girl claiming the heartrending backstory.[76] Some of the many dating shows are described in the Table page 30. In 2012, SAPPRFT decreed that only four dating shows should be permitted at any one time. Meanwhile foreign programming should be restricted and broadcasters were instructed to seek substitutes for light entertainment.[77] These have included documentaries and reality shows.

It was a Korean-originated reality show, *Daddy, where are we off to?* 爸爸去哪儿, which accelerated the rush to reality shows 真人秀. It tugged at the emotions aroused by absent, often workaholic fathers. Hunan TV has made several series of *Daddy* and even a feature film, pieced together from the television shows, which was a box office success. *C'mon Babe!* 来吧孩子, transmitted by Shenzhen Media Group, featured the individual, family and medical dramas surrounding births at a Shanghai hospital. Its independent producer also made the award-winning fixed-rig series *Stories in A&E* 急诊室故事, featuring gripping episodes from Shanghai Number 6 Hospital.

At the turn of the century, format and other factual entertainment shows were 'borrowed' copies of foreign programmes. Since the licensing of (UK) Fremantle's *Got Talent* to Shanghai Dragon TV in 2010, Chinese (multiplatform) broadcasters have been prepared to pay for IP, production expertise and original ideas, and to obey international trading terms. UK, Korean, US and lately Israeli generated format programmes have been bought; many more are based on foreign designs or made with foreign expertise. The import of formats has repercussions for both seller and buyer, as management systems, content development processes, production skills and creative culture all adapt.

The localisation of foreign formats has raised interesting issues. As we saw above, when *Who Wants to be a millionaire* was adapted for China, it turned into something very different. Dating shows have been adapted too. The young people involved do not major on looks – let alone nudity – but on the qualities and conditions needed to make a partnership for life. The British *Take Me Out* is exclusively for the young, whereas its Chinese version, *If not sincere, do not intrude* 非常勿扰, has contestants aged between 22 and 51. They are also average in looks and modest in background, unlike the glamorous British with whom few ordinary people could identify. Mentions of financial wealth and sexual attraction are curbed.

If not sincere's presenter, Meng Fei 孟非, is restrained and positive; he is assisted by two relationship experts. The fact that contestants from over 30 countries have taken part in the Chinese version, whereas the British original is exclusively domestic, suggests that the latter's may be much more parochial an approach.

This kind of television production has gone through several stages – copying, learning, modification and now indigenous creation. Although internationally established formats are still bought, leaders such as Zhejiang, Shanghai (SMG), Hunan and Jiangsu – and most recently CCTV – have sought to develop programme concepts systematically in-house, with the help of foreign development specialists. In 2014, SMG's development team came up with four ideas on a UK innovation course, all of which were made and broadcast within 12 months.[78]

Media people: an independent producer

After graduating from Peking University Dr Zeng Rong 曾荣 was a journalist at China Central Television. She took her MSc at the London School of Economics, was a Press Fellow at Wolfson College, Cambridge, and completed her PhD on comparative television journalism at the University of Westminster.

In 2012 Dr Zeng published *Television News and the Limits of Globalisation* and subsequently co-authored books on Chinese environment correspondents and government media handling.

Zeng founded Houghton Street Media (HSM) in 2012. HSM produces both factual entertainment and current affairs series for China Central Television and other television channels. It made the Chinese version of *The Gadget Show* transmitted by Shenzhen Television under licence, and the Channel also transmitted China's first 'fly on the wall' documentary show *C'mon Baby!* 来吧孩子！ This accumulated 80 million hits in two days. The two series of *Stories from A&E* 急诊室故事 (Shanghai's Dragon TV) have been awarded several international and national TV industry prizes/honours for creativity. *Stories from A&E* was eulogized in a letter to broadcasting senior management by the Deputy Prime Minister, as being invaluable and educational as to the pressures on the health service as well as exciting real life drama.

With dedicated programme development personnel and a permanent staff of 70, HSM in 2016-17 had several new LE series in production for online platforms as well as television broadcasters. The senior management team is all female, as are the heads of the concept development teams and the production managers.

A common funding model is for the producers to buy air space with the money they will earn from advertising, sponsorship and product placement. Alternatively, they receive some payment from the broadcaster (or air space) but share the revenues, or they simply receive spaces to fill with advertising in recompense. It is an approach suited to the way in which programme-making is developing, whereby independents or in-house production teams make the commercial case for a product rather than fulfilling the specifications of commissioning editors.

Content creation is not only affected by commercial competition or government regulation. Technological development has provided new platforms and, as people access their screen media on ipads and phones, new content providers have arisen, which eschew the television platform and make programmes for online distribution only. Sohu, PPTV, PPS and Aiqiyi 爱奇艺 all started by buying product made by others, but now also make their own. One of these is LeTV 乐视电视. It buys the on-line IP of popular TV dramas, for example the right to stream *Empresses of the Palace* 后宫甄嬛传. Its long-term strategic plan is to create an audience for its productions by selling its own mobiles, which are cheaper equivalents to the iphone. The main interface is set to on-line product provided by LeTV. In 2016 LeTV made its own coverage of the Olympics, presented by former CCTV Foreign Correspondent (and Portuguese speaker) Zhang Lan 张澜.

Media people: The creative executive

Nie Mei 聂玫 is Vice President of Hunan Broadcasting Systems 湖南广播电视台. Born in Hunan in 1969, she attended a local teacher training college from 1987 to 1991 before finding work at Hunan Economics Channel 湖南电视台经济频道, a subsidiary of Hunan TV. She has spent most of her career in Hunan TV, working through the roles of reporter, producer and manager, eventually becoming right hand of the celebrated President of Hunan Group, Ouyang Changling who drove the conglomerate into top position in the television firmament.

Ms Nie undertook professional in-service courses at the universities of Westminster and Oxford, England, and was responsible for a first group of Hunan producers undergoing 3-month briefings on broadcast entertainment production in England over 2005-7. Nie was responsible for Hunan buying, producing and transmitting the British format *Just the Two of Us* 名声大振, the first case of a foreign entertainment format being introduced into China. From 2010 to 2012, she was President of Qinghai Satellite Television 青海卫视, managing the first experiment in cross-provincial broadcast cooperation. Up to 2017, when she resigned, Nie Mei worked closely with President of Hunan TV Lu Huanbin 吕焕斌, taking responsibility for strategy, innovation and overseas expansion.

(Image source: Hunan Television)

3.4.5   Documentaries

Before 1949, documentaries introduced foreign worlds, after 1949 they were deployed for political mobilisation, in the 1980s they fed the 'culture fever' that ignited after the desperate decade, and in the 1990s many of them focused on ordinary people – a radical departure. In the same decade, *River Elegy* 河殇 was broadcast, the angry diatribe against what little was left of traditional culture, which it blamed for the failures which should more accurately have been ascribed to communism. It caused great controversy. It is described, in comparison to another, later, very influential documentary called *The Rise of the Great Powers* 大国崛起, pn p23.

Since 2010, the documentary format has been resurgent, with several new dedicated channels established.[79] From 2013, the regulator has published an approved list for documentary topics every six months. A huge audience of 660 million is reported for CCTV's documentary channel,[80] but that is only the best known. Shanghai's channel, 上海纪录频道[81] *inter alia,* commissioned an American intellectual and broadcaster to make a series analysing China's progress and whether its people are happy.[82] The most renowned documentary series to date is probably CCTV's *A Bite of China* 舌尖上的中国, which linked culinary customs and dishes to history and culture. Another popular series has been *Talking of Yangzi* 再说长江 which narrates the history, ecology and, socioeconomic changes around the Yangzi River.[83] Among the many documentaries dealing with current social issues are *The Mayor* 市长, directed by Zhao Qi 赵琦 and shown to international acclaim in 2014.

The revision of *Focus Reports*

Focus Reports 焦点访谈, or *Focal Point*, has at its height been one of the greatest media events of all time. It was created in 1994 by the Current Affairs Department of CCTV 评论部 to analyse factors behind the news, to raise hot social issues and to comment on what the citizenry write in of their concerns. Its investigative, evidential and populist approach was novel in the mid 90s, such that it was seen as 'democratic' and responsive. It attracted 300 million viewers regularly.

Political leaders were reported to, and themselves declared that they, pay great attention to *Focus Reports*, calling on all officials to watch it. Since that time the programme has gone through lacklustre periods and was less popular by 2016. Although critics blamed this on less interesting journalism, a consequence of political pressures, others simply cited the vast competition as the reason.

In 2013 *Focus Report* underwent its biggest revamp in 19 years. In the new version, episodes last 17 minutes as compared to the previous 11 minutes, and now feature two topics per episode instead of one. It promised to 'deliver more content with a longer running time', according to the presenter Lao Chunyan 劳春燕. It claims to pay more attention to the lives of ordinary people, trendy topics, and emphasises critical analysis.

There is now an emphasis on creating a more interactive and audience-focused programme, as the presenter no longer sits behind a desk, but stands facing and speaking directly to the viewer. The team of presenters, including two famous social commentators Bai Yansong 白岩松 and Yang Yu 杨禹, and comedian Guo Degang 郭德纲, help secure a wide audience. The programme begins with a screen of mind map diagrams with different themes and associated buzzwords in Chinese characters with the English translation, such as 'public opinion 舆论' and 'people's livelihood 民生'.

3.4.6   Public service

There are programmes that laud and reward good works and volunteering such as *Pro-Bono China* 公益中国 and *China Touched* 感动中国. With the same public service orientation are job programmes in which people present themselves to potential employers. *Job Hunter* 职来职往 takes the form of a glamorous talent show.

Although all Chinese television might be considered by outsiders to constitute 'public service broadcasting', the same could be said in much of Europe.

Nevertheless, there have been *official* public service channels since 1999. They were set up out of concern about the low cultural level of television content, then often consisting of cheap imports. Public service channels are expected to be part-subsidised by the commercial channels and part supported by local government. They are required to offer good quality children's' programming, to popularise high culture and to offer regional and local programming. Over the years there has been much discussion as to how to improve and fund public service TV, although the enthusiasts suffered a blow when Chongqing's initiative to promote it failed to attract audiences and was abolished after the fall of its progenitor, Bo Xilai. According to Taiwan academics Ming Yeh Rawnsley and Feng Chien-san, public service channels elsewhere have carved themselves niches by providing audience participation and serving local charities.[84]

Advertising [85]

China is now the second largest advertising market in the world. Advertising spend reached $94 billion in 2014 overtaking Japan as the number two admarket behind the US. Transnational advertising agencies have been quick to enter the market, either through foreign investment in Chinese advertising companies or by forming joint ventures. The gap between local and transnational knowledge of advertising and branding is narrowing. Most big advertising agencies have ties with China and getting established in China is considered essential; in fact, the world's biggest advertising agency, WWP, is also the biggest in China.

Advertising provides more than 80% of revenue for legacy media while online and mobile advertising are becoming close competitors. It has become the principal source of revenue for television, accounting for more than 90% of its income. CCTV has an annual auction of its primetime advertising slots a year in advance, which has become an important media event; the main regional companies follow suit. Concentrating advertising revenue on the most competitive television stations, such as CCTV and the chief provincial satellite broadcasters, is a growing trend. CCTV, with its huge audiences, is important to multinationals such as KFC and Kraft, with 30-second advertising slots on popular shows costing as much as $60,000. All advertisements have to be approved by the official China Advertising Association and are subject to censorship by the State and local regulations.

As to New Media, in 2016 online advertising grew 32.9% compared to 2015, reaching 290.27 billion yuan; mobile advertising grew 75.4%, reaching 175 billion year.

Since March 2004, foreign advertising agencies have been allowed to hold majority shares in joint ventures (JVs), increasing the share ceiling for foreign partners from 49% to 70%. Since 10 December 2005, when China joined the World Trade Organisation (WTO), wholly foreign-owned enterprises (WFOEs) have been allowed, gradually, to operate in advertising services.

In 1994 The State Administration for Industry & Commerce, SAIC 国家工商行政管理总局 issued the Advertising Law of the People's Republic of China 中华人民共和国广告法. In June 2012, SAIC released the 12th Five-Year Plan for the Development of the Advertising Industry 广告产业发展的十二个五年计划, the aim of which was to maintain an annual growth rate of around 12% and have ten or more large backbone advertising companies with annual advertising revenue of over 5 billion yuan; more than 50 advertising companies with annual advertising turnover of more than 1 billion yuan; 100 advertising companies with annual advertising turnover of over 100 million yuan. The Plan also foresaw the construction of 15 advertisement industrial parks, demonstrating a new stress on localisation in China's advertising industry.

A revised version of the Advertising Law was promulgated at the 14th meeting of the Standing Committee of the 12th NPC in 2015. The major change is that exaggerated claims and superlatives are banned.

3.5　Radio

Radio broadcasters

The principal broadcasters are China Broadcasting Network 中国广播网 (CBN), China National Radio (CNR) 中央人民广播电台 and China Radio International (CRI)

The leading regional radio broadcasters are owned by Shanghai Media Group 上海东方传媒集团 (usually abbreviated to 上海文广), and Shenzhen Media Group 深圳广播电影电视集团.Shanghai Radio has many channels, including a Western classical music channel 经典 947, and a Chinese classical music and drama channel 戏剧曲艺, which is sometimes hosted in Shanghainese. These two channels transmit live concerts every two weeks, the programme on 经典 947 is 星期广播音乐会, usually played by the Shanghai Philharmonic Orchestra 上海爱乐乐团.

Shenzhen Media Group (SMG) is a conglomerate created in 2004 and comprises Shenzhen TV 深圳电视, Shenzhen Film Studio 深圳电影制片厂, Shenzhen City Radio 深圳城市广播 and Television transmission centres 电视传播中心. 'The company operates four radio stations and 12 television channels, including a satellite TV channel, a high-definition TV channel, a mobile TV channel, a DVD pay channel, a shopping channel and seven terrestrial TV channels'. It has many subsidiaries. A growing number of its channels are in the local languages, Cantonese 粤语, Hakka 客家话 and Chiuchow 潮州話.

These conglomerates aside, the leading individual stations by income from advertising are: Jiangsu Radio Traffic Net 江苏交通广播网 (FM101.1); China National Radio 1 (Voice of China FM106.1) 中央人民广播电台 1 套中国之声 and Zhejiang Communications Voice (FM93) 浙江交通之声. Programme examples in Table page 106.

At an all-industry conference in 2005, it was noted that, whereas provincial television stations had been able to escape administrative boundaries through their satellite channels and create national markets for themselves, the same was yet to happen with radio.[86] Despite deregulation, relatively few of the radio stations were commercially successful.[87] The conference identified a huge unexploited market for radio in the countryside, but little initiative in exploiting it. At the same conference, radio stations declared their intention of reforming their management and production processes in order to take advantage of new opportunities.[88]

As with television, radio stations are organised along the lines of the political structure. Perhaps two thousand of them[89] are essentially government organisations operated at the various administrative levels. Although the number of stations grew during the 1980s, radio went into decline as television expanded. Then, early in the new century, social changes brought radio back into vogue. The ever-growing number of car drivers provided a market, which was further expanded by the habit of listening on mobile phones . Businesses, needing more and cheaper types of advertising than were otherwise available, turned to radio. Further deregulation took place as the wealthier radio stations were allowed to make their own news and current affairs programmes, which had previously been mandated from the centre.

Some radio programmes[90]

My car has something to say 我的汽车有话说 belongs to Hangzhou Transport Economics Radio 杭州交通经济广播, FM91.8, transmitted daily since 11th April 2005, 11:00-12:30. It is a live, interactive, 'query programme' involving consumers, drivers, transport companies and the authorities. The public can text, call or message on the Internet to get to the host, Yu Hu 于虎, famed for his incisive mind and speaking style. As knowledgeable about law as about cars, he helps drivers with many varied queries. He reveals the traps laid for consumers by the car industry and teaches the consumer how to navigate the hidden rules. His successes have made his show the top rated radio programme in Hangzhou 杭州.

Face to Face with the Consultant 名医面对面 is a daily health service programme from Guangdong Southern Life Radio 广东南方生活广播. It has been transmitted, 15:00-16:00 every day and Sunday 09:00-10:00 since 28th February 2013. The programme cooperates with 26 leading local hospitals, such as Guangdong Provincial People's Hospital 广东省人民医院. It popularizes useful medical knowledge, offers the latest service messages from the hospitals, discusses health care policy and facilitates communication between doctor and patients, public and hospitals. It is a pathbreaking multimedia broadcast programme combining radio, video and website. The public can listen to the radio, or watch video on line, use weixin 微博 to obtain the contents, and also interact with the programme team through weixin 微信.

Dong and Wu Together 冬吴相对论 is a weekend money programme, 11:30-12:00 from CNR Business Radio. The style is relaxed, humorous and down to earth. The two hosts are Liang Dong 梁冬, formerly of Phoenix Television 凤凰卫视 and Wu Bofan 吴伯凡, editor of *21st Century Business Review* 21世纪商业评论. The programme analyses current social and economic issues, and explains complicated financial stories lucidly.[91]

Green new world 绿色新天地, is a farming programme from Yunnan Rural Radio 云南农村广播. Transmitted every working day 8:00-8:30, 12:00-12:30 and 19:00-19:30, it spreads new agricultural information and introduces technology to farmers; it listen to farmers, helps them fix their problems, explains the latest government policies and keeps farmers in touch with what is going on in the wider agricultural world.

Fukien Opera 闽南听戏台 belongs to Xiamen Fukienese Radio 厦门闽南之声, transmitting daily 06:00-07:00. There are five themes: *Leading Artistes and Selections*, inviting the audience to enjoy various types, schools and outstanding performances; *Opera Express*, introducing different traditional operatic traditions from all over the country; *Singing Coach* invites experts to teach listeners. Then there is the latest *Opera News*, explanations of opera culture from the clothing and makeup to the props; in *Hard practice in the theatre*, singers are interviewed for their behind the scenes anecdotes and there are introductions to genres with their own peculiar characteristics such as Taiwanese Opera 歌仔戏 and Li Yuan Opera 梨园戏.

The China Radio Association 中国无线电协会 was established in 2009 for promoting cooperation, policy making and good practice.[92] It welcomed Hong Kong investment into China National Radio 中央人民广播电台 and Beijing People's Radio 北京人民广播电台. SAPPRFT now aims for more state investment, to improve programming for the rural population.

100% of the population can now receive radio, and advertising expenditure has increased, although radio still receives only 3% of total advertising spending.[93] The fashion for learning English has had people turning to radio to follow English Language courses and listening to the English programmes on China Radio International 中国国际广播电台. The table on p105 lists the principal broadcasters, led by China Broadcasting Network. Internet radio is becoming increasingly popular, which means that income from advertising is likely to grow.

3.6   Discussion

From this sketch of the main media we find a number of features which distinguish them. China is a big country with many variations of culture, language and economy, so any generalisations must be rather abstract. In theory all media are 'public service' , with commercial exigencies secondary.

What constitutes public service is decided by Party and regulator. They determine the approach and main topics to be covered in drama, news and current affairs, with varying degrees of precision according to proximity to the centre. The media are governed with greater or lesser intensity according to political circumstances. Because they are now mainly commercial, in matters where the Party or state regulator has no purview they are shaped, as elsewhere, by perceptions of what the market wants and what advertisers need. Managers must please two masters.

Local media are supervised locally. Providing that the Organisation Department of the Party has done a good job in selecting and appointing personnel, the sub-provincial units will be managed by people who conform ideologically and are ready to resist commercial pressures to deviate from the norms. Although independent broadcast production and freelance writing would seem to open a cleft or two in the carapace, the indies and freelancers would not be in their positions if they were not already at one with the consensus.

Regulators, censors and editors are not necessarily disaffected. From the point of view of the Organisation Department, they are all part of the media world. It would be thought not only normal but a mark of success for an outstanding programme director or journalist to spend part of her or his career as a government spokesman or regulator.

Some of the best journalism may well be produced for Restricted Circulation Publications (RCPs). Producing RCPs is a matter of pride for professional journalists because they may well influence policy and the author may be consulted by policy makers.

When they see themselves as part of the establishment, writers, directors, producers and reporters seek to be critical constructively, and at their best they have a profound sense of responsibility about the possible effects of what they publish on the people concerned and the wider society. References to 'screaming journalism' notwithstanding, sensation and scoop are not highly rated.

Online newspapers and social media may be deepening peoples' sense of citizenship. No longer is it only the literate families who feel they constitute a policy world, but everybody who wants to join in. This brings us to New Media, at which we will now look.

What's in the magazines?

Details	Example (a principal article or story)
Name 故事会 *Storytime* General Pocket sized stories, scandalous, whimsical and moral	Sample feature: *An Intimate Relationship* A headmaster has a friendly relationship with a monk, whom he reveres as a spiritual adviser. One day, soon after he has guiltily agreed to take a cut on the sale of substandard schoolbooks to his pupils, he finds the monk is avoiding him. The headmaster realises that the monk knows about the corrupt transaction and is turning away from his erstwhile friend. Remorseful, the headmaster reverses his decision on the schoolbooks. Just days after this the local director of education calls him in to offer him promotion, because he is 'the only headmaster who has not been involved in a scam to sell substandard textbooks'. Filled with gratitude, he goes to the monk to thank him for his unspoken criticism. The monk is surprised, since he claims to know nothing of the scam: 'It was all in your own heart'.
Name 知音 *Best Friend* General Reports of personal and family predicaments	Sample feature: *Suicide from shame* 1. A PhD student is married to a man who does not know that he is impotent. With her mother's encouragement, she conceives by another man, but then, consumed by shame and guilt, she commits suicide. Sample feature: *Who dares buy a flat from someone's mistress?* 2. A young man is sold a flat at a knock-down price by a former girlfriend, whom he believes to be doing him a favour. It transpires, however, that this flat was a gift to her from a married lover, who has died leaving his family destitute, unless they can obtain ownership of the flat. Legally, it belongs to the young man, but morally?
Name 家庭 *Family* General 64 pages of profiles, quirky life, sociology ('why do we like sword fighting tales?') romance, business, psychology, culture ('the art of resignation' or 'what happens to those brilliant Americans who fail in the elections?')	Sample Feature: *A miscarriage of justice and the ten-year road to redress.* In May 2003 a 17 year old girl hitched a lift on the truck owned by a Mr Zhang and his nephew, respectable and successful local traders. Some hours after they had dropped her in Hangzhou her naked body was found. Within days the two Zhangs were arrested on suspicion of rape and murder by the local police, who failed to check evidence but proceeded to beat them savagely until they confessed. In 2004, despite the court finding no DNA evidence, the men were convicted and sentenced, one to death (later commuted) and the younger to life. When the younger arrived at the prison in Xinjiang he continued to protest his innocence. This came to the attention of a prison officer who tried to reopen the case, but without success. The officer's decency buoyed up the prisoner who read up on cases in *Democracy and Law* in the prison reading room, and one day in 2008 came across an earlier instance, the exposure of a false confession extracted by the very same brute who had beaten one out of him. In 2010, after talking with the prison officer, a lawyer agreed to take on the case

108

	pro bono, and started the complicated appeal proceedings on the grounds that the court had seen no material evidence, but had convicted on the basis of a confession that was now suspect; he also requested that the traces of male DNA found on the two separate murdered girls should be compared. Frustrated with the slowness of his application, the lawyer publicised it in 2011 through the Hangzhou media. The following year it was agreed that the case be reopened and in March 2013 the appellate court found the two Zhangs not guilty.
Name 读者 *The Reader*	*Sample feature: I can't study so I'm off back home* This is a rambling tale of a student's changing relationship with her parents and her reflections on the future. As she grew older, their relationship changed. Then came a day when she realised that her parents did not understand what she was studying and could not help her anymore; how she coped with their urging her to find a boyfriend; how her parents are as critical and demanding of their child as they are of themselves. She finds her mother has grey hairs, and this sets her off worrying as to how she can support and help them as they get old. She recalls how her grandparents' memories faded and they constantly repeated themselves, recalling the high hopes they had had for their children, her parents, when they were young. Our student is sent to the villages to do some research and finds many old people bereft of their children and grandchildren who have moved to the cities to earn and cannot get back regularly, and is upset about the loneliness of the old and the apparent 'Westernisation of our relationships'. To many of her peers, their own lives are quite detached from that of their parents; the intimate involvement in each other's lives and the security and happiness that this provided to both parties is being lost. Children are abandoning their parents. She thinks that although today she does not want them involved in her life there will be a time when she is leading them by the hand as they too reminisce over her childhood, endlessly repeating themselves. So she pulls herself together and determines to be a good student and live a clean life, not giving in to the temptation to laze about or forget her family responsibilities. 'I must get myself into the position that I can one day say to my parents, "Don't worry, I'm going to look after you"'.
Name 三连生活周刊/ *Lifeweek*	Cover feature: *Corruption's Production Line: Reciprocity and Covert understandings*, with a short essay and several related articles. Other topics covered: Putin's pro-natalist policies; the Shanxi scandal of phenylamine leakage polluting Henan and Hebei; an investigation into a huge fire in Shanghai. The relevant edition had extensive coverage and analysis of the US elections.
Name 新世纪 *New Century*	Cover feature: *The Next Ten Years: political reform, turning round the economic model, a society of laws, openness and innovation, social fairness……what a host of problems, where will we start?* Articles on all these issues, plus features on Dong Yongan, former Director of Transportation in Henan, 'the very model of a repeatedly corrupt official' and one on the disappointment felt by specialist environment lawyers at the reformulation of the environmental protection laws.

Name 博客天下/*Blog Weekly*	Selected features: 1. The US and North Korea may be sworn enemies, but recently important US guests have been visiting the enemy: will that change anything? 2. The UK's Minister of Trade is criticised for going to work in an official car rather than using public transport. 3. The founder of Alibaba, Ma Yun, and why he will not accept nomination for Congress or the CPPCC.
Name 中国周刊 *China Week*	Selected features: 1. Unforeseen disaster: An investigation into the bird flu epidemic in Shandong, Jiangsu, Anhui, Zhejiang, Fujian, Taiwan and Shanghai. 2. North Korea: Is war coming?
Name 人物/ *Portrait*	Cover feature: *Whence comes freedom?*, with fine photographs from Brazil, North Korea, the USA, Jinan (Shandong), the Philippines and Mexico, intended to evoke different concepts of freedom, and 17 pages of associated essays. Discussions of individuals and their concerns: an entrepreneur, the retired Pope Benedict, Nuo Kang, 糯康, a drug gangster from the Mekong area, and how he comported himself on trial. An essay from an academic wishing that people who immigrate to China do not do so just for money; another asking 'what contribution do Buddhist monks make to our happiness?'
Name 芭莎男士商业 *Harper's Bazaar*	Selected features: Profile of the house of Rothschild; one-page interviews with entrepreneurs, an English professor, a YouTube innovator. Which countries have the most magnates? Reports on Peking opera actors, a painter, and (a big one) the CEO of Lianxiang Group about its 30-year history of international operations.
Name 财经国家周刊 *Economy & Nation Weekly*	Cover feature: *Finance is 'Idling'*. In-depth analysis of the failings of the financial sector adequately to support the economy, plus reports on media coverage of the recent Sichuan earthquake.
Name 财经 *Caijing*	Cover feature: *The time for choice: Inspiration from the 20th anniversary of Comrade Deng's Southern Progress* An eight-page critique of present directions, under the slogan 'The only way to dissipate our woes is reform'. The main article is by Zhou Ruijin, a leading journalist who played a part in promoting Deng's reform agenda in the newspapers of the 1990s. Now he writes that vested interests are the main hindrance to further progress. Other articles: • Understanding the logic of China's economy. • An interview with the British minister of finance about membership of the EU. • Putin's difficulties (in Russia). • Reforming Wenzhou's informal banking system. • The limited progress of budgetary law reform.

	• The need for national strategy to safeguard the very small enterprises. • The 'white hats' who fight the hackers in cyberspace • 'India's hazards are greater than China's', by a Yale professor who is non-executive chairman of Morgan Stanley. • The need to grasp banking reform: if the last eight years were about system reform, the next need to be about reforming the mechanisms. • The importance of strengthening legal processes in budgetary and financial issues. • Leakgate: the case of the Yunnan medicine *baiyao*, in which its closely guarded secrets were found on US websites. What this tells us about cyber security in China, the activities of hackers and how we should be countering them, how investigating them, and the construction of an Internet law. • Analysis of the case of Zhang Jiameng, former Mayor of Zhoushan and Vice Chairman of the Zhejiang CPC Standing Committee, recently sentenced for corruption. • Resolving doubts about the RMB offshore market.
Name *Insight China* 小康	Cover feature: *The New Policy for Holding Xinjiang Together: In part, it is raising standards of living, in part it is stabilisation. A year or more ago Xinjiang was turbulent and several times was the focus of attention, not only in China, but throughout the world.* Articles within the magazine: 1. Secretary (of the Xinjiang Party) wants changes in how Xinjiang is run. 2. Speeding up the improvement in people's living conditions. 3. The anti-terrorism policy. 4. Looking in depth at the fundamentals of Xinjiang stability. 5. Getting Xinjiang's delinquent children back home. Other articles in this edition include: • The social sickness behind the riots in England. • The Prince of Kungqu opera. • The last person from the Beiquan Middle School crippled by the • earthquake. • 'I am studying to be an undertaker': The funeral business. • Today's major issues in education. • Professor Xiong Jiaqi on China's failing universities. • How Weibo bigwigs tore away the curtain from the officials' Weibo.

Notes

[1] See, for example, Moore, Malcolm (2016) 'The rebel Chinese newspaper which dares to challenge the Communist party line'. [Online]. Available at: http://www.telegraph.co.uk/news/worldnews/asia/china/9905781/The-rebel-Chinese-newspaper-which-dares-to-challenge-the-Communist-party-line.html (Accessed: 10 January 2016). Cases of people who have been imprisoned, journalists in Hunan and students at Peking University among them, for trying to set up a newspaper, are detailed in He Qinglian (nd, probably 2006) *The Fog of Censorship: Media Control in China*, p25, available at http://www.hrichina.org/sites/default/files/PDFs/Reports/HRIC-Fog-of-Censorship.pdf

[2] The Head of the London Hub of CCTV is called 'Controller' for day to day purposes, but her rank, and the established rank for that particular post, is Deputy Bureau Head 副局长。

[3] Sun Wanning 'Rescaling media in China: the formations of local, provincial, and regional media cultures', *Chinese Journal of Communication* Vol. 5, No. 1, March 2012, 10–15, pp 13.

[4] Ibid., pp11.

[5] The bifurcation is not as clear as I may have made it sound, after all, the *Jiangsu Daily* carries advertising but cannot survive on that, let alone on cover price. Moreover the commercial media are circumscribed politically though not in such a manner as to impinge on profitability.

[6] Scotton, JF. Xinhua (2010) The voice of the Party. In: Scotton JF, Hachten WA. (eds.) *New media for a new China.* Oxford: Wiley-Blackwell, Chapter 9.

[7] Liu, B. (2010) New strength of competition and innovation: China's independent television production. In: *Conference of the International Communication Association: Matters of Communication* 22-26 June 2010, Singapore.

[8] Luo, Jun 骆珺, Correspondent with Xinhua News Agency London Bureau (Politics, Foreign Affairs, Royal) personal communication, 12 February 2013.

[9] Shirk SL. (2011) Changing media, changing China. In: Shirk SL, (2011) (ed). *Changing media, changing China.* New York: Oxford University Press.

[10] *Liberation Daily* was published in the redoubt of Yanan from 1941-47 and then revived in Shanghai in 1949.

[11] Zhao Yuezhi has written about this extensively in Zhao (2000) and Zhao (2008).

[12] 胡正容 Hu, Zhengrong (2010) 社会透镜，新中国媒介变迁六十年 *Society's lens: sixty years of vicissitudes for the Chinese media.* 北京 Beijing：清华大学出版社 Tsinghua University Press, pp 307.

[13] Zhao, Yuezhi (2012) Understanding China's Media System. In: Hallin, DC and Mancini, P. (eds.) *Comparing media systems beyond the western world.* Cambridge: Cambridge University Press, pp 170-173. See also Zhao (2003) and Zhao (2008).

[14] Ke, G. (2010) Newspapers: changing roles. In: Scotton, JF and Hachten, WA (eds.). *New media for a new China.* Oxford: Wiley-Blackwell, Chapter 4.

[15] Li Hong carried out the survey of newspapers dated 23 April 2013 and weekend papers dated 5 May 2013 and Verada Liu examined the main stories for differences in treatment. The sample was too small (and allowance needed to be made for the particular model of *Global Times*) but indicated that there may be culturally distinct ways of reporting which should be rewarding to study. My own review of a range of local newspapers, *Suzhou Weekend, Modern Express* (Jiangsu), *New People Evening News* (Shanghai) , *Nanjing Morning News* and *Golden Tomb* (!) *Evening News* (Nanjing) suggests to me the same, but also that what in the Anglosphere would be regarded as 'high culture' has much more of a place in China's local press.

[16] 7 December 2013.

[17] Pavlik, JV. Running the Technological Gauntlet: Journalism and New Media in de Burgh, H (ed) (2005) *Making Journalists: Diverse Models, Global Issues* London: Routledge p 263

[18] Lee, Chin-chuan, He, Zhou and Huang, Yu (2006) 'Chinese party publicity Inc.' Conglomerated: the case of the Shenzhen press group in Media, Culture and Society volume 28: pp 581–602, pp 568.

[19] Lu Ye, quoted in Ibid., pp 584

[20] Sun, a student, was beaten to death in a police cell where he had been taken as a suspected vagrant. The ensuing outcry led to changes in the law on vagrancy.

[21] Zhao (2008), pp 296. She also writes (p52 that registration of various periodicals criticising the 'neo-liberal agenda' was cancelled. They included *Pursuit of Truth* 真理的追求and *Midstream*中流.

[22] Ibid., pp 319.

[23] Gong, Qian, Sarah (2015) 'An emerging middle class public sphere in China? Analysis of news media representation of "self text declaration"' in Rawnsley, Gary D. and Rawnsley Ming-yeh T.(eds.) *Routledge Handbook of Chinese Media.* London: Taylor & Francis, pp 255.

[24] Ibid., pp 256 and pp 258.

[25] Ibid., pp 254.

[26] Lee, Hsiao-wen (2015) From control to competition, a comparative study of the party press and the popular press. In: Rawnsley, Gary D. and Rawnsley Ming-yeh T. (eds.) *Routledge Handbook of Chinese Media*. London: Taylor & Francis.

[27] Ibid., pp 128.

[28] Zhao (2008), pp 92-93.

[29] Chen, Guidi and Wu, Chuntao (2006) *Will the Boat sink the Water?* London: Public Affairs Ltd, pp 42-61.

[30] http://www.theguardian.com/commentisfree/2013/nov/02/chen-yongzhou-weibo-china-struggles-media (Accessed: 17 March 2016)

[31] This section is based on the research and interviews of Mi Miao.

[32] It is not only locally originated websites that must be compted with. Aside from Chinese language websites from abroad such as FT and *The Guardian*, there appears to be a growing audience for English language online newspaoers. Gavin Essler, Managing Editor of Britain's *Daily Mail* was startled to find, in 2012, that he had a 'significant' readership in the PRC, and promptly flew to Guangzhou to discuss with the Nanfang Group how he might launch a Chinese edition.

[33] Yang Xing, Editor-in-Chief, Hangzhou Daily Press Group. Interviewed by Mi Miao; December 2012 杨星 杭州日报报业集团集团副总编辑、都市快报总编辑.

[34] Ibid.

[35] These processes are explored comprehensively in Pavlik, John V (2008) *Media in the Digital Age*. New York: Columbia University Press, pp103-29. See also his magisterial overview, with McIntosh, Shawn, (2011) *Converging Media: A new Introduction to Communication*. Oxford: Oxford University Press.

[36] Mi Miao (2015) 'How newspapers respond to technological change : a comparison between the UK and China', PhD Thesis, *University of Westminster*, 2015. For further discussion of these developments, see Thurman N., Making 'The Daily Me': technology, economics and habit in the mainstream assimilation of personalized news. *Journalism: Theory, Practice & Criticism*.12(4); 2011.

[37] http://bbs.peoplc.com.cn/bbs/, quoted by Li Jingyu 李径宇. Interviewed by Mi Miao; December 2012. 中国新闻社《中国新闻周刊》副总编辑兼执行主编 Deputy Editor-in-Chief & Executive Chief Editor, China News Weekly.

[38] Li, Shiheng 李世恒. Interviewed by Mi Miao; December 2012. 北京青年报社党委副书记、纪委书记 Vice Secretary, Party Committee and Secretary, Discipline Committee, *Beijing Youth Daily*.

[39] Wang, Songmiao 王松苗. Interviewed by Mi Miao; December 2012 检察日报社总编辑.

[40] Chang, Ping (2014) Scottish exercise of democracy becomes antidemocracy fodder in Chinese press. In: *South China morning post* 17 September 2014, pp A15.

[41] Tuchman, G. (1978). *Making News: A Study in the Construction of Reality*. New York: The Free Press, pp184. I am indebted to Vivien Marsh for pointing this out.

[42] Ibid., pp ix.

[43] http://mt.sohu.com/20150330/n410527051.shtml (Accessed: 1 February 2016).

[44] Li, S. (2011) *The new generation of lifestyle magazine journalism in China: the professional approach*. PhD thesis. University of Westminster, London. [Online]. Available at: http://westminsterresearch.wmin.ac.uk/10089/. (Accessed: 9 March 2016) .

[45] Li, S. (2011) *The new generation of lifestyle magazine journalism in China: the professional approach*. PhD thesis. University of Westminster, London. [Online]. Available at: http://westminsterresearch.wmin.ac.uk/10089/. (Accessed: 9 March 2016).

[46] Kavita K, Yang F. (2009) International women's magazines in China: global and local perspectives. *Chinese Journal of Communication*, November 2009, pp 348-366.

[47] Chen, P. (2010) Magazines: an industry in transition. In: Scotton JF, Hachten WA. (2010). *New media for a new China*. Oxford: Wiley-Blackwell.

[48] Wang (2011), Jiang (2009): Cited in: Lu, Nan (2013) Reading women's magazines: identity negotiation in the construction of femininity among Chinese new women; pp 33. Hong Kong Baptist University: Research proposal for PhD candidature, provided to the author; June 2013.

[49] Kavita K, Yang F. (2009) International women's magazines in China: global and local perspectives. *Chinese Journal of Communication*, November 2009, pp 348-366.

[50]. The expression 'cultural cringe' is used to explain the adoption of the habits of one culture by members of another culture, because they feel overawed by it, or at least by the prestige engendered by successful soft power.

[51] http://mediaconv.com/pdf/FIPP%20World%20Magazine%20Trends%202012-2013%20-%20China.pdfhttp://mediaconv.com/wp-, see also content/uploads/2015/01/WMT-2014-China-amended-print-221214.pdf (Accessed: 1 February 2016).

[52] Zhu (2009) p 236. Phoenix' audience is mainly located in the capital and Guangzhou. In principle reception of Phoenix and the other services is limited to Guangdong plus hotels and certain other subscribers, but in fact reception may be more widespread. Phoenix is often seen as a competitor to CCTV, with more freedom and variety. See Zeng, Rong (2012) *Television and the Limits of Globalisation: BBC and Phoenix Today*, Buckingham: U of Buckingham Press. US media corporations such as News International and AOL Time Warner sell programmes to China and also have set up channels to 'target' China generally. See Chan, Joseph M. (2009) 'Towards Television Regionalisation in Greater China and Beyond' in Zhu, Ying and Berry, Chris (2009) *TV China*, Bloomington: Indiana UP, pp 15-39

[53] Barboza D. (2008) *Olympics are ratings bonanza for Chinese TV*. [Online]. New York Times. 2008 [cited 3 January 2012]. Available at: http://www.nytimes.com/2008/08/22/sports/olympics/22cctv.html?scp=1&sq=%22Chinese%20TV%20hits%20jackpot%20with%20games%22&st=cse (Accessed: 17 March 2016),

[54] Researchers have started to analyse the roles of Chinese overseas media representatives. At the 2015 IAMCR conference, Jiang Hei and Huang Kuo presented a paper *The role reflection between a journalist and a public diplomat: A case study of Chinese overseas correspondents*. Available from: fjiangmedi @ ahoo.com, Department of Communication, the Institute of Journalism & Communication, Chinese Academy of Social Sciences (CASS), Beijing, China.

[55] *Southern Weekend*, 25 January 2013.

[56] See: http://yule.sohu.com/20141017/n405190685.shtml (Accessed: 10 February 2016). Audience figure was 11.06% (first half year of 2014).

[57] Zhu, Ying (2012). *Two billion eyes: the story of China Central Television*. New York: The New Press, pp 15-17.

[58] Rawnsley (2015), pp 469.

[59] http://www.taipeitimes.com/News/taiwan/archives/2015/11/08/2003631975 (Accessed: 10 February 2016). In later editions, presumably once the speech had been analysed, it was shown in full.

[60] 胡正容 Hu, Zhenrong (2010) 社会透镜，新中国媒介变迁六十年 *Society's lens: sixty years of vicissitudes for the Chinese media*. 北京 Beijing：清华大学出版社 Tsinghua University Press, pp 302, 305.

[61] Dong, GP and Shi, AB. (2012) Chinese News in Transition: Facing the Challenge of Global Competition. In: 史安斌 Shi, A. (ed.) 国际传播研究前沿 Leading-Edge Studies on International Communication in Tsinghua University. 北京 Beijing：清华大学出版社 Tsinghua University Press, pp 189.

[62] Yu Dan 于丹 （2008）*Confucius from the Heart* 论语感悟, 北京：中华书局

[63] 12th Sichuan TV Festival: Introduction, 12th Sichuan TV Festival; 2013.

[64] Zhu Ying, Keane Michael and Bai Ruoyun (2008) *TV drama in China.* HK: Hong Kong University, pp xiii.

[65] Liu, B. (2010) New strength of competition and innovation: China's independent television production. In: *Conference of the International Communication Association: Matters of Communication,* 22-26 June 2010, Singapore.

[66] For an analysis of the competition see Zhu, Ying (2009) 'Transnational Circulation of Chinese-Language Television Dramas' in Zhu, Ying and Berry, Chris (2009) *TV China,* Bloomington: Indiana UP, pp 225 et seq.

[67] Zhu, Ying (2009) pp 221 and 226.

[68] Huang Yeh-chien in Zhu et al (2008), pp 13.

[69] Zhu et al (2008), pp 8.

[70] Scotton JF, Hachten WA. (eds.) (2010) *New media for a new China.* Oxford: Wiley/Blackwell, pp 91.

[71] See Zhu Ying (2008) Television in Post-Reform China: Serial Dramas, Confucian Leadership and the Global Televison Market , London: Routledge

[72] Zhu (2008), pp 52.

[73] The exploits of Di Renjie have been rendered into English in a series of novels by Robert van Gulik.

[74] For example: *Sun Yat-sen* 孙中山 1986 *Marching towards the republic* 走向共和 2003 十月围城 *Bodyguards and Assassins* (an HK film) 2009.

[75] de Burgh, H, et al. (2012) Chinese television 'internationalisation' and the search for creativity. *Creative Industries Journal,* 4(2).

[76] Paul Jackson, former Head of Comedy, BBC. Lecture at Tsinghua University; 13 October 2013.

[77] Zeng Rong, personal communication; 25 October 2013.

[78] They were: *King of Comedy* 笑傲江湖, a comedy version of X Factor, in which celebrity judges evaluate amateur performers from various backgrounds and crown one with the title 'King of Comedy'; *Ladder to Heaven* 天梯, a show based on the idea of an 'elevator pitch' – participants seeking investment have the time of an elevator ride to promote themselves or their products or services; *Sweet Secret Dates* 蜜密约会, a dating show similar to the British programme *Blind Date*; *Top Dog* 狗狗冲冲冲, a dog talent show in which dogs and their owners work together to win obstacle races to gain the title of 'Top Dog', testing the bond between dogs and their owners.

[79] There is considered to be a renaissance of documentary today. See 何苏六 He Shuliu （ed.） (2013) 中国纪录片发展报告 *The Annual Report on the Development of Chinese Documentary* Beijing：社会科学文献出版社 Social Science Academic Press. Leading channels are Chongqing Science and Education 重庆科教频道, Golden Eagle Documentary 湖南金鹰纪实频道, Liaoning Radio and Television North 辽宁北方频道, Tianjin Science and Education 天津科教频道。

[80] Cao, Qing (2015) The politics and poetics of television documentary in China. In: Rawnsley, Gary D. and Rawnsley Ming-yeh T.(eds.) *Routledge Handbook of Chinese Media.* London: Taylor & Francis, pp 355-356.

[81] Analysed in several publications by Berry. See Berry, Chris (2009) Shanghai Television's Documentary Channel: Chinese Television as Public Space' in Zhu, Ying and Berry, Chris (2009) *TV China,* Bloomington: Indiana UP pp 71-89

[82] Kuhn, RL. (2012) China's challenges 中国面临的挑战, Shanghai: Wuan Publishers 上海五岸传播有限公司.

[83] see: http://baike.baidu.com/link?url=21E0PtvI2_lmynOaufdexiukpItmPGwG0BN5m45nU3i_R_p5xC7 -JjOtac7MCzUL-ZbJbghazagtiXYLVfR-LzkvWN9LLv66JyQfgym8nmq (Accessed: 17 March 2016).

[84] Rawnsley Ming-yeh T. and Feng Chien-san (2015) Public service television in China. In: Rawnsley, Gary D. and Rawnsley Ming-yeh T.(eds.) *Routledge Handbook of Chinese Media*. London: Taylor & Francis, pp 298-313.

[85] The sections on New Media advertising and advertising agencies were researched and written for the author by Dr Giovanna Puppin.

[86] 徐来见 Xu Laijian (2006?) 中国广播发展的瓶颈及对策 *Bottleneck and counter-measures: the development of Chinese radio.* [Online]. 2006? [cited 23 October 2013]. Available at: http://d.g.wanfangdata.com.cn/conference_6354918.aspx (Accessed: 17 March 2016).

[87] Zhou Xiaopu 周小普(2006) 广播产业发展及体制、机制改革 *System and mechanism reform and the development of Chinese broadcasting.* Beijing: 中国广播电视学刊 China Radio & TV Academic Journal, pp 13.

[88] Ibid, *passim*

[89] It is very unclear as to how many there are; estimates range wildly from 200 to 3,000.

[90] This section was researched by Li Yingying.

[91] http://blog.sina.com.cn/s/articlelist_1591039221_0_7.html

[92] Global Media Market Intelligence (G2Mi.com). Growth in digital radio accelerates the Chinese radio sector. London: Heernet Ventures Ltd; 1 December 2012.

[93] In the first quarter of 2012, 'the radio industry adspend grew by 12% annually to reach RMB 4,800 million. Finance, business and services, and automobiles were the leading adspend categories, totalling RMB 918 million, RMB 828 million and RMB 657 million, respectively. In H1 2011.....Radio advertising showed annual growth of 24.3%'. [Ref: Global Media Market Intelligence (G2Mi.com). Growth in digital radio accelerates the Chinese radio sector. London: Heernet Ventures Ltd; 1 December 2012].

4   China's Babel: New Media

Everywhere New Media are transforming how and with whom we communicate and what information we can access or have thrust upon us. Nowhere is this more true than in China. Relationships are changing, facts and rumours cannot be hidden, people and events are exposed when before they might never have come to light. These possibilities change different societies in different ways. How do they affect the authoritarian, communitarian and reticent society that China has been for much of its recorded history? Do netizens relate to each other differently? How are politics being affected? Will New Media be the means by which China is finally homogenized and abandons its resistance to 'universal' norms? Is the Great Firewall successful? We do not know the answer to all these questions but we can chart some of the more obvious developments.

4.1   Exposure

If you YouTube and type in 'My Father is Li Gang' 我爸是李刚 you will find a rap song and pictures from a 2010 story which has become an archetype, to say nothing of gigabytes of comment. The story 'My Father is Li Gang' must be every parent's nightmare. Here it is:

Your son is driving your car on the campus of his university.

He's been drinking, and he knocks down two girls. One is killed, the other seriously hurt.

Your son doesn't do the decent thing. Oh no!

He tries to get away. But he fails. His car is surrounded by angry students while he sits there.

They call the police. Is the boy contrite? Not a bit of it. When the cop comes to nab him, he says 'You can't touch me! My father is Li Gang!'

So? Li Gang is a big cheese in the city, a senior police officer. Once upon a time, under Mao Zedong and before the Internet, the son's boast would have worked. When the gap between powerful and powerless was much greater, no one dared to upset a relative or friend of the bosses. But today people protest and the central government logs the protests as legitimate manifestations of grievance. They sue, and sometimes they win, and they publicise through the Internet what the media are too constrained to broadcast or publish. Hooligans are nervous.

Not only did the phrase 'My father is Li Gang' become a rap song, it become a popular figure of speech; Jane says to her flatmate: 'You've left a mess in the kitchen' and he replies: 'My father is Li Gang'.

The case of Sun Zhigang

The best known example of web posts mobilising opinion is the case of Sun Zhigang 孙志剛, a young migrant who died in custody and whose case was taken up posthumously, but with such fervour and general outcry that the government abolished the *Custody & Repatriation Ordinance* 收容遣送.

In March 2003, Sun Zhigang, a 26 year old graduate of Wuhan University, was stopped and searched in Guangzhou. Because he was not carrying his identity card and residence permit, he was taken into custody under the ordinance which required that the police detain persons unable to show valid documents. Some days after his detention, Sun was found dead, and an autopsy revealed this to be the result of a beating. His father speculated that his son had remonstrated and thus infuriated the police, who had decided to teach him a lesson.

As soon as the circumstances of Sun's death reached the public domain, it became a cause célèbre on the web, and was taken up by the local paper, *Southern City News* 南方都市报. Law academics opined that the *Ordinance* was unconstitutional. In June the Prime Minister announced that the *Ordinance* had been abolished and replaced by *Measures for assisting vagrants and beggars with no means of support* 城市生活无着的流浪乞讨人员的救助管理办法, a more humane response to the problem. The police involved were tried and punished, but so also were the editor of *Southern City News* and some of his colleagues, though the latter were released from prison very smartly.

This case is often interpreted as an example of the Chinese government's rapid reaction to issues broached on the Internet, as well as of its relationship with newspaper editors.

The local authorities tried to prevent discussion of the case in the offline media, but this only redoubled the efforts of the netizens to recycle it. They were so successful that the whole nation was scandalised that people with powerful parents thought 'in this day and age!' 这个是什么时代! that they were above the laws of the land and morality. This reaction suggests a change in the relationship between citizens and authority. Predictions that because of the Internet and social media in particular, revolution is imminent, may be misplaced, just as dire warnings that new media are becoming tools with which the politicians manipulate us may be exaggerated. But changes there are, and they are illustrated by several well-known cases.[1]

- In 2007 netizens mobilised public opinion against a paraxylene plant proposed for the city of Xiamen and stopped it being built. Because of this, it is now difficult for authorities to refuse consultation on controversial proposed developments. According to the respected website *China Dialogue*, 'This is generally considered a victory for public participation; the central government listened to environmental concerns and the Xiamen municipality worked to protect the city. More importantly, the events established a new type of activism, which focused on a single issue in order to change governmental habits and the law. For officials, this will mean new rules on how they act'.[2]

- A family of victims of urban development held out over three years for greater compensation for the loss of their home. A picture of their house posted online, sticking up like a nail in a cleared building site, moved millions of netizens. The Chongqing nailhouse dwellers 重庆钉子户 eventually won the compensation they were seeking.

- Netizens exposed the collusion of civil servants and police with employers to exploit and enslave child workers in Shanxi brick kilns 山西 砖窑 and obliged the authorities to deal with the issue.

- In 2014, at Yue Yuan Industrial Holdings in Dongguan, shoemakers were angry about the underpayment of contributions to a retirement fund. They used messaging apps to get each other out on strike and in doing so showed that industrial relations have changed: QQ enabled them to create numerous overlapping groups. Weixin 微信 has a 'look around' function so that they searched for people they knew nearby and could create invitation-only groups. 30,000 workers went out on strike.[3]

Since then there have been innumerable cyber events or reports that have caused furores. Many observers suggest that, in particular, the Sun Zhigang case (detailed on page 117) shows how Internet activism can influence the policymakers, in effect becoming part of the policy world in ways that the other media cannot, except through RCPs. Netizen anger over the Sun Zhigang case obliged the authorities to change laws and police procedures; Athina Karatzogianni and Andrew Robinson, in their studies of cyberconflicts, have found similar cases.[4]

People in positions of responsibility have lost them on account of being outed through New Media. An air hostess tweeted that she had been subjected to abuse by a senior soldier and he lost his job. On Weibo 微博, the first equivalent of Facebook, an official from Hubei was reported for building an office the size of the (U.S.) White House, at a time when the local government claimed it could not afford desks in its schools. The desks were provided forthwith. The Director of Health and Safety in Shaanxi was photographed wearing expensive watches, which led to him being investigated and tried for corruption. A mature official was filmed in bed with a teenager said to have been trained and supplied by a contractor, and the film went viral. And so on.

Prior to the eruption of the Internet, the authorities had been accustomed to

119

keeping problems quiet and never washing dirty linen in public. Now they, and anybody else who incurs the interest of netizens, have to deal with the probability of exposure and to find new ways of relating to their online critics, as we will see below. But first, let us map out this world.

4.2 The Chinese Internet

When commentators outside China mention that there is a 'separate' Chinese Internet, they can make it sound like an accusation. They appear to dislike the repudiation of globalization that a 'separate' Internet implies, although few object to a corporate intranet. Yet, now that the USA-owned versions are being denounced for publishing vile and degrading material, terrorist propaganda and bomb kits, Chinese policy does not seem so contrary. In the case of Facebook, commentators are concerned too at the medium's political bias[5] and there is home grown criticism at Google's financing of academics to influence the political environment.[6]

China's netizens are not cut off from the global Internet, though they have to make an effort to get there, but the government's selective pruning has made it possible for indigenous equivalents of USA-originated Google, Twitter, Facebook and so forth to grow strong and ensure that new media, owned and managed from China, can develop.

As Michael Schudson, the American sociologist, has suggested, the media of communication take on different characteristics according to the cultures in which they are deployed.[7] Similarly 'The ways in which a new technology is used depend on pre-existing conventions and social relations',[8] thus the Internet may be applied in culturally specific ways, if it is not dominated by foreign models at the outset. Internet specialist Yang Guobin finds that Chinese use of the Internet has very particular aspects, both because of the impetus of the government to promote and manage Internet use, and the ways netizens use it to extend their daily habits.

The intensity of Chinese social life, which involves a great deal of regular interaction between familiars – meals together, present giving, mutual support, finding ways to reinforce networks – is reflected in online habits.

Urban populations routinely share their social lives, work or other information through texts, verbals, photos or video. The importance attached to interpersonal relationships (see Chapter 5), the urgency of work routines and the lack of a clear distinction between working and private life are all factors. E-commerce and online marketing are also advanced, and now include private trading through

Weixin 微信, called we-commerce 微商. It is predicted that soon more online transactions will take place in China than in the rest of the world combined.[9] Weixin is more than just an e-commerce app; it is an essential tool of work and friendship among all age-groups, whereas its equivalents are currently less exploited in the Anglosphere,[10] even among the under-thirties. It hosts family chatrooms which keep different generations in touch with what each other are eating, viewing, thinking, hour by hour. Students and schoolchildren run online study groups via Weixin as a matter of course. Some court cases are now conducted through it.[11]

Text Messaging Humour

Learning Chemistry in China
How Chinese learn Chemistry: by eating rice we discover paraffin; from ham we know dichloryos; by eating sausage we try tonyred; from trying eels we imbibe prophylactics; by enjoying hotpot we learn about formaldehyde; in candies we meet sulphur; in vegetables we find cupric sulphate; from beer we learn about methanol; with milk powder we discover melamine.
Getting a job
Two medical school graduates apply for a hospital post. The director asks Graduate A, 'What is your treatment for a person who is stung by bees?' He answers, 'It's very simple, apply some disinfectant to his skin'. The director shakes his head, and asks the same question of Graduate B. B replies that the patient has to stay in hospital for at least one week for his blood, EEG, electrocardiogram, Colour Doppler Ultrasound, MRI, etc. to be checked. The Director is satisfied, and tells him, 'You've got the job!'
Pig's dream
'A pig wants to change into a human being. God asks him, 'What job do you want to do? Do you want to be a docker?' Pig says, 'Too heavy.' God asks, 'How about being a peasant?' Pig says, 'Too heavy.' 'How about business?' Pig says, 'I am not very numerate.' God asks, Then what do you want to do?' Pig says, 'I want a job which requires only eating, drinking, gambling and having sex.' God is astonished at his answer and says, 'Now I know, you want to be a civil servant.'
Education and crime
Q: Which higher education institution in the world has the highest crime rate among its graduates? A: The Central Party School.
Pollution
According to unreliable sources, due to the recent heavy smog in Beijing, many lovers lost each other. And many couples who had intended to get divorced are forced to become reconciled, since they get lost on the way to the Divorce Office.

Borrowing from a colleague's experience, here is an imaginary, but realistic, scenario illustrating a Xian professional's dependence on New Media at New Year:

Using a Huawei smartphone with two simcards, one for her employer's work, one for her own affairs, Ms Zhang will spend much of her day in conference in several Weixin groups working on different projects; documents and video clips will be passed round and she will voice her contributions or write them as convenient, in three languages. When she wants news updates, she will flick to Sohu; for communication with foreigners there is regular email, and she will arrange her flight to see her parents at the weekend through ctrip. She books a restaurant for a lunch meeting and orders the dishes through its illustrated app, to be ready on arrival.

While in the taxi, booked via her DiDi app, she may peruse a dating site, continue with the online game based on a Three Kingdoms story from 1800 years ago that she started yesterday or read a big V [SM celebrity] who has millions of followers.

She pays for the meal via the wechat scanning system.

It is Chinese New Year, so not surprisingly her mobile receives a red envelope [gift of money] from her boyfriend. Then she joins in a battle over red envelopes in the family chat room. Later, she will have her daily video call with her parents.

Towards evening, she posts a series of witty emoticons to the colleague who thanked her for lunch with a self-drawn cartoon. Then she orders a gift for her boyfriend in England on Taobao, the biggest online retailer in the world (bigger than Amazon). The book she ordered yesterday on DangDang has arrived (she is old fashioned enough to prefer paper books to electronic ones). She curls up to read it in bed but interrupts herself to open the door for delivery of the meal she selected via Baiduwaimai 百度外卖. Since the food arrives late, she will only pay half the bill.

After her meal, she decides to treat herself by participating in an on-line auction. After a complicated process of certifying her identity, she starts bidding for a jewellery set.

Tuning in to the annual New Year Gala on television, she finds a code on the screen to scan. Once she does this, she gets an opportunity to try her luck in grabbing red envelopes and other random gifts from the networks. Then curiosity gets the better of her good taste and she glances at some lives 直播平台, mainly teenage girls showing off in the hope of attracting gifts.

Before going to sleep, she will receive a Weixin with a recording of her boyfriend reading her a Tang Dynasty poem, followed by a virtual bunch of pink roses. She will thank him with a spasm of busy emoticons.

Netizens have been quick to exploit the means provided by Weibo and Weixin to be gregarious at high speed, to forward, post and cross post pictures and videos, more flexible and comprehensive than their overseas equivalents. The Internet cafes of the early 2000s have been superseded: there are now 700 million-plus people in 'mobile Internet cafes'. As in society generally, where Chinese are renowned for creating 'pseudo families', so netgroups 微博群 are rife because of the 'functions that encourage user interaction and community building'.[12]

In 2014 the Cyberspace Administration of China (CAC) 中央网信办 was set up as a body separate from the State Council Information Office.[13] It answers to the Coordinating Group for Internet Security and Informationisation 中央网络安全和信息化领导小组, chaired by President Xi himself. (We should recall that his predecessors also considered the Internet of fundamental importance to China's economic growth). The rapidity and efficacy of government initiatives are believed to have had great benefits to the economy;[14] China recently overtook the USA as the largest e-commerce market and, of the top ten Internet companies, six are from the USA and four are Chinese.

The government censors for subversive content. The 'Great Firewall' has been erected as a virtual boundary, selectively separating Chinese cyberspace from the outside. There is a system of Internet control and monitoring, blocking or filtering of selected information from outside China and censoring information inside.[15] Using both human power and software technologies, the 'Great Firewall' filters keywords and blocks selected foreign websites. Netizens find their way around these controls in creative ways.

There are two other aspects of Internet use that appear to be manifestations of particular cultural proclivities. One is that Internet literature has vastly expanded the field of creative writing and transformed publishing, in a fusion of the heritage of literary culture with modern technology. A thumbnail sketch of this is to be found on pp125-6. Secondly, as Yang suggests, the focus on airing grievances is 'very Chinese' and the way the Internet is used for this harks back to the tradition of big character posters or complaints and petitions gummed onto walls.[16]

4.2.1   The blogospheres

According to Xiao Qiang 萧强, Editor of *China Digital Times* 中国数字时代, blogging first appeared in China in 2002, when the Beijing technology writer Fang Xingdong 方兴东 coined the word bo ke 博客 for 'blogger' and encouraged his readers to register on blogger.com.[17] The number of weblogs has risen sharply in the past decade and in 2015 estimates put the number of active monthly bloggers

123

at upwards of 222 million.[18]

The earliest notable Chinese equivalent to Twitter was Fanfou 饭否, launched in May 2007, but closed down by the Chinese government after the 2009 Urumqi Riots, along with microblogging services not based in China, including Twitter. After the British riots of summer 2012, the British government toyed with doing the same with the latter, but desisted. One of the characteristics of microblogs that makes governments fearful is the speed with which information can be diffused[19] and the anonymity afforded to those viewed by authority as troublemakers.

Development has been rapid.[20] The number of microbloggers increased four-fold between 2012 and 2015.[21] Sina Weibo, the most popular microblogging site, has 140 million users, 50 million of them active monthly users, with 10 million new accounts opened each month.[22] Many opinion leaders have a blog or microblog account. The celebrity artist Ai Weiwei 艾未未 was recruited by Sina Weibo in 2005 and reportedly had 17 million readers until his blog was closed down in 2009.[23]

Several successful campaigns have been run on Sina's microblog service. At least one child was reunited with his parents after pictures of street children were uploaded to that site.[24] When the authorities tried to restrict release of the names of those killed by collapsing school buildings during the Sichuan Earthquake, Ai organised a crowd-sourcing exercise 公民调查 to reveal those names.[25] On a famous occasion when the new CCTV headquarters building caught fire, it was not the conventional media that reported it, but microbloggers.[26]

While surveys show that 85% of bloggers' comments concern personal matters[27] such as hobbies, pets or clothing,[28] political commentary is becoming increasingly common.[29] Several events in 2011 caused rashes of comments among Weibo users, expressing public outrage and criticism of officials.[30] In July a bullet train crashed at Wenzhou 温州, killing 40 people.[31] Within 10 days there had been 26 million comments from netizens, providing more accurate information than was conveyed by other media and denouncing the official handling of the matter.[32] In October 2011 there was an outcry in China when passers-by ignored a child who had been run over twice in the street and later died.[33] Later that year, news of unrest, sparked by a land dispute in the village of Wukan 乌坎村 in Guangdong, spread quickly on Weibo. Searches relating to the protest were later blocked.[34]

Microblogging is remarkable on account of its speed and scope and because it can be so concise; written Chinese, being pithy, is the ideal language for it. Short messages with links can spread like wildfire. The authorities have commanded sites/suppliers 'to monitor content and remove materials deemed sensitive. News media are banned from reporting online material before verification'.[35]

One of the most notable features of China's new media has been the number of scandals exposed by angry microbloggers. Netizens trawl for malpractice in order to expose corruption and abuse of power. This approach to investigating and exposing individuals has acquired the name 'Human Flesh Search' 人肉搜索. In one notorious and contested case, named after Guo Meimei 郭美美, a girl whose post of herself sparked a flesh search, there were accusations of misappropriation of Red Cross 中国红十字会 funding (see p158).[36] Members of Congress have used Social Media to campaign for budgetary transparency 预算透明度,[37] and there has been a national debate on the hukou 户籍 system[38] and its effect on children's education.[39] The Bo Xilai 薄熙来 case was discussed extensively until many posts were deleted.[40] Film director Zhang Yimou 张艺谋 was exposed as having broken family planning laws, after which he was convicted and fined.

To explain contradictory reports of apparently selective censorship, it is sometimes remarked that 'élite' people who blog or use Weibo encounter no difficulties from officials no matter what they write, while people who have good contacts among the authorities may find themselves censored but suffer no other repercussions. It is those at the bottom of society who are most at risk from vindictive officials and outraged censors. Others, however, point to the ways in which sympathy has been mobilised on behalf of 'nobodies', including a peasant youth ensnared by dishonest law enforcement officers trying to prove he was operating an illegal taxi service,[41] and a university applicant who failed to get into her chosen college because the admissions office had lost her application. After the publicity, she got into the college.[42]

Offline journalists in China often use blogs as an outlet for expressing the kind of views that cannot be aired in the traditional media, Chris Berry, specialist in Chinese films, puts it thus: 'We know that mainstream journalists run blogs in China very often precisely to have a space where they can say a little bit more than they can say in the *People's Daily* or wherever it is they work. The government would not tolerate them revealing something regarded as a state secret, but it will tolerate them discussing things a bit more online than it would on air'.[43] Thus blogs are not confined in the way that newspapers and television programmes are. There is more criticism, according to an analysis of 'almost 6,000 news articles from nine mainstream daily newspapers in Beijing, Shanghai and Guangzhou, and more than 500 news-related blog entries relating to these stories'.[44]

Although it is generally thought that Chinese officials pay attention to the blogosphere and take netizens' views into account when formulating policies,[45] it is not the case, according to Internet specialist Rebecca MacKinnon, that 'ordinary, articulate citizens' are significant. It is, rather, the small number of influential 'bridge bloggers' who are trusted to help interpret, and often translate, local online discourse, who matter.[46]

Web Literature[47]

Beside the hundreds of millions of web-users and the huge scope for access to information, censorship may be insignificant. Emphasising it might blind us to other, perhaps more important, particularities of the Chinese New Media.

One such is online novels. The first novel written for and published, in 1998, on the Internet was *My First Intimacy* 第一次的亲密接触 by Cai Zhiheng 蔡智恒. By 2009, there were reports on hits to websites amounting to several hundred million a day, and over several thousand writers composing. 'Qidian.com, 起点中文小说网, China's largest Internet literature website, has more than 36 million registered users and provides a huge amount of reading material. Average page-views per day often hit 400 million, which indicates that Internet novels are increasing in popularity.' Zhao Ganlü's *Elevator Encounter* 赵赶驴电梯奇遇记, 'which begins in a malfunctioning elevator, where the eponymous hero and his beautiful female colleague are temporarily stranded ... scored an impressive 100 million hits on the net'.

Web fiction includes science fiction, fantasy, horror, social critique and romance, An example of a fantasy/horror web hit, *The Ghost Blows Out the Light* 鬼吹灯, is about tomb robbers and combines fact, fiction and suspense.

In 2010, Chen Peng 陈鹏 published *Eilikochen: A Memoir of Living in Kyoto* 京都生活记 on Sina Weibo, becoming the inventor of the micro-novel. In 2011 Sinaheld a micro-novel essay contest, and initial entries rapidly surpassed 1.4 million articles, of which as many as 200,000 were micro-novel submissions. Not only were unknowns eager to submit their entries, but one after the other, well-established authors joined in too, and a few overseas compatriots tried their hands.

Online novels are usually serialised, and require payment of a reading fee per segment. For approximately 2,000 words that a reader clicks through, a fee of a few cents is charged, to be shared (in the case of Qidian and others) 70/30 between author and website. So as to earn higher royalties, online novels tend to be very long, well over several million words, and lasting for three to five years. Micro-novels, on the other hand, are free. The authors are limited to 140 words or less, which obliges them to turn their books from lengthy sagas with millions of words to something rather more concise.

Another genre, Internet essays, has caught leaders' attention. At a 2014 State Forum on Arts and Literature, President Xi praised and encouraged two young web writers, Zhou Xiaoping and Hua Qianfang. Zhou's works include: "Please Do Not Fail this Era!" (请不要辜负这个时代), "Your China, Your Party" (你的中国你的党) , "Youth, do you really know your country" (少年，你真的了解这个国家么). In Zhou's widely discussed "Nine Tricks of the United States Cultural Cold War" (美国对华文化战的九大绝招, 2014)he argues that United States uses the Internet to subvert China and its culture.

Hua's works are well known for carrying "positive energy" and conveying Chinese dream. His fictional "Our Journey Is The Ocean of Stars"(我们的征途是星辰大海)made his name, using internet language to retell modern history.

Content

Offline literature in the 1980s and 1990s was always critical, often iconoclastic, and ready to escape from the confines of the publishing industry. The trend away from paper publishing not only has influenced content but has also attracted authors to being published exclusively on the Internet, only later printed and placed on bookshop shelves. According to the Rome-based analyst, Serena Zuccheri, there is a great deal of rebellion against convention and authority, but although it might be subversive, it is not *samizdat*。 She writes: This current does know limitations and restrictions, but it is quite wrong to classify it as clandestine literature. By no means always does the web lend itself to clandestine narrative. Indeed, I would say that [] it operates as the mirror of a new epoch and a new generation, reflecting a country at the forefront and quite unafraid of change. Media censorship bothers itself with other matters.[48]

As to the audiences, web literature addresses itself to three distinct 'symbolic worlds': Greater China, Intellectual China and, especially, Diaspora China.

Under the Banyan Tree 榕树下 has become a market for editors and authors. It has its own radio programmes and conferences, literary prizes, partnership with *Shanghai Literary News* 上海文藝出版社 and sponsors. In 2002, Bertelsmann Book Club bought 65% of the site but it has since become part of the Shanda Group 盛大互动娱乐有限公司. It is claimed that readers' enthusiasm has brought profits for Internet writers too; in 2008, for example, one named 'I eat tomato' earned more than 2 million RMB while ten other Internet writers netted more than 1 million rmb [in one] year.

The consequences for society at large are interesting. The need for traditional literary journals is less; dependence upon contacts made through universities, societies and personal ties is less. Publishing houses can be circumvented. And what might have been stifled by the old modes of publishing is shooting through China - a literary renaissance.

4.2.2   Search engine Baidu

Just as China has established its own versions of social media, so it has its own search engines. Baidu 百度 handles more than 82% of all Internet searches in the PRC.[49] It was founded in 1999 by Li Yanhong 李彦宏, a graduate of Peking University who set up the website after returning home from working in the USA's Silicon Valley. It is now one of the world's richest Internet companies,[50] while Li is named the country's richest man.[51] He has become the inspiration for a new generation hoping to become Internet entrepreneurs.[52] Baidu was listed on the New York NASDAQ stock exchange in 2005.[53] In addition to its search engine function, Baidu offers chat rooms, music downloads, videos and an online shopping mall.[54] In 2015 it had around 190 million Monthly Unique Visitors, a market value of more than $72 billion and had nearly double the Internet search revenue of its main competitor, Google (China).[55] According to the *New York Times*, 'Baidu capitalised on the national fervour for chat and invented a tool that allows people to create instant discussion groups based on popular search queries. Now, when users search on baidu.com for the name of the basketball star Yao Ming 姚明, for example, they are shown not only links to news reports on his games; they are also able to join a chat room with thousands of others and argue about him. Baidu's chat rooms 百度贴吧 receive as many as five million posts a day'.[56]

Baidu makes it possible for Chinese Internet users to access foreign programming and news.[57] However, it 'has gained a reputation in the West for censoring search results, as well as for its tussles with major music labels over its controversial practice of "deep linking" to pirated music tracks hosted on other websites. In February, the US trade representative named Baidu as one of the world's "notorious markets" for piracy and copyright infringement'.[58] Notwithstanding this, Microsoft has contracted with it to offer users its English language search engine, Bing.[59] Google (China) has a 11% market share, compared with Baidu's 79% market share.[60]

There are more question marks over Baidu, especially since the death in 2016 of a cancer patient, Wei Zexi 魏则西。It is alleged that the hospital which treated Wei was at the least innappropriate. Wei's family had identified it from recommendations on Baidu, which is alleged by some to be irresponsible in its lucrative promotion of suspect companies, including hospitals. Baidu is being investigated by the Cyberspace Administration.

Other search engines include Panguso 盘古搜索, from Xinhua News Agency, China Mobile, and Jike 即刻搜索. Jike.com, established in 2010 by *People's Daily* and *People's Daily Online*, was re-launched in 2011 with the aim of competing with Baidu and becoming fully commercial and profitable.[61] It attracts criticism for bias and self-censorship.[62]

4.2.3 Relationship with foreign providers

Ever since Carl Crow published his *Four Hundred Million Customers*[63] in 1937, international businesses have longed to sew up the Chinese market. With over three times the number of mouths noticed by Crow, and a rapidly growing proportion of them on the Internet, the urge is still great.[64] But Microsoft Corp and others complain of numerous obstacles, among them of a lack of clarity and predictability when doing business with China,[65] and unhelpful foreign policies and regulations.

In 1999, Yahoo! introduced a Chinese language version of its website, with email and blogging, and set up an office in China. In 2000, Google also produced a Chinese language version, but from 2001 Baidu quickly overtook both.

Since 2002, Internet service providers have to agree to self-censor to be permitted to operate. Daniel Drezner, of Tufts, USA, School of Law and Diplomacy, states: 'Starting in 2000, China passed a series of laws criminalising the production or consumption of 'unauthorised' political content. In July 2002, China was able to persuade more than 300 Internet service providers and web portals, including Yahoo!, to sign a voluntary pledge promising to refrain from producing, posting, or disseminating pernicious information that may jeopardise state security and disrupt social stability. The central government also re-routed attempts to access search engines like Google to search engines owned or regulated by the government'.[66]

In 2004 a Hunan journalist, Shi Tao 师涛, used his Yahoo! account to leak a CPD instruction on how to deal with information on 'the 4th June event' (i.e., the Tiananmen Massacre) and other issues. He was arrested and sentenced to ten years in jail. Reporters Without Borders revealed that Yahoo! had handed over Shi's email address to the Chinese government.[67] In 2006, Google set up a Chinese version of its search engine, Google.cn, under an arrangement with the authorities that required it to delete search results on banned topics.[68] There was a great deal of adverse publicity about this decision in the Anglosphere. According to the *New York Times*, Google could not obtain an official list of blocked sites from the authorities, so it had to develop its own.[69] Following that, Microsoft obeyed a government request to close the blog of a well-known writer, Michael Anti (Zhao Jing 赵静), despite the its servers being based on foreign soil. Google eventually decided it could no longer struggle with the censorship rules; after attacks from Chinese hackers, the company announced in 2010 that it was moving its Internet search engine to Hong Kong. In 2012 Google stated that several of its online services had been blocked in mainland China, including its search engine and Gmail. Later that year, Google declared that it 'was changing its search service in China, so that it will warn users when they are using terms likely to trigger interference from the authorities, and suggest ways around the censorship'.[70]

Although Twitter remains generally blocked, access is possible. In March 2010, well-established blogger Lian Yue 连岳 began publishing a serialised novel on Twitter, reported as being the first Chinese language novel posted in this way.[71]

4.2.4   News

Since 2000, the net and mobile media have become ever more important information providers, commercial news websites separate from government have sprung up, and blogs, microblogs and other social media have become leading sources of news . Many people, especially the under 30s, access their news online not from online newspapers[72] but from portals such as Sina 新浪, NetEase (163.com) 网易, TencentQQ 腾迅 and Sohu.com 搜狐 which are owned and managed by private Internet companies. Most of these companies were set up in the 1990s with venture capital. Besides news portals, they all run other Internet services. NetEase's profit mainly comes from online gaming. TencentQQ has the instant messaging service QQ. These privately owned news portals respond to the market more quickly than websites owned by Party news groups *Chinanews* 中国新闻网 and *Xinhuanet* 新华网. Their flexibility tends to lead to bigger market shares: Sina now dominates the microblogging market in China, while TencentQQ has the biggest slice of the instant messaging business.

Since 2014, the major news organisations have launched mobile apps. Journalists can use their smartphones for online live broadcasting through social media platforms and apps, while audiences can send live comments and interact with journalists.

These operations have limitations placed upon them. According to the *Regulation on Publishing News on News Portals* 互联网站从事登载新闻业务管理暂行规定, comprehensive portals that are funded by non-news service providers may provide news already published by approved providers, but cannot publish news gathered by themselves or others.[73] They do, however, sometimes produce their own content on soft subjects such as lifestyle, health, sport and entertainment. They differentiate their wares by offering add-on services: NetEase 网易 with e-mail, Sina 新浪 with blogs and microblogs, and Tencent 腾讯 with its instant messaging service QQ.

The first successful portal in China, Sohu 搜狐, is still the nation's third most visited portal 门户 website. Established by a graduate of Massachusetts Institute of Technology, it provides a search engine and online video gaming 线上游戏, along with other services.[74]

In summary, the Chinese increasingly access news in different ways from those in the Anglosphere, through large commercial providers which do not source their own news but pay for its provision to customers by selling other services.

4.2.5   Social networking

People in China spend about 6% of their time social networking, via sites such as TencentQQ, Sina Weibo, Tencent Weibo, Renren 人人网 and Kaixin 开心网. The leader is QQ, with over 286 million users, who register using their real identities.[75] Kaixin and RenRen were leaders until 2010, when they were overtaken by Sinaweibo. Tencent QQ has the biggest free instant messaging system. Weixin, introduced above, is used by hundreds of millions, either as individuals or in groups. The author's work unit consists of 8 core members, whose weixin group 微信朋友圈, set up 7 years ago, is used to obviate meetings, deliver instructions, verbalise or write messages, review documents and share ideas and concerns. Many other groups are set up annually to work with the managers of specific projects. Chinese students have long had their own worldwide groups. Around 900 million now have a QQ account, which also gives them access to QQ's many other services, including games and blogs.[76]

130

4.3   Participation in politics

In the eighteenth- and nineteenth-century Anglosphere, the wide diffusion of printing enlarged the numbers of those with access to information and education, enabling more people to join the public sphere and sometimes even to be connected with what we would now call the 'policy world'. These effects were not immediate, although they happened much faster than in the culturally distinct areas of mainland Europe. The gradually acquired freedom to talk and write paved the way for the electoral democracy that would institutionalise the participative society.

The Anglophone political classes have had high expectations of New Media as agents of political change elsewhere. The 'Arab Spring' was for a time taken as proof of its efficacy in undermining unsatisfactory governments.[77] Since then, thoughtful studies of the matter from several different angles, published in the edited book *New media, old news: journalism and democracy in the digital age*, came to the more sober conclusion that the political significance of New Media is overstated and their influence on existing channels of political communication detrimental.[78] The mere capacity to communicate and to create networks, and the ability of previously voiceless people to communicate, are not the whole story. The delivery, diffusion of and access to information may be even more important drivers of change, particularly when people have more time available and are better informed, in part thanks to the Internet. The dissatisfaction felt in most countries with their politicians is surely related not only to their mistakes or corruptibility, but to the self-empowerment gifted by the Internet. Just as citizens can, unless prevented by regulations, bypass traditional gatekeepers such as physicians and lawyers by informing themselves from the Internet, so many question the expertise of professional politicians, preferring the opinions of specialists to those of gatekeepers. The latter may often be less knowledgeable than they are themselves.

New Media are involving ever more people in debate and discussion. The speed and simplicity of microblogging 'has helped netizens to publicise and express their discontent'.[79] Harvard researchers have found that, 'Contrary to previous understandings, posts with negative, even vitriolic, criticism of the state, its leaders, and its policies are not more likely to be censored.' What gets the censors goat, is, rather, anything likely to mobilise people to collective action.[80] Whether this amounts to a 'public sphere' is a question explored in Chapter 5.

In a considered examination of the ways in which social media might be influencing politics, Lars Willnat, from the US University of Kentucky, and colleagues find that there is evidence that more Internet use is associated with higher levels of political engagement. [81]

Online news portals and websites in rank order

1	腾讯网	Tencent	www.qq.com
2	搜狐	Sohu	www.sohu.com
3	新浪	Sina	www.sina.com.cn
4	网易	163	www163.com
5	凤凰网	Ifeng	www.ifeng.com
6	新华网	Xinhuanet	www.xinhuanet.com
7	中华网：	China.com	www.china.com
8	人民网	People	www.people.com.cn
9	央视网	cntv	www.cntv.cn
10	中国网	China.com	www.china.com.cn
11	东方网	Eastday	www.eastday.com
12	和讯网	Hexun	www.hexun.com
13	中国新闻网	Chinanews	www.chinanews.com
14	大众网	dazhong	http://www.dzwww.com/
15	红网	rednet	www.rednet.cn

Since 2016, with the increasing use of smart phones, less and less people access news from websites. Reading news from Apps or from the wechat channel has become usual among all age groups

In China, the form which political engagement is likely to take is joining the CCP. Willnat explains that 'claims that social media are altering the balance of power between the Chinese government and the public often are unsupported…'.[82] Quite so. In one study of reactions to the dismissal of the CCP Secretary of the city of Shanghai, it was found that only about one in 10 posts were critical of the government's actions. 'The Internet in this case was hardly subversive'.[83] It could, however, be argued that although text messages may not be directly politically subversive, they are culturally and ideologically subversive because they undermine the monopoly of ideas. Willnat and co note that this has not been tested empirically.[84]

There are ways in which Social Media may influence politics other than by increasing participation in debate. Observers believe that the authorities pay attention to what is being said, especially when they think it reflects widespread dissatisfaction. Although they know that bloggers are mathematically unrepresentative, they suspect that they might easily take their protests further, and they are acutely aware that they may have large followings. Former US minister and China specialist Susan Shirk suggests that authoritarian governments are particularly likely to take bloggers into account because they do not have elections and other kinds of polls to warn them of popular unease.[85]

The politics focus of Western academics may be misplaced. The ways in which social media affect netizens' lives as friends, lovers, consumers, dog owners, temple-goers or workers are arguably more important. Willnat points to a potentially fruitful line of inquiry by writing that '…instead of assuming direct effects of online usage on political change in China, we need to pay more attention to social and cultural factors that might interfere in such a relationship'.[86]

4.3.1   Nationalism

The War of Biaoqingbao 表情包大战 took place in 2016. It was an emotional campaign against the Taiwan Independence movement, organised through Baidu's largest message board 贴吧, with 20 million members. Teams divided up tasks. There were those collecting information about the pro-independence side, teams making stickers, translation teams, monitoring Facebook teams, recruiting teams and so on.[87] Accusations against foreign governments that they were colluding in Taiwan independence had those governments responding against the fake news.

There had been precedents for this kind of campaign. In 2008, riots in Tibet and Tibetan areas of China were supported by demonstrators around the world. They were orchestrated through the Internet. The same would be true of riots in Xinjiang the following year, 'despite all the surveillance technologies to which the state has access'.[88] The rioters held that China was a colonial power wrongfully oppressing the indigenes. The government countered that the riots were either the expression of hooligan elements or were orchestrated by secessionists abroad. Demonstrations disrupted the Olympic torch relay which was taking place in many countries, and they fired the anger of Chinese students in the West, who used social media to mobilise their own protests against Tibetan expatriates and their supporters.

On the web, students established a website especially to expose what they regarded as the propaganda and distortions of the 'Western media' about Tibet, and prejudice against China generally. It was named anti-cnn.com.[89] In effect, they co-ordinated a global event which has 'driven the Chinese government to stress the Tibet issue in its diplomacy with the United States, Europe and other countries'.[90]

From this and other cases, we have learnt what Chinese netizens think, and whether it accords with the views of their leaders. Nationalist views have been very evident, with attitudes to France (over the Olympics), Japan (over the Diaoyu

Islands and school textbooks which allegedly whitewash militarism) and the USA (reconnaissance plane and other provocations[91]) expressed far more vehemently than in the conventional media. Pre-Social Media, some observers had thought that fervid expressions of nationalism were organised by the political class, but they soon realized their mistake.

4.3.2 Ideological defiance

Social Media have provided opportunities for challenges to the CCP's 'northern narrative' that the Party and nation are one and that love of country equals love of Party. Ma Yiben notes that it is Internet historians who have re-evaluated the Nationalist Party (KMT)'s role in the Anti-Japanese War.[92] This has been a portentous development, because it has undermined the boast that the CCP was the sole hero of the conflict. Historians outside China have long questioned CCP claims, stating that the brunt of the fighting was borne by the KMT. CCP legitimacy is based upon its history as 'liberator' from imperialism and capitalism, as much as upon its providing stability and growth. The re-evaluation has made this tendentious.

Other issues are raised by people accessing differing versions of events. Li Xiguang 李希光 has pointed out that, under present conditions, the public 'can reconstruct and revise the official media accounts of events in ways that directly challenge the version of political reality presented by the mainstream press'.[93] The case he uses to illustrate his point is a notorious incident in which a US reconnaissance aircraft collided with a Chinese aircraft over Chinese territory. Before the mainstream media had featured the incident, the AP report had already been posted on a Peoples' Daily website *Strong Country Forum* 强国论坛 (SCF) and a busy discussion ensued. Very soon, Chinese websites and chat rooms were full of information lifted and cross-posted from Western sources.

Some 11 days later, the *People's Daily* printed the Chinese President's statement concerning the USA's 'letter of regret', indicating that it served as an apology. The public, however, was at odds with the President's interpretation of the letter. 55 per cent of postings on the forum argued that, in truth, the American government had not apologised to China, even though this was a precondition set by the Chinese government for the release of the American pilot. Credence was given to this claim when US media reported that their President and Secretary of State denied apologizing, contradicting the official Chinese position.

After these reports were posted on SCF, over 90% of postings indicated disbelief of the Chinese government.[94] Some stated that there had been a betrayal by officials who, benefiting personally from US-China trade, wished to smooth everything over. A further point made by Li[95] is that contributors to the online debate may have included overseas Chinese with access to other news sources, which may thus have been influencing the Chinese political agenda. After all, the SCF is a subsidiary of the main Party organ, yet it has become a site on which the Party's interpretations are disputed.

Human Flesh Search

While the Anglophone world worries about cyberbullying, cyberharassment and internet defamation, and how these unpleasant phenomena can be policed and their perpetrators brought to account, China has given birth to a form of investigation which can have devastating effects on the target and which may influence how we all project ourselves: Human Flesh Search 人肉搜索 (HFS).

The use of all available means to expose titillating aspects of a person who has somehow come to the attention of journalists is familiar, but HFS goes further, in that it involves the collaboration of many, perhaps multitudes, of people, crowd sourcing data with the intention of humiliating the victim. Sometimes the target may be deserving of exposure if he or she has abused office or been dishonest; but cyber exposure is not a court of law, there is little opportunity for self defence.

The paradigm case is that of a civil servant called Yang Dacai, Director of Work Safety in Shaanxi on August 30th 2012. Attending a traffic accident which involved many deaths and grievous injuries, he was photographed by bystanders at some point smiling. Posted on the web, the pictures of him smiling infuriated netizens who took this as a sign of callousness; they proceeded to subject Yang to HFS. Checking various photographs against each other, the searchers found him wearing a variety of different, very expensive, watches. They opined that he could not possibly have bought them on his salary and deduced corruption. These accusations caused the Discipline Inspection Commission to start an investigation into Yang and his assets; after the investigation was concluded Yang was dismissed.

Yang was not the first official to been drawn to the attention of netizens through an apparently innocuous event. In 2008 the Head of the Land Office in Nanjing made some comments about the property market that raised netizens' ire; he became a HFS target and it was found that he owned more than could reasonably be explained such that the Commission investigated him and eventually he was sentenced to 11 years in prison on conviction for bribery. Others have been punished following photographs of their high jinks being posted on the internet.

Li concluded that 'Chinese citizens turned to the news sources of the very nation with which they were in conflict for information on how to interpret events. Setting the press and public agenda for another country through media and the Internet has become a new form of "soft power" in international politics'.[96]

Those overseas Chinese suspected by Li may include many of the most severe critics of China, among them the Falungong, the prohibited meditation sect, whose newspaper claims to have distributed one of its texts to 2.3m Chinese users, and drawn 15 million into its campaign to renounce CCP membership.[97] There are now innumerable critics of Chinese politicians, using Social Media from abroad, of which the most famous at the time of writing is probably the property tycoon Guo Wengui 郭文贵 who specialises in attacking Wang Qishan 王岐山, Secretary of the Central Committee for Discipline Inspection.

Another phenomenon which undermines official accounts is the capacity of social media to 'upscale', that is, to take events or issues that are local and turn them, rapidly, into national or international ones. Ai Weiwei 艾未未 and his criticisms have become globally famous because of cyberspace. Tibetan radicals may be defeated physically but they can continue their struggle through the Internet, organising protests around the world. The Internet makes widespread exposure possible, expands the numbers involved in debates, mobilises, and facilitates alliances.[98]

4.4   Government reaction

Professor of Film, Chris Berry, suggests that 'nobody in China turns on the mainstream media expecting to find a surprise. So there's an intensity around the Internet in China that doesn't quite exist in the West, because there isn't a demand for it in the same way'.[99] While the government has encouraged the Internet at all stages and seen digital developments as essential to China's intellectual and material economies, it has also shown a not necessarily successful determination to strengthen control, and has threatened to punish people who spread 'harmful' information online.[100] As we will see in Chapter 6, pornography, incitement to crime and gambling are targets, as are damaging rumours and political opposition. In many areas, social media users are required to 'register their real names' 实名制 on accounts.[101] This is not, however, a uniquely Chinese phenomenon, it seems that Internet anonymity may be doomed the world over for a variety of reasons.[102]

The challenge has not been met only by tightening controls. The authorities themselves participate in New Media. State and Party organs are well represented on the Internet; most national and local government organs and their subsidiaries have websites, Sinaweibo blogs and weixin accounts. By the end of 2012 there were more than 176,000 Party or government micro blogs.[103] 60% of web-users in China report having used them to express opinions intended to 'supervise' government activities.[104] If you want to get advice on living safely in the capital or to see the latest doings of the police on video, you could do worse than access *Peaceful Beijing* 平安北京. A State Council app, launched in 2016, was announced as a channel for government/citizen interaction and way of getting the public involved in government decision-making and in providing feedback on draft policies.[105]

There has been much talk of accountability and transparency, which might never have taken place without the Internet. Moreover, initiatives such as Freedom of Information legislation, the conducting of opinion polls, putting information about local government decision-making on the web, and instituting press conferences all imply that functionaries should modify their work style to an ever-more co-operative one.

Internet Development

1987	First Internet connection
1999	2% of citizens are web users
2000	The three largest web portals, Sohu 搜狐, Sina 新浪 and NetEase 网易, are listed on the NASDAQ 纳斯达克
2004 Jul	87 million web users; rate of increase 27.9%
2005 Dec	Internet population surpasses 100 million
2008 Jul	253 million web users, China surpasses US in total web users
	350 million cell phones
	300 million blogs
2009 Dec	384 million web users: i.e., 28.9% of citizens are web users; 233 million Internet users access Internet on a mobile phone, accounting for 60.8% of total Internet population
2011	513 million web users
	356 million people using mobile phone to connect to Internet
	917 million mobile phone subscribers
	Internet is prime source of information for 85% of citizens in China
	cf 66% for television and 61% newspapers
2012 Dec	564 million web users: i.e., 42.1% of citizens are web users
	420 million people use mobile phone to connect to Internet
	309 million people have microblog accounts, of which 202 million access their accounts on mobile phone
	242 million people use online shopping
2013 Jul	Users 591 million,44.1%: Mobile phone reached 464 million, 78.5%: rural users 27.9%, 165 million. The total number of domain names was 14.7 million, The total number of Chinese sites rose to 2.94 million
2014 Jan	Users 618 million, 45.8%: Mobile phone users reached 500 million, 81.0%. The proportion of companies using office computers was 93.1%, the proportion of Internet use was 83.2%. The proportion of online sales, online purchases were 23.5% and 26.8%, using the Internet to carry out marketing activities was 20.9%
2014 Jul	Users 632 million, 46.9%: Mobile phone users reached 527 million, 83.4%. The proportion of Primary, Secondary education and below in the Internet users was 12.1%, rose 0.2 percentage points compared to the end of 2013, while the proportion of college and above declined 0.3 percentage points.
2015 Jan	Users 649 million, 47.9%; Mobile phone users reached 557 million, 85.8%; tablet usage reached 34.8%; TV Internet usage is 15.6%.60.0% of Chinese Internet users holds positive attitude for sharing behavior on the Internet; 43.8% users said they liked to comment on the Internet; 53.1% users think they are relatively or very dependent on the Internet.
2015 Jul	Users 668 million, 48.8%: Mobile phone users reached 594 million, 88.9%.
2016 Jan	Users 688 million, 50.3%: Mobile phone users reached 620 million, 90.1%.
2016 June	Users 710 million, 51.7%: Mobile phone users 92.5%

A study carried out among Hangzhou officials[106] suggests that social media could be the catalyst for such change. Asked about the deluge of denunciation on the web, respondents spoke of engagement, not suppression; of transforming emotion into reason, of dealing with the negative, and of accepting the right of the media to investigate ('netizens have every right to criticise'). As one of them put it, 'what we want to learn is how to create participation and conversation, how to avoid confrontation'. Communication between government and the governed was now presented as a matter of how to share information and encourage participation. One put the matter succinctly: 'In the past we told people what to think; now we think things through together'. [107]

Such is the predicament of well-meaning officials as they grapple with the New Media and information environment. Given the Party's ultimate power over the means and content of communication, plus the authoritarian tradition, their ability to build the new relationships that they predict may be limited.

4.5   Transformation of offline media

The diversifications and adjustments noted above have had an impact on the offline media too. The activist Liu Xiaobo 刘晓波 wrote in his essay, 'The Internet and I':[108]

'Internet opinion has gradually become the main force of monitoring and supervising by opinion. Whenever there is a major public disaster, the broad Internet opinions will more or less influence the attitudes of the traditional media and the government. First, Internet opinion is pressing the other media to be more open and diversified in providing information. An important indicator of the degree of openness of any media is whether they can keep up with Internet information and opinion. Next, the government can control the traditional media, but they cannot control the Internet in total. The scandals that are censored in the traditional media are disseminated through the Internet to form a powerful Internet opinion and the government has to be concerned about the hearts and minds of the people. Therefore, they have to open up the release of information in certain areas, and the scandal-affected officials may have to appear in public to apologise to the victims' families and society as a whole.'[109]

Youku 优酷, the Chinese version of YouTube, carries many popular television shows and is a major competitor to other platforms Films and television series are increasingly made for the web, transforming entertainment and children's viewing. Video websites pay more than broadcasters for good drama and entertainment shows, and this is reportedly causing panic among the traditional media. Online TV entrepreneur Li Fa says: 'Although New Media are gobbling up the content of conventional media, they still need more content. In our country there has emerged the phenomenon of very high prices being paid for television drama. It seems that one episode can demand a million RMB just for one transmission on New Media. This price is much higher than that paid for airing on TV. Why? Because there is so much hot money invested in New Media. They are wealthy enough to use this cash to acquire dramas. If the industry was permitted willy-nilly to buy foreign film products, they'd go at it like crazy; it's because they so badly lack content, are so deficient in creative matter that they are in such intense competition with the TV companies'.[110]

Internet Memes

Memes, or ideas, pictures or expressions that transfer from blog to blog are thought to be particularly virulent in China because the language, with its innumerable homophones and evocative forms combines with a particularly ironical cast of mind.

River Crab 河蟹;	Homophone for harmonious, as in Harmonious Society 和谐, euphemism for censorship.
Are you happy today? 今天你幸福么？	CCTV reporters did a programme series investigating peoples' views on life and had the habit of asking what later became regarded as an absurd question.
Though I don't understand, I think its great! 不明觉厉	Used in Chaw Sing-Chi 周星驰's film The God of Cookery, it has come to be used in fake admiration of meaningless talk.
I'm off to buy a watch 我去买个表 or WQNMLGB	The Chinese expression 我去你玛勒隔壁 suggests you are going to have sexual relations with your interlocutor's loved one. The romanised logogram is also spelt WQNMLGB
check the water meter 查水表	In a TV series the police pretended to be checking the meter in order to gain entry. Now the expression refers to internet police.
I took an arrow in the knee 直膝箭	From a TV series, in which a character said he used to be an adventurer, until…… Now means some dramatic turn of fate.
绿茶婊 Green tea bitch	A girl who seems pure and honest but is a calculating go getter.
何弃疗 Why give up treatment?	Suggests your interlocutor is sick.
Yuan Fang, what do you make of it? 元芳, 你怎么看	In the TV series about Judge Dee, his colleague Yuan Fang is always asked what he reckons and Yuan responds, Sir I feel there's something strange going on.大人，我觉得此事有蹊跷
Brother Watch 表哥	A corrupt official (after an official who had a $10,000 watch)
Grab the luggage and run 细软跑	Used to describe the censors
草泥马 Grass Mud Horse	Pun on a crude expression, used to poke fun at censorship

Foreign shows are available on video content-sharing websites.[111] CCTV, Xinhua, China National Radio and China Radio International are the leading webcasters,[112] of which Xinhua is the provider of the most webcast news programmes.[113]

Since 2013, 4th generation technology has been widely used in mobile networks. Together with wider availability of Wi-Fi, this has led to more and more people consuming video content on mobile devices, so long as operators price access appropriately, and this is gradually changing the media scene.[114] China aims to be world leader in 5th generation technology.

One other development needs a mention, live streaming. There is now an industry of self made entertainment programmes. About 344million citizens follow live streams through apps such as Yingke Live 映客直播 and Miyou Live 蜜柚直播. Online hosts sing, dance and flirt with the audience through webcams, and the audience sends virtual gifts from watermelons and flowers to yachts and resorts which cost up to 3000 yuan each. Content varies from comedy to gross vulgarity, and even includes cosmetic surgery. In April 2016, the Ministry of Culture launched an examination of the industry with a view to banning live streaming platforms involved in pornographic, violent, gambling and crime inciting contents.

4.6   Afterword

In 2014 and 2015 China hosted the first World Internet Conference 世界互联网大, disdaining Anglophone criticisms and showing China to be a path breaker in cyberspace. Which it is. In a short space of time, Chinese have become the most intense users of New Media, comprise the world's biggest ecommerce market and are innovators in mobile services, with a vibrant online culture.

Chinese cyberspace constitutes a distinct but connected universe. To the extent that the government can manage it, the population is shielded from the foreign owned. Google, Twitter, Facebook, Instagram and Youtube are not invited to the party. The Head of the new Cyberspace Administration, Lu Wei, has repeatedly said 'I can choose who will be a guest in my home'.[115] He and his colleagues see the ownership of Internet businesses as an important determinant of the kind of ideological messages they convey, and they do not want foreign propaganda. Moreover, the Snowden affair[116] in which an American intelligence officer revealed details of US government interference in other countries, has made it credible to accuse the USA of being the greatest threat to Internet security, reinforcing China's position on 'Internet sovereignty'.

Some of the blockages – of Googlemail for example – affect people adversely: businesses selling overseas, students seeking to study abroad or researchers wanting to know what's going on in their field elsewhere.[117] This is frustrating but not a ruinous price to pay for being protected, or at least that's how one businessman put it.

Evgeny Morozov, the Belarussian writer on technology,[118] argues (mainly thinking of Russia) that from the perspective of those in power, there is much less to fear from their citizens' access to foreign media than they and their critics realize. This is partly because hostile or contradictory material is often discounted once it is easily available, and partly because politically subversive material forms a miniscule part of the vast flood of communication.

To some extent, both the state-inspired advance of the Internet and the authoritarian regulation of it reflect the political culture. This leads on to the question of whether such regulation limits critical thinking and poses a barrier to economic growth. From recent experience, it would not seem that it does, belying the assumptions of critics of the 90s who suggested that innovation and commercial success would be forestalled unless China become more democratic. In many fields – laser technology is often cited – Chinese ingenuity is at the global forefront.

The Chinese Internet reflects the culture in all its gregariousness and enthusiasm for interpersonal relationships and networks. But the media will also change that culture, although it is difficult to predict how. If the officials interviewed are to be believed, the relationship between governors and the governed is changing, moving towards a less hierarchical, perhaps even 'cooperative' model.

Will this have a fundamental influence on China's polity? It may well do, but only in the long-term and only if the government and Party fail to adapt their workstyle to the new realities. Yang Guobin 杨国斌 suggests that the nature of New Media is partly responsible for a different way of talking about current affairs. He contrasts the idealism, religiosity and intransigence of the 1989 protestors and their precursors way back to 1919, with the tone of commentary on the Internet. Online activism, he writes, is 'prosaic and playful'.[119] My own interpretation is that, as societies become both more secure economically and more participatory, the attraction of millenarianism ('Western democracy now!' 'Down with capitalists!') wanes and people think in terms of gradual, incremental reform rather than revolution. Things have been getting better in China, and as the sense of urgency evaporates, so extremism decreases. Perhaps people have learnt something from the disasters of the twentieth century – that revolutions invariably produce situations worse than what went before. New Media make citizens of netizens, draw them into the political world and give them a certain power over those in authority to the extent that Bai Yansong 白岩松 and other leading commentators on public affairs have referred to 'rule by media' 媒治. Transparency is being forced upon the governors, and they can be held to account and made to behave well as never before. As Bai Yansong has said: 'From rule by man to rule by law is progress, but there is still a long way to go from rule by media to rule by law'.[120]

If Chinese society was always particularly prone to networking and privileging interpersonal communication, the Internet has strengthened those predilections and empowered more and more people. For information they no longer need to rely on state media, and expertise is at a discount. Perhaps Chinese society, composed, as the anthropologists tell us, of innumerable interconnecting networks, was made for the digital world.

Notes

[1] de Burgh H. Verso la pagoda della gru gialla con il nostro ombrello bucherellato: riflessioni sul futuro dei media cinesi. Lecture given at *Universita degli Studi*, Milan; 27 December 2012.

[2] China Dialogue. Xiamen PX: a turning point? [Online]. 2008 [cited 11 February 2013]. Available at: http://www.chinadialogue.net/article/show/single/en/1626-Xiamen-PX-a-turning-point- (Accessed: 17 March 2016).

[3] Mason, Paul (2014) Striking Chinese workers are using 21st century tools to fight poverty and sweated labour. *The Guardian,* 15 September 2014, pp 5.

[4] See Karatzogianni, Athina and Robinson, Andrew (2015) A cyberconflict analysis of Chinese dissidents focusing on civil society, mass incidents and labour resistance. In: Rawnsley Gary D. and Rawnsley, Ming-Yeh T. (eds.) *Routledge Handbook of Chinese Media*, London: Routledge, for examples of how protests launched through the Internet have had results: protest against the building of a petrochemical plant in Ningbo was successful in forcing cancellation of the project within two days pp 225; a protest against the extension of a train line, which would reduce house values and pose a health risk; a hardline drive to enforce the one child policy in Guangxi resulted in protests which led to the reversal of policies; in Wukan energetic resistance to land seizures by resulted not only in the policy being reversed but also the villages be allowed to elect their own leaders pp 229.

[5] Herrman, John and Isaac, Mike (2016) Allegations of bias at Facebook stir backlash across the political spectrum in International New York Times, May 11, 2016 p19; Rutenberg, Jim (2016) Crisis at Facebook only highlights its power, *International New York Times*, Monday, May 23, 2016, p13

[6] Mullins, Brody and Nicas, Jack (2017) Google's Quiet Influence Campaign, in *The Wall Street Journal*, July 12, 2017, pp1, A6.

[7] Cited in Yang Guobin (2012) Chinese Internet? History, practice, and globalization. *Chinese Journal of Communication,* vol 5, no1, March 2012, pp 50.

[8] Ibid., pp 49 to 54.

[9] Beech, Hannah (2015) The other side of the great firewall, London. *Time Magazine,* pp 27. [Online]. Available at: http://intca.org/china-great-firewall/ (Accessed: 7 March 2016).

[10] Guo, Zhengbiao et al (2011) 'Sina Microblog: An Information-driven Online Social Network'. *International Conference on Cyberworlds*, Banff: IEEE, pp 160-167.

[11] Shi, Baoyin and Qi, Xin (2015) Henan judges conduct trials on WeChat. *China Daily*, 124/01/16, pp 4 (at Zhengzhou Intermediate Peoples' Court).

[12] Yang (2012), pp 50.

[13] The National Internet Information Office 国家互联网信息办公室 was separated off from the SCIO and made accountable to the State Council directly in May 2011. It was to advance the legal framework for Internet communication, support the development of news websites , and regulate traffic, including gaming and videos. Its first Director was Wang Chen 王晨. The SIO was subsumed into the CAC in 2014, and no longer exists as an independent entity.

[14] See, for example, *China Daily* on 16 December 2015 'Intertwining with traditional sectors to be key', pp C5 and other articles in the same section which assess the influence of the Internet on the economy, or predict its future.

[15] Yang (2012), pp 52.

[16] Ibid., pp 50.

[17] Qiang, Xiao. The 'blog' revolution sweeps across China. *New Scientist.* 24 November 2004.

[18] Available at: http://data.weibo.com/report/reportDetail?id=304 (Accessed: 6 January 2016).

[19] Sullivan, J. (2013) China's Weibo: is faster different? *New Media & Society.* 7 February 2013, pp 1-14.

[20] Barboza, D and Rusli, EM. (2011) Chinese site lists in US and its shares soar 29 per cent. *New York Times.* [Online]. 5 May 2011. Available at: http://dealbook.nytimes.com/2011/05/04/renren-raises-730-million/ (Accessed: 17 March 2016)

[21] Available at: http://data.weibo.com/report/reportDetail?id=304 (Accessed: 6 January 2016.

[22] Kiss, J. (2011) Weibo: the Chinese Twitter that dwarfs Twitter. *The Guardian.* [Online]. 15 July 2011. Available at: http://www.guardian.co.uk/technology/pda/2011/jul/15/weibo-twitter-china (Accessed: 17 March 2016).

[23] Berg, D and Strafella, G. A (2012) Twitter bodhisattva: Ai Weiwei's media politics. *Conference on Modes of Activism and Engagement in the Chinese Public Sphere.* Singapore: Asia Research Institute; 2012.

[24] Branigan, T. (2011) Web campaign aids search for China's lost children. *The Guardian.* 10 February 2011.

[25] Grube, K. (2009) Ai Weiwei challenges China's government over earthquake. [Online]. *ArtAsia Pacific*, 62. 2009 [cited 5 September 2013]. Available at: http://artasiapacific.com/Magazine/64/AiWeiweiChallengesChinasGovernmentOverEarthquake (Accessed: 17 March 2016).

[26] Sullivan, J. (2012) A tale of two microblogs in China. *Media, Culture & Society.* 2012; 3, pp 775.

[27] CNNIC reports. [Online]. [cited 3 September 2013]. Examples Available at: http://www1.cnnic.cn/IDR/ReportDownloads/201302/P020130221391269963814.pdf (Accessed: 17 March 2016).

[28] MacKinnon, R. (2008) Blogs and China correspondence: lessons about global information flow. *Chinese Journal of Communication*, October 2008; 1(2), pp 247.

[29] MacKinnon, R. (2011) China's 'networked authoritarianism'. *Journal of Democracy.* 2011; 22 (2), pp 5-16.

[30] Simpson, P. (2012) Chinese Internet users surge past half a billion. *Daily Telegraph.* [Online]. 17 January 2012. Available at: http://www.telegraph.co.uk/news/worldnews/asia/china/9019908/Chinese-Internet-users-surges-past-half-a-billion.html. (Accessed: 17 March 2016).

[31] China completes Wenzhou bullet train crash probe. *BBC News.* [Online]. 2011 [cited 29 January 2012]. Available at: http://www.bbc.co.uk/news/world-asia-china-16064581. (Accessed: 17 March 2016).

[32] Wu Changchang 'Micro-blog and the speech act of China's middle class: The 7.23 train accident case' in *Javnost : Communication and Class Divide in China*, Vol. 19 - 2012, No. 2, pages: 43-62. The author cites various other studies.

[33] Outcry in China over hit-and-run toddler left in street. *BBC News.* [Online]. 2011 [cited 29 January 2012]. Available at: http://www.bbc.co.uk/news/world-asia-pacific-15331773. (Accessed: 17 March 2016).

[34] China protest in Guangdong's Wukan 'vanishes from web'. *BBC News.* [Online]. 2011 [cited 29 January 2012]. Available at: http://www.bbc.co.uk/news/world-asia-china-16192541. (Accessed: 17 March 2016).

[35] Yu S. (2011) China Mobile eyes data goldmine: firm looks to tap potential revenue from SMS and Internet use as it attracts more subscribers. *South China Morning Post.* 14 October 2011.

[36] CNN.com. [Online]. 2011. Available at:http://articles.cnn.com/2011-07-06/world/china.redcross_1_netizens-china-red-cross-society-posts?_s=PM:WORLD.

[37] ChinaDaily.com. [Online]. 2012. Available at: http://www.chinadaily.com.cn/opinion/2012-10/23/content_15838082.htm) (Accessed: 17 March 2016); child abduction has been highlighted

(http://www.ministryoftofu.com/2011/02/chinese-professor-creates-microblog-to-end-child-abduction-and-forced-child-beggars/).

[38] Hukou is household registration denomination. Some European countries have household registration, tying citizens to their place of birth, but no longer has this the implications, for entitlement of education or benefits, of the Chinese system.

[39] ChinaDaily.com.cn. [Online]. 2012. Available at: http://bbs.chinadaily.com.cn/thread-814728-1-1.html. (Accessed: 17 March 2016).

[40] *BBC News*. [Online]. Available at: http://www.bbc.co.uk/news/world-asia-china-20765530 (Accessed: 17 March 2016).

[41] East South West North. The Shanghai illegal cab entrapment case. [Online]. 2009 [cited 3 September 2013]. Available at: http://www.zonaeuropa.com/20091025_1.htm. (Accessed: 17 March 2016).

[42] http://www.chinadaily.com.cn/china/2010-08/23/content_11186265.htm . [Online]. 23 August 2010 [cited 3 September 2013]. (Accessed: 17 March 2016).

[43] Berry C. Personal communication to Helen Briggs; 18 January 2012.

[44] Esarey A, Qiang Xiao (2011) Digital communication and political change in China. *International Journal of Communication*. 2011; 5, pp 298-319.

[45] MacKinnon R. (2008) Blogs and China correspondence: lessons about global information flow. *Chinese Journal of Communication*. October 2008; 1(2), pp 252.

[46] MacKinnon R. (2008) Blogs and China correspondence: lessons about global information flow. *Chinese Journal of Communication*. October 2008; 1(2), pp 242.

[47] I am obliged to Professor Michel Hockx for reading and commenting on this section.

[48] Zuccheri, Serena (2009) *Letteratura web in Cina* (Web literature in China) Rome: Nuove Edizioni Romane

[49] Perez, B. (2011) Baidu aims to promote Chinese interests in global web body. *South China Morning Post*. 15 September 2011.

[50] Barboza, D. (2011) Baidu to invest $306m in travel search site. *New York Times*. [Online]. 24 June 2011 [cited …]. Available at: http://dealbook.nytimes.com/2011/06/24/baidu-invests-306-million-in-travel-search-engine/?ref=baeducominc. (Accessed: 17 March 2016).

[51] Barboza, D. and Rusli, EM. (2011) Chinese site lists in US and its shares soar 29 per cent. *New York Times*. [Online]. 5 May 2011. Available at: http://dealbook.nytimes.com/2011/05/04/renren-raises-730-million/. (Accessed: 17 March 2016).

[52] Mi M. Personal communication to Helen Briggs; 27 Janaury 2012.

[53] *New York Times*. Baidu Inc. [Online] 2010 [cited 23 January 2012]. Available at: http://topics.nytimes.com/top/news/business/companies/baiducom-inc/index.html?scp=1&sq=Baidu%20China&st=cse. (Accessed: 17 March 2016).

[54] *New York Times*. Baidu Inc. [Online] 2010 [cited 23 January 2012]. Available at: http://topics.nytimes.com/top/news/business/companies/baiducom-inc/index.html?scp=1&sq=Baidu%20China&st=cse. (Accessed: 17 March 2016)

[55] Available at http://baidu.com.hypestat.com/ and http://www.chinadaily.com.cn/business/2015-12/11/content_22686526_4.htm#Contentp (Accessed: 6 January 2016).

[56] Thompson, C. (2006) Google's China problem (and China's Google problem). [Online]. New York Times. 23 April 2006 [cited …]. Available at: http://www.nytimes.com/2006/04/23/magazine/23google.html (Accessed: 17 March 2016)

[57] Levin, D. (2011) Chinese web search giant serves two masters. [Online]. *New York Times*. 17 July 2011 [cited …]. Available at: http://www.nytimes.com/2011/07/18/technology/chinese-web-search-giant-serves-two-masters.html?ref=baiducominc (Accessed: 17 March 2016)

[58] Levin, D. (2011) Chinese web search giant serves two masters. [Online]. *New York Times*. 17 July 2011 [cited …]. Available at: http://www.nytimes.com/2011/07/18/technology/chinese-web-search-giant-serves-two-masters.html?ref=baiducominc (Accessed: 17 March 2016)

[59] Barboza, D. (2011) Microsoft to partner with China's leading search engine. [Online]. *New York Times*. 4 July 2011 [cited …]. Available at: http://www.nytimes.com/2011/07/05/technology/05microsoft.html?ref=baiducominc. (Accessed: 17 March 2016)

[60] According to EnfoDesk, Baidu accounted for 79.48% market share, ranking top by revenue (including revenue from overseas but excluding revenue from channels), followed by Google China (11.91%) and Sogou(5.54%) in Q4 2014 in China.
See: http://www.chinaInternetwatch.com/12678/search-engine-market-overview-2014/#ixzz40Q0udmv1
The figures are very slightly different on
https://www.komdat.com/blog/china-market-update-search-engines-2015.

[61] offbeat China [Online]. 2013 [cited …]. Available at: http://offbeatchina.com/chinese-censor-to-taiwan-yes-we-dont-have-freedom-of-speech. (Accessed: 17 March 2016)

[62] cmp [Online]. 2012 [cited …]. Available at: http://cmp.hku.hk/2013/02/18/31356/. (Accessed: 17 March 2016)

[63] Crow, C. (1937) *Four hundred million customers*. London: Hamish Hamilton.

[64] Yu, S. (2011) Microsoft likens China market to 'Wild West': executive cites lack of rules, clarity. *South China Morning Post*. 22 February 2011.

[65] Donald Sull's book, *Made in China* (Boston, MA: Harvard Business Press; 2005), makes some very interesting points about unpredictability of the business environment in China.

[66] Drezner, DW. (2010) Weighing the scales: the Internet's effect on state-society relations. *Brown Journal of World Affairs*. 2010; 16(2).

[67] Reporters Without Borders. Information supplied by Yahoo! helped journalist Shi Tao to get ten years in prison. [Online]. 2005 Sep 06 [cited 10 November 2013 Nov 10]. Available at: http://en.rsf.org/china-information-supplied-by-yahoo-06-09-2005,14884.html. (Accessed: 17 March 2016).

[68] Helft, M. and Barboza, D. (2010) Google shuts China site in dispute over censorship. [Online]. *New York Times*. 22 March 2010 [cited …]. Available at: http://www.nytimes.com/2010/03/23/technology/23google.html (Accessed: 17 March 2016)

[69] Thompson, C. (2006) Google's China problem (and China's Google problem). [Online]. *New York Times*. 23 April 2006 [cited …]. Available at: http://www.nytimes.com/2006/04/23/magazine/23google.html?_r=0 . (Accessed: 17 March 2016)

[70] Google services blocked in China. [Online]. *The Guardian*. 2012 [cited 11 February 2013]. Available at: http://www.guardian.co.uk/technology/2012/nov/09/google-services-blocked-china-gmail (Accessed: 17 March 2016)

[71] China's first Twitter novel. [Online]. Allthingsd. 2010 [cited 11 February 2013]. Available at: http://allthingsd.com/20100311/china%E2%80%99s-first-twitter-novel/. (Accessed: 17 March 2016)

[72] By contrast, in the UK, the most popular news portals are the BBC's website, and the respective websites for the *Daily Mail*, the *Guardian* and the *Daily Telegraph*.

[73] CECC. Interim provisions on the administration of Internet websites engaged in news posting operations. [Online]. 2000 [cited 11 February 2013]. Available at: http://www.scio.gov.cn/zcfg/zcfg/Document/341490/341490.htm. (Accessed: 6 January 2016).

[74] Cao, B. (2011) Chinese stocks in the US: Sohu, Sina gain; China Mobile falls. *Bloomberg*. [Online]. 13 October 2011. Available at: http://www.bloomberg.com/news/2011-10-13/chinese-stocks-in-the-u-s-sohu-sina-gain-china-mobile-falls.html (Accessed: 17 March 2016)

[75] Barboza, D. and Rusli, EM. (2011) Chinese site lists in US and its shares soar 29 per cent. New York Times. [Online]. 5 May 2011. Available at: http://dealbook.nytimes.com/2011/05/04/renren-raises-730-million/. (Accessed: 17 March 2016)

[76] Available at: http://www.aliyun.com/zixun/content/2_6_7386.html, http://www.anfone.com/SJSJRJYHSLPX/2014-6/53964.html (Accessed: 17 March 2016)

145

http://zhidao.baidu.com/link?url=scnDqwglrr65778xskd5OHGzRVURpRboAFogMeNUjiv1dQSo
0HwsC8ccqUNgBy3A4L9G_LObUlj0o9Sb0SwiDMJIU3W9dmDaR8DA9CIU9c3 (Accessed: 6
January 2016).

[77] Krishnappa, S. (2011) Social media sites like Twitter deserve Nobel for pro-democracy protests
in Egypt, Libya & China? [Online]. *International Business Times*. 2011 Feb 22 [cited 1 May
2011]. Available at: http://www.ibtimes.com/social-media-sites-twitter-deserve-nobel-pro-
democracy-protests-egypt-libya-china-269321. (Accessed: 17 March 2016)

[78] Fenton, N. (2010) *New media, old news: journalism and democracy in the digital age.* London:
Sage.

[79] Sullivan, J. (2013) China's Weibo: is faster different? *New Media & Society.* 2013 Feb 07:1-14.

[80] King, Gary, Pan Jennidfer, Roberts, Margaret E. (2013) How Censorship in China Allows
Government Criticism but Silences Collective Expression in *American Political Science Review*
May 2013 https://gking.harvard.edu/files/censored.pdf, p1, accessed 310717

[81] Willnat, Lars, Lu, Wei and Martin, Jason A. (2015) Politics and social media in China. In:
Rawnsley Gary D. and Rawnsley, Ming-Yeh T. (eds.) *Routledge Handbook of Chinese Media*,
London: Routledge, pp 195.

[82] Ibid., pp 181.

[83] Ibid., pp 185.

[84] Ibid., pp 184.

[85] Shirk, SL (ed.) (2011) *Changing media, changing China.* New York: Oxford University Press,
pp 241.

[86] Kluver, R. and Bannerjee, I (2005) 'The Internet in nine Asian nations'. *Information,
Communication & Society* 8(1) pp 30-46) in ibid., pp 197.

[87] Chinese Netizen Chinese Netizens Flood Tsai Ing-Wen's Facebook Page With Anti-Taiwan
Independence Posts 21 January, 2016
 https://blogs.wsj.com/chinarealtime/2016/01/21/chinese-netizens-flood-tsai-ing-wens-facebook-
page-with-anti-taiwan-independence-posts/

[88] Lynch, Daniel (2010) The Study of Chinese Communication in the 2010s, in *International Journal
of Communication* 4, p 499. See also: Carter, L. (2015). *Let 100 Voices Speak: How the Internet is
Transforming China and Changing Everything.* London: IB Tauris.

[89] That there might be genuine Tibetan grievances was not considered by the Chinese students,
who concurred with the official line that Tibetan riots were simply acts orchestrated by foreign
enemies, see Wang X. Behind the great firewall: the Internet and democratisation in China. [PhD
thesis]. Ann Arbor, MI: University of Michigan, 2009. Available at:
https://deepblue.lib.umich.edu/bitstream/handle/2027.42/64681/wangx_1.pdf?sequence=1&isAllo
wed=y, (Accessed 19 March 2016)

[90] Shirk, SL (ed.) (2011). *Changing media, changing China.* New York: Oxford University Press,
pp 247.

[91] See, for example: http://www.globalresearch.ca/us-provocation-in-chinese-waters-the-
militarization-ofthe-south-china-sea/5484954 . It would be wise to consult differing websites.

[92] Ma, Yiben (2015) Online Chinese nationalism and its nationalist discourses. In: Rawnsley Gary
D. and Rawnsley, Ming-Yeh T. (eds.) *Routledge Handbook of Chinese Media*, London: Routledge,
pp 211.

[93] Li, Xiguang (2005) Who is setting the Chinese Agenda? The Impact of Online Chatrooms on
the Party Presses. In: *China sees the world sees China, Media and Power in China Today*, School
of Communication, Tsinghua University, pp 75.

[94] Ibid., pp 86.

[95] Ibid., pp 90.

[96] Li Xiguang. Interviewed by the author; April 2013.

[97] Karatzogianni, Athina and Robinson, Andrew (2015) A cyberconflict analysis of Chinese
dissidents focusing on civil society, mass incidents and labour resistance. In: Rawnsley Gary D.

and Rawnsley, Ming-Yeh T. (eds.) *Routledge Handbook of Chinese Media*, London: Routledge, pp 227.

[98] Ibid., pp 227.

[99] Berry C. Personal communication to Helen Briggs; 18 January 2012.

[100] Pierson, D. (2012) China's Internet users grow 12 per cent in a year, topping 500 million. [Online]. *Los Angeles Times*. 17 January 2012. Available at: http://articles.latimes.com/2012/jan/17/business/la-fi-china-Internet-20120117. (Accessed: 17 March 2016)

[101] Simpson, P. (2012) Chinese Internet users surge past half a billion. *Daily Telegraph*. [Online]. 17 January. Available at: http://www.telegraph.co.uk/news/worldnews/asia/china/9019908/Chinese-Internet-users-surges-past-half-a-billion.html. (Accessed: 17 March 2016)

[102] Waters, R. (2013) Online anonymity to be confined to virtual history. *Financial Times*. 2013 May 02.

[103] Available at http://english.cpc.people.com.cn/206972/206978/8188760.html (Accessed: 6 January 2016).

[104] Esarey, A and Qiang, Xiao (2011) Digital communication and political change in China. *International Journal of Communication*, Chapter 5, pp 298-319.

[105] Zhang Yue (2016) 'New app helps State Council reach out', *China Daily*, 27-28 February 2016.

[106] de Burgh, HW, Zeng, Rong and Mi Miao (2012) Responding to an Activist Public: Hangzhou Press Office Rethinks its Role. *Media, Culture & Society,* Vol 34, Number 8, November 2012.

[107] Ibid, p1013

[108] Liu, X. (2006) 我与互联网 刘晓波, English translation from: China Digital Times. 24 February 2006 [cited …]. Available at: http://chinadigitaltimes.net/2006/02/me-and-the-Internet-liu-xiaobo/

[109] Liu, X. (2006) op cit

[110] Li, Fa. Interviewed by the author; April 2013.

[111] Mi M. Personal communication to Helen Briggs; 27 January 2012.

[112] Scotton, JF. (2010) The impact of new media. In: Scotton, JF and Hachten, WA (eds.) *New media for a new China.* Oxford: Wiley-Blackwell, Chapter 3.

[113] Scotton, JF. (2010) The impact of new media. In: Scotton, JF and Hachten, WA (eds.) *New media for a new China.* Oxford: Wiley-Blackwell, Chapter 3.

[114] *China Daily*. East China cities launch commercial 4G network. [Online]. 4 February 2013 Feb 04 [cited 2013 Feb 11]. Available at: http://www.chinadaily.com.cn/china/2013-02/04/content_16199780.htm.

[115] http://www.bloomberg.com/news/articles/2014-11-21/whose-Internet-is-it-anyway-china-wields-more-influence consulted 030115.

[116] In 2013, Edward Snowden, a US National Security Agency employee revealed thousands of classified documents which, *inter alia*, exposed how the US government monitored foreign governments, companies and individuals. He then took asylum in Russia. The US government indicted Snowden for espionage but also announced some moves to assuage criticism of its cyberspying, for example by saying it would give up control over Internet names and addresses.

[117] Beech, Hannah (2015) The other side of the great firewall, London. *Time magazine,* pp 28 http://intca.org/china-great-firewall/, accessed 07 March 2016

[118] Morozov, Evegeny (2011) *The Net delusion: how not to liberate the world.* London: Penguin.

[119] Yang, Guobin (2009) *The power of the Internet in China.* New York: Columbia University Press, pp 85.

[120] Bai Yansong on CCTV's *News 1+1*, 13 April 2010.

5 The Networksphere

Monarchs of yore and Communist dictators tended to keep discussion of political and policy matters within a cabal of accomplices. Today, in many if not most countries, the policy world of those trying to input into decision-making is made up of many people and derives from a much larger constituency of citizens, participating to a greater or lesser extent in the public sphere 公共領域, where public opinion 民意 is formed. The participants are often active in civil society 公民 社会. Media provide the main space for public debate but there are other arenas, from theatre to academic seminars and professional associations to hobby clubs, whether inside or outside the media, on- or offline.[1]

This at least is typical of Anglophone and some European societies, in which it is widely assumed that such institutions and activities, seen as intermediate between state and citizens, are necessary elements of a participative, democratic, polity. And such a polity is seen as both modern and preferred.

As Eastern Europe recovers from Communism, domestic and international activists have been seeking to (re)create the institutions and habits that comprised public spheres and civil societies before their demolition in the 1940s and 1950s.[2] Observers of China have debated whether a similar process might be going on in China, whether the media are beginning to function in accordance with the Anglophone ideal and, if so, what this might presage.

5.1   The idea of civil society

Anglophones have defined civil society as the public realm that occupies the space between the state and the private sphere.[3] State and society are seen as separate.[4] Very early on in the development of the English, and some other European polities, people asserted rights and spheres of activity with which the state should not interfere.[5] Equality before the law and property rights were the soil in which civil society grew. Then, as Slavko Splichal , the Slovenian writer on public opinion, writes: 'The principles of publicness, personal freedom of communication, and freedom of the press were quintessential, not only for the emergence of the public sphere, but also for the development of civil society and the rise of democracy'.[6]

When, after the collapse of the Soviet empire in 1989, it became the vogue to discuss civil society and the public sphere, it was assumed that, shorn of Marxist dictators, all societies would or should have developed essentially as they had done in the Anglosphere. Over the last decade, with recognition of the indefatigable implications of culture, we have become chary of that assumption.

148

Investigative journalism

The pioneers of CCTV's *News Probe* expected their audience to consist of intellectuals, but editors rapidly realised that they had a huge following among the peasants and migrant workers. 'Large numbers of them call in with harrowing tales of exploitation, expropriation and corruption. All the calls are logged and the tales told are pored over for possible programme stories: brutality by policemen; a lottery scam; 'special' taxes imposed by officials; officials cutting down trees belonging to the local community; miscarriages of justice in the local courts; malpractice among registration officials leading to peculation in connection with residency and marriage procedures; overcharging by public utilities; underpayment of peasants for use of their assets; expropriation of public buildings in Peking; substitution at court when the accused are powerful people; theft of burial plots and arable land – these are just a few of the reports received and carefully recorded by NewsProbe's telephonists'.[7]

Today the investigative approach is mainstream in all branches of the media and has been stimulated, challenged and ruffled by revelation and criticism on the Internet.[8] The leading television shows are now engaged in tough competition, because the number of vehicles is so great.

According to Wang Keqin, 王克勤 'more and more reporters' have been engaged in the writing of exposés 揭黑报道; 'more and more media' have been engaged in the publishing of exposés; 'more and more' first-rate reports and regular columns [on investigative reporting] have appeared; investigative reports in China are showing an increasing degree of professionalism; investigative reporters are receiving more attention and respect [from society].[9] They reveal wrong, especially by those in positions of responsibility, create examples of good or bad practice, and may instigate legislation. Examples are provided in the tables yet the vehicles are now so numerous that they cannot be covered in great detail, particularly as every province has its own examples too.[10]

A close observer of investigative journalism in China, Zhan Jiang 展江, has identified seven movements or 'stages' in investigative journalism so far this century.[11] The fortunes of his object of study change almost from year to year, according, it would seem, to the political situation. Until 2002 there was a 'brilliant' period: for example, *Focus Report* revealed a coalmine disaster in Guangxi, and the collusion between mine owners and local officials; *Caijing* revealed 'shady deals' in the stock market; and *China Economic Times* 中国经济时报 disclosed the monopoly and corruption of Beijing's taxi industry.[12]

During 2003-4, three *Southern City News* editors were imprisoned, and yet the authorities allowed themselves to be influenced by the reporting of the Sun Zhigang 孙志刚 case. Xinhua News Agency revealed a series of accidents in the manufacture of traditional medicine. And yet, in 2004, the CPD prohibited the media from undertaking investigations in regions other than their own. The right to do this had heretofore been essential to journalists' ability to investigate at all, as it was generally regarded as unacceptable to report on sensitive home-town issues. To get round this, journalists had done swaps, by which they took tips from colleagues in distant provinces, and in return helped those same colleagues to publish in their own patch.

That year saw serious difficulties for several leading journalists. Two Editors from *Beijing News* 新京报 were sacked, as was an Associate Editor of *Southern City News*. It was the year of the *Freezing Point* 冰点 closure[13] and the dismissal of its Editor and Associate Editor.[14] During 2005, there were some high profile investigations of corrupt officials, and Wang Keqin 王克勤 exposed clashes between peasants and factory management in Hebei, as well as the extent of the AIDS scandal in a Hebei city. Nevertheless, according to Zhan, it was becoming much more dangerous to investigate and much more difficult to report. By 2006, only *Caijing* continued to investigate, and *Southern Weekend* compensated for its lack of investigations by expanding its opinion pages.

By 2007-8 the situation had improved, both because the potentially debilitating regulations on cross-provincial reporting were not enforced, and also because the Freedom of Information Act 政府信息公开条例 had been passed. Moreover, the Internet was starting to function as a constant reproach to the mainstream media and as a stimulus to report on what was becoming impossible to ignore. *Caijing* continued to produce good stories, hiding behind its identity as an economics and finance magazine. Its report, *Whose Shandong Energy?* 谁的鲁能?,[15] revealed a huge case of corruption, while Fu Zhenzhong 付振中 of Henan TV's City Channel exposed *The Hidden World of the Shanxi Brick Kilns* 揭开山西黑砖窑内幕第一人.

In March 2010, thirteen Chinese newspapers published a joint editorial, calling for reform and the future abolition of the household registration system. It was removed from websites, and the authors were admonished. *Caijing.com* revealed that the Governor of Hubei had snatched away a digital recording pen from a *Beijing Times* journalist, when she was trying to note what he was saying during a session of the National People's Congress. LI Chengpeng 李承鹏 published a book, *Chinese football: the inside story* 中国足球内幕, exposing corruption in the soccer establishment. The biggest development, however, was that the Internet, and Weibo in particular, were now driving investigative journalism. More and more revelations of official corruption and incompetence were emerging; the journalist's job was to try to keep abreast of the sources, which were now multitudinous.

From time to time a clear connection between investigative journalism and policy has been traceable, the best-known of which is the Sun Zhigang 孙志刚 case. As a result of critical reporting, ministers have resigned or been dismissed (e.g., the Minister of Health during the SARS revelations), though many would claim too few. It can be argued, nevertheless, that investigative journalists have had a profound influence on society, though not always directly on policy. They have brought into the public sphere a sceptical, revelatory approach, exposing to public view not only evils of which they could only guess, but how society actually works; subjected powerful people to criticism and accusation; used a rational, evidential style, rather than a literary one; and espoused impartiality 平衡报道, or at least detachment; and introduced techniques previously only associated with policemen.

Since civil society and public sphere have been particularly associated with the Anglosphere, it is worth looking at their foundations there before seeking manifestations in China. According to the political and social critic David Willetts, pre-modern English society, in which relationships were relatively detached, children left home early and inheritance was not necessarily within the nuclear family, required non-familial arrangements for protection and insurance. 'They were very effective in creating local and civic institutions'.[16] The forcing out of youths from the family home, thought quite barbaric by continental European observers, together with the personal as opposed to familial ownership of property and the protection of the law for property holders (necessary for a society without extended families) were preconditions of England's enterprise revolution, which preceded both the industrial revolution and overseas expansion. 'The vigour of historical civil society in England or the USA is not some universal trend. It depends upon some very unusual and shared features of our two countries. England and America share a similar civil society because they share the same (rather unusual) family structure'.[17]

Since China's family structures are very different, we might expect differences in the civil society that is re-emerging. In a similar way, economists have found explanations for China's economic take-off since 1991, the world's second great revolution in human wealth creation, in its cultural substructure.

5.1.1 Chinese characteristics

In recent years, people have asked why China has been so much more successful than many countries with greater resources, smaller populations or better infrastructure. To simplify, the answer is three-fold: first, much economic freedom and local decision-making were permitted in the 1980s;[18] secondly, the country opened itself to foreign trade and competition while ensuring that foreign capital could not stymie local enterprise; and thirdly, as it sloughed off its debilitating ideology, China was able to draw upon its traditional culture. This last claim would be a shock to most of the reformers and revolutionaries brought to life in Schell and Delury's *Wealth and Power*.[19] For many of these heroes of reform and revolution, China's culture was the main impediment to its renaissance. The contradiction can perhaps be explained by the fact that they had encountered neither Raymond Williams[20] nor Franz Boas,[21] and so for them 'culture' was what the wealthy did rather than Chinese modes of association. Since the work of those authors, we think of culture differently, and so, it seems, do Chinese politicians.

Media people: an Investigative Journalist

Image source:
http://gongyi.sohu.com/2013
1021/n388591125_6.shtml

Wang Keqing 王克勤 is known for carrying a small box containing a sponge soaked in red ink, which he uses to collect fingerprints from witnesses to confirm their agreement on the statements he compiles.

A peasant from the very poor Gansu Province, without any university education, he started his journalism career by writing propaganda stories for the local media, and then began working for the *Gansu Economics Daily* 甘肃经济日报.

After his uncovering of a fraudulent securities company in 2011, the newspaper was temporarily forced to close. Wang then joined *West Business Daily* 西部商报, but lost his job again over his investigations of local elections. He moved to the capital and spent ten years at *China Economic Times*. There, his investigative reports revealed that fake journalists were beaten to death by Shanxi coal mine owners, that six farmers were beaten to death during conflicts with the local authority in Hebei Province, along with other notorious scandals. Then there was his story on how a 'gross failure' to refrigerate vaccines in the Shanxi Province deaths and illness. This caused such a furore that the Chief Editor of the *China Economic Times* 中国经济时报 was fired.

Wang then joined the *Economic Observer* 经济观察 and set up an investigative unit, but a few months later he again incurred the anger of the authorities, and left the newspaper.

Let me again use the analogy of England. It used to be assumed that Britain had the industrial revolution and then became the world's first modern commercial society, whereas in fact, as the Cambridge Group for the History of Population and Social Structure found, 'the truth is exactly the other way round, we were already the world's first market society and were therefore ripe for the industrial revolution'.[22] The reason England was the first commercial society is largely to do with its particular family forms, as outlined above. As if in echo, economists studying China have argued recently that it is Chinese culture that has underpinned Chinese development.[23] Thomas Friedman put the point succinctly in the *New York Times*, in an article full of admiration for China's achievements in modernising its cities and its communications: 'They did not get all this by discovering oil, they got it by digging inside themselves'.[24] For modern societies, culture may well be a more significant predictor of development and ideology than economic conditions.[25] So what are the manifestations of China's 'culture'?

When contrasted with Anglophone societies and their famous individualism, obsession with private property and ancient traditions of shared law-making,[26] there are some distinctive 'rules' of Chinese culture which can help explain today's achievements: [27] putting before all things personal relationships and friendship 人际关系／人情／友谊, role respect (aka filial piety) 孝顺 in family obligations 家庭责任和义务,[28] communitarianism 集体主义;[29] honouring of authority and experience 敬畏权威和经验; respect for learning, and pragmatism 务实精神.[30] These comprise the 'grammar of action ' or ways of thinking and behaving towards which Chinese people are predisposed. [31] 'Confucianism' can be used as a shorthand term for these rules. Such traits are useful in building a commercial society. When Anglophones ask how it can possibly be that China is successful without having institutions like theirs, the answer is that it has institutions that are different but can be at least as effective. There is more than one path to modernity. President Xi's exhortations to defend and promote Chinese culture may be interpreted as expressions of awareness of this.

Yet this taxonomy of rules does not really do justice to the very distinct institutional foundations of Chinese society, distinctions that are identified in Hofstede's theory of Cultural Dimensions.[32] The founder of Chinese sociology, Fei Xiaotong[33] called the social system the 'differential of mode of association' 差序格局. In brief, a person is a member of a unit before he or she is an individual, the first one being the family. He or she progresses through life as a member of many other units or networks, towards which he/she has prescribed responsibilities which override duties to the self. People are not trapped in fixed categories. 'A person in the course of his or her life time moves from being a child obedient to parents, to being a parent expecting obedience, and so on.'[34] 'Obedience' today would probably best be replaced by 'consideration'.

The notion of equality is different from that encountered in Europe. Over a period of several centuries, Christian ideas of equality overturned assumptions of 'natural hierarchy', eventually animating reforms of the legal system and revolts against unrepresentative authority. In China there was equality of subjection to moral law, but that law institutionalised difference (of role rather than class prescription, let alone caste). Li Jin writes that even in today's China, how a person fulfils the role assigned within a network or community is deemed more important than the expression of individual personality. 'A person is not just John or David, but much more importantly a daughter, a sister, a wife, a mother, and aunt, a teacher, a colleague and so forth. This means that the person's existence is inevitably enmeshed in profound human relationships. As one develops and ages, then relationships and roles change. These relationships and their associated social and moral significance – not our biology – define our individual humanity'.[35]

Education reinforces this. Cambridge anthropologist Alan MacFarlane, as with Francis Hsu's *Americans and Chinese*[36] and Richard Wilson's *Learning to be Chinese,* suggests that a pupil at an English school is indoctrinated to become an individualist, independent of home and emotionally detached whereas in China, the character to be formed is one which accepts that it belongs to a community, is responsible to its parents, harmonious, and respectful of learning and of experience.[37]

5.1.2   Relationships

To make these abstractions more concrete, I will give a few instances of how culture affects attitudes and behaviour in China, in the media as elsewhere. Membership of the work unit is a more important aspect of life than it is normally expected to be for an Anglophone, and there is considerable emotional engagement with it. Among the advantages are low staff turnover and more long term investment by both employer and employees.[38] In a newspaper or website office, social life often revolves around the work unit. People expect to make close friends there, whom they will consult on every personal concern. It is not that this membership is the only one they have. There seems to be no contradiction in belonging to several networks at once[39] The culture predisposes its members to create new 'families', based on what Europeans might regard as nebulous ties such as being from the same school, province or town, or having the same surname. This distinguishes Chinese communitarianism from the 'amoral familism' found by anthropologists in Mediterranean societies, which celebrates inward-looking conservatism.[40] Once a network is formed, constituents get to know each other very well, including their family lives, love affairs[41] and personal habits. It may be precisely because the emotional bonds of members are so strong that rivalries between institutions and companies can be so intense in China.[42]

It is not surprising, then, that at least in small enterprises, employers do not take up just a few hours of an employee's time. They employ the whole person, and they choose employees not only because they have the right set of skills, but because they are perceived as having demonstrated moral worth and a sense of service.[43] Often they do not advertise posts, but employ individuals introduced to them by those with whom they have personal relationships, assuming that there will be shared values. This manner of appointment sets up obligations on both sides which may make disagreements problematic, reinforcing an existing instinct to cohere and be positive rather than negative.[44] The workshop or office is more of a community than an impersonal environment in which one happens to earn money. As political scientists Jonathan Unger and Anita Chan have shown in a study of the 'moral economy' of a state owned enterprise, this communitarian understanding is not just relevant to small and private businesses but could equally be the case in nationalised industry.[45]

The implications for politics and journalism are many. Anglophones assume the autonomy of individuals, but in China people tend to see themselves as members of a group first. Consequently, the norms of the group (or indeed the views of its leaders) are more likely to determine courses of action than the opinions of individuals.[46] Moreover, personal obligations can override professional values, which explains why a story can be spiked lest it upset a friend, or a friend of a friend.

One of the features of this kind of society is that business relationships have traditionally been based on trust.[47] Personal friendship or at least mutual respect is usually required to precede business.[48] Of course trust is essential to business transactions everywhere, but in the Anglosphere it is guaranteed by adherence to impersonal laws and contracts observed by both sides, whereas in China it is secured by a shared ethic as to how you behave towards those with whom you are in relationship. Anglophone businesses which have tried to get sales without participating in the preliminaries of meals, outings and gifts, have found this out very fast.

5.1.2.1   Networks

Networks, whether familial or otherwise, are subtly different from Anglophone civil associations. They bring people together with a common, often emotional, bond such as shared membership of a cultural group, lineage, temple congregation or college. The relationship predominates over the purpose. Moreover, 'pseudo families' are not so much civil associations as mutual support groups. In discussing civil society in the USA, Fareed Zakaria has noted that in the past, alumni of the great independent schools would trust each other in an analogous way because they were bonded by that common ground. He bewails what he terms the commercialization of many US institutions for having undermined such

154

cohesion.[49]

In his analysis of the leadership of the CCP, diplomat turned academic Kerry Brown reveals the networks to which individual members of the Standing Committee of the Politburo belong and the ways in which these may have assisted and managed their careers. He highlights the pressures from networks, incidentally noting that President Xi has been unusual in, as far as we can tell, keeping his family members from profiting by their association with him. This is a remarkable achievement in a society in which it is understood that any effective person must be beholden to groups by ties which are very hard to deny. Brown expresses the perplexity of many Anglophones at this phenomenon when he writes that 'this idea of belonging to someone in this way is, at least on the surface a strange one'.[50] He brings in Fei Xiaotong to help explain the power of networks, but the importance of these in today's politics have been analysed thoroughly by eminent Sinologist Lucien Pye, for whom 'the personalistic bonding of the political elite has turned out to be the most critical factor in holding the system together'.[51]

Because loyalty to relatives and networks take precedence over loyalty to abstractions, it has proved difficult to establish a concept of public service, adherence to professional ethics or a universal morality as opposed to loyalty to 'family' or leader. And this is despite CCP rhetoric and the best efforts of the KMT. Since, by tradition, abstract universal principles of morality are subsidiary to ethical principles governing relationships, to be dutiful is to serve well those involved in the relationship rather than an ideal. The word 'Socialism' is sometimes used as if it were an ethical concept and described in terms which make it seem like the Confucian notion of ren 仁, which is usually translated as 'benevolence', and is the nearest traditional Chinese ethics get to generalised altruism.

As an instance of what exists instead of the professional ethic, we might say that a Chinese investigative journalist performs his or her role by serving those whom journalists should serve, rather than because it is necessary for journalists to behave in a certain way. She or he may interpret the target of service differently, but for many it will simply be the person who appointed them. In various media at various times, there have been measures of success based on approval by different party leaders. If you please the leader you get high points and your point score at the end of the month determines your bonus.[52]

As we saw earlier, despite knowledge of and interest in the Anglophone idea of journalism and its professionalism, the doyens of the 'Golden Period' generally saw themselves as activists in the patriotic endeavour rather than as adherents to a professional creed (although the *Workers' Daily* was proud of its impartiality.[53]) In a similar manner, today's journalist will be honest and trustworthy to her colleague or the subject of her report, not because some ideal told her to treat everyone equally, but because she has entered into a relationship of trust. Trust derives from familiarity. In intercourse with those with whom you are familiar, if you are 'too' polite or you wish to formalise an agreement or share expenses, you may well be told "don't treat me like an outsider" 你这样，那就见外了.

Interpersonal relationships are also the means by which most activities are initiated. You start a business, get married or find a job through networks. An illustration of how this can apply to working in the media is found in an interview by Judy Polumbaum and Xiong Lei at *China Youth News* 中国青年:

'Reporting from the countryside made me understand a plain truth that when it comes to social relations in China, if you can open one link in a chain, it becomes possible to open all the links. For example: I need you and cultivate a good relationship. You trust me and invite me into your home. For Chinese New Year, I bring you cartons of cigarettes and a couple of bottles of liquor. The next day you take me to your maternal uncle's home, and your uncle takes me to his sister's, and the sister to her paternal uncle's. Thus the whole rural chain opens up. So you must be sincere and very nice to the first person you meet. If you offend him, you may ruin everything that could follow. Even in urban society, sometimes we have to act in this way. Say you want to interview someone, it is much more productive to get to know the interviewee through friends than through an official assignment and formal arrangement.'[54]

5.1.2.2 Roles and responsibilities

Another aspect of Chinese society which may inhibit the assertion of professional authority is the assumption of hierarchy. In Anglophone societies, deference is quite muted. Age and experience are often not given any particular respect and, over the past two decades, forms of address have eschewed differentiating styles in favour of a near universal use of the personal name. This is similar to the way in which 'comrade' became the only acceptable mode of address in 20th century totalitarian regimes. Thus hierarchy and differences in rank and responsibility are disguised, although power is no less cheerfully exercised. Chinese society has no embarrassment about hierarchy. Junior journalists see nothing shameful about submitting to the authority of their seniors, no matter how irritating, let alone in referring to them by their titles (eg. 'Editor-in-Chief 总编辑') and styles (eg. 'Respected 尊敬的').[55] In everyday speech an older colleague called Wang will be referred to as 'Elder Brother/Sister Wang' (王哥、姐) and a junior one as 'Young

Wang' （小王）. Professionals are not necessarily offended by submitting to authority or its version of events. In any case, hierarchy is tempered by the personalising of relationships.[56] The journalists who in 1989 joined protests demanding that they be not 'forced to lie' had been pushed too far; but it is unlikely they objected to the principle of authority influencing the media. Rather, they disliked the usurping of that power for nefarious ends.

The very concept of the equality of human beings was until recently quite a new one in most societies. Introduced into Europe by Christianity, its incorporation into secular life and law took place over several hundred years.[57] As European sociologist Larry Seidentop has shown, it was an outlandish idea in Europe for a long time. Not surprisingly, it has seemed equally odd to societies outside Europe in which a pecking order from the highest classes (or castes) stretched a long way to the bottom, where the 'hardly human' languished. Although this important idea has been seeded into China through Communism, the equality which modern Anglophones assume natural, can be incomprehensible in societies where it is due order that is deemed natural. Even the most nominally egalitarian of the CCP's past political campaigns were managed by an elite with plenary powers. Not surprisingly, therefore, it has taken some time for ordinary people to be participants in the media. Even now, while an expert will be tagged by his or her full name and title, a *vox pop* may be subtitled as 'villager', 'worker' or even 'poor person'.

Television events with audience involvement, showcases of common peoples' talents such as the *China Dream Show* 中国梦想秀, online newspapers seeking collaboration from readers and social media have all served to widen the group of those who participate in national conversations. They expect to have their voices heard, at least tentatively, on an equal footing with the leaders or the supposed experts. How has this affected traditional hierarchy?

Three investigations

Shanxi Vaccines

After many months of often difficult research, Wang Keqin 王克勤 reported in the *China Economic Times* 中国经济时报 of March 2010, how negligently stored and distributed vaccines had resulted in the deaths of at least four children and damage to 74 others. The vaccines had been left unrefrigerated, were harmful and should have been immediately destroyed but were administered to children throughout the province. This came about because the Shanxi Centre for Disease Control 山西省疾病预防控制中心 had entrusted vaccine manufacture and distribution to a businessman who had paid the Centre for Disease Control for rights to the sale and distribution of vaccines in the Province and had proved irresponsible.

Wang Keqin's report comprehensively documented the effects of the vaccines, and provoked widespread concern and anger. Shortly afterwards, the editor of *China Economic Times*, Bao Yueyang 包月阳, was relieved of his post. Although official sources stated that his dismissal was an unrelated coincidence, this was not generally believed. The main outcome of the report was the curtailment of an editor's career.

Anyuanding's Black Jails

Although petitioning central government is a frequently exercised right, it is one which infuriates some local officials, because they are disciplined if too many petitioners register complaints against them.

According to reporters from *Caijing* magazine and the *Southern City Daily*, published in September 2010, the Anyuanding Security Company 安元鼎保安公司 ran illegal detention centres in Beijing, which were very profitable and employed 3,000 'interceptors' to kidnap petitioners arriving in the capital to register grievances. These unfortunate people were incarcerated for up to a month until shipped back home, often suffering abuse or worse in the meantime. The company was paid up to 300rmb per person per day for 'taking care' of petitioners until they could be escorted home by police.

In an immediate response to the publication, Beijing City Public Security Bureau 北京市公安局 arrested two of Anyuanding's executives and charged them with unlawful detention.

The Red Cross in the digital pillory

The 6 August 2011edition of CCTV's *News Probe* began:

Guo Meimei 郭美美, a 20-year-old girl, posted pictures of herself on Sina Weibo showing off her luxury car and handbags and claiming to be the Commercial General Manager of the Red Cross, the country's largest charity. The pictures circulated widely and triggered public accusations against the Red Cross. The key question to be answered by this charity was: did Guo's wealth have any connection to the Red Cross and was the charity funding her lavish lifestyle? (*New Probe*, 6 August 2011)

This programme is a retroactive investigation, in which the reporters try to find out what really happened after netizens had claimed to have uncovered wicked doings at the Red Cross. China's largest charity came under ferocious attack in 2011 after Guo's posting. But was the assumption that Guo had got this money dishonestly from her supposed employers true?

At the end of the investigation, the reporter established:

a)   A director of a company associated with the Red Cross had resigned his job, but not because he himself had been found guilty of peculation — the accusations on social media were unfounded — but because his relationship with Guo and her behaviour had brought into disrepute both the Red Cross and the company.
b)   Guo Meimei had no connections to the Red Cross but this was ignored by the netizen public, for which her self-promotion was a catalyst triggering a vicious campaign against the charity, accusing it of corruption and supposed misspent donations in the past.
c)   Guo Meimei suffered a massive 'human flesh search', to dig out any sensational details about her and her wealth. The programme defined this as a violation of privacy.
d)   Many have ceased donating to the Red Cross.

This programme was not an investigation of the Red Cross, but of the way netizens seized the opportunity to attack the Red Cross and destroy its reputation unjustifiably, and without evidence. There have been other post-hoc investigations in recent years on *News Probe*, notably one about the corruption scandals in football which had, prior to the programme, been dealt with in a high profile trial which resulted in several football officials going to prison.

It may be that the paternalist and communitarian assumptions are giving way to, or may turn into, something more familiar to Anglophones, particularly as enterprises become more knowledge-based and participatory.[58] But still, because the relationships in Chinese organisations are so personal, even in huge organisations, when a senior decision maker moves post, many colleagues will move too, according to the principle of 'new king, new ministers' 一朝天子一朝臣. Media executives may be more like disciples than colleagues, and there are obligations anticipated for both the junior and the senior, as many a foreign professor or employer has discovered. [59] Hierarchy is clear, as are its responsibilities.[60]

Such deference contrasts with the adversarial attitude of many Anglophone journalists, who prioritise their independence in getting 'the truth' and reporting 'facts'. So too does the corollary that Chinese media workers are teachers before they are reporters and must tailor their output according to its moral implications and potential effects.

Here are some examples of how a particular sense of role informs Chinese journalists. At the end of a workshop on investigative journalism for young CCTV reporters in 2010, two Anglophone editors and a Chinese editor were asked to summarise the day. The Anglophones proceeded to describe the techniques that had been discussed and the criteria for effective revelation; how to get the scoop. When his turn came, Zhang Jie 张杰, then Editor of *Newsprobe*, made a rousing speech in which he related investigative journalism to enlightening and educating people to be better citizens and serve the common weal. His focus was entirely upon the higher purpose rather than the processes. He was enjoining the 250-odd youngsters, from whom would be selected a new wave of foreign correspondents, to grasp their roles as teachers and patriots.

In reporting the Kunming terror incidents of 2014 there were initially no mentions in the public media of the ethnicity of the perpetrators lest this inspire racism. In reporting the multiple terrorist attacks of November 2015, bloodshed in Paris was played down by CCTV lest it give heart to enemies and frighten citizens. In the same year, the *Global Times* demonstrated balance in pointing out that, while the slaughter of Charlie Hebdo journalists was unforgivable, it was provoked by vicious assaults on Islam. Observers of CCTV reports in Africa have noted a predilection for covering attempts to end conflict rather than reports from the conflict itself.[61]

Philosophers of the media have noticed these divergences from the Anglo-American way. As Shi Anbin and Dong Guanpeng, scholars from Tsinghua University, put it: 'Can our media transcend the limitations of our Western counterparts and find a more constructive alternative to the commercial model?'[62] Canadian academic Zhao Yuezhi speculates whether, given the disillusionment with 'Western' media today and questions over the 'sustainability of advertising dependent media systems', we might see convergence towards the Chinese model rather than homogenisation on Anglophone lines.[63] Students of anthropology might be sceptical.

5.1.3 Did China have a Civil Society before 1949?

Given what we know about civil society in the Anglosphere, it is reasonable to consider that it may configure differently in cultures such as we have been describing. Writes David Willetts, the English social policy-maker '…The extended non-nuclear family behind its walls is self-sufficient and turned its back on civil society. Generally, nuclear families mean a stronger civil society because individuals need support outside the family and turn to a rich network of clubs and friendly societies. People from inegalitarian nuclear family societies, like England, Denmark, and the Netherlands, are the likeliest to join clubs and associations.'[64] So, is there no civil society in China?

The main vehicles of investigative journalism and their slogans

Vehicle	Parent	Launch	Slogan
Southern Weekend 南方周末	Nanfang Group	1984	The best investigation is in-depth! 深入成就深度！
Focal Point 焦点访谈	CCTV	1994	Truth speaks out 用事实说话
Freezing Point 冰点	*China Youth Daily*	1995	Speak for the disadvantaged 为弱者讲话
News Probe 新闻调查	CCTV	1996	In pursuit of justice 探寻事实真相
Southern City Daily 南方都市报	Nanfang Group	1997	Voice of the citizenry 大众的声音
Caijing 财经	Stock Exchange Executive Council	1998	Independent standpoint, exclusive coverage, and unique perspective 独家，独立，独到
China News Weekly 新闻周刊	Chinese News Agency	2000	Progress with China 与进步的中国一同进步
New Beijing Newspaper 新京报	Guangming Group	2003	Responsible reporting 负责报道一切

Adapted from Haiyan Wang (2010) *Investigative Journalism and Political Power in China*. Reuters Institute for the Study of Journalism, Oxford: University of Oxford, by kind permission of the Reuters Institute.

Visitors to Hangzhou will be aware of the teahouse tradition, which Huang tells us amounted to a public sphere as early as 1270.[65] Pre-1949, China had many associations and organisations for business and philanthropic purposes that were barely touched by the state. They included chambers of commerce, schools and academies, kinship organisations, religious charities, cultural 'salons' for amateurs of gardening or literature, local militias, educational associations, clubs for practicing *qigong* and, especially, lineage and temple organisations which were 'examples of shareholding corporations which were extremely common in late imperial China'.[66]

American scholar Frederic Wakeman[67] shows us that local associations carried out innumerable public service functions, from charitable relief to fire-fighting, and local defence to education. Moreover, developments during the eighteenth and nineteenth centuries bear 'some similarities' to the public sphere described by Habermas in Western Europe. The associations may not have had the autonomy of English institutions but they were active and not part of government. It has suited the CCP to write off independent organisations pre-1949 as mere expressions of class interest but this is to belittle communities for which central government was far away, where towns and villages of necessity managed themselves, often efficiently and effectively.

Before its liquidation in the 1950s, Chinese civil society was different from that of the Anglosphere. Large, extended families enjoyed much collective activity and were plugged into many networks. China's civic associations will have been affected by that, even the professional guilds and reading and debating societies, of which thousands more were thrown up in response to the foreign threat in the late nineteenth and early twentieth centuries. As previously mentioned, Chinese are famously good at creating associations (earlier termed 'pseudo-families') based on relationships that would be regarded as nebulous in the Anglosphere. When away from the clan, members often feel the urge to replicate it.[68] Sociologist Fei Xiaotong referred to this propensity as 'the projection of consanguinity into space'.[69] But extra-familial associations may be less vital to people with extended families, because the family serves as welfare state, bank and consultant network. If, in addition, such associations are superfluous to politics because it is conducted through family networks, then Civil Society may exist but in a different way.

5.1.4 Does China have a Civil Society today?

In 2013 I visited a great mountaintop Taoist temple and monastery as the guest of a group of senior executives. They were MBA graduates of the same leading business school and mostly Party members. They consulted the monks on health and happiness, did a short course in qigong 气功 and listened to a sermon 布道. Several of the most senior executives also took part in the lengthy sung devotions, and almost all the visitors encouraged their children to kneel and pray. I was surprised, because Party members are not merely supposed to forswear religion for themselves but to proselytise atheism. Elsewhere religious organisations are an elementary segment of civil society, but what part they play or might play in Chinese society is difficult to fathom at present.[70] What is clear is that there is a revival of Buddhist and Daoist practices, that the proselytising by Christian missionaries has met with success and that Islam is also enjoying a revival, if the anti-religious propaganda in Muslim areas is anything to go by.

Synopses of recent investigations

Demolition in the public interest? 为了公共利益的拆迁？ *News Probe*

Residents in a suburb of Changshu, Jiangsu have just discovered that their right to the land on which their houses are built will be revoked within 15 days and their properties will be demolished. Yet the 800 or more houses have not been up for longer than ten years! The reason? So-called 'public interest', or rather the creation of a commercial and leisure centre.

Do we need a law to protect cats? 需要法律保护的猫？ *News Probe*

Exposing a cat dealer called Zhang Zhen'an in Shanghai, who claimed to provide up to 500 cats a day for to the larders of Canton. He also sources cat meat from other areas and has done so for 30 years. The programme investigates the theft, sale and processing of cats in Shanghai and Wuxi, and asks whether legislation could curtail this trade.

Crazy Usury 疯狂高利贷 *News Probe*

Usury is a perennial problem in China, as it is in most countries among the poorest parts of the population without access to banking [in the UK, usurers are called 'tallymen']. In Ongniud Banner (Chinese: Wengniuteqi), a suburb of Ulanhadhot (Chinese: Chifeng), Inner Mongolia, a debt of 60,000 RMB can become 700,000 RMB after a few months. In distress, more than 20 families in Wengniuteqi sold their herds and lands and left their homes because extreme rates of interest forced them into penury.

The 277 Fake Identities 277 个假身份 *News Probe*

Hebei province investigated a fraud crisis of fake identities in which, 277 pupils from two high schools were found to have used faked identification cards presenting them as the children of mining families, in order to get preferential treatment for university entrance exams.

Blood Shortage 血荒 *News Probe*

Hospitals in Kunming (population 6m) have been forced to postpone 90% of surgery, due to an unprecedented shortage of blood, according to the city's health authorities. Kunming has a stock of 20,000 millilitres of blood, far short of the minimum storage requirement of 400,000 ml for the city.

A New Generation of Peasants 新生代农民工 *News Probe*

An in-depth examination of new forces at work in peasant society. Unlike traditional city immigrants, the present generation of young peasants has been keen to get into the city, and they will not return, because they lack many of the skills required of traditional peasants. Over the Spring Festival over half of Foxconn employees (overwhelmingly from the rural areas) chose to stay away from their homes in the countryside. Their attitudes are very different from traditional city immigrants.

The Pain of Poyang Lake 鄱阳湖之痛 *News Probe*

The water level of China's largest freshwater lake, Poyang, has dropped to the lowest point in history, triggering a drought warning. This poses a threat to the water supply of Duchang County's 120,000 residents. Visitors find a parched lake-bed, dead snails and clams, and fishing ships that have run aground

---

The Real Face of Fake Journalists 假记者的真面目 *Focus*

Three 'reporters' visited a coal-mine in Huhehot, Inner Mongolia. They were coming for blackmail and deal-making, and merely posing as journalists.

Local Officials Whose Demolition Caused Death all still Hold Their Positions 拆出人命的地方官员果然个个还在 *Southern Weekend*

Local officials privately boasted about forced evictions and even about self-immolation. Neither this nor the deaths consequent on their actions will have the slightest impact on their careers. An extensive investigation in *Southern Weekend* confirms this.

Journalists Undercover in Foxconn, Exposing the Puzzle of Suicide of Employees 南方周末记者潜伏富士康探寻"八连跳"自杀之谜 *Southern Weekend*

In May 2010, seven young Chinese workers producing Apple iPads for consumers across the globe took their own lives, prompting an investigation into working conditions at the Foxconn factory in Shenzhen. A *Southern Weekend* intern took a job in Foxconn for 28 days in order to investigate.

162

*Who is in charge of the Henan Soong Ching Ling Foundation?*谁在控制河南宋庆龄基金会 *Southern Weekend.*
A scandal-ridden regional charity organisation, the Henan Soong Ching Ling Foundation, established to promote the welfare of children in poor areas is accused of spending a huge amount of money on illegal lending and other investments.
*An Investigation of Eight Uncharitable Lies by Lu Junqing and WECBA (World Eminent Chinese Business Associations)*卢俊卿及世界杰出华商协会 8 大谎言调查 *Southern City Daily*
China was hit by a second charity-related scandal, when questions swirled around the China-Africa Project Hope, founded jointly by the China Youth Development Foundation of the Chinese Communist Youth League and the World Eminent Chinese Business Association (WECBA), a group linked to billionaire Lu Junqing, and registered only as a private company in Hong Kong. Reporters from *Southern City Daily* carried out an investigation and discovered much evidence of fraudulent practice in the association's everyday operations.
Evil Road of 'The Black Men' 罪恶的黑人之路 Henan TV's City Channel
400 parents in Henan started an online campaign, appealing for public help to find their missing children. In the same month, Henan TV's *Metro Channel* journalist Fu Zhenzhong began to investigate at train and bus stations with a secret camera. He found that as many as 1,000 children had been kidnapped in Henan and sold as slaves to work in the brickworks of neighbouring Shanxi province. Henan Television broadcast this news story, and then the illegal brick kiln scandal hit the headlines and attracted the attention of the country's leaders. The government finally stepped in to rescue the enslaved labourers and arrested the illegal kiln bosses.

In his study of civil associations on both Taiwan and the mainland, Robert Weller has sought to understand whether Chinese culture is producing the kind of organizations which, like their apparent counterparts in the Anglosphere, might in time lead to a more democratic polity.[71] He notes that Anglophones have tended to assume that civil society is made up of autonomous individuals getting together once they have detached themselves from earlier traditional and religious loyalties.[72] Weber calls this the 'transition from traditional to rational' systems. Habermas too imagined an idealised version of civil society made up of autonomous individuals and critical thinkers. Weller suggests that Chinese civil society exists, but is not as those authors had in mind.

Sifting the ashes of traditional society, he shows us that there are multitudes of informal networks and that not all of them were smashed by communism. Some even managed to thrive. Ironically, the destruction of market society led to greater reliance on connections because they became essential for survival. When every decision is the responsibility of a politician, corruption can only increase.[73]

As market controls were relaxed in the 1980s, people started up businesses by mobilizing their networks and raising capital through kinsmen, neighbours, and friends. He considers that business relationships are 'embedded' in the informal social sector and that 'This is the heart of the claim for uniquely Chinese modernity'.[74]

Of what does this informal social sector consist? Well, grave cleaning and other rituals associated with ancestors have revived quickly.[75] South of the Yangzi, temple religion is once again widespread. Credit unions, local environmental associations and movements to promote healthy living or help the poor are also prominent. These revitalise cultural traditions, such as the conservation of resources for future generations.[76]

Another feature is that a very high proportion of activists and entrepreneurs are women, perhaps because their modes of association differ from those of males[77] and they are extending the nurturing impulse outside the walls of the home. This orientation differentiates them from the male-dominated (national) campaigning organizations normally seen as constituting civil society. We will come to these shortly.

Unlike the latter, 'informal' social groups in China maintain strong bonds with local community, kinship and religion which some analysts dismiss as 'premodern'. They do not threaten the state as they have neither the desire nor the ability to organize nationally. This does not, however, necessarily protect them from persecution.

Weller's evidence from both Taiwan and the PRC shows that even the worst abuse never fully succeeded in wiping out intermediate social organisations and that they have enjoyed a renaissance. In Taiwan, as soon as martial law was lifted, an abundance of civic associations 'formed almost overnight' and the same is happening on the mainland.[78]

These female dominated informal groups may or may not be included in the PRC figures which tell us that there are as many as 3 million 'social organisations' 社会 、社交团体 in China, of which about 60% are business or professional organisations, some 20% are academic and 15% hobby groups and welfare societies,[79] including choral societies, hiking clubs, literary circles and patient groups.[80] Huge amounts of public money are disbursed by local governments to such organisations.[81] 37% of the population are members of at least one, and 57% of the do some kind of volunteering.[82] Jessica Teets, China scholar from Vermont, suggests that the Shining Stone Community 社区参与行动, which involves city communities in providing help to migrants is an example showing that operationally autonomous civil society can exist within an authoritarian system.[83] Responsibility is shared between state and autonomous organisations, in a manner she terms 'consultative authoritarianism'.

More formally, there are 'Non-Governmental Organisations' 非政府机构 (NGOs) of which there are well over 140,000. The vast majority are government-organised GONGOs, (international) INGOs or student groups, while grassroots NGOs make up the remaining 4%.[84] Some observers attribute the government's support to the need to alleviate the burden of providing welfare.[85]

Media People: a satirist

Guo Degang 郭德纲 (bn 1973), a famous crosstalk comedian 相声演员, is widely credited with reviving the popularity of cross talk, an ancient Chinese performance art characterized by rapid wordplay that combines stand-up comedy with puns 双关语 and poetry.

Guo was born in Tianjin and began to learn the art of storytelling, 评书, from his master Hou Yaowen 侯耀文 when he was eight years old. He went to Beijing in 1995 and established the Deyun Society 德云社, a crosstalk performance community in 1996.

Guo makes great play of his grass roots 草根阶层; he is famous for insulting people and for sarcasm. His, northern, crosstalk is commonly compared with Zhou Libo's show which is very southern orientated. He has combined the traditional crosstalk with new performing forms. He has led his Deyun Society 德云社 to hold special theatre performances in the Army Theatre 解放军歌剧院, where the tickets sold out in very short time, and more than 20 million people watched the show online.

Image source:
http://news.xinhuanet.com/p
hoto/2013-
02/19/c_124361696.htm

Since 2016, Guo has expanded his career into light entertainment programmes, hosting shows such as *Top Funny Comedian* 欢乐喜剧人, *Floral God* 花样男神 and *The King's Pit* 坑王驾到..

Philanthropic organisations proliferate at national level; the most famous are Project Hope 希望工程, the Narada Foundation 南都公益基金会, SEE (Society Entrepreneur Ecology) 阿拉善 SEE 生态协会, the China Social Entrepreneur Foundation 中国友成企业家扶贫基金会 and the One Foundation 壹基金. These operations are not entirely independent of the state, cannot challenge it and are therefore not campaigning organisations. Restrictions on the operations of NGOs[86] mean that their main functions are education and raising awareness. In general, the rules of registration[87] make it difficult to get legal status, so some organisations live unregistered and therefore precariously.

Their situation is very different from that of the bodies that were permitted to remain, or set up to absorb existing ones in 1949: the official trades unions, women's and youth organisations and minor political parties. So far, these have demonstrated little spirit of their own.

To summarise, China has a traditional civil society that is very localised and detached from wider national or political issues, national civil organisations that can hardly be differentiated from government agencies and organisations that cooperate with the state to provide services to the needy. What it does not have, and perhaps never has, are representative bodies which can make cases to the rulers with the public backing of their members.

5.2 The idea of the Public sphere

The idea of a public sphere is usually traced back to the late eighteenth century in northern Europe and North America,[88] though in England guilds of craftsmen, associations of burghers and local magistrates met for discussion much earlier. Today's Parliament dates from 1265 and was preceded by the 6th century Witenaġemot. By the 18th century, as people became more affluent and society more layered, there emerged associations in which political rulers still had little or no involvement. Farmers or artisans, merchants or lawyers, would meet together to discuss issues of mutual concern.[89] In those days, the space for public debate consisted mainly of inns, coffee houses, salons, literary groups and societies, and debating clubs, as well as working men's mutual aid societies of various kinds. The idea that these phenomena could be understood as a 'public sphere' became the focus of interest in 1989, when *The Structural Transformation of the Public Sphere* was translated into English. To its author, Jürgen Habermas, a public sphere has three elements: A public made up of autonomous individuals who engage in rational debate, spaces where the public can gather for this purpose, and media of communication, such as newspapers and books.[90]

5.2.1.1 Did China have a public sphere before 1949?

Surely the culture of networking and the stress on personal relationships described above provide the ideal context for the kind of discussion that makes up a public sphere? So must China have had something of the kind? Applying the idea of public sphere to China is problematic because Chinese culture has not traditionally made the Anglophone distinction between state and society. The suggestions of an official may have originated in his local coterie, but they are enacted by good servants of the state. Disgruntled peasants petition. Concerned merchants network among families with the prince's ear. There is no 'official opposition'.

Anglophones today think of society as larger and more morally legitimate than the state,[91] but Chinese notions have the state 'occupying more of the moral ground than occupied by public activists in the West'.[92] When I have asked graduate students, mostly media professionals in their twenties taking a year out, what they think, they have suggested that they see China as a family and the national leaders as 'kind of' father figures. They most definitely reject the 'them and us' distinction between rulers and ruled. That said, this does not mean that they are not critical of the leadership. Like Hai Rui 海瑞 and Qu Yuan 屈原, the heroic officials of the past who castigated the throne, they could not envisage their relationship with the state as adversarial, but could imagine themselves remonstrating.

Black Journalism

Li Wenxue 李文学's involvement in the Da Vinci scandal is an example of the corruption of journalists. Da Vinci Ltd 达芬奇家居 is a Singapore-based company that sells Italian furniture to a wide market in China, and in 2011 was undergoing an investigation over the authenticity of its products. Li, a CCTV reporter, took advantage of the scandal, and abused his position of power to extort 1 million Yuan from Da Vinci. Jin Jing from Caixin 财新 states that Li went against the ethics of news reporting.[93]

He did this firstly by fabricating information presented in two episodes of the popular consumer programme *Weekly Quality Report* 每周质量报. Li stated that Da Vinci products are sourced from a factory in Guangdong, not Italy. Li falsified the identity of Peng Jie, an employee of the factory, presenting him as the manager. Panzhuang Xiuhua, the General Manager of Da Vinci Ltd, responded with fury, by questioning how a CCTV reporter could possibly confuse such basic facts. Moreover, Li 'deliberately ignored a statement from the Shanghai Administration of Industry and Commerce 上海市工商行政管理局(SAIC) that Da Vinci products had all the necessary customs paperwork at the time.' These two episodes had a negative impact on the reputation of Da Vinci Ltd. To resolve this quickly, Panzhuang Xiuhua paid PR company Media China 2.4 million Yuan to fight allegations against the smear. As part of this deal, Panzhuang was also instructed to transfer 1 million Yuan to Li via his Hong Kong account. They had met on the 19th July 2011, and according to Panzhuang, Li said 'he had more video clips relating to the investigation of Da Vinci, and he could either make a follow-up report or not. It was a set-up by Li, who threatened Da Vinci with the extra material he possessed.

Yu Guoming, Professor of Journalism at Peoples' University 人民大学, commenting on Li, attacked 'rotten apples' in the media just when the media are needed to play an increasingly important role in monitoring society.[94]

Kerry Brown,[95] diplomat turned academic specialist on China, says that there has always been active public debate in China, even during the most turbulent times in its history, however, the degree of publicness has been variable. Chris Berry, who writes on film and documentary in China,[96] argues that the very concept is questionable, as it postulates freedom as being an absence of government. While modern European thinkers can suggest that civilisation is the antithesis of the state, in the Chinese tradition civilisation is only possible because of the state, which obliges us to control our animal instincts, co-ordinates our interests with those of the group and assures us of fair treatment. The absence of the state is not considered idyllic, but barbaric.[97] Today's state chastens the rich and ensures that the media are not in their pocket.

It is likely that prior to the national crisis prompted by 19th century imperialism, participation in public affairs was restricted to officials, their families and their other networks. Policy ideas would have been discussed at home and on social occasions, and opinions transmitted, if at all, through the bureaucracy. The efficacy of such participation would have depended upon the intelligence and receptiveness of officials in a position to influence affairs, and their ability to transmit ideas to the levels where policy decisions were taken. Those guilds and societies with proposals would not have aired them publicly but advanced them through personal channels. This might be effective but it cannot be termed a 'public sphere'. It is very much what happens today, except that now everything is much more diverse and complicated, and the state makes great efforts to gather in ideas and opinions using a multitude of means. Whether the system works is dependent upon the channels of transmission and the recipients.

In times when the state is weak or hesitant, the sphere may be more public. Historian Frank Dikötter terms the period of the Republic (1911-1949) the 'Age of Openness', meaning not only that China was open to ideas and trade from abroad, but also that it was a society in which debate and opinion were possible. Indeed, he considers it to have been more democratic than most contemporary European countries, especially Germany, Russia, Spain and Italy.[98]

5.2.1.2   The public sphere since 1949

A polity based on Marxism does not countenance what are now regarded as essential components of a healthy and humane community: a public sphere and civil society. Marxists in power do not acknowledge that ideas or institutions can exist independent of class interests. Any association independent of the beliefs and power of the 'Party of the working class' represents the interests of the class enemy. This dogma has proved very useful to politicians wanting an excuse to repress ideas different from their own, or people who might expose their failures.

Thus in the 1950s the CCP got rid of the places and associations where people might talk, while reducing the media to uniformity. Anyone showing any enterprise or initiative not to the advancement of Party power was cut down. Temples, guilds, lineage organisations and other institutions that were the product of hundreds, perhaps thousands, of years of gestation were eliminated or perverted into state agencies. Although the process in Eastern Europe is well documented, the Chinese experience has been, until Dutch historian Frank Dikotter published his remarkable trilogy on China from 1945 to 1976, less well served.[99]

In the 1980s, at least among intellectuals and in the cities, a kind of variegated and vigorous public sphere returned to China.[100] Setting up what they called circles 圈子, salons 萨隆, editorial committees 编委会, academic associations 学会, academies 书院, or institutes of structural change 提谈所, they fell into three general classifications.

Some pressed for order and rationality in the political process, others espoused the continuity of traditional moral norms in reconstructing a modern culture for China, and a third group concerned themselves with de-politicisation and humanism.[101]

A Talk Show: *Mr Zhou live show*

From 1996 to 2010 the talk show *Tell it like it is* 实话实说 was feted as the most important site of discussion of public affairs in China. As other opportunities for discussion emerged, ratings declined and current affairs shows lost ground to entertainment programmes. In 2010 *Mr Zhou Live Show* 壹周立波秀 was launched.

As with the USA's *Conan, Mr Zhou live show* opens with a monologue by the presenter; both read from cue cards. The Conan set is much smaller and more intimate than Zhou's.

Like Conan O'Brien Zhou Libo 周立波 is an established entertainer. They both project dynamism, involving themselves in the music and dancing, making ironic and facetious comments and mimicking others. Zhou is remarkable for his historical and cultural allusions, for the patriotism that infuses many of his remarks and for trenchant criticisms of authority. He is an extraordinary performer, capable of long, captivating monologues in his Shanghai accent ,full of wit and sardonic observations of society's and authority's flaws and farces.

Mr Zhou live show episode running order[102]
The 45 minute episode starts with a voiceover explanation that the programme offers a new perspective on the world; a Gangnam style dance performance and then Zhou Libo then starts his monologue on the popularity of Gangnam style, comparisons between China and Korea, and the development of the music industry. 27 minutes in, he welcomes *Zhoujin xiaojie* 周瑾小姐, a female host, and both present a comic newsreel, as is usual. The newsreel features six headlines that joke about political and social issues. Thereafter, Zhou Libo returns centre stage to begin his commentary on the controversial issue of land sequestration. He ends the show performing a song.

Topics of Discussion
1. The Gangnam Style Craze
• Mocks the popularity of the song, deems it as coarse and vulgar. Compares it to Jiangnan 江南 music which is elegant and soft.
• Popular music is successful because it is a) simple and repetitive, b) incomprehensible (like Jay Chou songs), and c) funny and interesting
2. China and Korea
• Korea once belonged to China and has similarities in culture but China is a country with a glorious history of culture 文化大国, whereas Korea is small and insignificant.
• Joke about Britain importing television sets from China in the Thatcher years, and how Britain viewed China's lack of TV shows as backward. Now China is a real country of culture, because people in many countries watch *Mr Zhou Live Show*.
3. Popular Music
• The older generation listened to songs about the nation, the leader, whereas now songs are about all sorts of emotions and issues.
• Music is a gift of Heaven; one can get through difficulties with music.
4. Mock newsreel
1. Ridiculing politics as simply 'follow my leader'; deaths caused by alcohol poisoning, a professor claims people have a rapid rate of 'detoxing' harmful elements.'; jokes about difficulties of phone reception; fake currency, Mao's face on a dumpling and Russians being alcoholics.
5. Land Sequestration
Public anger caused by local governments bullying people to move out for development. Zhou cites two cases, accusing local government of bribery, murder, and destroying houses for personal gain. There is a lack of legal advice; the process is unjust.

Zhou pulls no punches, speaking directly to the camera as the voice of the people scolding officials and warning them that the issue will not go away. He castigates them in the words of Confucius, 'do as you would be done by' 己所不欲，勿施于人.

As for the media, long reduced to a pitiful rump of newspapers and magazines which merely recycled Party encyclicals, we have seen how, since the 1980s, they have been transformed by commercialisation, devolution of power, and the government's realisation that it had less to fear from ideas than it had imagined, and limited ability to control them anyway. The combination of these factors has given rise to modern media with varied values and perspectives, though still contained 'like a bird in a cage', as a popular quip has it.[103]

Some observers see signs of a 'virtual' public sphere in the transformation of the media and the increase in spaces for public discussion.[104] As to what people can talk about, in the words of Shi Yinhong, leading scholar at Peoples' University, 'with the exception of direct criticism of China's leader or the dominant position of the Communist Party, hardly any free expressions draw administrative punishment anymore. A published written opinion that is regarded by authorities as seriously violating some basic ideological doctrine or important state policy would result in punishment, but it would be levied against the publication or its publisher, rather than the author. This stems both from the intellectual world's great opposition to punishment of free expression, and from the government's unwillingness to publicize the offending writer (and his or her views) by creating a cause celebre.'[105]

The Internet, as we have seen, is providing a space for academics, political activists, dissidents and ordinary people to debate public issues, co-ordinate meetings, voice grievances and organise gatherings.[106] Thousands of shidu 失独, parents who have lost their only child, cooperate in dealing with some of the disastrous economic and social problems arising from the One Child Policy.[107] If you are daring, you can even access proscribed critics, including the Tiananmen Mothers Campaign 天安门母亲运动 and the Falungong 法轮大法.[108]

There is abundant evidence that online communication spaces, including chat-rooms, newsgroups and bulletin boards, are 'fulfilling important functions in China's nascent public sphere'.[109] They provide alternative spaces for public debate and the articulation of social problems, and they play a supervisory role in government affairs and public life.[110] The Internet has also helped social organisations to proliferate in China, and has made planning popular protest more practicable.[111]

Media and state working together are evolving to take account of a more aware and assertive public.[112] People no longer take injustice and scandal lying down. This is exemplified by the Weiquan Movement 维权运动, a group of courageous lawyers who defend religious and ethnic minorities and struggle to see the law implemented and upheld by authority, particularly over environmental issues.[113]

Investigative journalism was the exclusive preserve of élite channels during the 1990s. Then regional and local commercial media joined in , and finally social media extended to everyone, at least in principle, the ability to shed light on abuses perpetrated by powerful interests and to set the agenda for offline media.[114] And the traditional opinion-formers have been bested.

It may be that, in contrast to the 19th century or the pre- and immediate post- 1989 periods, intellectuals have lost their special status. Doers – business people, the enterprising and creative officials – are accorded greater credibility. So the intellectuals settle down to 'feed on the emperor's grain' and, according to Zhao, to promote market economics and self-realization through money-making.[115] In 2008 though, some intellectuals stepped back into their traditional role of admonishers of those in power, when launching Charter 08, a call for the application of universal values rejected by the Party as 'westernizing'.

So far we have considered the public sphere as if it were monolithic, but recent observers have suggested that there are actually multiple public spheres. Wang Haiyan finds that journalists create 'contesting public spheres' revolving around particular clubs or bars.[116] Xing Guoxin discovers one in a Zhengzhou 郑州 workers' meeting hall,[117] and then finds out that migrant labourers have a 'counter public sphere' online.[118]

5.3   The environment as a public issue[119]

Concern about environmental issues has been a particularly important factor in leading ordinary citizens, as well as activists sometimes connected with transnational campaigners, to demonstrate and publicly debate.

The first 30 years of CCP rule left an appalling legacy of environmental destruction and mismanagement. Since then, rapid economic development has exacerbated environmental problems, ranging from algal blooms and chemical spills to droughts, floods and sandstorms.[120] According to the World Bank, 16 of the 20 cities with the worst air pollution on the planet are in China, while two thirds of its 656 cities suffer water shortages. Between 2001 and 2005, more than half the seven main rivers contained water considered unsafe for drinking, on average.[121] Many Chinese are well-informed about this and officials no longer seeks to hide the overall picture from them.[122]

As the authorities have become more concerned, so have citizens.[123] In the most recent year for which numbers are available,[124] the Ministry of Environmental Protection (MEP) 环境保护部 received 616,122 letters of complaint.[125] There were a great many disputes and demonstrations recorded, increasing from 8,706 in 1993 to 74,000 in 2004.[126] In 2005, SEPA 国家环境保护总局 (the precursor to MEP) recorded 51,000 environment-related protests and demonstrations.[127] In 2012, *People's Daily Online* reported over 100,000.

A women programme

Many television programmes focus on female issues whether dramas, soaps or current affairs and the prevailing image of woman emphasises independence and enterprise. Of about 100 programmes intended exclusively to appeal to women, talk shows are thought most influential. Compared to the British programme *Loose Women*, the Chinese equivalent, *Her Village* 女人天下, concentrate on women rather than general social issues .

Her Village profiles those who have struggled to succeed in their chosen profession and gives a platform to explain how they manage. In the example the theme is how to balance work and motherhood, and in particular how to care for babies while working. The programme highlights how the Internet, particularly *Weibo,* helps women to voice opinions and share information.

Her Village stresses the positive and gives people ideas on how to improve their lives and learn from others. *Loose Women*, on the other hand, might deal with criminality, alcohol consumption and other social issues.

Her Village[128]
This episode of 38 mins starts with an introduction to actress Shen Jiaojun 沈傲君 and her mother. The elegant host Yang Lan 杨澜 then begins with the tagline, *better self, better future* 更好的自己更好的未来. Two co-presenters also comment and ask questions throughout. Shen Jiaojun arrives to discuss a campaign to raise awareness of problems encountered by 背奶妈妈 (women who collect milk at work, to return home to feed the baby) and the issue of breastfeeding. The host then invites Kele Mama 可乐妈妈,a popular blogger on motherhood and breastfeeding, to speak. Later the director of Johnsons Baby is invited to promote the online network for mothers and a new product, a breastfeeding-notice door tag. The promotional video for the tag is screened. Yang Lang ends the show.

The topics of Discussion
1. **Breastfeeding**
- breastfeeding campaign; need for facilities for women who breastfeed.
2. **'Working Mother' – is this a double identity?**
- how to balance work with motherhood, eg how to deal with an energetic child after a tiring day of work.
- *Shen Jiaojun* criticises celebrity mothers who indulge in conspicuous consumption for children.
3. **Celebrity mothers**
- *Shen Jiaojun* tells of meeting with other celebrity mothers to discuss topics such as education and managing child behaviour
4. **Online network for mothers to share experiences, and a campaign launch**
- *Kele Mama* talks on managing work with motherhood.
- The director of Johnsons Baby and the manager of New Mother Band 新妈帮,
- Campaign for a doortag to notify people that a room is being used for breastfeeding
- Yang Lan ends with uplifting words on the delight of having children.

According to a report from *Caijing*, during the 11th Five-Year Plan period (2006-2010), over 300,000 petitions on environment matters were received by the government, which prompted the re-examination of 2,614 administrative decisions. The number of Chinese environmental protests has increased by 29% annually since 1996. Less than 1% of environmental cases are resolved through legal channels.[129] Assessments (EIA). One result was a new Regulation on Public Participation in Environmental Protection in February 2006. This was the first legal document enabling public participation in the policy-making process .In 2005, 56 NGOs wrote an open letter supporting SEPA's sanctions on 30 large infrastructure projects, which did not have official Environment Impact Assessment.

Is it too much to imagine that as the environment impinges on the consciousness of more and more people, not only are attitudes to the environment changing, but also attitudes to society and to political arrangements? Today, the authorities' concern over the environment, has led to them indulging, even encouraging, exposure. Pollution in the main cities has regularly been the front-page story of many newspapers, and leading current affairs magazines also led with pollution scare stories. Newspapers have weekly 'green' supplements, focusing on exposures. It is now expected of journalists to point to failings in environment protection and legitimate for citizens to do the same. It is acceptable to question decisions that appear to damage the environment, commonplace to form pressure groups to defend it, and axiomatic to demand transparency and accountability in its name.[130]

In the words of one Environment Correspondent: 'The reporting of environment issues is having a profound effect on our country. The government sees the need to create consensus around the issues, and therefore opens them up to public discussion and debate; news and information is opened up and a spirit of participation is fostered.'[131]

5.4   The future of the public sphere

We have noted many ways in which people are conversing, arguing, organising and participating. In comparison with the Anglosphere, Chinese commentators and public intellectuals may be, as Kerry Brown says 'much more circumscribed in their areas of engagement and the way they articulate things. They have to be much more cautious, they have to think politically all the time in ways that we don't have to' But they are always talking. The masses became the audience once media commercialisation took place. Now they are the citizens. Does all this constitute a public sphere in the Anglophone sense?[132]

I believe that the term 'networking sphere' better encapsulates the kind of society described above. The various 'public spheres' that constitute the networking sphere take different forms and are assertive in different ways from their

Anglophone counterparts. The civil society that underpins it relies upon personal relationships and intercommunication to get ideas moving and things done. The media lubricates both. Zhan Jiang 展江 believes that what distinguishes China's public sphere is that it is media-driven in a way that is not the case elsewhere: happenings, opinions, associations and fashions come about just because of the media.[133] Our 'deliberative democracy 商议民主 takes place in the media', he posits.[134] What Chinese people might mean by democracy will be discussed in Chapter 7.

We have seen that the Chinese mode of association ensures that civil society is different from that of the Anglosphere. The public sphere is different too, on account of the place of the state, cultural characteristics and how the media function. Public expression of views is more guarded than in the Anglosphere and more deference to authority is required.

'Contesting public spheres' are appearing . Does this mean that the loyalty that is such a feature of the Chinese mode of association is morphing into a wider social consciousness and concern for the public weal?[135] As LSE anthropologist Stephan Feuchtwang puts it, 'Can these relations of reciprocity and obligation become the basis for a local political life that checks the demands of powerful central state, and the ruthlessness of the capitalist economy?'[136] We might go further: is the Chinese mode of association a more effective foundation for a vigorous civil society than the individualism of the Anglosphere?

That depends on whether and how the Chinese mode of association is evolving. Yan Yunxiang, in 2003 and subsequently, writes of the individualization of Chinese society, identifying the weakening of bonds within families and between families and other networks.[137] Today, according to the author of *Deep China*, Arthur Kleinman, individuals are more interested in their personal happiness and well-being than the success of the family.[138] He describes various phenomena as related to the 'shifting focus from responsibilities to rights, from self-sacrifice to self-realisation, and ultimately from collectivity to individuality'.[139] The Chinese today are more likely to share 'the image of an enterprising self' and to perceive people as individuals making decisions about and for themselves independent of others. The self of 'personal interest' is no longer submissive to the 'self of the collectivity' as in the past, although the authorities continue to laud collective ethics and ignore or criticize growing individualism.[140]

Could this amount to an evolution from status-based relationships to contract-based ones,[141] to 'individuating' as the society evolves from a 'vertical system of relationships' to a 'lateral system of contracting individuals'?[142] If these mutations are indeed taking place, do they imply that a new moral world is coming about, and perhaps a new political world too?

The Wenzhou train crash

On 26th July 2011, Bai Yansong 白岩松, China's most famous journalist and the presenter of its best-known current affairs show, *One plus One* 一加一 was suspended from his work. Although no public announcement of the reason was provided, it was generally assumed that this was because he had expressed incredulity at the explanation given by the Railways Ministry spokesman for the high speed rail crash that had taken place at Wenzhou 温州 on 23rd July 2011

The Wenzhou crash in which a high speed train travelling at an unexceptional speed collided with a stationery one on the same track, was generally blamed on signalling failures. It was initially the technology that was at fault, but when in December the full report was issued, human error was pointed out and several dozen people lost their jobs. Although any crash with 40 dead and many injured is serious, by international standards China has a good safety record – according to one US observer, better than that of, say, the USA or India.[143] The issue that inflamed people in China was less the crash itself than the authorities' handling of it. The consequence was insubordination by some of the media.

The government immediately understood that, quite apart from the lives lost and those injured, the import of the crash would be to influence attitudes to high speed rail in China and to China's burgeoning HSR technology industry, along with its plans to sell abroad. Senior leaders rushed to the site with condolences, an inquiry was promised and at least two senior local officials were immediately sacked. However, the spokesman's explanations were muddled, and the local authorities took the eccentric step of burying the evidence – the smashed carriages, still containing the effects of the passengers – within days, In addition, the CPD attempted to stop the media from raising difficult questions or linking the crash to the conviction, a year before, of the then Minister of Railways for corruption in the awarding of HSR contracts. The public outcry on Sina Weibo was unprecedented. The foreign media berated the Chinese authorities, with David Bandurski writing in the *New York Times* that

'the political culture of expediency and secrecy is the root cause of this and other tragedies, from food and mine safety to violent property demolition'.[144]

From the perspective of an observer of media, the Wenzhou Train Crash offers an example of how the government failed to deal adequately with a public relations crisis, as well as an illustration of the growing irascibility of the media.

Kleinman and other observers are surely right to note that greater mobility of all kinds is changing how people relate to each other. The media connect people of different backgrounds and attitudes with each other on an equal footing, and in associations which bear no relation to those of the past. Volunteering and protesting may do the same, although it is possible that some of the new forms of association are actually based on old ones. The fact that people are relating to different others for different purposes does not necessarily mean that the mechanisms of communitarian behaviour are changing. While social media introduce new relations and enlarge existing networks, they also deepen and solidify existing ones.[145] New Media appear to intensify familism.

My own experience of working with Chinese media inclines me to notice the surviving characteristics as much as the new formulae. Moreover, since the Chinese mode of association – despite the pressures it impose on associates–is a bulwark against alienation, anomie and powerlessness, I tend to believe that people will resist its disintegration, just as they survived attempts to destroy the family in the 1950s and 1960s. More scientifically, after a review of studies, Feuchtwang writes that 'we can conclude that the differential mode of association is still a strong characteristic of Chinese society, but that it has changed and expanded considerably, as morally trustworthy relations are created and maintained across far greater expanses of social relationships, while forming a counterpoint to the even greater expansion of purely instrumental and anonymous economic relations'.[146]

The implication for the public sphere would appear to be that it will maintain Chinese characteristics and be more aptly described as a *networking sphere*. How this might impinge upon the development of political institutions is discussed in Chapter 7.

Notes

[1] Gripsrud J, Moe H, Molander A, Murdock G. (2011) Introduction: discovering the public sphere. In: Gripsrud J et al. *The public sphere.* London: Sage.

[2] First the Nazis, then the Communists, sought to eliminate, often by actual liquidation, those in leadership positions and the trained professionals in most spheres. See Applebaum, Anne (2012) *Iron Curtain: the crushing of Eastern Europe,* 1944-1956. London: Allen Lane. In her history of Eastern Europe under Communism, Applebaum has documented the destruction of civil society and the public sphere.

[3] Sima Y. (2011) Grassroots environmental activism and the Internet: constructing a green public sphere in China. *Asian Times.* 2011; 35(4).

[4] Brook T, Frolic BM, editors (1997) *Civil society in China.* New York: ME Sharpe.

[5] Described more fully (and drawing upon scholarship) in 戴雨果 de Burgh H (2013) 你所不了解的西方故事, *The West you really don't know.* 南京 Nanjing：江苏人民出版社 Jiangsu People's Publishing

[6] Splichal S. (2012) *Transnationalization of the public sphere and the fate of the public.* New York: Hampton Press, pp 81.

[7] de Burgh H, Xin X. (2003)News Probe: what does it tell us about Chinese journalism today? *Medien Journal.* 2003; 30(2-3): 52-66.

[8] There is a genre of book which reviews and evaluates this kind of journalism. For example: 连玉明,武建忠 Lian, Y. and Wu, J. (2011) 中国舆情报告 *The Report of Chinese Public Opinions.* 中国时代经济出版社 China Modern Economics Publishing House, 陈夷茁 Chen, Y. (2011) 民生新闻案例解读 *Case Studies Of Citizen News.* 重庆大学出版社 Chongqing University Press and 曾国华 Zeng, G. (2006) 中国式调查报道 *Chinese Muckrakers.* 南方日报出版社 Nanfang Daily Press. In addition there are the collections of investigations published by the media themselves, eg 新闻调查栏目组 News Probe (2006) "调查"十年 News Probe 1996-2006. 三联书店 Joint Publishing and 南方报业传媒集团南方传媒学院 Nanfang Media Group (2012) 南方传媒研究 Nanfang Media Research. 南方日报出版社 Nanfang Daily Press.

[9] Wang, H. (2010) *Investigative journalism and political power in China* (Reuters Institute Working Paper). Oxford: Reuters Institute, University of Oxford.

[10] For example, see SMG's news channel 新闻综合频道, and in particular a programme called One Seventh 七分之一, transmitted every Sunday evening. The author is grateful to Tang Ju for drawing this to his attention.

[11] The examples cited here are taken from Zhan Jiang, with whom the author had an extensive discussion on 12 January 2013, and who subsequently sent the author his lecture notes.

[12] ibid.

[13] Bingdian (Freezing Point), the weekly supplement of *China Youth Daily* 中国青年报 was closed down after it featured a reinterpretation of nineteenth-century Anglo-Chinese history.

[14] Lu Yuegang. Personal communication to author and Xin Xin; 2004. Lu had just been sacked as Associate Editor of the 'Freezing Point' section of China Youth Daily.

[15] Li Qichan et al 李其谚 王晓冰. Whose Shandong energy? 谁的鲁能? In: *Caixin* 财新. [Internet] **2007 年 01 月 08 日** . Available from: http://magazine.caixin.com/2007-01-08/100080339.html

[16] Willetts, David (2010) *The Pinch*. London Atlantic Books, pp6. He draws upon the Cambridge Group for the History of Population and Social Structure.

[17] Ibid., pp 19.

[18] Much of the success has been attributed to the 'Town & Village Enterprises' TVEs (see L Brandt, T Rawski (eds.) (2008) *China's great economic transformation.* Cambridge: Cambridge University Press, pp 57; also H Lai (2008) *Reform and the non-state economy in China.* New York: Palgrave, pp 16, 233, 248-9.

[19] Schell, Orville and Delury, John (2013) *Wealth and Power: China's Long March to the Twenty-First Century* New York: Random House.

[20] Raymond Williams laid the foundations of cultural studies with his *Culture and Society,* (London: Chatto and Windus, 1958) and other works. 'Culture is ordinary' and 'culture is a whole way of life' are expressions attributed to him.

[21] Franz Boas explained differences between human societies as being functions of culture. He introduced the concept of 'cultural relativism' . He is often regarded as the founding father of modern anthropology.

[22] Willetts (2010), pp 11.

[23] Perkins DH. (2000) Law, family ties and the East Asian way of business. In: Harrison LE, Huntington SP. (eds.) *Culture matters: how values shape human progress.* New York: Basic Books. See also Berger Peter L. and Hsiao Hsin-Huang Michael (eds.), (1988) *In Search of an East Asian Development Model* New Brunswick, N.J.: Transaction Books. Tai Hung-chao, (ed.) (1989) *Confucianism and Economic Development: An Oriental Alternative?* Washington, D.C.: Washington Institute Press. Chung-Hua Institution for Economic Research (1989) *Conference on Confucianism and Economic Development in East Asia* Taipei: CIER Press. Vogel, Ezra F. (1991) *The Four Little Dragons: The Spread of Industrialization in East Asia* Cambridge: Harvard University Press. Jochim, Christian (1992) Confucius and Capitalism: Views of Confucianism in Works on Confucianism and Economic Development. In: *Journal of Chinese Religions*, no. 20.

[24] Friedman TL. (2008) *New York Times.* 27 August 2008. Quoted in Zhang Weiwei. *The China wave: rise of a civilizational state*, Hackenstack, NJ: World Century Publishing; 2011, 7.

[25] The key texts are those of Emmanuel Todd, (1985) *The Explanation of Ideology.* Oxford: Blackwell; and *The Causes of Progress.* (1987) Oxford: Blackwell. These describe the ramifications of the exogamous community family. For China in particular, see C-Y Chiu, Y-Y Hong, (2006) *Social psychology of culture.* New York: Psychology Press.

[26] Anthropologists are reasonably clear about the unusual individualism and egalitarianism of Anglophone culture, which sets it apart from most others. See, for example, MacFarlane A (1978) *The Origins of English Individualism: The Family, Property and Social Transition*, Cambridge: Blackwells and Cambridge Univ. Press

[27] Max Weber famously blamed Confucianism for China's failure to develop capitalism. However, he was thinking of the anti-commercial, self-cultivating ethic of the leisured classes, ideas which hardly applied to the mass of those who practised the behaviours that I (following scholars in anthropology) identify as the 'rules' or popular Confucianism. To blame a small number of etiolated gentlemen for a failure to have an industrial revolution is rather like blaming the British élite's love of country houses on that nation's relative economic decline.

[28] It is curious how early Western observers of China accord with modern sociologists. For an overview of these characteristics, insofar as they may be relevant to the media, see Zeng Rong, *Television news and the limits of globalisation: BBC World and Phoenix Television today.* Buckingham: University of Buckingham Press; 2012: pp.9-12.

[29] The term 'grammar of action' is derived from Social Rule System Theory, a sub-set of New Institutionalism.

[30] England's comparable great period of growth also took place because of economic freedom and local decision-making. Its people were more individualistic than China's, which meant that they could not benefit as much from family solidarity and networks as Chinese do, but they too were extraordinarily pragmatic. The great inventions which made possible the Industrial Revolution were made by those who had never been to university and had not studied science, but had good maths and grammar plus an enterprising and enquiring attitude. (This is a quotation from 戴雨果 de Burgh H (2013) 你所不了解的西方故事, *The West you really don't know.* 南京 Nanjing：江苏人民出版社 Jiangsu People's Publishing: Chapter 1)

[31] As few other than Americans know, Alexis de Tocqueville wrote some of the most perceptive sociological observations of other cultures that have ever been produced. The first volume of *Democracy in America* was published in 1835. His writings not only help us to understand the USA today, and whence it has come, but also the relationships between different cultures.

[32] Hofstede, Geert (2001) *Culture's Consequences: comparing values, behaviors, institutions, and organizations across nations* Thousand Oaks: Sage.

[33] Fei Xiaotong (1992) *From the Soil: The Foundations of Chinese Society*, Berkeley: U California Press.

[34] Feuchtwang Stephan (2015) Social Egoism and Individualism. In: *Journal of China in comparative perspective* volume one number 1 June 2015, pp 143 to 160, pp 148.

[35] Li, Jin (2012) *Cultural foundations of learning, East and West.* Cambridge: Cambridge University Press, pp 37.

[36] Hsu, Francis (1986) *Americans & Chinese*, Honolulu: University of Hawaii Press

[37] MacFarlane, A (2015) *A Modern Education* Cambridge: Cambridge Rivers Press p65 He quotes Hsu, Francis (1986) *Americans & Chinese*, Honolulu: University of Hawaii Press on p 67.

[38] See Bretton, John and Gold, Jeff (2012) *Human Resource Management: Theory and Practice*, Basingstoke: Palgrave MacMillan, pp 519-20.

[39] Nakane, Chie (2013) *Japanese Society.* London: Pelican, pp 22.

[40] Fei Xiaotong contrasts 'Western' and 'Chinese' and reveals by doing so that he was not familiar either with other East Asian societies (which closely resemble China in these respects) or with those 'western societies', for example, Greece and southern Italy, which may well be more like China than they are like Northern Europe, an insight which further helps us to grasp that supposedly 'universal' ideas about civil society are probably parochial. See Banfield, Edward (1958): *Amoral Familism: the moral basis of a backward society.* Glencoe, Ill.: The Free Press and Campbell, John (1964) *Honour, Family, and Patronage: A Study of Institutions and Moral Values in a Greek Mountain Community.* Oxford, England: Clarendon Press.

[41] For a very graphic illustration of the involvement of work colleagues in personal life, see Chi Li's novel *Coming and Going*, in which the protagonist, a successful businessman, is visited by his own former boss plus his wife's former boss and upbraided for wishing to divorce her. 池莉 Chi Li (2009) 来来往往. 北京 Beijing：十月文艺出版社 October Arts & Literature Publishing House. I

came across a real life situation while working with Hunan TV which illustrates ways of thinking that probably seem incredible to modern Anglophones. When a particularly strong-willed and independent producer 'Sally' announced she would have a baby out of wedlock, shock waves went around her colleagues in Hunan TV. If Sally were to give birth, not one of her superiors would ever again attain promotion. That's the rule. Of course her colleagues tried to talk her out of it. But when it seemed that she was pregnant, the discussion changed: who could be persuaded to marry her? And if necessary, whose wife could be persuaded to divorce her husband so that he might marry 'Sally' and save everybody's careers? Many dinners were shared chewing over this issue.

[42] Forming groups facilitates collective working, as studies of Chinese students abroad have demonstrated (see Lamb, Bernard (2007) 'Foreign Students: Their Effects on UK Higher Education', in de Burgh, H, Fazackerley A and Black, J (eds.) (2007) *Can the Prizes Still Glitter? The Future of the Universities in a Changing World.* Oxford: University of Buckingham Press). The template for the facility for collectivity probably lies in collective parenting and is the norm in East Asian societies, although possibly being undermined by urbanisation. Whereas children in Anglophone societies are brought up by two, or increasingly, one parent, in China the job is shared and the child becomes habituated to moving in a sometimes quite extensive circle of adults from birth. Grandparents, aunts and uncles all have potentially unlimited responsibilities towards the child, and obligations never cease with age. In fact, it has often been noted that although the family is recognised in both China and the Anglosphere, both as the gateway of happiness and as the building block of society, it is filial piety that is the Chinese cement, rather than marital fidelity, as in the Anglosphere. [filial piety is not a good translation of xiao 孝, which might be better rendered as 'role respect']

[43] In episode 51 of the TV series *Good Husbands* 大丈夫, an entrepreneur defends an employee charged with being inefficient on the grounds that she is a longstanding friend and with the words 'a good heart is more important'.

[44] After acting as External Examiner on a PhD which I found interesting, I wrote to the head of media at one of China's leading universities, a longstanding associate, that the examinee might be worth meeting. I was embarrassed when he promptly engaged her as a lecturer on the strength, as he put it 'of your recommendation alone'.

[45] Unger, Jonathan and Chan, Anita (2007) 'Memories and the Moral Economy of a Stare-Owned Enterprise' in Lee, Ching Kwan and Yang Guobin (eds) (2007) *Re-envisioning the Chinese Revolution* Stanford : Stanford University Press

[46] For a thorough discussion of this, see Fei Hsiaotong (1992) *From the Soil, The Foundations of Chinese Society*, Berkeley: University of California Press, pp 21 et seq.

[47] Tong Chee Kiong and Yong Pit Kee (1998) Guanxi Bases, Xinyong and Chinese Business Networks *The British Journal of Sociology* Vol. 49, No. 1 (Mar., 1998), pp. 75-96

[48] Hamilton, Gary G. (2015) What Western social scientists can learn from the writings of Fei Xiaotong. In: *Journal of China in Comparative Perspective* Vol 1 Number 1 June 2015, pp 143 to 160. Hamilton, pp 126, describes the 'ideal' of how Taiwan business people organise their business dealings. The owner and the wife are the inner core, around which is an inner circle of confidantes and other concentric rings of contacts.

[49] Zakaria, Fareed (2007) *The Future of Freedom.* London: Norton.

[50] Brown, Kerry (2015) *The New emperors: power and the princelings in China,* London: I B Tauris, pp 25.

[51] Unger, Jonathan (ed) (2002) *The Nature of Chinese Politics, from Mao to Jiang*, Armonk: ME Sharpe. This volume is the best illumination of the spirit of Chinese politics that exists to date. Others who have shed light on the cultural dynamics include Chiu, Chi-yue and Hong, Ying-yi (2006) *Social Psychology of Culture.* New York: Psychology Press.

[52] As opposed to the system ostensibly held to in CCTV, whereby your points depend upon the number of transmissions, audience and sales. In most newspapers reporters' pay is linked to the number of stories published.

[53] Lee (2005), pp 111.

[54] Jin Yongquan, quoted in: Polumbaum J, Xiong L. (2008) *China ink: the changing face of Chinese journalism*. Lanham, Md: Rowman & Littlefield, pp 63.

[55] In big state-run media units where managers may take little interest in their employees, relationships are likely to be more fractious and hierarchy may be resented by those on the bottom.

[56] In a detached relationship, hierarchy may be unpleasant and divisive, whereas it need not be so where the relationship is warmer. Hierarchy between parents and children should be entirely positive and in no way diminish mutual respect and affection; similarly with teachers and pupils.

[57] Chinese scholars have long noticed the connection. 'from the concept of God, who is actually the symbol of universal organisation, two important corollaries have emerged. One is that everyone is equal before God, and the other is that God treats everyone with equal justice' in Fei, Hsiaotong (1992) *From the Soil, The Foundations of Chinese Society*. Berkeley: University of California Press, pp 72.

[58] Changes are afoot, at least in big enterprises. Guthrie [Guthrie D. (2006) *China and globalisation*. London: Routledge, pp 294] states that, increasingly, 'in the work unit, labour relations have been formalised with formal recruitment procedures, proper contracts, organisational rules, grievance procedures and representation'. He also makes the point that 'the vast majority of labour disputes settled by arbitration on mediation are decided in favour of the workers who filed the suits' [Guthrie, pp 294].

[59] As an employer of several Chinese, I was at first bemused when I got a dressing down from some of them for not having taken upon myself the responsibility of finding a husband for an unmarried woman whom her colleagues considered to be approaching the age after which finding a husband would be impossible.

[60] Although the society is more flexible than, say, Japanese, in this regard, nevertheless ranking consciousness is greater than in Anglo-America. This is very noticeable to Anglophones holding meetings with Chinese organisations; those who speak first and most are senior, the juniors hold back. Present in the early days of several new creative companies involving young Chinese (almost invariably at least partly educated in the Anglosphere), I noticed that a ranking system, with the appropriate nomenclature (older sister, younger man), immediately comes about. It would be wrong to think that this kind of acknowledgment of authority gives untrammelled power to the bosses – far from it. Leadership has many restrictions and obligations placed on it by group consensus, so that the leader leads as often as not by influencing the consensus; s/he is less likely to issue formal orders than use persuasion exerted in person-to-person contact. Ranking consciousness sounds, at least to Anglophones, rather negative, but when re-conceived as acknowledgment of responsibility and authority, respect for education and achievement, then it may seem more positive. There are some telling illustrations of the power of relationships and how they trump what Anglophones would consider to be morality, in Leslie T Chang's (2008) *Factory Girls*, New York: Picador, pp 193.

[61] Personal communication with Marsh, Vivien, 2015.

[62] Dong SG, Shi Anbin. Chinese news in transition: facing the challenge of global competition. In: Thussu DK, editor. *Media on the move: global flow and contra-flow*. London: Routledge; 2006: Chapter 11: 190.

[63] 7. Zhao Yuezhi (2012) 'Understanding China's Media System'. In: Hallin, DC and Mancini, P (eds.) *Comparing media systems beyond the western world*, Cambridge: Cambridge University Press, pp 172.

[64] Willetts, David (2010) *The Pinch*. London Atlantic Books, pp 20.

[65] Huang, Philip CC (1978) *The Development of Underdevelopment in China*. New York: ME Sharpe, pp 3.

[66] Weller, Robert P (2001) *Alternative Civilities: Democracy and Culture in China and Taiwan*. Boulder: Westview, pp 27-32.

[67] Wakeman, Frederic (1993) The Civil Society Public Sphere Debate, Western Reflections on Chinese Political Culture. In: *Modern China*, April 1993, 19, 2, pp 108-138. See also: Rowe, William T. (1993) 'The Problem of "Civil Society" in late Imperial China' in *Modern China*, April 1993 19, 139-157.

[68] In a class situation, not only will the teacher's wife be called 'teaching mother', but older and younger students or senior and junior students will call each other 'older sister', 'younger brother' and so forth. In companies, the boss is called 'teacher' or 'older brother', and a sponsor or patron will often be referred to as 'older brother' or 'older sister'.

[69] Fei, Hsiaotong (1992) *From the Soil, The Foundations of Chinese Society*. Berkeley: University of California Press, Chapter 12, pp 123.

[70] Although Wielander tells us that Christianity is influencing society's values in unexpected ways (Wielander, Dr Gerda spoke on 26 November 2013 at the University of Westminster to launch her book: *Christian Values in Communist China*. London: Routledge; 2013).

[71] Weller (2001)

[72] Ibid., pp 135.

[73] Graphic descriptions of how corruption blighted the lives of factory workers before the 1980s are contained in Lee, Ching Kwan (2007) 'What was socialism to Chinese workers?' in Lee, Ching Kwan and Yang Guobin (eds) (2007) *Re-envisioning the Chinese Revolution* Stanford : Stanford University Press

[74] Ibid., pp 69.

[75] Ibid., pp 86. Several of my students report that their parents have joined in the rebuilding of family temples in which every earlier generation gets a tablet and hours of pleasure are gained from study of the genealogy.

[76] Ibid., pp 118.

[77] Ibid., pp 72.

[78] Ibid., pp 136-7.

[79] Ngo T-W (2011) Introduction: civil society, citizenship, and popular resistance. In: *Contemporary China Studies – Economy and Society*. III. In: Ngo T-W, editor. Civil society, citizenship, and popular resistance.

[80] Wang and He (2004), quoted in Teets JC. (2013) Let many civil societies bloom: the rise of consultative authoritarianism in China. I. March 2013, pp 6.

[81] Thornton PM. (2013) The advance of the party: transformation or takeover of urban grassroots society? *China Quarterly*. March 2013, pp 9.

[82] Tsinghua University NGO Research Centre, 2006.

[83] Teets JC. (2013) Let many civil societies bloom: the rise of consultative authoritarianism in China. *China Quarterly*. March 2013, pp 27.

[84] Sima Y. (2011) Grassroots environmental activism and the Internet: constructing a green public sphere in China. *Asian Times*, 35 (4).

[85] Ibid. See also: All-China Environment Federation. *Summary report on the development of China's environmental civil society organisations in 2008*. [Online]. All-China Environment Federation; 2008. Available at: www.acef.com.cn and Stern, Rachel E.(2013) Environmental Litigation in China, Cambridge: Cambridge University Press.

[86] Xie L. (2009) *Environmental activism in urban China: the role of personal networks*. London; New York: Routledge; pp 4, 21.

[87] 1989 Regulation on the Registration and Management of Social Organizations 社会团体登记管理条例 1989 年 10 月 13 日国务院第四十九次常务会议通过 1989 年 10 月 25 日国务院令第四十三号发布自发布之日起施行.

[88] Gripsrud J, Moe H, Molander A, Murdock G. (2011) Introduction: discovering the public sphere. In: Gripsrud J et al. *The public sphere*. London: Sage.

[89] Roberts JM, Crossley N, (eds.) (2004) *After Habermas: new perspectives on the public sphere*. Oxford: Blackwell/Sociological Review.

[90] Yang, G. (2011) The Internet and civil society in China: a preliminary assessment. *Contemporary China Studies – Economy and Society*. III. In: Ngo T-W, editor. Civil society, citizenship, and popular resistance.

[91] Brook T, Frolic BM, editors. (1997) *Civil society in China*. New York: ME Sharpe.

[92] Ibid.

[93] *Wang, J, 2012.* 达芬奇回应李文学:材料均有证据佐证称欲把其更名为"芬达奇, Caijing, *[online] Available at: (http://politics.caijing.com.cn/2012-01-02/111587462.html) (Accessed 22nd September 2013)*

[94] Gao, Y et al, 2012. Corruption and Journalism: the case of Da Vinci, *Caixin* [online] Available at: (http://english.caixin.com/2012-01-04/100345676.html) (Accessed 20th September 2013)

[470] Brown, K. Personal Communication; 15 January 2012.

[96] Berry C. Personal communication; 18 January 2012.

[97] Ibid.

[98] Dikötter, F. (2008) *The Age of Openness: China before Mao*. Berkeley, CA: University of California Press.

[99] Frank Dikotter *The Tragedy of Liberation*, *Mao's Great Famine* and *The Cultural Revolution: A Peoples' History 1962-1976*. Preceding those there were, however, some remarkable testimonies, for example Shapiro, J and Liang Heng (1984) *Son of the revolution*. London: Fontana and Thaxton, Ralph A. (2008) *Catastrophe and Contention in Rural China* Cambridge: CUP .

[100] From 1978-9 courageous people created the Democracy Wall （see p53. According to Zhao (1998: 75) According to Zhao (1998: 75) in1980 Deng Xiaoping also abolished the four great freedoms 四大自由 enshrined in the Constitution (speech, air views, debating, poster-writing 言论自由, 观点自由, 辩论自由, 大字报写作自由)

[101] Yan Jiaqi and Gao Gao (1996) *Turbulent Age, A History of the Cultural Revolution*. Honolulu: Shaps, pp xii.

[102] Episode transmitted by Hunan Broadcasting System on 12th August 2012 at 00:10 and researched by Stacey Ng.
http://www.iqiyi.com/zongyi/20121230/72ea2a04f17d3585.html#curid=328023_ce9b07d5e0b640
388dac76ecb443c003

[103] Zhan, Jiang (2011) Environmental journalism in China. In: Shirk SL. (ed.) *Changing media, changing China*. New York: Oxford University Press, pp 116.

[104] Yang, G. (2011) The Internet and civil society in China: a preliminary assessment. Contemporary China Studies – Economy and Society. III. In: Ngo T-W. (ed.) *Civil society, citizenship, and popular resistance*. See also Splichal, S. (2012) *Transnationalization of the public sphere and the fate of the public*. New York: Hampton Press.

[105] Shi, Yinhong (2004) The Issue of Civil Society and its Complexity, Chapter 18. In: Sato Yoichiro (ed) *Growth & Governance in Asia*, Honolulu: Asia-Pacific Centre for Security Studies, pp 230.

[106] Ngo, T-W. (2011) Introduction: civil society, citizenship, and popular resistance. *Contemporary China Studies – Economy and Society*. III. In: Ngo T-W, editor. *Civil society, citizenship, and popular resistance*.

[107] Fong, Mei (2016) in London : *The Sunday Times Magazine*, 3 January 2016, pp 28.

[108] Tai, Zixue. (2006) *The Internet in China: cyberspace and civil society*. New York; London: Routledge (Taylor & Francis Group).

[109] Yang, G. (2011).

[110] Ibid.

[111] Ibid.

[112] Zhan, Jiang (2011) Environmental journalism in China. In: Shirk SL. (ed.) *Changing media, changing China*. New York: Oxford University Press.

[113] Nicola McBean, speaking at the Said Business School, Oxford University on 20th February 2016, reports that there has been an unprecedented crackdown on these and other rights organisations http://www.rights-practice.org/en/about.html

[114] Ibid., pp 116-117.

[115] Zhao, Yuezhi (2012) 'Your Show's Been Cut: The Politics of Intellectual Publicity in China's Brave New Media World'. In: *Javnost: Communication and Class Divide in China*, Vol. 19 - 2012, No. 2, pp 101-118, also quoting Xu Jilin (2010).

[116] Wang, Haiyan (2013) *Journalism, Activism and Counter-public Sphere in China: A Case Study of a Contentious Journalist Community in Guangzhou,* A Thesis Submitted in Partial Fulfillment of the Requirements for the Degree of Doctor of Philosophy in Communication, HK: The Chinese University of Hong Kong.

[117] Xing, Guoxin (2012) Online Activism and Counter-public Spheres: A Case Study of Migrant Labour Resistance in Communication and Class Divide in China. Javnost – The Public, Vol. 19 – 2012, No. 2: 63-82.

[118] Xing, Guoxin (2011) Urban Workers' Leisure Culture and the 'Public Sphere': A Study of the Transformation of the Workers' Cultural Palace in Reform-Era China. *Critical Sociology,* November 2011 vol. 37 no. 6: 817-835.

[119] This section is adapted from de Burgh H, Zeng R. (2012) *China's environment and China's environment journalists: a study* Bristol: Intellect, which also contains a much fuller contextualisation and history of the environment movement in China.

[120] Liu, J and Diamond J. (2008) Revolutionizing China's environmental protection. *Science.* 2008; 319:37-38.

[121] World Bank/State Environmental Protection Administration of China. 2007. Cost of pollution in China: economic estimates of physical damages. [Online]. Washington DC: World Bank; 2007 [cited 31 July 2013]. Available at: http://siteresources.worldbank.org/INTEAPREGTOPENVIRONMENT/Resources/China_Cost_of_Pollution.pdf (Accessed: 17 March 2016).

[122] Economic growth has improved basic living conditions, feeding, housing, health and employment, and brought some 400 million people out of poverty. If economic growth continues, the situation of the 200 million people still living on less than one dollar a day should soon improve.[World Bank/State Environmental Protection Administration of China. 2007. *Cost of pollution in China: economic estimates of physical damages.* [Online]. Washington DC: World Bank; 2007 [cited 31 July 2013]. Available at: http://siteresources.worldbank.org/INTEAPREGTOPENVIRONMENT/Resources/China_Cost_of_Pollution.pdf (Accessed: 17 March 2016). However, the environmental problems linked to economic growth are themselves causing economic loss. Elizabeth Economy writes of 'the terrible price' that the environment has paid 'for this impressive transformation' in the opening passages of her book, [Economy EC. (2004) *The river runs black: the environmental challenge to China's future.* London: Cornell University Press.], adding that it is 'impinging on continued economic development, forcing large-scale migration, and inflicting significant harm on the public's health'.

[123] Well discussed in Yang G, Calhoun C. (2007) Media, civil society, and the rise of a green public sphere in China. *China Information*, pp 211-235.

[124] There are other figures, but they are confusing and disputed. For instance, see a January 2013 report from Danwei, http://www.danwei.com/a-report-on-mass-incidents-in-china-in-2012/ (Accessed: 17 March 2016).

[125] SEPA.(2006) China Environment Statistical Report. 2006; Part 2, pp 24.

[126] Caijing. The annual growth rate of environmental protests has been up to 29% in China, but less than 1% of environmental cases are resolved through legal channels. [Online]. 2012 [cited 24 March 2013]: 62. Available at: http://politics.caijing.com.cn/2012-10-27/112233970.html (Accessed: 17 March 2016).

[127] Ma, Tianjie (2008) Environmental Mass Incidents in Rural China: Examining Large-Scale Unrest in Dongyang, Zhejiang. *China Environment Series*, The Woodrow Wilson International Center for Scholars.

[128] Episode transmitted by Hunan Broadcasting System on 12th August 2012 at 00:10 and researched by Stacey Ng.
http://www.iqiyi.com/zongyi/20121230/72ea2a04f17d3585.html#curid=328023_ce9b07d5e0b640
388dac76ecb443c003

[129] *Caijing*. The annual growth rate of environmental protests has been up to 29% in China, but less than 1% of environmental cases are resolved through legal channels. [Online]. 2012 [cited 24 March 2013]. Available at: http://politics.caijing.com.cn/2012-10-27/112233970.html (Accessed: 17 March 2016).

[130] de Burgh H, Zeng, R. (2011) *Environment and China's environment journalists: a study.* Chicago: Intellect/University of Chicago Press; Bristol: Intellect.

[131] Respondents in this study requested, and have received, anonymity.

[132] Ngo, T-W. (2011)

[133] For an extraordinary compendium of what is going on in this field, see 连玉明&武建忠 Lian Y and Wu J (2011) 中国舆情报告. *Public Sentiment: the report* 中国时代经济出版社. Beijing: China Modern Economics Publishing House.

[134] Zhan, Jiang, lecture at the China Media Centre, London, February 2013.

[135] This kind of evolution took place in Medieval Europe; perhaps the modernisers are right and that other societies go through the same gestation. Siedentop, thinking of the ancient (Mediterranean) world, describes 'the restriction of affection to the family circle', that the most important thing in life was fulfilling roles ascribed by the family, that the individual was a piece of that family and 'neither the master of his property nor of himself'. He then investigates how 'moral intuitions' changed, over several hundred years, to those advanced by Christianity, which would become the basis of secularism and the Enlightenment. (Siedentop op cit pp 117) Is China undergoing an analogous process, which would affect all its institutions?

[136] Feuchtwang (2015), pp 151.

[137] Yan, Yunxiang (2003) *Private Life under Socialism: Love, Intimacy, and Family Change in a Chinese Village, 1949-1999* Stanford: Stanford University Press.

[138] Kleinman, Arthur (2011) *Deep China*, Berkeley: U of California Press, pp 45.

[139] Ibid., pp 47.

[140] Ibid., pp 8.

[141] MacFarlane, Alan (2015) *A Modern Education.* Cambridge: Cambridge Rivers Press, pp 33, 52-3,55, 66-67, 75-76.

[142] Ibid., pp 75-76.

[143] Zeliger R. You think this weekend's Chinese train crash was bad? It's nothing compared to India's deadly rails. [Internet]. *Foreign Policy*. 2011 July 25 [cited 2013 Aug 26]. Available from: http://blog.foreignpolicy.com/posts/2011/07/25/you_think_this_weekend_s_chinese_train_crash_
was_bad_it_s_nothing_compared_to_india

[144] Bandurski D. *New York Times*, 2011 Jul 28.

[145] My students in the UK are typically messaging their parents everyday and can keep in touch with their cousins (important because so few have brothers or sisters) and aunts and uncles with regularity denied previous generations.

[146] Ibid., pp 158.

6 Defending Identity : Managing Ideas

Although Confucianism and Marxism are at odds in many fundamental ways, the workstyles of their adherents have been similar enough to make for a painless transition for the patriot students who built the Communist Party of China. The elitism of the Bolsheviks appealed to those brought up to be members of a Confucian ruling class and the ideological conformity seemed natural. Although Marxists abjured traditional ethics, once in power they became moralistic. Both philosophies were suspicious of commerce and of the depraving influence of the profit motive. The guidance of ideas and information was axiomatic for both, although Marxists, unlike the Confucians, justified the suppression of heterodoxy on the grounds that all ideas are renditions of class interests.

The media belong to the state apparatus; the state apparatus is directed by the Party. In sight of the foreign diplomat, business negotiator or citizen, are the Finance Ministry or the courts or the universities or creative enterprises. Yet strategic and personnel decisions in all of these and others are made by a parallel organisation, the Party, at every level of social or economic activity. Lucien Pye complains that the line between politics and administration that is normal elsewhere is blurred in China.[1] Zheng Yongnian, Head of Singapore's East Asian Institute, likens the Party to the Emperor, whose agents can interfere in every branch of administration, while Frank Pieke, of Leiden University, refers to it as the superego of governance and its pivot, the mysterious Zhongnanhai leadership compound, as the 'Sacred Void'.[2]

Today, control of the media is justified less by the Marxist theory than as a defence against enemy propaganda, dysfunctional lifestyles and subversive values. As International Relations academic Daniel Lynch writes, 'China's leaders do believe that they should be inculcating standards other than just material ones, they have an idea of what a socialist spiritual civilisation should promote'.[3] President Xi emphasises Chineseness: 'We should carry forward and foster the traditional morality long cultivated and developed by our ancestors'.[4]

To the Confucians as to the Marxists, Anglophone individualism is unpleasant and undesirable, a consequence of capitalism's turning people into wage slaves and customers rather than of liberation. Commercial values corrupt and vulgarise, business people should not be allowed to influence the culture when their motivation is profit, and short termism and hedonism are threats to survival. Faced by Anglophone 'hegemony' Confucians have come to believe that the 'site of political battles' is cultural: they have to fight spiritual pollution. And all this in a country where the drive to get rich has propelled China to becoming the most successful economy in the world!

Media People: head of a propaganda department

Zhu Yi 朱毅 After being head of the Propaganda Department of the city of Wuhan, an important industrial centre of 10million people, Zhu was promoted to Member of the Standing Committee of Hubei Provincial People's Congress and Secretary General of the Party Committee.

Zhu began his career in 1981 and joined the CCP in 1985. He was appointed as Deputy Secretary of the Wuhan City Committee of the Communist Youth League of China in 1993. Four years later he was deputy secretary of the CPC Wuhan Jiang'an District Committee. In July 2005 Zhu was elevated to serve as member and Secretary-general of the Standing Committee of Wuhan City Committee of the CPC. He attended part-time postgraduate courses after entering employment and obtained his master's degree.

Image source:
http://zt.cjn.cn/zt2011/bn/rm
tt/201201/t1606251.htm

Several books by Zhu Yi have been published, on aspects of Wuhan history and culture; married to an architect, he is an amateur of Chinese traditional furnishings and porcelain.

While defending these values at home, neo-Confucians also promote their view of how information in the wider world should be managed. Li Congjun, President of Xinhua News Agency, wrote on this theme in the *Wall Street Journal* in 2011. He notes that the world's information and communications channels are dominated by the rich, the powerful and the entrenched. He seeks a global media organization, rather like the UN, to promote fairness. He wants respect for diversity, transparency and equality for all countries. The unspoken but underlying belief was that Anglosphere propaganda crowds out other voices and serves the purposes of the old hegemons.[5] While waiting for international action, the Chinese authorities limit the influence of foreign media at home.

6.1 The Central Propaganda Department (CPD)

Nationally, the most important agency for setting the media agenda is the Central Propaganda Department 中共中央宣传部 of the CCP. This body is widely considered to be as powerful as, if not more important than, the Central Organisation Department 中国共产党中央组织部, which manages the appointment of those who run Party, government, state enterprises and armed forces and is therefore a potent influence on the media. Its power is illustrated by an event in early 2011. As was widely reported, Prime Minister Wen Jiabao visited the State Petitions Office 国家信访局 to show his concern that petitioners 上访者 against injustice were not being treated appropriately by many local authorities. The Central Propaganda Department criticised the Prime Minister for doing this, a surprising but not unprecedented revelation. The year before, it had been reported that Wen had had parts of his speeches censored on 'at least four occasions in recent months'.[6]

Quoting a Party publication, David Shambaugh comments that its definition of the CPD 'means that virtually every conceivable medium that transmits and conveys information to the people of China falls under the bureaucratic purview of the CCP Propaganda Department. This includes all media organs, all schools and educational institutions, all literary and art organs and all publishing outlets'.[7]

The CPD is responsible for (a) issuing instructions on content, (b) the professional development of content managers (editors, publishers) and (c) monitoring the content of communications to ensure that they do not cross the official line on topics that the Party considers important. It is particularly interested in books, films or other publications which touch on foreign policies, the leadership, minorities and religion. It has units at every level of administration, and local newspapers and broadcasting channels must take account of them. The CPD answers for the *xitong* (the network of information and cultural institutions) and to the principal decision-making body in China, the Standing Committee of the Politburo of the Central Committee of the CCP 中共中央政治局常委会. However, the strategic body for the whole *xitong* is the Leadership Group on Informatization, created in its present form in 2001 and currently chaired by President Xi.

6.2 Responding to a new environment

Since 1978, the CPD has been faced with a number of challenges. In the 1980s, it became clear not merely that people no longer believed in the state ideology, but that few of the traditional methods of mobilising support or promoting the values so forcefully propagated in China actually worked after the Cultural Revolution (1965-75). By 1989, journalists were demonstrating in the street for freedom of information and 'freedom not to lie'.[8]

The leadership of the Party was shaken by the Tiananmen Square Massacre of 4th June 1989. In its analysis of the causes and repercussions, it decided that much of the blame lay with the Party's failure to remember that 'thought work' is the basis of everything.[9] This, according to the leadership, had permitted pernicious ideas to take hold, in particular what they regarded as the fraudulent concepts of electoral democracy and freedom of the press. The Party's position was that in 'the West' only the rich enjoyed democracy and freedom to speak. Those who had been seduced into thinking otherwise were dupes of the foreign ruling classes and needed re-education. Journalists and culture workers were ordered to go down to the factories and villages to learn from the people, to remind themselves that the media serve the Party, the authentic representative of the people. 'Western freedom' was projected as a chimera.

The tone of speeches from senior leaders was uncompromising. Not only was ideology to be returned to as the bedrock, but the CPD was to have its powers and authority enhanced. Politburo member Li Ruihuan 李瑞环[10] told the media that their job was to promote stability, provide less politics, and include more stories to attract the interest of ordinary people, motivating them to work towards China's economic development.

In an inspired analogy, New Zealand writer Anne-Marie Brady likens the hold of the Propaganda *xitong* in China today to that of the medieval church in Europe.[11] Its lofty mandate is to attend to things spiritual and normative, to guide the minds of the people onto the right paths, and in particular to ensure that its emissaries, those employed in the media, do not deviate. For Brady, whereas in Christendom the Church's authority has withered away, the propaganda *xitong*, far from being an organisation whose usefulness in the era of the market society has passed, has become ever more important. This has come about because the Party has understood that it is not by force but by persuasion that it must now exercise power. The system itself has adopted advanced theories and modern techniques in order to influence attitudes and behaviour. Although it has reinforced its existing methods of control, it has implicitly acknowledged their limitations and exercised them in a more restricted and considered manner.

The media report an ever expanding repertoire of topics; very few areas are out of bounds. The exposures of failures, corruption and problems as yet unidentified by the government were in the recent past mainly confined to the RCPs. More and more revelations of this kind have found their way into the public media as investigative journalism has been encouraged. [12] CCTV has televised the confessions of even very senior malefactors in an extended series of documentaries. Chat shows and opinion columns have multiplied, and journalism has been stirred and stimulated by the social media. Opinion polls are regularly conducted at both national and local levels by the Public Opinion Office of the CPD and its lower tier equivalents. The results feed into policy-making and sometimes into the media. Starting with *Strong Country Forum* (see p139), the CPD began using the Internet to set agendas, marshal opinion and direct discussion.

6.3   Instruments

Mao Zedong and his henchmen, like Marxists elsewhere, abolished China's legal system as an impediment to their total power over every person and everything. When the devastation produced by Communism was to be reversed, the economy to be revitalised and foreign trade re-commenced, laws were found to be necessary once more. Today the legislature is the National Peoples' Congress but it is often argued that the de facto legislating body is the State Council and there are other authorities which have effective legislating powers, in theory restricted under the NPC's Legislation Law of 2000.[13]

No media law has been enacted. Policies and regulations are created through orders issued by executives and agencies rather than through formal law-making.[14] Administrative orders are classified into two types: the Administrative Directives 行政指令 issued by the State Council, the status of which is second to law, and the Administrative Rules 行政法规, issued by SAPPRFT.[15] The rule-making process is 'not open to public engagement', but results from negotiation and co-ordination between different State Council departments, according to Chin Yikchan, who studies Chinese law at Oxford.[16]

Regulation is not confined to these two categories of administrative order. There are also Internal Normative Documents 内部规范性文件, which include directives issued either by the State Council or SAPPRFT, the legal status of which is determined by the courts. They are the result of negotiations between SAPPRFT, its local bureaux and media organisations.[17]

Such instruments do not have the same authority as their equivalents in Anglophone societies. Decisions taken by senior Party officers carry more weight than any written documents, whether they be laws, rules or directives. This approach to governance, or *workstyle* 作风 is discussed extensively by Heilmann and colleagues in a volume which attributes it to Mao's 'guerilla policy style, [which] stands in stark contrast to democratic norms of political accountability, legal consistency and procedural stability'.[18] They assess that the principles underlying governance are flexibility and pragmatism, lack of dogma or universal rules, the use of interpersonal relations and reliance on conformity in society at large.[19] They interpret this *workstyle* as reflecting the influence of Mao and the continuance of a revolutionary approach, but it seems to me that its basic features are congruent with the characteristics of traditional society and governance that we identified in Chapter 5. This would suggest that Mao was a conduit rather than an innovator. As the University of Washington's Gary Hamilton assures us, emperors of the past did not tend to make laws but sent out reminders as to what the fundamental laws of nature said about the models for right conduct of government.[20] We will return to this question in Chapter 7.

In practice, no matter what might be enacted by the NPC or enshrined in the Constitution, managers will tend to take their lead from the pronouncements of the most senior Party leader. In the absence of such pronouncements, the speeches of the officer responsible for the propaganda *xitong* will have the force of law. This can make life difficult, as media workers have to second guess their bosses rather than check a handbook.

Some sociologists go so far as to explain these phenomena by defining China as a *relation-based* rather than *rule-based* society.[21] Day to day control is not exercised in a completely predictable way. It varies according to circumstances, such as foreign policy exigencies. domestic crises, the personalities and politics of the leadership of the moment, who happens to be the editor at any particular time; and the local context, if the media involved are not national. Examples of the exercise of control are therefore not necessarily typical of all times and places.

There is, however, a system which is adhered to in ordinary circumstances. In the CPD, a small group discusses which matters are to be highlighted in the media during the forthcoming week and how current issues may be treated.[22] Once a decision has been made, the group calls in editors for 'synchronisation meetings' 同步会议 and then issues weekly guidelines. In the case of sensitive subjects, special instructions will be issued to publishers and editors as to which subjects cannot be covered and which ones should be. For example, on the anniversaries of major earthquakes, the CPD has been known to instruct the media to be positive and avoid negative material.[23] At various times, off-limits topics have included the gap between rich and poor, grain prices, the baby gender ratio and demonstrations. The angle to be taken in covering certain stories will be specified.[24] Particular forms of words are forbidden too, such as 'Fourth Estate' 第四个权利, though 'Fourth Department' 第四个部门 is acceptable. As in many other media organisations around the world, journalists and creatives are supplied with lists of approved formulations.[25]

Television documentaries and major newspaper features may be submitted for pre-publication review, but the most common point at which control is exercised is post-publication. It takes place at the regular meetings, when publications are analysed and evaluated, and editors and their staff are given guidance on how to handle themselves in future. The CPD carries out its monitoring responsibilities by using teams, often of retired officials, to read, watch and listen to all publications considered relevant. They also post content online in support of government positions. From time to time, managers in the media industries are obliged to attend away-days, at which they are made aware of the Party line on current issues and given guidance on how to deal with the issues.[26] There are many cases of editors being disciplined.[27]

6.4   Setting parameters

The current priorities of the Party are reflected in the media and this was very clear as the anti-corruption campaign initiated by President Xi got under way after his accession. The newspapers publish articles to keep the citizenry informed, to deter and contain and to encourage whistle-blowers. New Media is now the main means by which corruption is brought to the attention of the Discipline Commission, according to Xinhua. And drama, when it succeeds in attracting a large audience, can be used to promote the law-enforcement agencies and ensure that the message gets across nationwide.

Hunan TV's *In the Name of the People* 人民的名义, a 48-part drama series centring on the investigation of corruption, is a 2017 example. The effects of malfeasance on industrial workers, the flight of a senior official to the USA, the involvement of high and low are all there. *In the Name of the People* is not without precedent: *Heaven Above* 苍天在上 was the classic such series and there have been others such as *The Provincial Party Secretary* 省委书记, *Prosecution Nationwide* 国家公诉 and also series based on real events such as *The Great River Goes East* 大江东, *Without Blemish* 大雪无痕, *Never will I leave you* 绝不放过你. Ironically, although was put into production by Jiangsu TV, the local XCB prohibited transmission of *In the Name of the People*; more courageous, Hunan TV's President Lv Huanbin 吕焕斌 snapped it up.

A different example of positive interference was the way the media were required to provide upbeat stories about Uighurs, following violent incidents easily attributable to this Turkish speaking Muslim minority. *The Chinese Dream Show* 中国梦想秀 made a point of promoting Uighur dancer Gulmira Mamat in late 2014/early 2015 and this was one of many similar initiatives.[28]

The limits of revelation about social issues were evident in the case of *Snailhouse* 蜗居[29] This popular novel tells the story of young professionals struggling to buy a flat in the jungle of Shanghai's property market, so that they can provide their baby with a home where they do not have to share a bathroom and kitchen with numerous other families, each confined to one room of a shabby old tenement. The seediness of the property developers and their crooked agents, the power of unscrupulous employers, the corruptibility of officials, and the ease with which young women can be exploited are all dealt with, and in such a manner that the reader empathises with the protagonists and is moved by their plight.

Snailhouse was acceptable as a book, presumably because literature circulation is relatively restricted. When the television mini-series was screened, however, it was spiked midway. The reasons are unclear, but it would seem that while a very pessimistic portrayal of young couples might be acceptable if read by fiction enthusiasts, a television series would gain a considerably larger audience and could inflame many more passions against injustice, and against the gulf between the profiteering developers with their government accomplices and the rest.

CCTV New Year's Eve Variety Show

The CCTV New Year Gala 中国中央电视台春节联欢晚会 has the largest audience of any entertainment programme anywhere. Hosted by four favorite CCTV celebrity presenters, it is an eclectic mixture of traditional entertainment, modern pop, patriotic and nostalgic songs, dramatic skits and turns such as martial arts and acrobatics.

As in many other countries it has become the custom for families to watch the New Year Show together. For such a national showcase, selection of the acts is as Political as it is political; there are regulars, such as comic Zhao Benshan 赵本山; different sub-cultures and areas of China must be featured; there are usually acts in which foreigners show their proficiency in Chinese and there are usually one or two foreign stars. In 2013 Celine Dion, from an Anglophone country, co-performed one of the most famous of all modern pop-folk songs, *Jasmine Flower* 茉莉花, and Turkish belly dancers performed with Cossack partners. 2017 had more Variety Comic Routines than previously, with themes of national unity, family affection, traditional culture, honesty and friendship. "Tian Shan Love" is the first comic skit performed by actors of an ethnic minority. Apart from the main venue in the CCTV studio, there were also four live sub venues in Shanghai, Guilin, Liangshan, and Harbin which contributed live inputs.

Since the Gala tries to please everybody, and to showcase China to itself and to the world, it comes in for some jaundiced criticism from intellectuals and journalists.
Selected acts from the 2017 show:
Comic skit "*Big City and Small love* 大城小爱" (Liu Liang 刘亮, Bai Ge 白鸽 and Guo Jinjie 郭金杰)
Song "*Golden Crow* 金鸡报晓" (Air Force Blue Sky Kindergarten Arts Troup 空军蓝天幼儿艺术团)
Song with dance "*Song from Li Jiang River* 歌从漓江来"(Huang Wanqiu 黄婉秋，Zhang Xinzhe 张信哲，Deng Ziqi 邓紫棋)
Witty Skit "*Old Couple* 老伴"(Cai Ming 蔡明, Pan Changjiang 潘长江, Pan Binlong 潘斌龙)
Crosstalk "*New Escape from Tiger Mouth* 新虎口遐想"(Jiang Kun 姜昆, Dai Zhicheng 戴志诚)
"*Clapper talk* 快板表演" (Zhu Guangdou 朱光斗 Red Army Veteran)
Traditional Opera "*Pass the flame* 薪火相传" (Meng Guanglu 孟广禄, Yang Chi 杨赤, Wang Li 王荔, etc)
Ice dancing "*Flying dream in the snow* 冰雪梦飞扬" (Acrobatic Group of Harbin Winter Sports Centre)
Martial Arts "*Pride in China* 中国骄傲" (National Martial Arts Team 国家武术队)
Song and acrobatics "*City of Dreams* 梦想之城"(Li Wen 李玟 Lin Junjie 林俊杰 of the Shanghai Acrobatic Troupe 上海杂技团)
Presentation of exemplary families and social models 介绍全国文明家庭、道德模范代表
Song and Qipao Show "*Melody of black bamboo* 紫竹调-家的味道"(family of Wu Mengchao 吴孟超一家, family of Jiang Liping 姜丽萍一家，family of Liao Changyong 廖昌永一家, etc)
Song "*Unforgettable Night* 难忘今宵" (Li Guyi 李谷, Guan Mucun 关牧村, Gao Yin 高音, etc) This is the eighteenth and the customary final act.

Several of the novels of Yan Lianke 阎连科 are proscribed, presumably because of their negative depictions of politics before 1980. Yellow Peril 黄祸, an apocalyptic drama by Wang Lixiong 王力雄, in which China collapses and topples the world into nuclear war, is also prohibited, along with books about Zhao Ziyang 赵紫阳, the CCP General Secretary of 1989 and unflattering biographies such as *Mao, The Unknown Story*.[30] All of these, however, along with many other 'banned' books, are to be found on the bookshelves of (at least some) academics and officials.

Particular stories can be suppressed for no better reason than that their revelations might damage the editor's associates or local officials. Lee Hsiao-wen has shown how stories about mining accidents were spiked in several newspapers, even though they were initially researched by Xinhua. The now infamous Henan HIV scandal, brought to life in a vivid novel by Yan Lianke, was well known to national and local journalists for at least a decade before Wang Keqiang managed to publish his revelations in a newspaper.[31] He Qinglian has catalogued how local governments have pulled rank to suppress reports about infections, pollution and malpractices of many kinds.[32] There is nothing particularly Chinese about the phenomenon of suppression by political and business interests, but the fact that the media are part of the state apparatus makes it even more difficult to report unwelcome stories than it would be in other countries.

6.5   Mediating the Internet

The 'Great Firewall', introduced in Chapter 4, is an element in the Gold Shield Project 金盾工程 which devises strategy to protect China from nefarious influences, and organises a filtering system to stop access to foreign media. Further, a software known as 'Green Dam' is preinstalled on all Chinese computers and is used to block certain content and to report user activity to a central server. 2016 rules require foreign companies wishing to publish online to secure government approval and work through a 100% Chinese partner which is furnished with a licence. Servers, storage and technical equipment must be stored in China.[33]

Domain name registration is controlled centrally. As in Europe, Internet Service Providers are required to monitor their output and censor as advised.

Users of BBS websites and major web portals must register their real names. Skype is monitored and communications using sensitive terms are archived; the method deployed is 'very similar to that used by the US government'.[34] An addition to the regulatory weaponry is a rule that defamatory reports are criminal, if re-posted more than 500 times on the Internet. The first person to be charged under this rule may have been a youth in Gansu who allegedly spread false information about a local man's death, although he was released after an outcry.[35] In a notorious case of 2014, a certain Qin Zhihui 秦志晖 was sentenced to three years imprisonment for fabricating a much re-posted story that foreigners had been favoured by the authorities in accident compensation claims.

There were 113,000 Internet cafés by 2007, when the government put an end to licensing them out of concern that there was too much web-based gambling.[36] The authorities look for and close down sex and gambling sites, and websites selling illegal products such as drugs and fake examination certificates.[37]

Beijing Youth Forum

There have been many TV lecture series on every topic from natural history to business strategies. The most successful ever has been by media studies lecturer Yu Dan 于丹 who wrote and presented a series *Yu Dan's Insights into the Analects* 于丹《论语》心得 for the CCTV slot *The Lecture Room* 百家讲坛 in 2006.[38] Aside from gaining a huge audience, the accompanying book is believed to have sold, in official and pirated editions, over 10 million copies. Contributing to its enthusiastic reception was the fact that Confucianism could now be openly agreed to be the foundation of Chinese life, even on CCTV; that the presenter is stylish and inspiring both in her manner of presentation and in her ability to show the relevance of the philosopher to everyday modern life; that there is a dearth of moral and spiritual reference in society, where the state still is resolutely anti-religion.

The genre is being deployed online. *Beijing Youth Forum* 北青新讲坛 is a set of online lectures owned by *Beijing Youth Daily* aimed at providing a platform for "self-media" 自媒体 in which 'participants can express their ideas and thoughts'.

During the 40-plus, live, lectures so far there is a screen on which live microblog feeds can be shown, so that microblog users can comment on the topic and have their comments shown live on screen. 'Watching live microblog feed on the screen during a lecture is considered a powerful reflection of involvement. According to the official viewing figures for the *Beijing Youth Forum* there are more than 20 million followers on Microblog. This means that the images connected to any topic published through a microblog account can be seen by 20 million followers, quickly spreading to a larger Internet population'.[39]

Commentators are employed by the authorities[40] – mocked as the '5 Mao [50 cent] army' 五毛党 or sometimes the 'Water Army' 水军 – to join in discussions on chat rooms and web forums, and (presumably) report illicit content[41] as well as post content online.[42] At one university at least, students volunteer to monitor bulletin boards to guard against comments that might damage the reputation of the establishment.[43]

Ashley Esarey, the Canadian political scientist who has studied Chinese New Media extensively, notes that 'the state censors web traffic to ensure healthy social values, deter gambling, eliminate porn, punish swindlers, and excise the unhealthy views of religious cults, ethno-nationalists and democratic reformers'.[44] The responsibility for supervision lies with several public bodies, named on the charts on pp200 and 202. Local equivalents are tasked with overseeing local versions.[45] In May 2011, the (then new) State Internet Information Office was given the tasks of investigating and punishing violations of online content rules, and regulating content providers and telecommunications companies providing access to the Internet.[46] The regulator also checks news aggregation portals, lest they originate news.[47] In November 2016 a new law banned Internet users from publishing 'anything that damages 'national honour', 'disturbs economic and social order' or is 'aimed at overthrowing the socialist system'. Quite comprehensive.

At a strategic level, the government intends the Internet to be as far as possible a Chinese system, using Chinese language and subject to Chinese rules. It does not believe that there is a global free space, holding instead that the alternative to a Chinese system is one dominated by other powers. Rebecca MacKinnon, in her *Consent of the Networked*, suggests that companies such as Facebook and Google are like independent kingdoms, 'sovereigns of cyberspace'. She calls upon netizens to mobilise to hold them accountable and demand a 'social contract', plus regulations to prevent 'intermediaries' from having too much power over what we do or write.[48] The Chinese authorities would concur with her analysis, if not her solutions. This is why they have established the 'Great Firewall' 防火墙 to monitor connections to the global Internet and prevent China's access to unsavoury content, as they define it.

The New York Times[49] reminds us that 'when you use the Internet, it often feels placeless and virtual, but it's not. It runs on real wires that cut through real geographical boundaries. There are three main fibre-optic pipelines in China, giant underground cables that provide Internet access for the public and connect China to the rest of the Internet outside its borders. The Chinese government requires the private-sector companies that run these fibre-optic networks 光纤网络 to configure 'router' switches at the edge of the network, where signals cross into foreign countries. These routers – some of which are made by Cisco Systems, an American firm – serve as China's new censors'.[50]

Reporters without Borders, a campaigning organisation, avers that 'the Great Firewall combines URL filtering with the censoring of keywords considered "sensitive", ranging from "Tiananmen" 天安门 to the "Dalai Lama" 达赖喇嘛 to "democracy" and "human rights" 人权. In addition to filtering URLs, the authorities are monitoring the largest blog and microblogging platforms, from which they are removing numerous posts and comments. Assistance from foreign companies – mainly in the form of Yahoo! and Microsoft self-censored search engines – is making their job that much easier'.[51]

Notwithstanding these measures, those who wish to can bypass the controls by downloading and installing their own blogging software or by using VPNs.[52] One US journalist who interviewed eight students at Peking University for an article in *The New York Times* wrote that all but one had found and downloaded a proscribed documentary.[53] My students at Tsinghua University claimed to be able to access any site in the world they fancy. Writing in the *New Scientist*, Xiao Qiang notes that bloggers can re-publish and spread banned information very quickly, sometimes using code words 代称 to continue conversations about subjects which would normally be blocked.[54]

Media workers and creatives who travel abroad take advantage of Twitter, Facebook and so forth as soon as they leave China but do not appear to chafe at the restrictions at home. In lively discussions about censorship, among students abroad, there is always a large majority in favour of it. And although Anglophones might find this shocking, even 'victims' can say that they regard the dangers of unlimited free expression on the Internet as outweighing the benefits. In this they probably have allies among parents around the world.[55]

A certain defence, or at least comprehension, of the Chinese government's position comes from Evgeny Morozov, the Belarussian democracy activist based in the USA. He argues[56] that censorship of the web has occurred (or will do) in all societies, because ordinary citizens push for it. Parents do not want their children exposed to pornography and violence, businesses want their copyrights protected, individuals are concerned about identity theft and malicious 'human flesh searches' 人肉搜索, cyber bullying worries schoolteachers, local communities want to deny gangsters access to the web, ethnic and religious minorities want to be protected from abuse, and the police want to restrict incitement to disorder.

Mozorov's views are shared by some US academics in *The Offensive Internet,*[57] which calls for regulation and policing of the intermediaries, who at present get immunity from Section 230 of the [US] Communications Decency Act.[58]

The Chinese authorities are just as much pressured by people with the foregoing concerns as Anglophone politicians, though the latter choose to attribute iniquitous motives to censors in countries with which they disagree. Morozov notices that US President Barack Obama lectured China on the virtues of free media when he was in Shanghai, whereas in the USA he warned of their dangers.[59]

6.6   Access to information

A Freedom of Information Law was enacted after years of discussion in 2007, whether to promote transparency as a move against corruption, to help squash the rumours and false information with which the web abounds or simply in acknowledgement of the impossibility of keeping a lid on information in the era of the Internet. While exploring foreign examples during the 1990s, the authorities introduced 'open government' programmes, and promoted discussion about freedom of information legislation being implemented elsewhere in the world.

Freedom of information is to be achieved through two main policies. The first is requiring authorities at different levels to make information available on matters within their purview. This covers all regulations, particularly information on emergency planning, cost of public services including economic and social programmes, government budgets and decisions, urban planning, land requisitions, and demolition plans. The authorities are also obliged to publish the results of investigations into environmental protection, public health, and food and drug safety.

The *Freezing Point* case

When, in January 2006, its editors were sacked, *Freezing Point* 冰点周刊 had appeared as the weekly supplement to the Party-affiliated newspaper *China Youth Daily's* 中国青年报 for 11 years, with a daily circulation of more than 400,000. Not only were its articles recycled in many other newspapers but television programmes picked them up, they were collected into books and had become compulsory reading for the students in many universities. In 2005 *Freezing Point* was selected as medium of the year by the best known websites.[60]

By 2006, according to Li Datong 李大同, the editor, it had failed to follow instructions in three cases. First, it had published the article "Battle and Victory of Pingxingguang" 平型关战役与平行关大捷 which for the first time revealed that in the 1930s the Nationalist army 国民党军队 had fought a serious war of many casualties against the Japanese, whereas the CCP had claimed the credit. Secondly it had published an essay by columnist Lung Ying-tai 龙应台, 'The Taiwan you do not know', an implicit rebuke of the PRC's hostility to her country. Thirdly there was an essay in memory of Hu Yaobang 胡耀邦.

The last straw was an article by a university teacher from Zhongshan University 中山大学 which suggested that the anti-foreign Boxer Movement 义和团运动 of 1898-1901 was not 'progressive' but 'reactionary' and xenophobic. At issue, according to Lung Ying-tai, was how history be taught. Should it be a long rant about the abuse of China by nasty foreigners and thus a celebration of victimhood and resentment? Should it emphasise the events that inflame passions against the US and Japan to the extent that politicians are terrified of seeming insufficiently patriotic?[61]

Lung believes that these attitudes are instantiated in schoolbooks and the offline media, and now reflected and reinforced on the Internet.[62] This is unhelpful for two reasons. First, if history is distorted, with everything about pre-1949 China presented as negative, and foreigners to blame for it, then people will have little insight into what leads to progress. Secondly, the 'Maoist' interpretation of history has no place for humaneness, tolerance, freedom of expression, and the rule of law.[63]

Lung has lived in Germany and is conscious of the influence of interpretations of history on politics. Scarred by the lessons of World War II, many Europeans have become more sensitive to others: witness the concern for human rights, multiculturalism and the championing of cultural identity. Italy gives freedoms to the Tyrolese, Spain to the Catalans, England to the Scots; England also defends the rights of two warring identities in Ulster. But when, after World War II, European countries were establishing the rule of law, trying to diminish violence and increase reconciliation, China's rulers not only jettisoned legal and moral restraint, but also promoted a vengeful view of recent history.[64]

Despite this, there are all over China people reading and writing periodicals such as *Freezing Point*, who are rethinking the past for the sake of the future. In March 2013, *Freezing Point* resurfaced, launching its Wechat account with daily content since August 2015. The *Freezing Point* case was a skirmish in the very slow transformation of engrained assumptions.

The second is the 'request function', by which citizens are given the right to request access to information. But there are established habits of withholding information, on the pretext that 'class traitors' or 'foreign enemies' might make nefarious use of it. Although this is often merely a cover for official laziness, it may take a long time to eradicate. In any case, critics suggest that the 'request function' is attenuated in scope, not giving adequate opportunities or rights to citizens.[65]

6.7   Regulation

The way in which the Chinese government deals with the media has often been regarded as a Soviet legacy. Thus it has been assumed that, as Marxist ideology and precedent lose their hold, so the system they underpinned will disintegrate. Yet although Marxist ideas are less pervasive today, the attitudes of authority to thought and information have not necessarily changed very much, perhaps because they sit well with traditional statecraft as well as the cultural predilections that we noted in the last chapter.

A story about regulation

This is an illustration of the type of problem thrown up by the somewhat unsystematic system of Chinese media regulation. 'Mrs Lei', a woman from Nanjing, Jiangsu province, advertised her daughter Gan Lulu 干露露 on the Internet to gentlemen desirous of an attractive companion. Through the website, where photographs of the girl, wearing very little clothing, were posted, many men got in touch and invited her out on dates.

Before long, the website had come to the attention of the general public and was being discussed in newspapers and on radio and TV shows. Some regarded Mrs Lei's activities as tantamount to prostitution, while many saw them as demeaning.

Jiangsu Television's Education Channel has a Question and Answer programme, happily named *Bang Bang Bang* 棒棒棒, which was among many that discussed the story. By that time the younger daughter, Gan Maomao 干毛毛, was being advertised in the same way and the programme featured a debate between a studio audience and the originator of the project, Mrs Lei, and both daughters. The studio discussion was heated and the mother became very angry with some of her critics, verbally hitting out at them and using foul language.

Very rapidly, SAPPRFT decided that this was improper and reacted with this statement:
'Jiangsu Education TV's Question and Answer programme, *Bang Bang Bang*, [] violated national broadcasting regulations, amplified ugliness, undermined media ethics and created a negative social impact.'
SAPPRFT demanded that Jiangsu TV axe the channel – not just the programme – for an indeterminate period as a punishment for breaking regulations on indecency and obscenities. The difficulty was that there were no explicit regulations on either of these topics; they are implicit. Media professionals were angry at what they considered a draconian punishment, a blatant example of *killing the chicken to frighten the monkeys* 杀鸡儆猴, as they would put it.

Two presuppositions widely adhered to throughout Chinese history are that the media must support authority, and that government has a duty to use the media at its disposal to educate and inform the public as it sees fit.[66] Thus there were already government initiated media campaigns under the Republic, which greatly intensified when the CCP took power. They continue to be used to encourage approved attitudes and behaviour, although they are fewer and milder than in the past. Every city government will have a section responsible for spiritual development 精神发展 and civilised comportment 文明行为, which will promote cleanliness, courtesy and good behaviour among citizens, through agitation, competitions and public events.[67]

Observant visitors will notice billboards instructing local inhabitants how to behave. In January 2016, billboards all around the centre of the capital promoted solidarity between the generations. I received a pretty sticker to remind me what to aim for, which included civility, justice, integrity and friendship. Officials who are this attentive to behaviour understandably regard it as their duty to ensure that opinions are guided and that morally subversive information is excluded from publication. There is, in other words, a general assumption in the culture that the authorities will be deeply concerned as to how citizens think and behave.[68]

6.8   Morality and the public

In an essay reflecting on his experiences of television chat shows, the novelist, blogger and youth hero Han Han 韩寒 described his fury at discovering, on a programme purporting to discuss his own writings, that members of the audience had been primed to attack him and provoke dissension. To add insult to injury, they had not even read his works!

'On that programme, *How They Moved Me*, I stated that I disliked the stirring up of conflict on television programmes; good programmes should direct their attacks towards real problems and inequities in the world, rather than manufacture dissension among studio guests. Today's programme makers only reckon a programme works if it produces discord and conflict. If this goes on, we will soon see satellite TV producing a programme in which they urge loving couples to divorce, and it'll be called 'I smash, I smash, I smash smash smash.'[69]

He is criticising the tendency to tabloidisation, which we met earlier as 'eyeball journalism' and 'screaming media',[70] and which causes widespread concern. A journalist and academic castigates it in the following terms:

"The journalistic business model of the highly commercialised media can be simplified as 'screaming journalism', which means that whenever people open a newspaper, [or] turn on a TV channel, they would scream out, 'OMG! What a horrible bombing' or 'My God! What a terrible beheading' or 'OMG! The 82-year-old professor married a 20-year-old student' or 'OMG! He committed suicide', or 'OMG, Zhao had an affair with a massage lady'."[71]

A leading professor of media studies, on being asked whether Taiwan's 'free media' offered China a model for the future, expressed a general anxiety when he replied:

'Taiwan has public media, but the majority of the media of Taiwan are commercial. That's why they have many different voices. But there are two problems. One is that the media are overly commercial. Because it's a small island, a small market, with too many TV channels, the competition is ferocious. They have more than 120 channels, many of which are entertainment or news channels. They compete within this small market, so that the news programmes are becoming more and more 'tabloid'. They are increasingly sensationalised, yes, even more so than the Anglo-Saxon media. Even Taiwanese scholars criticise this. They describe today's Taiwan media with three Chinese words 'Sexual', 'Sensational', 'Bloody' 色情 , 煽情 , 血腥'.[72]

Thus, those January 2012 regulations[73] can fairly be described as a response to widespread moral concern. If they are censorship, then the BBC Guidelines on taste and decency also constitute censorship (though by the media class[74] rather than by the ruling Party). What actually occurred was that SAPPRFT ordered broadcasters to reduce the number of entertainment programmes and increase the time allocated to news and current affairs, to encourage other types of programme production such as documentaries, and to limit commercial breaks.[75] The main reason was concern at the trashy and vulgar nature of many of the entertainment programmes, and their promotion of greed and celebrity. However, it is possible that SAPPRFT was also anxious about the success of regional television companies competing for audiences with national 'public service' CCTV, and therefore wished to remind the broadcasters, daily growing richer from advertising income, that they were subject to higher authority.

In a further effort to raise the tone of television production, more regulations appeared in Autumn 2013, although they were not then formally promulgated. They caused a considerable change to broadcasters' established *modus operandi*. In each quarter of the year, there is now only one talent singing show permitted the satellite channels, which must bid for the slots. In future, each satellite channel will be permitted to buy only one new format from abroad . News, documentary and animation programmes are all to occupy more of the satellite channels' air time.[76] The broadcasters had to cudgel their brains to devise programming that would attract advertisers yet not offend the regulators, and it is to this that the explosion of documentary and reality shows can be attributed.[77]

Chart of regulatory agencies

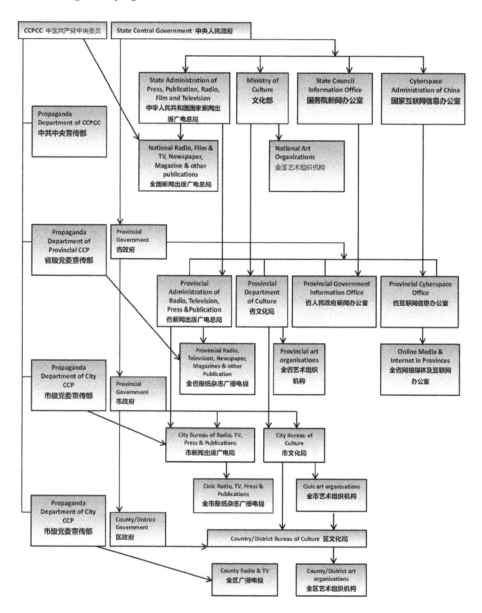

6.9   Culture

Aside from taste, there is also the issue of cultural pollution.[78] While conservatives in the Anglosphere often bemoan the vulgarisation of culture consequent on the commercialisation or industrialisation of music, art and literature, they at least cannot complain that it is foreigners who are to blame. Yet for much of the rest of the world, the powerful culture industries, supposedly reflecting Anglophone values and promoting Anglophone interpretations of the world, are agents of imperialist subversion undermining their identities. According to a 2016 Pew Attitudes Survey, 77% of Chinese believe that their way of life needs to be protected against foreign influences.[79] The fight to get UNESCO to pass, in 2005 and against strong US objections, its Convention on the Protection and Promotion of the Diversity of Cultural Expression was an illustration of that view.[80] Chinese academic institutions now have a specialism called 'Research into Cultural Security', putting this on a par with 'Food Security' and 'Military Security'.[81]

In the eyes of China's regulators, who are probably representative of their compatriots in the pride they take in Chinese values as the foundation of society, not only are these products culturally unacceptable, they also create markets for the other industries of their parent cultures. They do this by appealing to atavism and hedonism, fashioning the consumers they want and at the same time driving out indigenous cultural product, or at least they will if they are permitted to do so. In defence therefore, the authorities limit the importation of foreign films (and their transmission online), deny foreigners the right to invest in much of the media and require that co-productions obey Chinese strictures on content. Aside from violence and content that presents 'loose living' as 'natural', the depiction of gross individualism and nihilism as 'normal', or the implicit presentation of an objectionable way of life as the cynosure, are also unacceptable.[82] The censors are undeterred by the absurd positions into which this can put them. Transmission of a successful and admired US comedy, *The Big Bang Theory*, was halted in 2015 until some vulgar references could be expunged, murder scenes have had blood and close-ups expunged, a film in which villagers in wartime were shown fraternising with the Japanese occupation forces was banned, time travel met with disapproval, and a fly-on-the-wall documentary about babies being born, *C'mon Babe!* 来吧孩子 was spiked for indecent exposure in 2014 but restored a year later after frenzied lobbying.[83]

Children's programming is stringently controlled. In 2013 the country's most popular animated cartoon, *Happy Goat and the Big Bad Wolf* 喜羊羊与灰太狼 was censored for violence and unacceptable language. The regulators said that children had imitated the offensive behaviour. Perhaps on account of the not so happy *Goat*, discussions were held between SAPPRFT and animation producers, with the latter promising not to produce unsuitable content. Following a further case of naughty soft toys in the programme *Watch out for the Bear* 熊出没, SAPPRFT announced that it would publish Standards for the Content of National Animation. 国产电视动画片内容标准.[84]

202

Regulatory agencies – what they do

Ministry of Culture 文化部
The Ministry of Culture executes cultural policy. It promotes and protects the arts of all kinds, including architecture, literature, folk arts, music and dance, as well as television and film. It manages national monuments, museums, archives and regional culture centres.

The State Administration of Press, Publications, Radio, Film and Television 国家新闻出版广播电影电视总局
Formed in 1989 from several existing bureaux (as SARFT) and amalgamated in 2013 with GAPP (see below) , SAPPRFT supervises the management of state owned enterprises in the media and directly manages China Central Television, China National Radio and China Radio International; it owns a number of corporations making film and television products; it also handles agreements with foreign media organisations.
Its supervisory functions include researching and proposing media policy, drafting laws and regulations, auditing imports, approving new production units, examining and censoring all films, permitting and distributing licences for films, formulating the various technical policies and standards; assigning radio and television frequencies.

SAPPRFT can also concern itself with content. In 2007, it suspended the talent show *First Heart-Throb* 第一次心动, declaring that it was full of 'stunts and sensationalism', and instructed the publisher, Chongqing TV, to discipline the staff responsible. Following this, local branches supervising Guangdong TV and Shenzhen TV suspended similar shows. In 2012 it issued instructions on the degree and scheduling of light entertainment television. Confusingly, since several organisations appear to be doing this job, SAPPRFT also gets involved with supervising the Internet. In 2009, it issued a directive pointing out the categories of content prohibited online, including violence, pornography and whatever might 'incite ethnic discrimination or undermine social stability'.

General Administration of Press and Publication (GAPP) 中华人民共和国新闻出版总署
GAPP licensed and regulated news, print and Internet publications and their distribution. Its most high profile operation is the National Office for the Suppression of Pornographic and Illegal Publications. It houses the National Copyright Administration. In March 2013 GAPP was merged into SAPPRFT .

The State Council Information Office (SCIO) 国务院信息办公室
In May 2011 SCIO announced it was hiving off its Internet functions into this new department to manage registrations and approvals and all manner of Internet access issues as well as online gaming, online video and online publication industries. It investigates and deals with violations of the law.

Ministry of Public Security 公安部
The MPS is tasked with filtering and monitoring the Internet.

In August 2015, the Ministry of Culture (note, not SAPPRFT) issued a blacklist of Internet musical productions, asking Internet companies to remove 120 songs and accompanying music videos which featured lewdness or violence, encouraged law-breaking or were subversive of public morality'.[85]

At the same time, SAPPRFT reiterated that it would ban anything that could be interpreted as impairing national integrity, revealing state secrets, besmirching the nation's reputation, fanning race hatred, undermining the state's religious policies, threatening public order, promoting licentiousness, gambling, violence or criminal activity, defaming others or damaging public morality.[86] Film-makers were instructed to delete distortions of history, no matter what the country, the slighting of national heroes, sexually explicit material, depictions of violence and cruelty, pictures, atmospheric sounds, music and script causing fear, and anything advocating destruction of fauna or the environment, or encouraging the use of alcohol, cigarettes and other addictive or unhealthy substances.

Worldwide, one of the principal arguments against censorship is that the guardians of public morality cannot be trusted not to abuse their powers and use them to their own advantage. China's authorities are often accused of using censorship to protect the Party from embarrassment, to maintain a version of modern history that it would undermine the credibility of the CCP to expose as myth, and to prevent publicity about the business affairs of leading families. This is quite easy in a country whose official ideology is still Marxism-Leninism.

6.10   Marxist-Leninist justifications

Lenin used Marx's superstructure theory to close down the media of Tsarist Russia, which had prepared the ground for his revolution, lest they prepare the ground for another one. Following him, the early Chinese Communists identified the media as a mere expression of the ruling class, whose nature and culture were determined by the prevailing economic system. In this view, people and their ideas are products of the economic system, and a ruling class consists simply of those who have commandeered the most resources. The media are its voices.

Individuals and agglomerations of individuals grouped by interest, religion or ethnic difference, occupation or culture, reflect economic circumstances, and will automatically change their behaviour as economic circumstances change. If this appears to be happening too slowly, the thugs can be called in to help them conform. Although discredited today, this theory was convincing to many in the past as an explanation of how the world worked and as a justification for destroying 'the system' and liquidating or 're-making' its members through brainwashing 洗脑.

Brainwashing was a legitimate process in China for the first 30 years of CCP rule, when the utopian vision advanced by the CCP required people who didn't join the ranks of the 'disappeared' to be re-made. A 'new man' had to be created for a 'new world'. The media were responsible for keeping people thinking about the world in the manner that the Party required. Thus media should reflect the interpretation of events or facts imposed on them by the Party, rather than the more haphazard interpretations, reflecting the politics and prejudices of writers and producers, to which the Anglosphere is accustomed. Drama, documentaries and other media genres were also expected to have themes proposed or approved by authority. In China today the range of themes and topics that escapes censorship has expanded greatly but limitations still cause frustration.

Media People: a broadcasting unit Party Secretary

Before being appointed head of Nanjing TV in 1997, Zhou Li 周莉 had had no television experience, being moved from the Chairmanship of the Nanjing Federation of Literature. In 2003 she became President of Jiangsu Broadcasting Group, since when Jiangsu has become a leading broadcaster, rivalling Hunan TV.

Under Li's leadership Jiangsu TV produced the respected current affairs show *Distant from Zero*, 零距离, the country's most successful dating show, *If not sincere, don't bother me!* 非诚勿扰, and a soap, *Big Brother's Joy* 老大的幸福. During that time, the Group also produced three successful feature films: *Nanking! Nanking!* 南京！南京、*The Making of the Nation* 建国大业、and *Ten Years' Siege* 十月围城.

In 2012 Li resigned from Jiangsu TV and the 10th Jiangsu Political Consultative Conference, then became a member of the 11th Jiangsu Standing Committee of the Provincial People's Congress.

Image source:
http://tv.sohu.com/20071219
/n254179654.shtml

The intelligentsia finds particularly unacceptable the curtailing of discussion of controversial issues of Chinese history and politics. The Cultural Revolution was discussed openly in the 1980s and many memoirs were published, the Great Leap Forward too. Now these subjects are largely taboo and the National Museum's modern history section, *The Road of Rejuvenation* 复兴之路, mentions none of the horrific campaigns that caused so much suffering and killed so many.[87] Even the remarkable book of investigative history, *Tombstone*, is banned and can only be read on the mainland in pirated editions.[88] The persecutions of the 1950s have never been acceptable for discussion, although the iniquities of that era are implied, in, among others, the novels of Mo Yan.[89] The purpose of censoring discussion of these periods is this: factual evidence of the destructiveness and oppression of the first thirty years of CCP rule might sow disillusionment as well as undermining the legitimacy of the Party.

Another aspect of censorship is that religion is absent from the media, as from education. Given that China is undergoing a religious revival which involves hundreds of millions, this might be thought extraordinary. Yet the Communist Party, which has ceased persecuting religion with the fanaticism that was usual before the 1980s, in its hostility was merely carrying to barbaric extremes anti-religious policies that were initiated in the late 19th century when the ruling classes first came to believe that religion required eradication that China might become 'modern'.[90] It has taken generations for the rulers to accept that religion is not contradictory to modernisation, and indeed may be an essential ingredient of a stable transition to modernity. Nevertheless, permitting publicity for expressions of religion is still a step too far.

Media people: the man who heads CCTV

Image source: http://www.gapp.gov.cn/gov public/4236.shtml

Nie Chenxi 聂辰席 graduated in computer programming from Fudan University in 1980. From graduation he was an official in 2006, when he was appointed Head of the Hebei Propaganda Department. He became Deputy Governor of Hebei Province in 2011. From 2012 to 2015 he was Deputy Minister of the State Administration of Radio, Film and Television (SARFT).

In 2015 Nie was appointed President of China Central Television CCTV, replacing Hu Zhanfan 胡占凡 who had been a radio journalist for 28 years, rising to Vice President of China National Radio (CNR) in 1999. Hu had also been Deputy Minister of SARFT, before becoming Editor-in-Chief of a major national newspaper, *Guangming Daily* from 2010. Hu's inaugural speech at CCTV became a hot topic in the microblogosphere, when he was quoted as stating that 'some journalists do not position themselves as the Party's propagandists, but regard themselves as professional journalists. This is quite wrong.' 一些新闻工作者，没有把自己定位在党的宣传工作者上，而是定位在新闻职业者上，这是定位上的根本错误。 He is also widely quoted as saying that it is 'wrong to think that there is a contradiction between being the mouthpiece of the Party and being a good journalist'. 一些人认为强调党性和喉舌作用会影响新闻报道的客观性，会影响按新闻规律办事……这是非常错误的，也是十分片面的.

Nie likewise stressed the political functions of CCTV. In January 2016, gave a speech on "The Five Consciousnesses" that all CCTV employees should implement. The first is 'political awareness'. They should always follow the correct political line and lead public opinion. 始终牢牢把握正确政治方向和舆论导向 The second is innovation, the third pubic service 不断提高服务大局、服务人民的能力和水平. The fourth consciousness is improving international awareness and the fifth is a sense of urgency 切实增强忧患意识，在应对挑战、破解难题中不断开创发展新局面。On February 19 2016, President Xi visited CCTV Beijing headquarter's central control room and listened to Nie's report on CCTV's work. President Xi also did a video call with the CCTV American hub and held a discussion with the national news' production team.

From the 1920s onwards, journalists have been fully aware of the main alternative theory of the press, i.e., the liberal interpretation, which maintains that the media are a public space, where free journalists vie to provide timely and impartial information in order to enable people to make informed judgements about politics and society.[91] The weaknesses and limitations of the liberal argument have, however, always been so obvious as to undermine its defence against the attacks of the Marxists.

Today, the CCP continues to maintain that the Western media are no more than expressions of economic and political interests. This is a convenient way of avoiding engagement with criticisms of China. That some of them are motivated by commercial competition or political malice is surely so, and their shortcomings are evident;[92] but the theory that they are all simply an expression of economic interests is not credible. The old theory too simple. It is also an impediment to the recognition of media roles in society and to the introduction of a media law.

6.10.1 Rejecting universalism

So far we have discussed control of the media as if it were, on the one hand a bureaucratic manoeuvre typical of Marxist executives and, on the other, a series of technical responses to social problems. Since the ascent to power of President Xi Jinping, the approach to the media has become more coherent. In a series of pronouncements, including his book on governance and those made during his motivational visits to national media in February 2016, he has re-asserted a traditional vision.

According to this view, the principal role of all media is to communicate the Party line in a manner representative of China's culture. They are the front line of defence against subversion. They must be vigilant against the 'universal values' promoted by the USA and its allies, which are simply expressions of cultural imperialism and propaganda tools for the denigration and subversion of China.

Western analysts of globalisation could slight such a views as outdated. Early castigations, notably by critic of American domination, Herbert Schiller,[93] of the destructive, homogenising and above all commercialising influences of globalisation have given way to what many consider to be a more balanced view. This is that the old idea of how culture is transmitted is hypodermic, and therefore simplistic. Life is more complicated than that and culture changes. Audiences are not dupes but accept and reject of their own volition. Manuell Castells, a Spanish sociologist, has lauded the power of local culture to resist the centrifugal force of capitalist globalisation. John Tomlinson, analyst of cultural imperialism, tells us that 'another story can be told that globalisation, far from destroying it, has been the most significant force in creating and proliferating cultural identity.'[94] 'Glocalisation' or the adaptation of international concepts to local conditions is now thought of as a potent force.[95] Daya Thussu, who studies India in particular, shows as that contraflows are complementing and even supplanting the hitherto dominant Anglophone mass media exports. With the rise of the BRICS, the imbalance of power slated by Chinese critics is being redressed.[96]

Media Studies luminary David Morley, though, in *Globalisation and cultural imperialism reconsidered*, argues that the fundamental facts about globalisation have not changed. The forms of foreignness available for import are still mainly Anglo-American, if not exclusively so.[97] He analyses cultural imperialism, old and new, and concludes that the USA has no serious rivals.[98] Critical intellectuals and Chinese regulators are not the only people who see culture as a weapon. Morley shows that popular culture was seen early on as not a mere support for foreign policy but as a direct instrument of it.[99]

Media people: The minister

Image source:
http://news.xinhuanet.com/e
nglish/special/18cpcnc/2012-
11/15/131977282_11n.jpg

Liu Yunshan 刘云山 (1947-) is 5th-ranked member of the Politburo Standing Committee, First Secretary of the Secretariat of the Communist Party of China Central Committee中国共产党中央书记处, Chairman of the CPC Central Guidance Commission for Building Spiritual Civilization中国共产党中央精神文明建设指导委员会and President of the CPC Central Party School中共中央党校(since January 2013).

Liu was a teacher in Inner Mongolia Autonomous Region 内蒙古自治区from 1964 to 1968, and joined the Party in 1971. From 1975-1982, he worked as a reporter and division head in the Inner Mongolia Autonomous Region branch of Xinhua News Agency. Liu was deputy party secretary of the Communist Youth League中国共产主义青年团1982-1984 and then deputy head of the Propaganda Department宣传部of the CCP Committee of Inner Mongolia Autonomous Region 1984-1987. Thereafter he was promoted to Secretary General of the CCP Committee of Inner Mongolia AR where he served from 1987 to 1991. He spent three years (1989-1992) taking courses part-time at the Central Party School.

Liu was transferred to the capital in 1993 as Deputy Director of the CCP Propaganda Department (1993-2002). He became Director in 2002，being succeeded by Liu Qibao 刘奇葆 in 2012 when he was elected to the Standing Committee of the Politburo. A 'youthleaguer' 团派, that is one of those who has made his career through the Youth League, as did Hu Jintao, he is regarded as an arch leftist whose inclination has been to be as repressive towards the media as he dare.

Even those who agree that China is threatened by American values might assume that President Xi has a hopeless task, trying to resist and even replace a *zeitgeist* supposedly transmitted by the media of the most powerful nation the world has ever seen. Moreover he is doing this while shoring up an identity which is already malleable and porous, thanks not merely to foreign penetration but also to vandalism by his own Party, with younger generations adapting selectively in the manner famously called 'bricolage'. In terms of cultural artefacts, fashion and architecture, Chinese cities are at least superficially cosmopolitan. Where exactly is this ideal cultural identity that is to be protected and proselytized? What is it that is at risk of being subverted?

Opponents of 'Westernization' claim that a modern Chinese identity is emerging, with the sloughing off of the Russian carapace, expressing traditional ideas in modern terms. 'Socialism with Chinese characteristics', for example, might better be thought of as 'Chineseness with socialist vocabulary'.

When they talk of their culture being undermined, proponents of the return of Chineseness do not appear to be talking of material culture as much as those attitudes and behaviours which we described in Chapter 5 as 'characteristics'. It is not the woman's clothes that they want to proscribe, but the particular way she is tempted by Western values to express femaleness; not the boy's toys but how he relates to his grandparents; not the journalist's actions as much as her reasons for being a journalist in the first place. The political order is seen as a by-product of culture and the means by which it is to be defended.

As he cleaned out pigsties during the Cultural Revolution, Deng Xiaoping may have realised that Marx had been wrong to imagine that capitalism would pauperize the workers. In fact, as we know, it has enriched them beyond his imagination. What Deng's successors have understood is that capitalism can have other reprehensible consequences, as Schumpeter predicted. The remaining Communists and the Confucians in China appear to agree what they are and that they should be forestalled. They include the 'creative' destruction of community and identity, the conversion of citizens and partners into selfish individualists, consumerism over environmental sustainability, the dislocation of lives subjected to constant change and pressure, the appeal to hedonistic values through advertising, the cash nexus; the corruption of public service and social instincts, and short term profit-making replacing responsibility to the future. These are the viruses of capitalism. Even as it harnesses peoples' urge to get rich, or at least moderately well-off, China must resist the subversion of its society by such values. This is not only because they are destructive of the good society, but because they are the means by which the foreigners want to subject China and add it to their hoard of colonies or client states.

If socialism, defined as government providing material advancement, stability and welfare in the interests of the majority, is to succeed, authoritarian government is axiomatic. Although the enterprising are valued and their enrichment is respected, by contrast to the times where Marxism was the bible, they are not to imagine that this gives them special rights, still less that they can suborn officials. The same goes for intellectuals and journalists.

Even if the majority of media workers are content with such leadership, there will always be conflict between the CPD and those creatives and journalists who are sure that they know better than their colleagues the regulators, as in a famous stand-off between *Southern Weekend* and the local Propaganda Department in December 2013, recounted on pages 225-6. But we should not imagine this is a bigger issue than it is. From a collection of profiles of Chinese journalists, *China Ink*, we see that for many and perhaps most reporters and editors, this conflict is not a major part of their lives. It is possible to be a professional journalist in China without clashing with the authorities.[100]

Today, what is said at home or among friends is of little interest to those authorities. But they arrogate to themselves the right to police all public communication. This is to be expected, in a society whose core value is what I have termed communitarianism. Moreover, overt censorship is often not really necessary, or just something the more clumsy officials do, since self-censorship comes naturally to those who believe (often subconsciously), that their main duty is to act appropriately to their roles.[101]

Management of the media today is less Marxist than Confucian.

Notes

[1] Pye, Lucien W. (2002) 'Factions and the Politics of Guanxi' in Unger, Jonathan (ed) (2002) *The Nature of Chinese Politics, from Mao to Jiang*, Armonk: ME Sharpe, p40.

[2] Pieke, Frank (2016) *Knowing China A Twenty First Century Guide* Cambridge: CUP pp140-143

[3] Lynch, Daniel C (1999) *After the Propaganda State*. Stanford: Stanford University Press, pp 13.

[4] Xi, Jinping (2014), *The Governance of China*. Beijing: Foreign Languages Press, pp 178.

[5] Li, Congjun (2011) Toward a New World Media Order: We need a mechanism to coordinate the global communications industry, something like a 'media U.N.'. *Wall Street Journal*, 1 June 2011. http://www.wsj.com/articles/SB10001424052748704816604576335563624853594 (Accessed: 3 February 2016).

[6] Moore, M. (2010) *Chinese leader's speech 'cut by the censor's invisible hand'*. *Daily Telegraph*, October 14.

[7] Shambaugh, DL. (2009) *China's Communist Party*. Berkeley: University of California Press, pp 107.

[8] Polumbaum, J. (2009) The tribulations of China's journalists after a decade of reform. In: Lee, Chin-Chuan, editor. *Voices of China: the interplay of politics and journalism*. New York: Guilford Press.

[9] Brady, A-M. (2007) *Marketing dictatorship: propaganda and thought work in contemporary China*. New York: Rowman & Littlefield, Chapter 1.

[10] Dong, SG. (2009) *Governing China with the news: television and national development in China since 1958*. Unpublished PhD thesis. University of Durham, pp 111. [Online]. Available at: http://etheses.dur.ac.uk/2161/1/2161_169.PDF?UkUDh:CyT (Accessed: 17 March 2016).

[11] Brady, A-M. (2007) *Marketing dictatorship: propaganda and thought work in contemporary China*. New York: Rowman & Littlefield, Chapter 2 & passim.

[12] Tong, J. (2011) *Investigative journalism in China*. London: Continuum, passim.

[13] See 'Law', chapter 33 of de Burgh, Hugo (2006) *China Friend or Foe*. Cambridge: Icon, pp 177-80. Also Chen Jianfu (2008) *Chinese Law: Context and Transformation*, Leiden: Marinus Nijhoff

[14] Zhao Yuezhi (2012) writes that this is intentionally done to circumvent Congress, where discussion would lead to debates on press freedom and constituional rights. See pp 154-5.

[15] The situation is rather more complicated than that and is more fully described in Zhao (2008), Chapter 2.

[16] Chin, Y-C. (2007) From the local to the global: China's television policy in transition. In: Kops, M and Ollig S. (eds.) *Internationalization of the Chinese TV sector*. Berlin: Lit Verlag, pp 221-

240. For more detail on these and also on classified directives and other documents, see He Qinglian (nd, probably 2006) *The Fog of Censorship: Media Control in China*, available at http://www.hrichina.org/sites/default/files/PDFs/Reports/HRIC-Fog-of-Censorship.pdf

[17] See http://www.javnostthepublic.org/media/datoteke/chin4-2003-5.pdf

[18] Heilmann, Sebastian and Perry, Elizabeth J. (2011) *Mao's Invisible Hand: The Political Foundations of Adaptive Governance in China*, Cambridge: Harvard U Asia Center, p 14

[19] This is my paraphrase of the arguments presented in Chapter 1 of ibid.

[20] Hamilton (2015), pp 139.

[21] Li, Shaomin (2009) *Managing international business in relation-based versus rule-based countries*. New York: Business Expert Press, pp 19-32.

[22] For a detailed escription of how 'unified news coverage' is achieved, see He Qinglian pp33-35, He Qinglian (nd, probably 2006) *The Fog of Censorship: Media Control in China*, available at http://www.hrichina.org/sites/default/files/PDFs/Reports/HRIC-Fog-of-Censorship.pdf

[23] Van Pinxteren, Garrie (2013) *Foreign media on China: beyond positive and negative reporting* at https://www.clingendael.nl/publication/foreign-media-china-beyond-positive-and-negative-reporting accessed 290517

[24] Zhao goes into detail on the methods in her section on Government Regulation in Zhao (2008), pp 26-28.

[25] The use of language to confine and channel thought is examined in detail in Schoenhals , Michael (1992) *Doings Things With Words in Chinese Politics, Five Studies*, Berkeley : U of California University of California Institute of East Asian Studies. Chapter 2 describes Party circulars which detail exactly how people and events may or may not be termed; chapter 4 analyses guidelines to journalists. The latter are still used and help journalists self censor appropriately. Such circulars are still issued, as indeed they are in the BBC and state media organisations elsewhere.

[26] http://www.freedominfo.org/features/20070509.htm#3

[27] The Chinese media reported on the Savile case, the Lord McAlpine case and the pranksters at the London hospital, as well as the lurid details of the hacking scandal.

[28] https://www.youtube.com/watch?v=rnO-DstdbBg (Accessed: 2 February 2016).

[29] 六六 Liu Liu (2007) *Snailhouse* 蜗居. 武汉 Wuhan: 长江出版社 Changjiang.

[30] Chang, Jung and Halliday, Jon (2005) *Mao: The Unknown Story* London: Vintage

[31] 阎连科 Yan Lianke （2005） 丁莊梦 *The Dream of Ding Village*. HK：文化艺术出版社 Yishu Publishers.

[32] He Qinglian (nd, probably 2006) *The Fog of Censorship: Media Control in China*, pp44-48, available at http://www.hrichina.org/sites/default/files/PDFs/Reports/HRIC-Fog-of-Censorship.pdf

[33] Barboza, D and Mozur, P (2016) New Chinese rules on foreign firms' online content *The New York Times*, 19 February 2016

[34] Scotton JF. and Hachten, WA. (eds.) (2010) *New media for a new China*. Chichester: Wiley-Blackwell, pp 35.

[35] Yu, H. (2014) China confronts the online rumor mill. *The New York Times,* 7 January 2014.

[36] Scotton, JF. (2010) The impact of new media. In: Scotton JF. and Hachten, WA. (eds.) *New media for a new China*. Oxford: Wiley-Blackwell, Chapter 3.

[37] Scotton, JF. (2010) The impact of new media. In: Scotton JF. and Hachten, WA. (eds.) *New media for a new China*. Oxford: Wiley-Blackwell, Chapter 3.

[38] Varriano, Valeria (2011) Confucio in TV risponde alle domande di un presente inquieto, in Pozzi, Silvia (ed) *Confucio re senza corona*, Milano: O Barra, pp151-198

[39] Li Shisheng, Vice Secretary of the Party Committee, *Beijing Youth Daily* interviewed by Mi Miao, October 2012

[40] Shirk, SL. (2007) *China fragile superpower*. Oxford: Oxford University Press. See also Mozur, Paul (2016) China's Web tainted by fake posts in *International New York Times*, 20 May 2016, p16 which reports a study of official interventions in social media.

[41] Bandurski, D. (2008) China's guerrilla war for the web. *Far Eastern Economic Review*. 2008 Jul/Aug, pp 41-44.

[42] The Water Army, also known as the 'Internet Navy' 网络水军, consists of those paid to post online by businesses wanting to boost their products, or by PR firms working on their behalf,; in the Anglosphere the process is known as 'astroturfing'.

[43] Ibid.

[44] Esarey A, Qiang Xiao. (2011) *Digital communication and political change in China*. International Journal of Communication 5 (2011), 298–319

[45] Xiao, Qiang (2011) The rise of online public opinion and its political impact. In: Shirk SL. (ed) *Changing media, changing China*. New York: Oxford University Press, pp 202-224.

[46] Wines, M. (2011) China creates new agency for patrolling the Internet. New York Times, 5 May 2011.

[47] Scotton, JF. (2010) The impact of new media. In: Scotton JF. and Hachten, WA. (eds.) *New media for a new China*. Oxford: Wiley-Blackwell, Chapter 3.

[48] MacKinnon, R. (2012) Consent of the networked: the worldwide struggle for Internet freedom. New York: Basic Books, pp 165.

[49] Thompson, C. (2006) *Google's China problem (and China's Google problem)*. [Online]. New York Times., Ap 23 . Available at: http://www.nytimes.com/2006/04/23/magazine/23google.html (Accessed: 17 March 2016).

[50] Ibid.

[51] Reporters Without Borders. *Internet enemies China*. 2011 [cited 21 January 2012]. Available at: http://en.rsf.org/Internet-enemie-china,39741.html (Accessed: 17 March 2016).

[52] VPNs have recently (February 2017) been targeted such that they may be of less service in future.

[53] La Franiere, S. (2009) *Tiananmen now seems distant to China's students*. [Online]. New York Times. 21 May 2009. Available at: http://www.nytimes.com/2009/05/22/world/asia/22tiananmen.html?pagewanted=1&fta=y (Accessed: 17 March 2016).

[54] Xiao, Qiang. (2004)The 'blog' revolution sweeps across China. *New Scientist*, 24 November.

[55] In the UK the Child Exploitation and Child Protection Centre is calling for censorship of Facebook.

[56] Morozov, Evegeny (2011) The Net delusion: how not to liberate the world. London: Penguin.

[57] Levmore, S. and Nussbaum, M. (eds.) (2010) *The offensive Internet: speech, privacy and reputation*. Cambridge: Harvard University Press.

[58] Section 230 of the USA's Communications Decency Act gives immunity to operators on websites and other types of interactive computer service.

[59] Morozov, Evegeny (2011) *The Net delusion: how not to liberate the world*. London: Penguin, pp 240.

[60]蔡明燁 Tsai Mingyeh (2010) 小書房大天地 Little bookshop, Big World 台北：立緒文化事業有限公司 pp224-233

[61] Isabel Hilton reports that in Shanghai in 1974 her university campus was festooned with banners proclaiming eternal friendship between the Japanese and Chinese people. Nobody talked about and quite likely never knew about the Nanking massacre. It was after 1989 that both the Japanese invasion and the Opium Wars were harped upon.. The summer palace, looted and burned by the Europeans in 1860, has been carefully preserved to emphasise the way in which China was subjected to humiliation. 'Monuments to Japanese war atrocities and Chinese resistance have sprung up across the country.' Hilton, Isabel (2011) China: at war with its history in *Prospect* October 2011, pp50-54

[62] The history curriculum has been undergoing change in recent years. In particular, peasant uprisings are no longer given the prominence they once were, openness to foreign countries is emphasised and ordinary people's yearning for stability and unity is stressed. Marxist history, while

not yet jettisoned, is recognised as too formulaic. There are heated discussions among intellectuals about the failure to commemorate and therefore learn from the cultural revolution. See:

Yuan, W. (2006) *Modernization and Chinese history textbook* 现代化与中国的历史教科书问题. [Online] Available from: http://bbs.tianya.cn/post-no01-32461-1.shtml [Accessed 01 August 2013]

[62] http://www.gapp.gov.cn/govpublic/4236.shtml accessed 250216

[62] 国家新闻出版广电总局 (no date) 聂辰席个人简历. Available at:
http://www.gapp.gov.cn/govpublic/4236.shtml Accessed: 24 February 2016

[63] Lung, Y. 龙应台(2006) 请用文明来说服我. *Please convince me with civility*Taipei: Times Press

[64] These issues are not exclusive to China; perhaps they apply in every country. For a view of tendentious history teaching in the USA, see Loewen, James W. (1995). *Lies My Teacher Told Me: Everything Your High School History Textbook Got Wrong.* New York: The New Press.

[65] See comments about SARFT's later announcements in *Global Times*:
http://www.globaltimes.cn/content/725442.shtml (Accessed: 17 March 2016).

[66] MacKinnon, SR. (1997) Towards a history of the Chinese press in the Republican Period. *Modern China.* 23(1):3-32.

[67] Citizenship education is being studied by several academics. See Kerry, John Kennedy et al (2013) *Citizenship Education in China: preparing citizens for the Chinese century?* London: Routledge for several fascinating essays.

[68] Martin Jacques discusses this in (2009). *When China Rules The World.* London: Allen Lane, pp 81-84.

[69] 韩寒 Han Han (2012) 青春 *Springtime.* 长沙 Changsha: 湖南人民出版社 Renmin Chubanshe, pp 22.

[70] Li, Xiguang (2008) *Journalism in transition.* Beijing: Tsinghua University Press.

[71] http://bbs.people.com.cn/bbs/, quoted by Li Jingyu 李径宇. Interviewed by Mi Miao; December 2012. 中国新闻社《中国新闻周刊》副总编辑兼执行主编 Deputy Editor-in-Chief & Executive Chief Editor, *China News Weekly.*

[72] Hu Zhengrong. Interviewed by the author. Peking; 10 November 2012.

[73] Efficiently summarised in:
http://www.marbridgeconsulting.com/marbridgedaily/archive/article/50698/sarft_curbs_satellite_t v_entertainment_programming (Accessed: 17 March 2016)

[74] The concept of the media class as a social interest group with its own ideology and objectives was first introduced in Oborne, Peter (1999) *Alastair Campbell: New Labour and the Rise of the Media Class.* London: Aurum.

[75] SARFT 国家广播电影电视总局. [Online]. 2011. Available at:
http://www.sarft.gov.cn/articles/2011/10/26/20111027084748180633.html (Accessed: 17 March 2016)

[76] Zeng Rong. Emailed discussion with the author and Nino Cirone. 4 November 2013.

[77] According to *Southern City Daily*, no more than one format show may be imported by each satellite channel and only one singing competition show may be aired during prime time in one season (yes, one per quarter in the whole country). Full text available at:
http://epaper.oeeee.com/A/html/2013-10/20/content_1954225.htm (Accessed: 17 March 2016)

[78] A representative work on this topic, from the Academy of Special Sciences, is A Study of Culture Security in the Age of Globalisation by Li Jinqi, published by CASS Publishers in 2008. 李金齐，全球化时代的文化安全研究，中国社会科学出版社

[79] http://www.pewglobal.org/2016/10/05/2-china-and-the-world/ Accessed 31 July 2017

[80] http://unesdoc.unesco.org/images/0014/001429/142919e.pdf, Accessed 06 April, 2016

[81] Readers of Chinese will find the arguments clearly laid out in, for example, Li Jinji (2008) 李金齐 Studies in Cultural Security in the Age of Globaliation 全球化时代的文化安全研究 Beijing : Academy of Social Sciences 北京： 中国社会科学出版社

[82] Asked whether she could justify her claims about violence in US media, a SAPPRFT official directed me to this website on 22 December 2015: http://www.aafp.org/about/policies/all/violence-media.html (Accessed: 22 December 2015).

[83] 'Exposing female flesh' was the reason given to the producers, however no formal ruling ever provided a clear explanation.

[84] 群众路线网 Mass Line, [website], 2013, http://qzlx.people.com.cn/n/2013/1023/c366722-23303489.html, (Accessed: 14 March 2016).

[85] The titles of some of them perhaps explain their place on the black list: 'Clear off to someone else's bed', 'swing those buttocks', 'farting' , 'you're just a whore'; 'prostitute', 'not going to school, 'one night stand', 'little girl's first time' , 'foul society', 'excreting' and 'suicide diary'. The inclusion of 'I love Taiwan Girls' 我爱台妹 is explained less by the music and lyrics, a dreary and repetitive rap song, suggesting the singer's sexual obsession, than by the video in which girls perform erotic movements for his delectation. In general, the black list appears to consist of songs devised for the adolescent boy market. See: https://www.youtube.com/watch?v=ZQ8mn5fS5_M (Accessed: 18 August 2015)

[86] SAPPRFT was in effect re-stating rules set out in 1997, see http://www.mps.gov.cn/n16/n1282/n3493/n3823/n442104/452202.html (Accessed: 12 March 2016).

[87] More on this from Isabel Hilton, (2011) *China: at war with its history* in London: Prospect, October 2011 pp50-55

[88] 楊繼繩 Yang Jisheng (2008) 墓碑 - 中國六十年代大饑荒紀實 *Tombstone: An Account of Chinese Famine in the 1960s*. Hong Kong: Cosmos Books.

[89] 莫言 Mo Yan (2006) 生死疲劳 *Life and Death are Wearing Me Out* Jilin: Zuojiachubanshe 作家出版社.

[90] The terrible, indeed grotesque, story of the destruction of what Johnson calls 'one of the world's richest religious traditions' is summarised in Johnson, Ian (2011) China Gets Religion! In *The New York Review of Books*, December 22, 2011 pp55-58. Therein Johnson reviews several books on the subject.

[91] Discussed thoroughly in Curran, James and Seaton, Jean (1981 and many subsequent editions) *Power without Responsibility* London: Fontana.

[92] For a list of recent books on the flaws of the Anglophone 'free' media, see Endword, note 21.

[93] Schiller , Herbert(1969) *Mass Communication and the American Empire*. New York: Keeley.

[94] Tomlinson, John (2003) Globalisation and cultural identity. In: Held, David (2003) *The Global Transformations Reader*, 2nd Edition. London: Polity.

[95] The leading chronicler of glocalization is Victor Roudometof, with his (2016) *Glocalization, A Critical Introduction* London: Routledge

[96] Morley, David (2006) Globalisation and cultural imperialism reconsidered: old questions in new guises, in Curran, James and Morley, David (2006) M*edia and cultural theory*. London: Routledge, pp 30-43, pp 35.

[97] Ibid., pp38

[98] Ibid., pp 40; the Appardurai quotation is from Appadurai, A. (1996) *Modernity at Large*, Minneapolis: University of Minnesota Press, pp 31.

[99] Ibid., pp 34.

[100] Polumbaum, J. and Xiong, L. (2008) *China ink: the changing face of Chinese journalism*. Lanham, Md: Rowman & Littlefield, pp 3 and passim.

[101] Hamilton (2015), pp 139.

7 The Future and Its Past

Although politicians continue to use the vocabulary and deploy the tools of Marxism, it has been discredited in society at large and is no longer adequate as justification for authoritarian rule or suppression of free speech. While some may pine for 'Western democracy' it would seem that the narrative that is replacing Marxism explains authoritarian rule as being an aspect of Chinese tradition, the essential tool to protect and preserve Chinese civilisation at risk of subversion or worse from aggressive powers. While such rule has its defects, so does the alternative. The best of both worlds, it is thought, can be achieved by getting the authoritarian model to mutate into a more participative polity, variously termed 'consultative democracy' 'deliberative democracy' or 'guardianship democracy'.

7.1   Marxism in the departure lounge

Although there remain theoreticians at work in the ideological strongholds of the Party,[1] even the heirs of those who benefited from 'liberation' hardly seem to take Marxism seriously. As Shi Yinhong 时殷弘 of Peoples' University (a CCP foundation) has written:

> '…the most remarkable manifestation of civil society in China is found in the alienation of society from the state's ideology, belief system, political culture, and "official discourse." Political indoctrination courses and their examinations have long been viewed as repugnant by undergraduate and postgraduate students, who muddle through them with the least amount of effort. There is hardly any private subscription to the central and local Party newspapers, magazines and journals. The Chinese Communist Party's propaganda-producing departments are viewed as the least prestigious party institutions by intellectuals. Political functionaries are regarded in most places as cadres possessing no specialized or professional skills who make their living with "empty talk."[2]

In everyday life, people refer to traditional moral values and suggest that they uphold them. Teachers cite Chinese philosophers, primary school classes study both national philosophy 国学 and the Confucian virtues 思想品德, novels and telenovelas reflect a society rooted in Confucian and Buddhist notions. The brutally suppressed Falungong 法轮功 movement was a wildly popular expression of traditional Chinese mores, suppressed because of its perceived political interference rather than for its beliefs. The numbers of practitioners and their variety of ages, social classes and localities, were testimony to the resilience of traditional culture and Marxism's failure to appeal to present generations, let alone to inspire them.[3]

President Xi, who is the first leader to give a speech in commemoration of Confucius' birth,[4] makes more references to Confucian thinkers in his speeches than to any other category.[5] And yet, university professors who have history curricula written for them by the XCB curse Xi's 'Maoism' as do Editors obliged to instruct their neophytes in 'Marxist' ideas of the media.

Organisation: The Chinese Communist Party

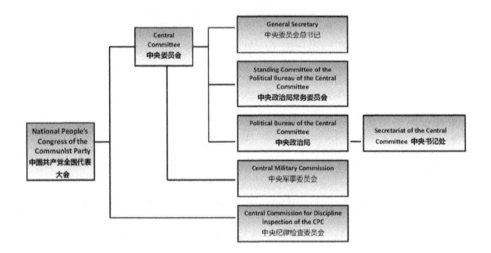

Xi, accused by some intellectuals of 'having missed out on education, knows only Maoism', takes selectively from Marxism (which some now dub a 'Western religion'), eulogises facets of Mao which are most 'Chinese' and wants to fuse Marxist practices and Confucian precepts. He castigates corruption but does not see it as a concomitant of the system established by the Marxists. Rather he believes that the corrupted have not adequately cultivated virtue.[6] He extolled Bo Xilai's extra-legal methods of cleaning up Chongqing, which were reminiscent of the Maoist past and shocked his peers. In 2016, it was being claimed that the anti-corruption drive that Xi has instituted was in the same mould.

Xi represents a strand of thinking that still matters. It was exemplified by Wu Banggu 吴邦国, the second ranking member of the 16th and 17th party congress Politburo Standing Committee, when, according to Kerry Brown, he set out the five 'noes': no multi-party system, no liberalisation of thinking, no tripartite division of responsibilities into party, state and courts, no federalism for China and no privatization.[7]

Demonstrating that the Party is a coalition of differing views, Wu's colleague, the then Prime Minister Wen Jiabao, simultaneously advocated the rule of law, a reduction of absolute power and its concentration, reform of the party and state leadership system, the promotion of social fairness and justice, the maintenance of judicial impartiality and independence, and the safeguarding of democratic rights including the right to vote, to receive information, and to supervise and participate.[8]

Brown has a nice illustration of how Marxism might remain the state religion, but be irrelevant in practical matters. Zhang Dejiang 张德江, then Zhejiang Party Secretary, later Vice Premier, in 2001 published an article entitled 'We must make it clear that private businessmen cannot be enrolled in the Party'. That year, they were.[9] Marxist nostrums had already become mere incantations.

7.1.1 Marxism dysfunctional

Why has Marxism lost its hold? The most obvious explanation is simply that it did not work. Far from propelling China into the modern future, ideology not only wrecked the economy but also took China back to a past of arbitrary power involving the utter subjugation of the people to the ruling elite.[10] George Orwell satirizes such a consummation of revolution in his novel *Animal Farm*.

Where it is recognized, this 'great leap backwards' is generally blamed on Mao Zedong, just as apologists once blamed Russia's bloodbaths on Stalin. But more reflective observers see him as only the conduit. It was Marxist ideas that, as in Russia, dislocated the economy and provided moral justification and motivation for the brainwashing, killings and assault on the visible past. They did this for various reasons. First, Marxists did not see pre-communist legality and moral constraints as the products of struggles by the weak to protect themselves with rights.[11] They characterised them as impositions by the ruling class which had to be swept out to make way for 'peoples' democratic dictatorship', an oxymoron if ever there were one. Thus the communists abolished a legal system which, as the historian of Chinese legal institutions, Philip Huang, has shown, by no means deserved to be dumped.[12]

Second, Marx did not see people as individuals or as members of cultural and family groups which had evolved their own responses to the challenges of life, cultures which should be respected. Instead, he saw them as members of universal classes and the products of particular economic circumstances which would, and should be, superseded. Individuals merely reflect social conditions and are not themselves significant. These two tenets licensed the liquidation of millions as 'former people'[13] and gave grounds for the employment of the psychopaths and murderers who join the executive ranks of all totalitarian regimes. The contempt

217

for (certain categories of) human beings engendered by Marxism would reach its apogee in the rule of Pol Pot in Cambodia, although the numbers who suffered were greater in the USSR and China.

The Marxists' failure to understand how economies work and the significance of the legal, moral and interpersonal frameworks for them led to such inhumane experiments as collectivisation in the Soviet Union and the communes in China.[14] The idea that a complex economy supporting millions of people in vastly different areas with vastly different needs can be directed from a central office imposing a great plan is fatuous to the modern mind. Yet this was an article of faith for the revolutionaries of the 20th century, for the leaders especially because it justified the expropriation of the many and the ascendency of the few. When policies caused the reverse of what was boasted, famine instead of plenty, chaos instead of productivity, journalists and creatives dared not say so for fear of being branded proponents of capitalism.

Historical determinism was another core belief. Marx's background was Judeo-Christian and for both religions, for we should term Marxism a secular religion, heaven on earth (utopia) will be brought about by faith and the coming of the saviour. In the manner of Christian missionaries and preachers over previous hundreds of years, Communists everywhere promoted Marxist ideas as the one truth, offering a supposedly scientific explanation as to how utopia would come about once the proletariat ruled the world and had swept away all impediments, namely old ideas and 'former people'. The media were essential tools in the necessary changing of thinking.

Since the new world was inevitable, all the Marxian activists were doing when they assaulted 'old' ideas and institutions was acting out their historically determined roles and giving predestination a helping hand. In a country in which Buddhism, Islam, Taoism and Christianity had cohabited for dynasties, religious tyranny in the Lenin style was introduced. Fanatical hatred of other religions was a hallmark of 20th century totalitarian movements, and has been revived in the 21st century by Islamic State.[15]

Chinese people cogitating over their country's future have come to these conclusions less, we can surmise, by reading foreign books than from their own reviews of their country's recent past. For market labourers as for university students, Marxism is the state religion which gets in the way of open discussion and acknowledgment of reality. It is not only that its interpretation of the world is dysfunctional.[16] It is increasingly seen as something foreign and, through some curious logic, disassociated from Mao Zedong. The 'Great Helmsman' can still be venerated, particularly by the poor (from whom he made the comfortable classes learn the facts of life) and those who have lost job security under 'marketisation'. The idealism with which people sacrificed themselves for the CCP in the early years, the heroic endeavour of the Long March and the expulsion of the foreign oppressors tend to be attributed to Mao *despite* his failures. 'Humankind cannot bear very much reality'.

Organisation: The Party Branch

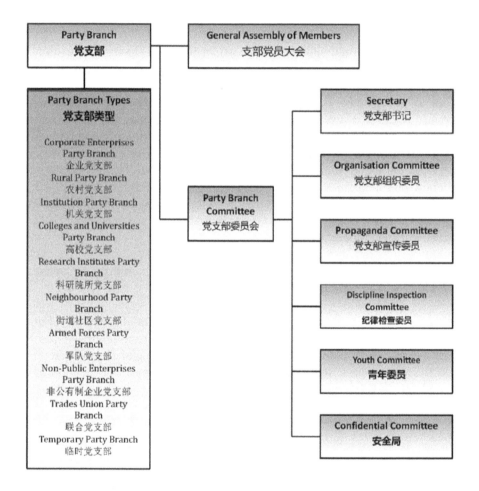

7.1.2 Re-reading history

Communism, or the practical application of Marxism, can today be perceived as a variant on the utopianism which germinated in Europe in the 19th century and swept through much of the world in the 20th. The enthusiasm for communism among Chinese intellectuals in the 1920s and 1930s was part of a transnational phenomenon, as student politicians everywhere, needing a guiding philosophy for their activism, seized upon a easily graspable solution for all ills. The countries most impervious to it were those with relatively capitalist economies and comparatively participative polities. The Anglosphere was resistant. The Chinese were particularly susceptible because Marxism offered a blueprint for the resurrection of the nation and its modernisation as well as a rejection of 'the West'. It was also sedulously promoted by Russia as an instrument of her aggressive foreign policy.[17]

The key tenet of this utopianism – some prefer the term *modernism*, as used by the Italian artist Marinetti in the *Futurist Manifesto* – was that a revolution by the enlightened should repudiate the contemporary order as the first stage in the creation of a classless and moneyless society. Powered by this idea, revolts ensconced regimes whose privileged élites, under the banners of 'progress' and 'modernisation', subjected their subjects to unparalleled violence and repression. They justified this by assuring their supporters that a glorious future was just around the corner, a society from which all evils would have been purged. Politicians find ideologies that will propel them to power and call them truth. In retrospect, the twentieth century was the age of repudiation, in which demagogues dismantled not only oppressive institutions but whatever protection and comforts had been afforded by traditional society.

In Edmund Stillman and William Pfaff's inquiry into 20th century totalitarianism, *The Politics of Hysteria*, they ponder:

> 'To destroy a city, a state, and Empire even, is an essentially finite act; but to attempt the total annihilation – the liquidation – of so ubiquitous but so theoretically or ideological defined an entity as a social class or racial abstraction is quite another, and one impossible even in conception to minds not conditioned by Western habits of thought. …Yet such have been the stated ambitions of the two political movements, communism and fascism, which have convulsed the middle years of our century.'[18]

How did Chinese fall for the fantasy of utopia? From the mid-nineteenth century onwards, seeing their country exploited and bullied by foreign powers, the educated families which traditionally supplied the civil service candidates from among their sons sought a way to restore China to wealth and power so that she might see off the imperialists. There were many different ideas – constitutional monarchy and American style democracy were both popular – and some sought a compromise between Chinese tradition and participation. Many of the formerly proscribed writers of the Republic, including Hu Shih 胡适 and Chou Tsojen 周作

人, have been republished in China in recent years and have fertilised discussion of how to 'move on'. When they were alive, they could not compete with the organisation and zealotry of the Communists. The latter had answers to everything, supposedly based on a science of progress, and a mobilising ideology that repudiated the West and promised that China would supersede capitalism.

7.1.3   Chineseness versus Marxism

While we cannot easily imagine the practicalities of how China might 'move on', it is not difficult to see why Marxism failed to take hold, even aside from its incompetence.

For traditional society Confucian nostrums provided the ethical matrix. Unlike the monotheist religions, Confucianism neither demanded exclusivity – you could burn a joss stick to a local saint or go to a church while being a good 'Confucian'[19] – nor did it evangelise. Whereas Christianity and Islam have often claimed universal validity and worked towards the destruction of other religions and heretics, Confucian China left metaphysical matters to individual taste. Provided adherents did not threaten the social order, it has been quite feasible to be a Confucian and invoke Buddha, the Daoist masters, Jesus Christ or other assorted 'saints'. Called pragmatism or permissiveness by some, pantheism by others, this aspect of traditional Chinese society offers a model of co-existence.

The Marxists were not only exclusive, they were also crusading, attempting to impose a militant vision of progress on others. A greater contradiction with traditional Chinese values could hardly be imagined. According to the Scots philosopher John Gray,[20] it is Christianity that is responsible for making people think that we can be masters of our destiny and for Marx's claim that we can create heaven on earth. 'The humanist belief in progress is only a secular version of Christian faith'.[21]

Another borrowing from Christianity is universalism. 'If only one belief can be true,' says Gray, 'every way of life in which it is not accepted must be in error'.[22] Thus when Lenin and Mao destroyed those who thought differently, they were not merely eliminating inconvenient rivals. They were reflecting the belief of the positivists, by whom Marx was deeply influenced, that 'there is but one God'.

The conviction that human society is inevitably heading towards a Communist or racist paradise, in which the chosen people (proletarians or Aryans in twentieth-century Europe; peasants/workers/soldiers in Asia) will have happiness without end was also contrary to traditional Chinese ideas of history. They acknowledged material development but not moral improvement. Traditionally, Chinese thinkers

221

had urged people to live up to the (perhaps mythical) high standards set by their forebears, rather than to imagine that they might overtake them. By contrast, the myth of progress derives from the Jewish-Christian tradition of millenarianism. In pointing out the adverse consequences of that belief when it is used as a rallying cry, and in using the word 'myth' to describe it, critics are not suggesting that progress in the sense of improvements in our material conditions or knowledge or behaviour does not occur. Rather, they are asserting that the belief that progress is unilinear and permanently changes our moral attitudes, has no basis in evidence. It is just a myth, or, more properly, fallacy. The grisly fate of societies that have elevated progress to a religion should be warning enough against Marxist prescription. The 20th century experience of abuse and slaughter of millions, justified by 'scientific' ideas and carried out by the most 'modern' and 'progressive' regimes, should clarify that technological progress does not automatically bundle moral improvement.

Consultative democracy

The political commentator Professor Hu Angang 胡鞍钢 has explained, in a *China Daily* essay, how the 12th Five Year Plan was developedover a long period of consultation which involved nine steps methodically taken.[23]

In 2008 three organisations were tasked by the National Development and Reform Commission (NDRC)国家发展和改革委员会 to evaluate the 11th five-year plan in mid-term. These three organisations were the Centre for Domestic Affairs at Tsinghua University 清华大学国情研究中心, the Development Research Centre of the State Council 国务院发展研究中心 and the World Bank office in China. In December the NDRC, having also carried out an opinion poll, reported its findings.

After this, the NDRC fixed on 20 issues and arranged for experts to brainstorm. Several thousand such experts examined these issues for a whole year in order to come up with proposals as to what the overall strategy of the 12th five-year plan should be.

In 2010 the third step took place. This was the actualization of the guidelines for the plan, itself followed by a fourth step which was the writing of a consultative draft, during which suggestions were collected from a wide variety of sources and included in the draft.

Simultaneously an expert committee, which had been established originally five years before, deliberated on the consultative draft and advised drafting team. A draft plan was completed at the beginning of 2011. Thereafter the expert committee took soundings on that draft.

The eighth step took place in early 2011 when Prime Minister Wen Jiabao solicited opinions from society at large.

The final two steps comprised the presentation of the draft of the National People's Congress and, once the National People's Congress approved it, it goes to the State Council for promulgation and implementation.

The writer concludes that this is the largest policy consulting and research activity conducted anywhere in the world.

In March 2013, the newly-elected chairman of the CPPCC pledged that 'China will promote consultative democracy and will not copy Western political systems under any circumstances'.

I have emphasised the negative and destructive aspects of Communism. On the other hand, the rhetoric of equality and democracy, though betrayed, has surely seeped into the minds of ordinary people. The attempt to atomise people, tear them away from relationships other than the state, has not succeeded but has probably left people much more self-aware. We can ask ourselves whether a similar process of democratization is happening in Chinese society today as took place in Anglo-Saxon England or medieval Europe before the Renaissance. There, the moral intuitions generated by Christianity, the equality of all and individual relationships with God, penetrated the general consciousness and stimulated criticism of the contemporary order.[24]

Thus in China today, protests are not necessarily just the desperate rising of helots wanting to replace one set of rogues with another. They are assertions of the right to take part and to hold the powerful to account. And even irritable intellectuals and wealthy bourgeois who are snobbish about the Party and its functionaries, consider that they too are stakeholders and expect to be consulted, even if in reality they don't want to waste time on politics.

7.2   Taking the place of Marxism

The Peoples' Daily Online has helpfully produced a précis of President Xi's statements on the media.[25] In them, he not only enjoins them to recognize their mission in the great work of rebuilding China, but also reaffirms the Marxist view of the media. The leaders continue to speak Marxism, partly because to abjure it would throw the nation into confusion and raise unwelcome questions about the Party's past, partly to obviate a 'real' communist opposition occupying that space, partly because it is not politic to admit that 'socialism with Chinese characteristics' has been shorn of Marxism, and possibly even because some elements of the Marxian vision are still serviceable. Xi's identification of the destructive and dehumanising aspects of capitalism, its global aggressiveness, its promotion of inequality and the commodification of every aspect of culture and relationships are aspects of his thought that still appear to have purchase among thinkers in the Party.[26]

For the less reflective, it is the socialist message, rather than the Marxist method, that remains. Because of that, Marxism can continue to inspire, particularly those who have risen from poor backgrounds to serve the state. On visits to London, officers of the Peoples' Liberation Army pay their respects at the tomb of Karl Marx in Highgate Cemetery, dressing in suits and ties brought especially for the purpose.[27]

Yet for most people, daily practices appear to be reflecting tradition more and more.[28] 'Role respect' 孝, which English speakers have translated as 'filial piety', is a code of duty which ensures the care and happiness of the very young and the very old. Its prescription educates children in the virtues, and situates the individual within a caring community of relatives and within a story of those will come before and after.[29] It is constantly referred to and indeed depicted on street hoardings. Confucian practice has evolved and elders are now likely to share decision-making. At the recent wedding of a returned student, the bride rode in a palanquin and her groom on a horse, according to 19th century formula, but they were treated as equals and treated each other in the same way. Instead of bowing to a portrait of Chairman Mao and dedicating their marriage to the state, as their parents would have done, the young couple made obeisance to their two sets of parents and ancestral tablets together. Ready-made steles for each of the '100 surnames' can now be bought off the peg, along with ancestral tablets before which you can burn joss at home if there is no longer a convenient temple. It is claimed that, in the southern provinces, a great many family temples have been rebuilt.

The media reflect this. Characters in television series have been found to express Confucian codes of benevolence and filial piety[30] or simply to assume traditional extended family values, as with the series *A Good Husband*, mentioned earlier. Street exhortations have been part and parcel of Chinese life for hundreds of years, with the CCP making a great deal of use of sloganeering. Today, public signage less and less reflects Marxist or Leninist ideas, but instead displays Confucian aphorisms. In the Deng era reform policies were advertised with such catchphrases as 'Raise high the banner of Socialism with Chinese characteristics' 高举中国特色社会主义伟大旗帜. Under Hu Jintao there was a slow transition to the theme of harmony.[31] Here is a typical example, photographed in the capital:

> the country and you should treat each other with a mother's profound affection 祖国母亲恩情深 [picture: baby carried on back of mother]

The most important series of slogans are those which repeat the values which, by contrast with class struggle, communist utopia or economic determinism, are now those of the state:

> The key values of socialism are 社会主义核心价值观: 富强 affluence and strength, 民主 democracy, 文明 civility, 和谐 harmony, 自由 freedom, 平等 equality, 公正 justice, 法制 legality, 爱国 patriotism, 敬业 professionalism, 诚信 sincerity, 友善 kindness [often accompanied by pretty pictures of jolly families of three generations]

224

In the suburbs of the capital, taking up spaces previously reserved for political slogans, are direct quotes from indigenous philosophers, including Confucius and Mencius.[32]

What can be written only in novels

What people actually believe, as opposed to what they might officially espouse, is changing. This is clear from the, relatively uncontrolled, fiction, much of which subverts orthodoxy.

Many depict social issues: Liu Liu 六六 describes the struggles of the middle class, Chi Li 池莉 and Wang Hailing 王海鸰 deal with social pressures on personal life. Others are deconstructing the history of Communism: Mo Yan's 莫言 *Life and death are wearing me out* 生死疲劳 is one long exposure of the failure of Communist Party policies from 1949-1978; Yu Hua's 余华 *To live* 活着 provides a gripping account of the tragedy of the Great Leap Forward as it affected one community, carrying on the work of the long-banned but now popular Zhāng Ailíng 张爱玲, who hated the dehumanisation of China after 1949.[33]

But it is Yan Lianke's 阎连科 depiction of an ambitious young politician's quest for advancement during the Cultural Revolution, *Tough like water* 坚硬如水, that carries a fearsome message about Chinese politics and perhaps about politics in general. Yan gives us the seizure of power in a village by the young, ambitious Gao. Because there is no mechanism for the transition to a new generation or interest group, he uses cruel methods and causes damage to many people in order to get his gang in and replace the existing power holders. The interests of the citizenry and society are completely ignored, although he always claims that he is motivated only by idealism and zeal to serve the people. It is a brilliant exposition of the mind of a certain kind of politician, whose motivations and behaviour may be similar the world over, though limited and channelled by the system in which he or she has to operate.

Modern novelists like Yan are rethinking the past in the way that the mass media cannot – yet. There is not yet a Truth and Reconciliation Commission, but the first steps are being taken towards truth in history.

The reinstatement of Confucianism in education has been going on since the early 1990s when many small independent schools calling themselves Confucius Academies opened. In 1993 two articles were published in the leading national party newspapers, in effect 'legalising' the movement.[34] Two years later at the annual National Consultative Conference (CPPCC), a group of scholars called for the establishment of schools specializing in the study of the Chinese classics.[35]

Today there are many academies but the main impact of the Canon is probably in the generality of schools in which *guoxue* classes have become a significant component. To bring the older generation up to speed, universities and private colleges have also set up such classes. Communist Party personnel take *guoxue* courses.

In 2014 the Ministry of Education required more lessons on traditional culture to be added to the curriculum in both primary and secondary schools. This occurred at about the same time as the Peking Education Committee reduced the amount of English which needs to be studied in the high school curriculum.[36]

7.2.1 Governance

Traditional political theory, although authoritarian, was not despotic. According to Confucius and Mencius, the ruler's task is to look after the people. If he fail in that, he loses the mandate entrusted to him by heaven and can be deposed. He was enjoined to model himself on the Emperor Yu the Great 大禹 (c. 2200 – 2100 BC), whose first responsibility was controlling floods lest they threaten the peasantry He was expected to commit himself to the welfare of his subjects, and civil servants had the right of criticism and rebellion when they thought that commitment unfulfilled.[37] Such, at least, were the ideals.

Being selected through heredity and often subjected to malign influences in the court, the Emperor was a potential weakness in the system. With the exception of the founders of dynasties, Emperors were often only parts, if very important ones, of the machinery of government. They were condemned to fulfil specified roles and hemmed in by conventions, institutions, demands and relationships. Amusing evocations of this are offered in the popular TV drama series *The story of Wu Mei Niang* 武媚娘传奇 (2015), the saga of China's great female Emperor. It depicts Li Shimin 李世民 (598-649), when Emperor of Tang 唐太宗, as a man who, though one of the most powerful personalities in history, is circumspect in showing his preferences even among the women of his own harem. He has to navigate court and national politics as much as any minister.

Southern Weekend

Southern Weekend (南方周末 *Weekend South, Southern Weekly*) is the flagship product of the Southern Daily Group (SDG), which in 2010 attempted to buy the USA's *Newsweek* magazine, owned by *The Washington Post*. Founded in 1984 by the Southern Daily Group, SDG, it soon became a national newspaper and one of the few known outside China.

The first editor raised issues of direct concern to ordinary people which were not covered by the 'Party newspapers' so that its circulation, with 3 million mainly private subscribers, rapidly overtook that of the *Southern Daily, Guangzhou Daily* and the more popular *Yangcheng Evening News*.

After 1989 many publications diminished critical commentary and sensitive investigation, but *Southern Weekend* kept going. He Qinglian[38] offers three reasons to explain its survival during the 1990s: First, the newspaper was extraordinarily profitable; and this was very welcome, because the SDG was itself in competition with two other newspaper groups, and could not risk losing these readers. Second, the editors were crafty: they rarely investigated issues in Guangzhou, but responded to information from outside their own area, and through frequent apologies and self-criticisms, they managed to survive. Third, the Guangdong government was then in the pocket of a sympathetic Marshal Ye Jianning, a general of the Civil War, of whose immense prestige regional officials were in awe.

Things were to change after Li Changchun came to power in Guangdong in 1998. According to He Qingling, the media analyst, before 1999 *Southern Weekend* published many reports critical of 'monopolies in the banking, public utility and communication sectors, but very few [such] reports after that.'[39] Thereafter investigations concentrated on relatively small fry, mainly business people, rather than officials. Sectors with less clout than the banking or heavily capitalised utilities, such as education, health or agriculture, were featured together with relatively easy targets, such as brothels or commercial rip-offs. Even these proved too much for the authorities; in 2000 Editor Jiang Yiping (who had succeeded Zuo Fang) was obliged to resign.

Worse was to come.[40] In 2001 *Southern Weekend* published an article about a gang of criminals in which it named, as being equally criminal, two very senior political figures. The CPD then engineered the dismissal of some leading journalists, and a year later followed this with another purge when the editors proposed to publish an article about corruption in an establishment charity, Project Hope.

On 3rd January 2013, *Southern Weekend* published its New Year message, 'Chasing dreams'. The theme of the editorial was 'guaranteed constitutional rights', an idea frequently mentioned in a recent speech by the newly-elected General Secretary of the Party, Xi Jinping. Nevertheless, the local CPD was displeased and substituted its own version for that written by the journalists.

As the New Year message of *Southern Weekend* is a famous landmark, even before the edition had been published, netizens had already seen the planned New Year message such that, by 2nd January, there were two versions available online. One of them, 2,200 words long, was written by journalist Dai Zhiyong 戴志勇, and was regarded as the original piece. Entitled, 'China's dream, constitution's dream 中国梦，宪政梦', it called for guaranteed constitutional rights. The second version, entitled, 'The 'dream' is our acknowledgment of what ought to happen' 梦想是我们对应然之事的承诺, is thought to have been edited and adapted by the Guangdong CPD. The latter version praised the achievements of the Party and government, but there was a much softer tone on constitutional rights. It was regarded as a compromise between Party and newspaper.

On the night of 3rd January, *Southern Weekend*'s official microblog account announced that the CPD had interfered by adding lines, changing the title and topic of the New Year's message, and so forth, without consulting the frontline editors. Heated discussion, mainly critical of the CPD and even calling for the resignation of its Director, followed hour by hour, and celebrity bloggers as well as many journalists joined in, until on the night of 6th January, journalist Zhang Hua announced on his microblog that he and his colleagues were going on strike.

On 8th January all the Party newspapers were asked to re-issue an editorial published in the *Global Times* the day before. It indicated that the CPD was not behind the changes to the New Year message, adding that activists outside China's media industry – including US-based blind lawyer Chen Guangcheng – had been 'inciting some media to engage in confrontation'. *Southern Weekend* resisted publishing this. In the 10th January edition, *Southern Weekend* announced that the staff strike was over.

Southern Weekend has survived today, a big, stimulating newspaper of many sections, but friction with the authorities is continuous. Critics see it as endangering social harmony and 'washing dirty linen in public', while its supporters regard it as a either a beacon of good journalism or a standard bearer for reform.

When the Emperor was a conforming part of the machinery, China enjoyed a system of governance admired by Enlightenment Europeans, who had nothing like the efficient civil service selected largely through public examination.[41] The principle was meritocratic even if the practise was not always consistent. The ideal is heroic and celebrated today, in shrines to such great exemplars of justice as ministers Hai Rui 海瑞 and Qu Yuan 屈原 and in constant references to the frugality and irreproachability of Di Renjie 狄仁杰 and Bao Qingtian 包青天 (see p54). Unfortunately, while many young officials in the 21st century may start out with the intention of emulating them, swearing fealty to high ideals as in episode 7 of *In the Name of the People*, the pitifully low salaries and opportunities for gain mean that the temptations to abuse their offices are many.

In the later dynasties, central control was maintained through personnel management and clear definitions of responsibility. Policy was arrived at by discussion, to which local officials contributed through their regular reports. This is still a fundamental feature of officialdom. Since local officials were responsible for local welfare, economic well-being and critical evaluation of government initiatives, they were active participants. But 'Once policy was decided, each official had the duty of carrying it out in complete and meticulous conformity with the ruler's intention.'[42] Today this approach is called 'democratic centralism', an essentially Soviet label for a traditional Chinese technique of government.

Practice was pragmatic, flexible and undogmatic. Sebastian Heilmann considers this attitude to still be typical today. As reported in Chapter 6, he generally attributes this approach to Mao, yet also notes that aspects of it are congruent with traditional thought.[43] The Empire was bureaucratic, yet bureaucracy functioned according to rules different from those which Anglophones normally associate with bureaucracy. When Mao called for a Cultural Revolution he was not likely to change the workstyle, because those who replaced the hierarchy adopted one even more relationship-dependent and arbitrary than what had preceded it. It was moral values and learning that he disrupted, not workstyle.

In traditional society, the esprit de corps of the civil service and its sense of duty made it possible for officials to put pressure on the court and check irresponsibility. [44] Within the bureaucracy, there were checks and balances amounting to mutual surveillance. This was institutionalized in a Censorate, founded during the Qin Dynasty (221-207 BC), which at its best investigated the execution of policy and its abuses. During the Tang Dynasty (618-907), censors could act without permission of their masters. They investigated, reported and initiated judicial action, leaving judgment to others. Their sources were protected. 'The longevity of China's political system must be credited in significant degree to the power and vigilance of the Censorate' writes the Sinologist, English Kracke.[45]

Principles of Confucian government were reasserted when Deng Xiaoping and colleagues sought to build an administration fit for purpose. In the 1990s, they reintroduced recruitment through written examination, supplemented subsequently by peer review and other criteria. Once again, Chinese officials are selected and promoted on merit and supervised through the detailed records 个人档案 kept of their performance by a command centre (today the Central Organisation Department 中组部, which determines senior appointments). The provincial equivalents control the lower level positions. Censorial functions, in particular investigations of corruption, are performed by the Party's *Central Commission for Discipline Inspection* 中央纪律检查委员会,with local equivalents, and investigative journalists can be this organisation's accomplices.

Aside from the vast extension of competencies and therefore the content of the civil service examinations, the most obvious difference between the earlier and present systems of governance is that the Party has been battened on to the structure. It is not that there is much that is unfamiliar about the Party's activities at each level, but those activities – ideological work, education and training, policy making – would in the past have been undertaken in-house by the civil service. The bifurcation between Party and State is only partly real, however, since their leaders are generally the same people. An able official will alternate between state and Party appointments throughout his or her career. A township head who has done well will become the township Party Secretary; the next step would be Deputy County Head and if that goes well at he or she will enter the executive and thence become County Head. From there, the next elevation is to be County Party Secretary. Movement from state to Party position at the same grade is considered to be a promotion.

And what do these officials actually do? Political philosophy gives priority to the responsibility of the rulers for the social and economic conditions of the people, rather than for their individual liberty or political participation.[46] Hence the resonance, to the political class of the 20th century, of 'socialism'. Today, socialism in China seems to mean a political system that identifies the material conditions of the citizenry as the first consideration, that to which all modern governments of left and right aspire. Something similar has been the object of Chinese government since long before European intellectuals theorized socialism.

It is possible therefore, to perceive both the aims and the practice of the nominally Communist state as a reinvigoration of traditional governance, not only in its institutions but also in its values. The violent oppression of 'class enemies' and other vile initiatives modelled on Bolshevik savagery appear to be over. Officials go to London or New York for professional development one day, and to Yenan on another. And the 'Emperor' is now selected from within the bureaucracy rather than superimposed upon it by a family.

7.3   How do we account for these 'cultural' dispositions?

How can it be claimed that an overthrown mode of governance is making a comeback? Only if it is acknowledged that polities, at least at steady-state, are reflections of the cultural substructure. In the Anglosphere, critics of China account for its resistance to 'Western' ideas by suggesting that introducing electoral democracy would threaten 'crony capitalism', that the bourgeoisie are very comfortable with repression of the lower orders thank you, that the intellectuals have been bought over with sinecures and the right to pontificate in the media, and that media workers, who would otherwise be natural critics of an unfair regime, are paid or cowed to be mouthpieces. Yet these are not sufficient explanations. Authoritarian politics, with claims to egalitarianism, have been facts in both Nationalist and Communist China as well as in Singapore. Today's Taiwan may be the exception, and be a valuable demonstration that Chinese societies are amenable to electoral democracy. Taiwan is very small though, so the analogy with the PRC may be inaccurate, and its political parties may function differently from their Anglophone counterparts, even if there are superficial similarities.

The characteristics of Chinese society identified in Chapter 5 offer a plausible explanation. But how are we to account for those characteristics and their endurance? When 'Confucianism' was abolished, they persisted, suggesting that the ideology was not the originator of the culture but a reflection of it. Here Todd's *family hypothesis*[47] is serviceable, especially when considered in the light of its success in elucidating ideological and economic development in many parts of the world.

According to Todd, the differential mode of association and complementary characteristics of Chinese society are epiphenomena of the substructure. Family relations, according to his hypothesis, set the parameters for politics. So the Chinese political system is a reflection less of the economy or even of the Russian instruction manual which was absorbed in the 1940s, than of the primordial family form. This determines how individuals relate to each other and their parents, what their expectations are and their assumptions as to how power is exercised. 'Unconsciously but inevitably, each generation absorbs those parental values which define elementary human relationships: between parents and children, between cousins, between husband and wife. The power of the reproductive mechanism springs from the fact that it does not need to be conscious or expressed: it is automatic and has its own internal logic'.[48]

Todd suggests that, at the moment that the Communist Party was attacking and attempting to destroy the family, it was actually transferring its characteristics to the state level. Filial devotion was co-opted to the state; the nation was now the family and all were equal under the paterfamilias, whether the Great Helmsman or Comrade Xiaoping. Any loosening of the bonds, in other words freedom, was perceived as chaos and instability, the worst of all possible worlds. Party branches were to provide the fraternity formerly enjoyed in the extended family and had power over their subjects' lives, even deciding whom they might marry.

Since those observations, the Party's grip has loosened and the family has waltzed back out of the graveyard. This matters because it is the particular family form and its norms that account for the grammar of Chinese society that was discussed in Chapter 5: personal loyalty as truth, the iron grip of family and friendship obligations, communitarianism, the honouring of authority and experience, and pragmatism or the rejection of ideals or ideologies that distract from the practical exigencies of family survival.[49]

In other words, equality before impartial law and the idea of rights attaching to the individual regardless of role, which are twin bases of the Anglophone polity, are exotic to traditional Chinese society. It may be, though, that these ideas, which were once foreign to European societies too, have penetrated China via communism, which preached them without practicing them. Thus the communitarian-orientated China might be giving way to what Kleinman, as we noted in Chapter 5, refers to as 'individualism'.[50] However, the existing evidence of how China's governance is evolving does not confirm Kleinman's theory,[51] or that it is shared by those to whose ideas about the future we now turn.

7.4   Thinking through the future

The most common criticism made abroad is that China is not 'democratic', yet today the Chinese discuss 'democracy' incessantly.[52] Surveys suggest that most people in China believe that their civil liberty and political freedom have increased since 1979. A content analysis of *People's Daily*, the official newspaper of the CCP, showed a growing number of articles critical of the government from 1978 to 2001. It also found that 'democracy is now portrayed in the official newspaper of the CCP as a universal value to be embraced by all. Moreover, debates on the issue of freedom, human rights and religion have flooded the newspaper. The focus of the debates is no longer whether these concepts are suitable for China, but rather what method should be adopted and what timing is appropriate for their introduction'.[53]

In 2012 the outgoing Prime Minister made a point of calling for political reform which would involve separation of state from Party, an independent judiciary and more grassroots elections. People claim to want 'democracy', it seems, partly because they fear that their political system has weaknesses that can only be ameliorated by democratic participation, and partly because they see that in the wider world governments without electoral democracy are not regarded as legitimate. Back in the 1980s, much decision-making had already been devolved to local authorities and private enterprise.[54]

A 1987 law, confirmed in 1998, introduced elections for village government and required that elected officials make their accounts public every six months.[55] Deng Xiaoping predicted general elections in fifty years.[56]

Organisation: The executive[57]

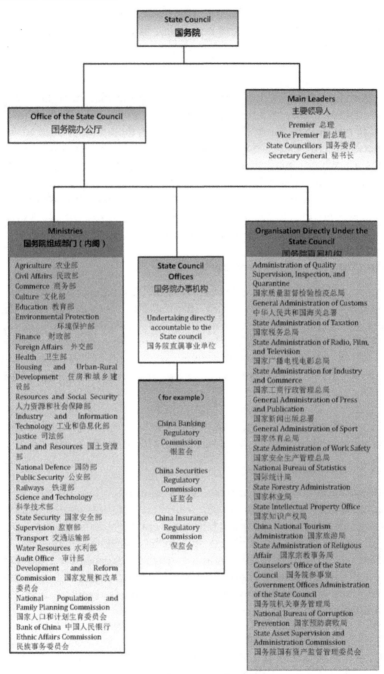

Apple University academic Doug Guthrie argues persuasively that the ruling class is 'anything but' unwilling to make political changes and has used 'economic reforms as a way of accomplishing political reform'.[58] What it has not done is countenance sudden, large-scale change. Aside from the philosophical attitudes, there are at least two practical reasons for this.

First, in the 1980s some people argued for 'Liberal Democracy'. They too were revolutionaries, hopeful of sweeping away the past and creating a brighter future without very clear plans as to how their objective might be achieved. This was twentieth-century politics, because it proposed another utopia, to be brought about by revolution. It filled Party leaders with fear, we may surmise, first because they stood to be wiped out and, second, because many of them had understood more clearly than those further from power, the dangers of utopian politics.

They knew better than the students what damage had been done to China since 1949, and feared chaos and even civil war. Some wanted to bring back constitutionality and the rule of law. They would succeed in doing so by arguing that such changes were necessary to economic development, but 'of course they fundamentally changed politics'.[59]

7.4.1 Electoral democracy's critics

The second reason for a cautious approach is misgivings about 'Western style' electoral democracy. This seems as common among intellectuals as officials, and with good reason: elections do not always produce leaders with the wellbeing of their electors at heart. Chinese intellectuals remind foreign interlocutors that democracy brought Hitler to power[60] and that many European countries jettisoned democracy in the first half of the twentieth century in favour of dictatorships of one kind or another. They also point out that it is democratic regimes that have been the most aggressive since the Second World War. Serbia was democratic when it launched the Balkan Wars; the USA showed over Kosovo in 1999 that it had no respect for the international legal order. In this and the previous half century, the USA and its democratic allies have reduced several countries to wreckage and subverted or destroyed order elsewhere, most bloodily in the Vietnam War (1955-75) and the assault on Iraq,[61] (2003-?). The 'Pivot towards Asia', which appears today to be a central plank of US foreign policy, is regarded as targeting and attempting to contain China.[62] Aggression is seen, rightly or wrongly, not only as a consequence of elected politicians being suborned by capitalists, but also as populism: ambitious politicians marketing themselves through big gestures or distracting the electorate from their domestic failures. The inference is that should China's millions come to select their rulers, the world might regret it, since the masses are far more radical and nationalistic than their current leaders, wise officials who have worked their careers through the bureaucracy with realistic understandings of the limits to, and potential repercussions of, policy.

Such scepticism is incredible to most Anglophones because they are committed to the belief that the only legitimate form of government is electoral democracy. Our forebears and those European political thinkers who debated which form of government might be best were more open-minded.[63] They understood that the electoral democracy that Anglophones blithely advocate today evolved in particular North European societies in which necessary preconditions were already established. To the modern Chinese, the lesson to be learnt from 'the West' is not that electoral democracy is essential to further development, but that it may be its product.[64]

Electoral democracy is not just viewed with suspicion because democracies are thought to be aggressive, but also because it only works if certain prior conditions are met. Participants need to already share values of equality before the law, a prizing of freedom, a sense of public service, and perhaps the empathy which Christianity has engendered.[65]

Without such foundations, 'free' elections in China might be nothing more than a ritual. The rule of law and free speech preceded electoral democracy in Anglophone societies,[66] and universal enfranchisement in fair elections was only achieved after centuries of debate and struggle.[67] Intellectuals can be categorical about this. Oxford's Rana Mitter points out that some 'argue that liberalism and pluralist democracy are purely Western ideas that can only be built on the specific basis of 300 years of post-Renaissance European experience'.[68] In discussion, it is common to be told that there are countries today which do not conform to strict Anglophone notions of electoral democracy, yet they are 'free' in that people are not subjected to arbitrary treatment and can speak their minds. In other words, electoral democracy is not an essential condition for freedom.

More topically, the problems of the USA and the European Union are cited as illustrations of the inability of elected politicians to think long-term on issues such as the environment, or to take action on controversial matters such as immigration or international affairs because they are focused on their own careers and the next election. Anglophone democracy is said to suffer from the excessive influence of big business, corrupt electoral practices, distortions of policy to please or create particular electoral constituencies, failure of elected representatives to represent the voters when their interests clash with those of the political class and ideological commitments by career politicians lacking the practical experiences which could temper them with realism. It is willingly admitted that Chinese governance suffers from the overwhelming importance of personal access and relationships, but these are problems thought to be found everywhere.

Media people: a controversialist

Image source:
http://news.xinhuanet.com/e
nglish/special/18cpcnc/2012-
11/15/131977282_11n.jpg

Bai Yansong 白岩松 is the leading news commentator and journalist. Graduating in journalism from Beijing Broadcasting Institute 北广 (now Communication University of China) in 1989, he first worked in newspapers and radio before moving into television news. While at CCTV he served as the lead anchor for *Focus Reports* 焦点访谈 and *Oriental Horizon* 东方时空, where he gained national fame. He was also involved in establishing several news commentary programmes, including *Timeline* 时空连线 and *News 1+1* 新闻仪一加一, the latter being China's first live news programme of that kind. *News Weekly* 新闻周刊 is a 45 minutes' programme reviewing the social problems behind the most discussed issues in the week. He has also written several books, including *Painful and Happy* 痛并快乐着, *Yansong goes to Japan* 岩松看日本 and *Happy now?* 幸福了吗?

Bai is regarded as representing the liberal élite in modern China, and has not been afraid of controversy. In 2008 he expressed his public opposition to the Carrefour boycott in an article entitled, 'Don't punish yourself for others' mistakes 不要拿别人的错误来惩罚自己', on his sohu.com blog (16th April 2008). This immediately provoked criticism and condemnation from the public and the news media, including Xinhua. In 2011, Bai used his show *News 1+1* to criticise the Railways Ministry spokesman over the Wenzhou train crash of 23rd July and expressed the public's discontent over the government's lack of openness in the aftermath of disasters, with vehemence. The next day he was suspended and then the programme was suspended for a week. This in turn brought criticism, from intellectuals and retired officials, of the Propaganda Department's handling of the media and information in general. Among them were the former editor of *People's Daily*, Hu Jiwei 胡绩伟, who denounced the closure of *News 1+1*.

Finally, behind many of these suspicions of 'Western democracy' lies the refutation of the Anglophone idea that state and society are distinct and even in opposition. As Lee Chin-ch'uan puts it, 'the Confucian tradition holds that benevolent rulers…are best qualified to represent and take care of the interests of their subjects.'[69] Even those who condemn the present decision-makers consider it right that government has taken the lead in economic development. The state is seen as promoting liberty, making press freedom possible and defending the interests of the majority against private ones.[70] The, admittedly somewhat ingenuous, point has often been made that media ownership is far more widespread in China, where thousands of work units or local governments control one or more media, than in the USA with a few rich proprietors.

So when they are leery of democracy as practised elsewhere, what do thoughtful Chinese mean by democracy when they plan for it in their own country? It seems that they mean consultation and consensus, not that all power should be in the hands of those chosen through the ballot box, whose actions may be swayed by fashions or electoral marketing.[71]

7.4.2   Ideas about political reform and democracy

Various Chinese thinkers, observing Anglophone democracy and aware of the cultural differences, have sought to identify ways in which more political participation might emerge organically in Chinese society. The head of an important political think-tank, Hu Angang (see p223) believes that the means used to canvass opinion and share policy-making today provide the answer: 'consultative democracy'. Others are concerned with the lack of accountability and want transparent participation. He Baogang 何包刚, a widely published writer on Chinese democratisation, has reported both on the theorists who are seeking 'deliberative democracy' in China, and on the practical measures which are been undertaken to develop deliberative and participatory institutions, of which there are many examples.[72] Columbia political scientist Andrew Nathan has shown us that we cannot assume that traditional Chinese culture is antithetical to democracy.[73]

Daniel Bell,[74] a political philosopher at Tsinghua University, has done most to explore what forms democracy might take in a China trying to develop institutions congruent with its culture and circumstances. He argues that 'there are morally legitimate alternatives to Western-style liberal democracy',[75] and finds that Chinese thinkers are looking for better solutions to the apparent need for greater political participation than those on offer from the Anglosphere. They aver that in all polities political decision-making is left to an élite, 'guardians' whom, the citizens, wanting to concentrate on their own affairs, families and communities, hope will be both educated and public spirited.[76] The point of a selection system is to find the best and most public-spirited people to oversee the administration of society and to hold the administrators to account. Elections are one way of do these things, but they may not be the best way and may need to be qualified or supplemented to limit the unforeseen consequences to which they can give rise.

While in China people fear that their present system makes corruption likely, they also note that Western elections now produce anything but 'the rule of the wise'. Societies need leaders who consider long-term consequences of present day decisions.[77] It is reasoned that the mandarinate, or corps of well-educated and dedicated officials, can do this better than the electoral democracy of the Anglosphere.

So those advocating 'democracy' are thinking of gradual, piecemeal reforms, such as revamping the Chinese People's Political Consultative Conference (CPPCC) 中国人民政治协商会议, which brings together experts and able people from different walks of life. The CPPCC could be given more power to hold government bodies accountable.[78] Were selection to the CPPCC transparently on the basis of ability or even by examination then it could be regarded as legitimate. Even in 'the West' elections are not the only means of attaining legitimacy: the monarchs of Europe are legitimate without ever having been subjected to the ballot box, as are US Supreme Court Judges.[79] Journalistic interrogations and investigations are possible in the Anglosphere because they and their profession are considered legitimate. In China journalists are well placed to render the powerful accountable and transparent in their dealings, once the principle is accepted in society at large, because the best of them are likened to the outspoken scholar-officials of history. They are already half way to becoming an arm of good governance.

In short, what is meant by democratisation in China is not necessarily what is meant in the Anglosphere. Bell has taken his exegesis further, suggesting that the 'China Model', which he sees as emerging, is one in which there will be electoral democracy in the villages and townships, but strategic decision-making will be kept in the hands of a (what is in effect) a Confucian mandarinate. This will be held to account by the modern equivalent of the Censorate, to which he might have added investigative and analytical journalism, and rendered legitimate because entry is through an open and uncorrupted examination system. He argues that this system best reflects the Chinese aspiration for a combination of 'democracy' and 'guardianship'.[80]

In taking a more idealistic and intransigent position, some, such as the Nobel prizewinner Liu Xiaobo 刘晓波, appear to belong more to the generation of 1989 than to the pragmatists, sceptics and gradualists of today. He bases his criticisms of the establishment on morality, denouncing the fact that self-interest has taken the place of law and conscience, and condemning the hedonism of society.[81] This is not particularly disturbing to the authorities, who say very much the same. It is Liu's radicalism, his desire for sweeping change, that makes them nervous and probably assures him of limited purchase inside China. He calls for people to 'risk their lives in struggle'.[82] Ai Weiwei, whose name is often linked with Liu in the West, may be more disliked for what William Callahan calls his 'warrior narrative' than his opinions.[83]

Thus, just as attitudes to democracy are conditioned by cultural assumptions and pragmatism, so despite day-to-day frustrations with limitations on the media or regulation of the Internet, most of the talk in China is of piecemeal enhancement.

7.5   Summary

If a major crisis were to force multiparty politics on China, we might see an approximation to electoral democracy as the Anglosphere understands it, in form if not always in substance. If, on the other hand, pressure from below and altering perceptions among the ruling groups bring about incremental changes, we may see institutions gradually evolving to become more participative and allowing more open discussion and transparency. Such developments would make them more accountable even without national elections. The media would need to become bolder and detached from the Party, which it could do without turning into a copy of the Anglophone media.

If it is the case that, from within, ways are emerging to make politics more participatory without adopting the Anglophone model, then we should not expect revolutionary changes in how China's media operate. They derive their norms not only from the political- economic system, but also from the substructure, that which we rather loosely call culture. We could not expect Anglophone journalists to abandon their adversarial instincts in favour of 'happy journalism' or 'constructive journalism' unless the elemental culture were fundamentally transformed. So it is with their Chinese counterparts. Independent-minded media workers may continue to feel frustrated when they compare themselves with their Anglophone equivalents and many will jibe at the obtuseness of censors, yet they will not necessarily be opponents of the system, but simply those who want to make it work better.

Notes

[1] These include the journal of the Central Committee, *Seek Truth* 求是 and the Central Compilation and Translation Bureau 中央编译局, Literature Research Centre of the Central Committee 中央文献研究室, and the Central Party School 中校.

[2] Shi, Yinhong (2004) The Issue of Civil Society in China and its Complexity. In: Sato, Yoichiro (ed.) *Growth & Governance in Asia*. Hawaii: Asia-Pacific Centre for Security Studies, Chapter 18, pp 228.

[3] It is exactly because of the Falungong's appeal across classes and regions that the authorities feared it, once it had demonstrated an ability to organize nationally. Religious or semi-religious movements – the White Lotus, the Taiping, the Boxers, the Communists – have been powerful subversives in modern Chinese history.

[4] Xi, Jinping (2014) Xi Jinping's Speech in Commemoration of the 2,565th Anniversary of Confucius' Birth. ChinaUSFocus, 24 September. Available from http://library.chinausfocus.com/article-1534.html [Accessed 25 February 2016].

[5] Sun, X. (2014) *Xi Jinping's 300 References*, 30 November. See http://news.sina.com.cn/c/2014-10-30/024831066011.shtml [Accessed 25 February 2016]. CHECK AGAIN

[6] Brown, Kerry (2015) *The New emperors: power and the princelings in China*. London: I B Tauris pp 195.

[7] Ibid., pp 189.

[8] Ibid., pp 189.

[9] Brown, ibid., pp 174.

[10] Lynch, Daniel C (1999) *After the Propaganda State*. Stanford: Stanford University Press, pp 231. Lynch also quotes writers who see 1949 as an interruption in China's development. However Lynch appears to believe that this is not so.

[11] In my exposition of Marx's ideas I am drawing on David Conway's (1987) *A Farewell to Marx: An Outline and Appraisal of His Theories* London: Pelican. Professor Conway generously reviewed my synthesis and approved.

[12] Huang Philip C. C. In his *Chinese Civil Justice, Past and Present* (New York: Rowman & Littlefield, 2010) Huang has described the unnecessary rejection of traditional Chinese law by China's own lawmakers, from the late Qing to the Republic, and then not only in the People's Republic up to the 1980s but even since. He also shows that there is continuity in legal reasoning, with profound implications for the present and future of law-making and judicial process.

[13] The expression 'former people' is a Russian one and is chillingly explained in Figes O. (2007) *The whisperers: private life in Stalin's Russia.* London: Allen Lane. CCP were more varied: 'black elements', 'stinking ninth' and so forth were applied to whole families and professions.

[14] According to Zhao Yuezhi, leading party theorist Xie Tao repudiated the Bolshevik Revolution as being wrongheaded from the start Zhao (2008), pp 348.

[15] On the so called Islamic Fundamentalists and their similarities with utopian ideologies of 20th century Europe, see *Gray, John (2010) Al Qaeda and what it means to be Modern* London: Faber & Faber

[16] Intellectuals have often, out of political tact or because they have been out of touch with modern currents of thought, formulated their criticisms and proposals in Marxists terms. On this, see Leonard Mark (2008) *What does China Think?* London: Fourth Estate.

[17] Moreover, the Russian rulers were concerned about instability in the former Qing Empire, both because of the potential for trouble across the very long land borders between the two empires (millions of refugees from Lenin's tyranny had fled into China), and because of the potential advantages of exploiting such instability. The Russians were also concerned that China should not be swallowed up by the British Empire or divided between the various other imperialists who were gobbling up concessions. They arranged for Outer Mongolia to detach itself and become its satellite; they busied themselves in East Turkestan (Xinjiang) and much of North China, where they competed for influence with the Germans, British and Japanese. The British threatened Tibet. Today, awareness of this history accounts for the inordinate fear that Chinese policy-makers have of foreign subversion in Central Asia, as much as does more recent US aggression in Vietnam (1955-1975) or Iraq (2003-)

[18] Stillman, Edmund and Pfaff, William (1964) *The politics of hysteria: the sources of 20th century conflict*, London: Victor Gollancz, quoted in Gray, John (2010) *Al Qaeda and what it means to be Modern London*: Faber & Faber, pp 117. Note how they equate Fascism and Communism. Both movements derived from the same roots and functioned in much the same ways, justifying our lumping them together as 20th century 'utopianisms'.

[19] This approach was unacceptable to hardline Dominican Catholics when the Jesuits advocated that Confucianism was compatible with Christianity. The 'Rites Controversy' is relevant today as an illustration of 'Western' intransigence versus Chinese toleration.

[20] Gray, John (2002) *Straw Dogs*. London: Granta Books.

[21] Ibid., pp 89.

[22] Ibid., pp 126.

[23] Hu, A. (2011) Democratic process of planning. *China Daily*, 10 March. This is a précis of Hu's article Xinhuanet http://news.xinhuanet.com/english/china/2013-03/12/c_132227126.htm, accessed 2013 Oct 19.

[24] These processes are described best by Siedentop (2015).

[25] See China Media Project's website, http://cmp.hku.hk/2016/03/03/39672/, accessed 05 April 2016

[26] I am indebted to Leng Rong 冷溶, Director, CPC Central Committee Party Literature Research Center 中共中央文献研究室 for discussing these questions with me, Summer 2014

[27] Zhao Yuezhi argues that, despite all the changes, the Party 'continues to derive at least part of its political and ideological legitimacy from the Maoist revolutionary tradition' Zhao (2008), pp 37.

[28] I have rarely met a student who did not claim to go annually to visit the graves of her forbears, among the many other instances of the continuation (or revival) of tradition.

[29] O'Dwyer goes into these matters in greater depth. See O'Dwyer, Shaun (2003) Democracy and Confucian Values in *Philosophy East and West* 53(1): 39-63

[30] For example, Luzhou Li & Saskia Witteborn (2012) Confucianism in the Chinese media: an analysis of the revolutionary history television drama *In Those Passionate Days* in *Chinese Journal of Communication* Volume 5, 2012 - Issue 2 Pp 160-177

[31] *Qiu Shi* (2015). Building a Moderately Prosperous Society in All Respects: A Crucial Step for Realizing the Chinese Dream. *Qiushi* (English Edition), 7 (4), 21–26.

[32] (de Burgh and Feng in press). The Return of the Repressed: three examples of how Chinese identity is being reconsolidated for the modern world to be published in *Critical Arts: South-North Cultural and Media Studies*

[33] 余 华 Yu Hua (2012) 活着 To Live. 北京 Beijing : 作家出版社 China Writers Publishing House, see pp 78 onwards, for example.

[34] The Peoples' Daily published Guoxue quietly comes back to Peking University 国学,在燕园又悄然兴起 and the Guangming Daily published The charm of guoxue and the guoxue masters 国学和国学大师的魅力.

[35] 全国政协八届三次会议第 0003 号提案 '建立幼年古典学校的紧急呼吁'. http://www.huadingshuyuan.com/cn/news.php?show=detail&news_id=1278 (accessed 12 January 2017).

[36] 2013 年 10 月，北京市教委曾公布了《2014-2016 年高考高招改革框架方案》（征求意见稿），面向社会征求意见。北京市教委下设的教育服务咨询热线工作人员表示，目前最新的有关高招的政策就是北京市教委发布的《关于做好北京市 2015 年普通高校招生工作的通知》和《北京市 2015 年普通高等学校招生工作规定》等文件，都是 2015 年的政策。至于 2017 年高考高招的改革政策，目前并不对外发布。
http://edu.people.com.cn/n/2015/0601/c244541-27084479.html

[37] According to Siedentop (ibid., pp 206) the idea that monarchs should humbly serve their charges was astonishing in Europe when Gregory the Great advanced it in the 11th century. He subjected the secular sphere to the requirements of morality. Yet this had long been an essential principle of Chinese governance, though from different origins. Europeans had subjected rulers to moral laws (ibid p 199) even earlier: In AD 390 Ambrose excommunicated the Emperor for having ordered a massacre in Greece; in 1080 Henry the fourth did penance at Canossa. In 1644 in England Parliament that was responsible for executing Charles 1st for treachery.

[38] He, Qinglian (2007) *The Fog of Censorship*. New York: HRIC, pp 131.

[39] Ibid p133

[40] Ibid p137

[41] Kracke The Chinese and the art of government. In Dawson, Raymond: *the legacy of China*, pp 324. For a timeline of the development of the examination system see Bell, (2006) pp 81. The examinations took their present form following the reforms of Wu Zetian (AD 624-705).

[42] Kracke, op cit pp 319.

[43] Heilmann and Perry (2011), pp 15.

[44] Kracke op cit pp 310.

[45] Kracke op cit pp 321. As Kracke points out, comparing the fall of Rome and the collapse of Chinese dynasties, 'where Frankish rulers failed to restore the Roman fabric, the Sui and T'ang in China restored the Imperial forms so firmly that unity lasted, despite the fall of dynasties and foreign conquests…'Kracke op cit pp 334.

[46] Perry (2008), pp 37-50, quoted in Creemers (2015). pp 49.
[47] This is explained thoroughly in two books by Emmanuel Todd, (1985) *The Explanation of Ideology* . Oxford: Blackwell and (1987) *The Causes of Progress* Oxford: Blackwell. The family hypothesis, based on empirical data, posits ideologies and political systems as reflections of anthropological values. China's prevailing family form is that of the exogamous community family, characteristics distinct from, *interalia*, the Anglophone.
[48] Todd (1985), pp 12.
[49] Hamilton describes how the values are imbibed, pp 128: As children grow up they are continually socialised to recognise the legitimacy of the framework and to learn how to navigate their way around this world. This framework is known to everyone else in society and is used to interpret the actions of others, to judge them by how well they match the normative framework. Of course there are contradictions within that as there are in every society.(my precis)
[50] Kleinman, Arthur (2011) *Deep China*. Berkeley: U of California Press, pp 2.
[51] Kleinman makes very valuable points which can be used to back up the presumption, shared by Alan MacFarlane, that traditional Chinese social relations will give way to individualism. The evidence of the persistence of traditional mores, though, is strong. See, for example Pimental, E (2000) Just how do I love thee? Marital relations in Urban China, *Journal of Marriage and Family*, 62(1), pp 32-47.
[52] The sources for the discussion that follows are: M Leonard, (2008) *What does China think?*. London: Fourth Estate and J L Wu, K Yu, et al. (2011) 中国未来 30 年 *China in the next 30 years*. Beijing: Central Compilation and Translation Press.
[53] Shi, Tianjian and Lou,Diqing (2010) Subjective evaluation of changes in civil liberties and political rights in China. *Journal of Contemporary China*. 19(63), pp 175-199.
[54] Guthrie, D. (2006) *China and globalisation*. London: Routledge, pp 276-278.
[55] The Law on the Organisation of Village Committees 中华人民共和国村民委员会组织法 was piloted before being confirmed by the NPC in 1998.
[56] Gilley, Bruce (2004) *China's Democratic Future*, New York: Columbia University Press p 22
[57] The National Peoples' Congress 全国人民大会 is the supreme law-making body. Currently it has 8 permanent committees: Education, Science Culture & Public Health Committee, Environment & Resources, Finance & Economics, Foreign Affairs, Internal & Judicial, Law, Ethnic Affairs, Overseas Chinese Committees. Parallel to the Peoples' Congresses is the hierarchy of the Chinese Peoples' Political Consultative Congresses (CPPCC) 中国人民政治协商议全国委员会, the advisory chambers, also with its permanent committees.
[58] Guthrie, D. (2006), pp 296.
[59] Ibid., pp 296.
[60] This has been mentioned to me several times. I note that Liu Xiaobo has also made this point. See J-P Beja, Liu Xiaobo, Le retour de la morale. In: Cheng A. (ed.) (2007), *La pensée en Chine aujourd'hui*. Paris: Editions Gallimard, pp 147.
[61] Pan Wei. Conversations with the author at Peking University; April 2007.
[62] The Asia Pivot is described by *Time Magazine* as follows: 'The Pentagon is deploying more aircraft carriers, destroyers and submarines in the region and says it will deploy 60% of its overseas forces in Asia, up from the current 50% … The Air Force recently announced plans to move more fighter jets to Singapore, Thailand and India, and one official said bombers could eventually be stationed in Australia. Talks are underway with the Philippines about a substantial US presence there. A new force of 2,500 Marines is planned to be based on Australia's northern coast … These military moves delivered a clear message to China: ASIA PIVOT TARGETS BEIJING.' [Crowley M. Make way for China. Time. 21 October 2012, pp 23].
[63] Daniel Bell has reminded us how European thinkers of the past discussed democracy's strengths and weaknesses in a more detached manner than we do today, in his 2015 work, Bell, Daniel, A. (2015) *The China Model*. Princeton: Princeton University Press.

[64] Conversations with Minister Leng Rong, and others, summer 2014

[65] Pan Wei. Conversations with the author at Peking University; April 2007.

[66] See Yu, Keping 俞可平. (2011) Democracy in China: challenge or opportunity? In: 吴敬琏 Wu Jingzhuang et al (eds.) (2011) 中国未来 30 年 *China in the next 30 years*. Beijing: Central Compilation and Translation Press.

[67] Tang, Qingshan (2006) Deliberative democracy and village self government in China. Chapter 10, p 197. (See also other essays in the same volume). In: Leib EJ. (2006) *The search for deliberative democracy in China*. New York: Palgrave Macmillan.

[68] Mitter, R. (2004) *A Bitter Revolution*. Oxford: Oxford University Press, pp 307.

[69] Lee, Chin-chuan (1991) Mass Media, of China, about China. In: Lee, Chin-chuan (ed) *Voices of China: The Interplay of Politics & Journalism* New York: The Guildford Press, pp 7.

[70] Zhao Yuezhi discusses this in Zhao (2012) Understanding China's Media System. In: Hallin, Daniel C. and Mancini, Paolo *Comparing Media Systems Beyond the Western World*. Cambridge: Cambridge University Press.

[71] Discussed in Yu, Keping (2011).

[72] Tang, Qingshan (2006), Chapter 10, pp 197.

[73] Nathan, AJ. (1986) *Chinese democracy: the individual and the state in twentieth-century China*. Berkeley, CA: University of California Press.

[74] Bell, DA. (2006) *Beyond liberal democracy*. Princeton: Princeton University Press.

[75] Ibid., pp 8.

[76] Ibid., pp 150.

[77] Ibid., pp 158.

[78] Ibid., pp 175.

[79] Professional politicians have taught us to think that it is only elections that confer legitimacy, because it suits them that we discount intellectual authority, age, experience or custom, and the media have reinforced this by unthinkingly accepting politicians' self-evaluation.

[80] Bell (2015), passim

[81] Beja, J-P. and Liu, Xiaobo (2007) Le retour de la morale. In: Cheng A, et al (eds.). *La pensée en Chine aujourd'hui*. Paris: Editions Gallimard, pp 144.

[82] Beja, J-P. (2007), pp 145.

[83] Callahan, William *Citizen Ai: Warrior, Jester and Middleman*, Seminar at SOAS, 20 January 2014.

Human Rights

China has long been pilloried in the Anglophone media for human rights abuses and there certainly is evidence that police and security forces behave badly and that policy, for example over the Falungong, has in the recent past encouraged vicious abuse. There are human rights violations in many countries, though, and Anglophone critics can be selective as to which they choose to villify; China is held up to censure in such an insistent manner that it seems that this is part of a propaganda war. When China was seen as an ally rather than a competitor, the issue was ignored.[83]

To China this seems hypocritical, coming as it often does from countries which are causing suffering in the Middle East and Central Asia. Infuriated, China now issues an Annual Human Rights Record Report on the United States. 'The United States has long been in a violent, crime-ridden society with a severe infringement of the people's rights by law enforcement departments and with a lack of guarantee for the life of people, their freedom and personal safety.'[83] It also listed US human rights violations abroad, of which there is a vast number.

According to veteran journalist Frank Ching, part of the explanation for the widespread perception that China is deficient in human rights is that the two countries' ideas of human rights are different. China has provided relative security and freedom from want to more and more people every year since 1980; it is addressing numerous problems from which rich countries do not suffer and seeking to avoid their failings. People enjoy material goods and can be happy in ways that were, 30 years ago, possible only for the tiny Party elite. The authorities look around themselves and see immense progress and, not surprisingly in such circumstances, argue, and probably many citizens concur, that individual rights should always come after the good of the many and that society needs to emphasise responsibilities before rights.[83]

Ideas as to what is or is not moral change over time. Not long ago the USA practiced slavery, England tortured criminals publicly and in living memory Europe witnessed worse crimes against humanity than any ever previously recorded, orchestrated by the leaders of Russia and Germany. Many things that were quite acceptable a century ago are abhorrent to us today and yet we chastise societies which have not changed as fast as have we.

And China did not change as fast because, not only was China's moral growth stunted after 1949 but, as with Russia, it reverted to barbarism. Marxist denigration of the legal system as 'bourgeois legality' was used to justify appalling abuses, following the Communist conquest. Persecution of religion and indeed all ideas that did not concur with the Party's made life precarious, as did the fact that everyone became the serf of what was, in effect, a feudal state and had no right to change employer, let alone have recourse to trades unions. In recent years there has emerged a corps of dedicated lawyers who are committed to upholding civil rights and who are collectively known as the 'Rights Movement'维权运动. They, citing the declared aim of the leadership to re-establish a rule of law, struggle manfully against habits of lawlessness and brutality cultivated deliberately from the 1940s to the late 1970s. Great strides have been made in many areas such as the way suspects are treated in custody[83] and police officers and judges are both now increasingly professional and exposed to best practice from other countries. With many setbacks, the legal profession is trying to instantiate habits of lawfulness, but this is not easy in a country in which the power of the Party and its power holders can override all.

8   Endword: The Road of Rejuvenation?[1]

When President Xi visited the national media in February 2016, he exhorted them to remember that they exist to serve the Party. In the days following, study sessions 学习大会 *were held by their constituent departments in which employees were expected to give vent to their feelings* 发言, 发表自己的感想 *and describe how the President's encouragement had affected them. The dramatist or cameraman, editor or conductor on whom such sessions grate probably hanker for less Party control. Those who thanked the President for his moral guidance with fervour and re-dedicated themselves to their roles as flag carriers for the nation[2] may be more representative.[3]*

In the order that is emerging, China is set to be the richest country and, in time, to supplant the two hundred year predominance of the Anglophones in much of the world. The Belt and Road Initiative, by which China will provide infrastructure without which many poorer countries will not develop, will both ensure that Chinese design and construction has work for many decades ahead, and will transform languishing economies. It will confirm China's position as the driver of economic development the world over. Championing international trade, leading over the environment and creating supra national institutions, Chinese leaders are overturning perceptions of China and winning enthusiastic friends. It is tentatively involving itself in international issues independently of the USA, for example bringing Israeli and Palestinian leaders together and seeking to broker relations between Iran and Israel,[4] or negotiating over the South China Sea with ASEAN. Ordinary people see China as the coming lodestar: Chinese is already being studied in schools throughout the world, opinion formers and decision makers everywhere are making it their business to know what is happening there, and Chinese habits, pleasures and arts are infiltrating. China's media will make us aware of these changes and will report back about the rest of us to China.

It is not only because of China's wealth that a new order is emerging. An *idea* of China is being articulated.

In much of the world over the 1980s and 1990s there took place vast changes in perception and in how the world works, changes often attributed to British Prime Minister Thatcher and the USA's President Reagan. In time, the ascendancy of Deng Xiaoping may be considered to have been at least as critical because of the impact of his domestic reforms upon the world economy. Today, Xi Jinping is altering the environment in what may turn out to be an equally profound way. Although he makes ritual obeisance to some foreign thinkers – he leads, after all, a Communist Party – his inspiration comes from home.[5]

Ever since Deng Xiaoping turned a blind eye to the foreign ideology that he and his associates had tried to stamp on China since 1949, ordinary people have been trying to revive the civilisation of their forbears and reassert the essential beliefs by which Chinese society prospered for millennia, before the rise of Europe. The *guoxue* movement is one, public, manifestation of this; recognising the patriotism of the KMT is another; so too is the restoration of traditions, proprieties, temples and ceremonies. Even before 1949 many in the ruling classes assumed that 'China's ancient system of values could not offer a way to counter the West's military and industrial might'[6] and were zealous in destroying temples and customs; yet now officials join the masses in paying homage to the Yellow Emperor, legendary founder of China, in an annual ceremony. They talk no longer of progress into modernity, but of renaissance or return to past greatness interrupted by the West. In different ways all four leaders since Deng have moved a little further to accommodate the peoples' longings.

More, what President Xi and his advisers appear to be doing is turning a popular emotion into a state ideology, at first supplementing, then transforming beyond recognition the Party's *raison d'etre*. The ideology is to give direction and purpose to both government and governed. It is an equivalent of the religious faith that propelled the rise of the USA, or the sacred duty that sanctified late British imperialism. Unlike those ideologies, though, what he is conjuring is no messianic faith which threatens lesser breeds.[7] If China considers it has something to offer, it is as a shining city on a hill, which will win admirers by its very virtue, and not by sending gunboats or aircraft carriers to compel correctness.[8]

Confidence in China is also a reflection of the idea, implicit in much discussion, that China's successes of the last 30 years have come about as functions of Chinese culture rather than of learning from the West. That which kept Chinese civilisation going longer than any other human endeavour is seen not merely as a branding tool but as the fount of today's achievement. Bluntly, people increasingly reason, when China adopted 'Western' notions, such as Marxism, it failed to develop; once these were abandoned, China raced ahead. Such appears to be the often unspoken premise behind much of current Chinese thinking. The country's leadership has not only questioned taking lessons from abroad but also warned other countries to abjure foreign models.[9] This harks back to the notion, commonplace in the 19th century, of a choice being needed between total replacement of culture and mere adoption of skills and techniques from abroad, when it was referred to as the Essence and Technique Debate 体用. A revived phrase today is *use the skills of the barbarians to govern the barbarians* 师夷长技以制夷.

Confident that their own civilisation is at least the equal of the dominant Anglo

American one, we can foresee Chinese academics and pedagogues being more inclined to build on Chinese intellectual and artistic traditions to investigate and analyse the world rather than conform to Anglo-American norms. In the social sciences efforts are already being made to escape from Anglophone framings. Academics rail against Western dominance over social science theory which, they argue, has imposed structures of Western thought worldwide, while some say that Asia's economic rise has allowed Asian epistemologies to surface that 'emphasise cultural differences with the West rather than imitation'.[10]

After nearly a 100 years of denigration, following the 200 years in which Europeans overtook China in many fields such that Chinese intellectuals lost faith in their own tradition, it will take time for this rejuvenation to be fully realised. Nevertheless, today there is a shared will for a renaissance of Chinese civilisation, rather than simply a drive for wealth and power. Notwithstanding the efforts of critics abroad, and although, like every country, China has its share of the disgruntled, opinion polls register little alienation.

The media, including street media, are ever more Confucian in tone.[11] As we saw above, by contrast with class struggle, communist utopia or economic determinism, street media are reflecting the 'new' dispensation, with billboards that used to incite to revolt now having direct quotes from the sages, exhorting the moral life, implicitly rejecting the selfishness and callousness that many find around them and associate with 'Westernisation'.[12]

President Xi is devoting effort to revive the Confucian ethic among his executives, the sense of a code that constrained their imperial forbears with 'moral precepts and rules of correct conduct'.[13] Whenever addressing meetings of civil service and Party personnel, he repeats nostrums such as this quotation from around 1000BC.

'Government officials who are good at governing a country will treat the people as do parents caring for their children..........Hearing that the people are suffering from hunger and cold, they will grieve; seeing that the people are working too hard, they will be in pain.'[14]

President Xi holds that the socialist ideas previously attributed to Marx were part of the warp and woof of Chinese tradition. One of his advisers recently remarked that he wanted to stop teachers referring to the Enlightenment as a movement that took place in 18th century Europe; 'our Enlightenment took place much earlier, in the Spring and Autumn Period', he said.[15]

China is unique. At a session of the Central Committee at which the main topic was the Rule of Law, President Xi suggested a Chinese 'exceptionalism' in much the same way as anthropologists have described Anglophone exceptionalism:[16] 'Several thousand years ago the Chinese people trod a path that was different from other nations' culture and development', he said, and called upon the people to draw upon '5000 years of continuous Chinese culture'. This is both more than European-style nationalism, and less. It harks back to a pre-modern conception of China as 'the only true civilisation'.[17]

Sceptics dismiss the myths by which nations live as so much invention and irrationality, yet politicians who started with the desire to destroy inherited culture – Stalin and Hitler spring to mind – have ended up co-opting it in order to mobilise and motivate their subjects. Recently the rationalists and the universalists have had setbacks in Europe and the USA as their assumptions, that the nations of Europe should be conglomerated into a centralised empire, or that the job of Anglo American politicians is to usher in universal conformity rather than to serve their own citizens, have been called into question[18] as has the belief, dubbed by James Mann as 'The China Fantasy' that the country is gradually being converted into an obedient satrap.[19] Something similar is going on in China, where the rulers have grasped that their people want their country back. Universal values, Marxist pseudo science, historical determinism and the cult of progress are giving way to Chinese inclusiveness, underpinned by Confucian consensus.

So where does this place the media? The foregoing chapters have shown the roles played by the media in the transformation of this vast country from one superceded by Europeans in scientific and economic affairs to one that is intent to supercede them. In the process its institutions and beliefs have been buffeted and broken but have re-formed: The networking society of Fei Xiaotong's 'differential mode of association' has been turbo charged by the availability of digital media; imperial governance, in all its strengths and weaknesses, has been re-discovered, sharpened by Leninism; the codes of the Confucian Enlightenment have been shaken up, updated and purified of dysfunctional accretions and are to anchor Chinese men and women once more; the language has been enriched by modernity and is used with pride by many more people, no longer the tool and pleasure of a small elite. Of course there are recalcitrants; today's Chinese can get away to other worlds and, in the words of one colleague of Chinese parentage 'spend my life trying not to be Chinese'.

And the media? Before the 19th century it was assumed that the official media must support authority, and that government has a duty to use all media at its disposal to educate and inform the public as it see fit. Outwith the official channels were social media, then comprising storytellers and soothsayers, songs and the great popular and often subversive novels, a turbulent society.

Today, while anticipating that New Media will cause disruption, critics of China have characterised the official media as deficient because they do not perform the same functions as their own, but as we have seen, they perform different functions and, anyway, a clear-eyed comparison untrammelled by ideological prejudice, makes the differences seem less great.[20]

An Anglophone sense of superiority has been somewhat chastened in recent years both by the now widespread realisation that their media can be mendacious, and by the revelations of respected journalists themselves as to the failure of the media to live up to their claims.[21] In an inspired study, Bangkok-based analyst Jesse Hearns Branaman has gone as far as to compare the Chinese and United States press and to conclude that 'the media of all countries reflect elite views, use a narrow range of sources, and are almost impervious to ideas that would trouble the owners: all media are propaganda'.[22]

This requires two caveats, first, that there is great difference between different media and media vehicles in both countries as to their degree of subservience to culture and politics, and, second, that China is more systematic about ensuring that the media reflect elite views and a narrow range of sources, such that there is probably more pluralism in ideas in the Anglosphere, although ownership of the media is concentrated in fewer hands,.

The best of the Anglophone media have long been consumed even by their most vehement opponents on account of the relative detachment and fidelity to facts that, sometimes, set them apart from much other media. This is that which differentiates them from other media.

For media lie on a spectrum from free to unfree on which none inhabit the far zone of freedom and on which the position of any one country's media shift according to political climates; consider how different have been USA media after Watergate from those of the McCarthy era, Germany in the 1900s as against the Germany of 1933 or English media preceding and following the ascendancy of News International.

China's media have changed over the last century many times and at the time of writing they are being permitted less independence, such that the insight, offered over 50 years ago by President Liu Shaoqi after the disasters of the Great Leap Forward, that the media are more useful to society, and indeed to the leadership, if they are given a long leash, will be parked for a while. To this writer, as to Liu Shaoqi, the authorities would better keep officials in line and head off local confrontations if China's media could continue to do what, at their best, loyal critics do elsewhere. The main agency for supervision of officialdom is the Party's

Discipline and Inspection Commission (DIC) but it is widely suspected of being insufficiently detached. A TV programme doubting the DIC's competence was spiked in 1998.[23] Effective media with a public service orientation and not cowed by power will propose workable alternatives to policies as a matter of course. Elite Chinese journalists are famously thorough and knowledgeable of their briefs; they can be sceptical, forensic in examination and find the weaknesses in the policymakers' cases. The proposals of power holders should be analysed, examined, and challenged. Measured criticism and dissent are needed. With little scrutiny and correction, governments can turn in on themselves, wasting time on power struggles, factionalism or self-indulgent feuding. They need to know that they are being watched.

At various times this has been the case: before 1949, in journalism and literature in the 1980s and, to an extent, in the 1990s as investigative journalism reached its apogee. Today, by contrast, the emphases on defending China's integrity against hostile propaganda from abroad and ensuring stability at home appear to be taking precedence.[24] Conformity is valued over constructive criticism, at least in central media. Whether this is so in the provinces is not clear.[25]

Meanwhile there is a case for China's media as legitimate but different. Tentative steps have been made to theorise them as constituting 'constructive media', drawing attention to their rejection of negativity, sensationalism and addiction to reporting epiphenomena. Advocates claim that such media are more responsible.

If China's political culture continues to consolidate into a modernised and democratised form of paternalism, the media will reflect that culture and reveal its contradictions. The purpose of this book has been to show that this system has its own legitimacy, even if, like all man-made systems it has flaws; its products are diverse, but they are constrained by a set of values and kept in order by a popular consensus about those values and about the right of the administrative elite to decide when those values are being adhered to. In some decades the media professionals will have more leeway, in other decades less. Throughout these periods, they remain instruments of China's rejuvenation as much as any arm of government, before they are expressions of creativity or commentary, and no matter that there are internal conflicts over interpretation.[26]

In the emerging world order, China's media will report on and inform much of the world; the world should know them.

Notes

[1] This is the title of the section of the National History Museum in Peking that deals with the 19th to 21st centuries.

[2] According to reports from my former students now at CCTV, a high proportion of those making such declarations in the CCTV sessions had studied at postgraduate level in the USA and UK.

[3] The position of CCTV employees is complicated by the recent (2016) revision of employee terms, which has alienated many from the service and driven 'hundreds' to leave state media for the private, online, sectors. Their irritation at CCTV's poor management does not necessarily imply alienation from the its goals.

[4] Matthews, Owen, (2013) Could China be the key to Peace between Israel and Iran? In *The Spectator*, 22 June 2013, p24.

[5] Some of his supporters and advisers are making a slightly different case, that Chinese and Western values can be brought into line. Thus Lai Hairong 莱海荣, of the Compilation and Translation Bureau of the Central Committee, has written extensively on this. See Skidelsky, Robert (ed) (nd) *Synthesising Chinese and Western Values*, London: Centre for Global Studies

[6] For a brief on the restoration of religion, see Johnson, Ian (2011) China Gets Religion! In The *New York Review of Books*, December 22, 2011 pp55-58.

[7] For the avoidance of doubt, please note that I use Kipling's expression ('lesser breeds without the law') to contrast Chinese and Anglophone approaches.

[8] Perhaps subconsciously fearing revenge for the damage they inflicted on China in the past, some Anglophones assume that China's military are being prepared to be aggressive. While it is certainly possible that a ruler might come to power – particularly if electoral democracy came to pass in China – who used them aggressively, as long as China is ruled by a Confucian bureaucracy focussed on domestic harmony, this is less likely. As an officer cadet said, interviewed by Steve Hewlett for BBC *Panorama* 'We have an army so that we can ensure that nothing like the Japanese invasion can ever happen again'. He was too polite to mention the barbarism of the European armies in China, whose exploits are known to every schoolchild, as is the treaty by which the USA required that every concession made to any other country be granted to the USA.

[9] Ringen, Stein (2016) *The Perfect Dictatorship: China in the 21st Century* HK: HKU Press *introduction*

[10] Liu, J. (2011). Asian Epistemologies and Contemporary Social Psychological Research. In N. Denzin & Y. Lincoln (eds), *The SAGE Handbook of Qualitative Research*, 4th edition. London: Sage, 213-226, p213. Michael Harris Bond and his associates on the psychology departments of Hong Kong were the first to recognise the inapplicability of many social science concepts to China. For example: Bond, M. H. (2010). Moving the scientific study of Chinese psychology into our twenty-first century: Some ways forward. In M. H. Bond (Ed.), *The Oxford handbook of Chinese psychology* (pp. 711-715). New York: Oxford University Press. More recently, there have been new attempts to distance China from 'Western' social sciences. These include: Xu, S. (2014). *Chinese Discourse Studies*. Basingstoke: Palgrave Macmillan and Liu, above.

[11] de Burgh H and Feng D, (in press). 'The Return of the Repressed: three examples of how Chinese identity is being reconsolidated for the modern world' to be published in 2017 in *Critical Arts: South-North Cultural and Media Studies*

[12] ibid

[13] Pye, Lucien W. (2002) 'Factions and the Politics of Guanxi' in Unger, Jonathan (ed) (2002) *The Nature of Chinese Politics, from Mao to Jiang*, Armonk: ME Sharpe, p40-41.

[14] Zhang Fenzhi (2015) *Xi Jinping: How to read Confucius and other Chinese classical thinkers*, NY: CN Times P32

[15] Kong Dan, head of the CITIC think tank, quoted to me by his associate Professor Li Xiguang on 17 May 2017.

[16] Tatlow, Didi Kirsten (2014) 'Xi Jinping on Exceptionalism with Chinese Characteristics' https://sinosphere.blogs.nytimes.com/2014/10/14/xi-jinping-on-exceptionalism-with-chinese-characteristics/ (Accessed 31 July 2017)

[17] For some thorough discussions of this topic, see Unger, Jonathan (ed) (1996) *Chinese Nationalism* Armonk ME Sharpe

[18] Most eloquently discussed (in relation to the UK) in Goodhart, David (2017)*The Road to Somewhere: The Populist Revolt and the Future of Politics*, London: Hurst & Company

[19] Mann, James (2007) *The China Fantasy*, New York: Penguin, p2 and passim.

[20] Media Studies academics have been slow to acknowledge that there are cultural differences in media systems; it was conventional to see the Anglophone system as the most 'advanced' version of a universal institution. The heretical idea was (probably first) mooted in Hallin, DC and Mancini, P. (eds.) *Comparing media systems beyond the western world.* Cambridge: Cambridge University Press, Chapter 10, passim

[21] Even before the News International scandal alerted the world to the criminal methods deployed by some journalists in the pursuit of stories of dubious value, many Anglosphere commentators had begun to see the conventional media as too negative, unethical and damaging to society. With critical analyses of the media by respected observers such as McChesney, Cook, Lloyd and O'Neill, the ideal of the dispassionate journalist wielding a 'sword of truth' lost purchase. An investigation of the investigators went further. With *Flat Earth News*, Nick Davies, drawing upon the evidence of US and British military and civil service personnel, as well as his own and other journalists' research, established that a very high proportion of the information provided by Anglo-American media about terrorism, the wars in the Islamic world, and the state of the countries in which Anglo-America had waged war, is fabricated and deceptive. Chinese observers welcome foreigners who confirm their impression that much reporting world issues, and of China in particular, serves a political agenda; the critique of the US media by Edward Herman and Noam Chomsky is staple fare for trainee journalists in China. (McChesney RW, Nichols J. D*ollarocracy: how the money and media election complex is destroying America.* New York: Nation Books; 2013; Cook TE. *Governing with the news: the news media as a political institution.* Chicago: University of Chicago Press; 1998; Lloyd J. *What the media are doing to our politics.* London: Constable; 2004; O'Neill C. *A question of trust: The BBC Reith Lectures 2002.* Cambridge: Cambridge University Press; 2002; Davies N. *Flat earth news: an award-winning reporter exposes falsehood, distortion and propaganda in the global media.* London: Chatto & Windus; 2008)

[22] Branaman, Jesse Owen Hearns- (2015) *The Political Economy of News in China, Manufacturing Harmony* Lanham: Lexington, p136. For a similar, earlier, opinion, see Lee, Chin-chuan (1991) Mass Media: Of China, About China. In: Lee, Chin-chuan (ed.) *Voices of China: The Interplay of Politics and Journalism.* London: The Guildford Press, pp 19

[23] Zhu (2009), pp 137.

[24] At present it seems as if steps backward are being taken – the way the anti-corruption campaign is going looks like a political purge; the rule of law has been suspended and the media are not being permitted to perform their censorial function. This can be a dangerous road for China as the enlightened patriots will lose hope of peaceful, incremental reform and enemies will enthusiastically seed the idea that only revolution will change China, that the old guard will never reform. The present government considers that its constituency is the poor, who are many and care little about political reform; however, in the course of pleasing them, the government may be not only be demoralising the good officials and the conscientious traders but suppressing the rise in living standards that the poor need. Communism did not work before when it punished the enterprising, the system staffers and the patriots; how much less will it work when vital parts of the economy are privately run and closely connected with the system staffers?

[25] A recent study of several million newspaper articles has found that references to President Xi's policies are relatively sparse in the provincial press. 'China's Newsmakers: How Media Power is Shifting in the Xi Jinping Era' will be published in *China Quarterly* in 2017.

[26] There are conflicts in many other arenas, for example over school textbooks or modern history. At the time of writing the CPD is trying to enforce a particular modern history course on university departments. 'Of course we ignore them and teach what our scholarship tells us is right' said an eminent Peking University historian, 'but I am afraid that the lower ranking universities conform'.

Acknowledgments

I wish to thank two people who have done much to introduce me to the Chinese media and other aspects of China. Veteran journalist, prolific writer and founding Dean of the Tsinghua School of Journalism & Communication, Professor Li Xiguang, is my teacher, as is Professor Hu Zhengrong, President of Communication University of China.

I have learnt a great deal from my students, whose student am I. Dr Mi Miao, Dr Li Hong and Dr Vivien Marsh all contributed to this book. Others who assisted are Bao Jiawei, Bao Shanshan, Dr Aurogeeta Das, Gao Yue, Cristina Goncales, Gu Yu, He Sijia, He Yuan, Dr Li Shuang, Li Yingying, Lavender Lin Yun, Liu Yumin, Lu Nan, Luo Jun, Stacey Ng, Pan Mengqi, Tang Ju, Yang Chen, Zhang Lan and Zhu Xiaowen. The staff of the China Media Centre, Chang Yiru, Virginia Cheung Man Ching, Guo Xu, Dr Wang Fang and Lorraine Xia backed me up with their customary kindness and efficiency while Alja Kranjec, helped and advised me ceaselessly in preparing the mss. Without the Communications and Media Research Institute and its founder, Professor Colin Sparks (now of Hong Kong Baptist University), or of our Dean, Sally Feldman, the work could not have been undertaken.

The manuscript has benefitted from the editing of Mary Hodge and of Johnny Acton. The latter read the whole mss as a 'typical reader' and advised. Initial scoping of the book was by Helen Briggs, who also undertook some interviews on my behalf, and whose research for a project on the environment in China has been incorporated by précis. To the President of Houghton Street Media 恒顿传媒, my former student Dr Zeng Rong, I owe many insights into Chinese society and governance, some of which have found their way into this book.

Colleagues who either agreed to be interviewed or read and commented on sections of the mss are Professor Chris Berry, Dr Kerry Brown, Dr Cao Qing, Professor David Conway, Professor Philip Deans, Dr Kent Deng, Professor David Gauntlett, Professor Michel Hockx, Professor Rana Mitter, Dr Frank Pieke, Professor Robert Rowthorn, Andrew Stirling, Professor Daya Thussu, Professor Wu Minsu and Dr Zhang Xiaoling. I have benefited from discussions with, among others, Bai Yansong, Chen Siming, Professor Cui Baoguo, Cui Yongyuan, Professor Dong Guanpeng, Li Yong, Dr Emma Lupano, Professor Pan Wei, Professor Canon Vernon White, Dr Giovanna Puppin, Professor Shi Anbin, Shui Junyi, Dr Si Si, Sun Wei, Sun Yusheng, Professor Wang Qisheng and Yang Rui. I am grateful to the anonymous peer reviewers, for their constructive comments.
I appreciate the efficiency and dispatch with which Christopher Woodhead, of the University of Buckingham Press, has executed the project. By his kind

permission, several excerpts from chapters 1 and 5 are to be incorporated into 'Domestic Context of Chinese Media's Globalization', in Thussu Daya, Shi Anbin and de Burgh Hugo (eds) *China's Media Go Global*, to be published by Routledge in 2018.

My heartfelt thanks are here extended to all those named. There are bound to be omissions and errors and for those I alone am at fault. I have expressed provocative and controversial interpretations of recent Chinese affairs which are mine alone; they do not represent the views of any of those listed above.

While writing this book, I also nursed to publication a book written by my mother during the Second World War when she served as a soldier in a foreign country.[1] As I read it, I admired her openness to and empathy for people and customs very different to her own. In writing about China, a world that for an Englishman becomes more diverse the more you learn about it, I have sought to emulate her approach. Thus this book is dedicated to her, my first teacher.

Hugo de Burgh

China Media Centre, London, 2017

---

[1] de Burgh, Lucy, edited by Mary Hodge, *My Adventures in Italy: An English Girl at War*, London: The History Press

Index